More Praise for *And*

> *"Polarity Thinking has revolutionized how we approach tough problems in our work."*

"Polarity Thinking has revolutionized how we approach tough problems in our work. There are countless moments – from making a big decision as a management team, to launching an issue campaign that requires navigating fraught political waters, to building deep and lasting coalitions, to building more inclusive and collaborative teams – in which we map out a polarity to push our thinking and hone our strategy. In today's complex world of politics and advocacy, identifying ways to better leverage key polarities has exponentially increased our impact. We are vocal evangelists and have shared the tool with countless customers and partners who have adopted it to increase the efficacy of their own progressive advocacy work!"

    Lanae Erickson
    Senior Vice President for Social Policy & Politics :: Third Way

> *"The fight for equity, inclusion, social justice and humanity ... can only be achieved when advocates and allies augment either/Or-thinking with both/And-thinking."*

"The fight for equity, inclusion, social justice and humanity is not an 'or' argument. It is a 'must' argument which can only be achieved when advocates and allies augment *either/Or*-thinking with *both/And*-thinking. These two volumes are uniquely divided between Foundations skill building in Polarity Thinking, and a wide variety of Applications of *both/And*-thinking. The two volumes contain critical information to help us all break the divisiveness that can result from only using *either/Or*-thinking."

    Eddie Moore, Jr., PhD
    Founder/Program Director, The White Privilege Conference

> *"Along with systems thinking, polarity mapping is an essential skill that should be part of the education of every human being on the planet, especially anyone charged with leadership responsibilities."*

"Polarity Thinking is one of the essential disciplines underlying our vital and never-ending search for win-win solutions to our many challenges and dilemmas. Barry Johnson has given us an invaluable gift in creating – and now deepening – this powerful tool. It can help us arrive at *And* solutions in a world that often seems hopelessly tangled in a bipolar dance within polarities. Along with systems thinking, Polarity Thinking is an essential skill that should be part of the education of every human being on the planet, especially anyone charged with leadership responsibilities."

Raj Sisodia
FW Olin Distinguished Professor of Global Business, Babson College
Co-founder & Co-Chairman, Conscious Capitalism Inc

> *"Polarity Thinking ... can move teams, organizations and communities from levels of languishing to thriving, from being stuck to getting unstuck."*

"The Polarity Thinking framework is a proven tool for leaders and teams using a powerful paradigm shift of supplementing *Or*-thinking with *And*-thinking. *Or*-thinking is alive and doing well in our chaotic and ever-changing workplaces. We constantly find ourselves in the trenches searching for solutions to the most intractable problems that, over time, can be exhausting and limiting for most. This book provides a second way of expanding our thinking that can move teams, organizations and communities from levels of languishing to thriving, from being stuck to getting unstuck. We use Barry Johnson's Polarity Thinking framework extensively at our center and the university to help people reach their full potential while transforming their lives and the lives of others. Individual and organizational well-being is uplifted when we start to think in terms of possibilities (*And*-thinking). These two volumes are complete with real examples of strategies to help you accomplish this and more."

Nance Lucas, PhD
Executive Director/Chief Well-Being Officer, Center for the
Advancement of Well-Being, George Mason University

> *"Polarity Thinking is, so far, the best 'answer' we've found to help leaders face the contradictions and ambiguities of a VUCA (Volatility, Uncertainty, Complexity and Ambiguity) world."*

"Polarity Thinking is, so far, the best 'answer' we've found to help leaders face the contradictions and ambiguities of a V.U.C.A. world. From the moment you assimilate the concept, the 'unhealthy tension' of ambiguity is replaced by a 'healthy tension,' a new dimension, full of perspectives and opportunities. *And*-thinking is innovative, resilient and effective."

> Ricardo Dellamea & Rosângela Angonese
> Senior Consultants, SEBRAE–Small Business Support Service,
> Paraná State, Brazil,
> Formal Practitioners of Polarity Thinking in Leadership Development Programs, the South of Brazil

> *"... a powerful tool to analyze, debate, and formulate movement strategies."*

"Polarity Thinking's Part *And* Whole matrix is a powerful tool to analyze, debate, and formulate movement strategies. The most powerful underlying component to the tool is the natural interdependency of the Part *And* Whole in which one does not exist without the other, and the existence of one requires the existence of the other. Often movement strategies and tactics can overlook the impact of change on the status quo that widens the gap between opposing sides. This misses the opportunity to see, acknowledge, and deepen the connectedness of the universal benefit of the good of marginalized people on all of humanity. While this is often interwoven into the philosophy of our work, our strategies and messaging often overlook explicitly expressing this interconnectedness. Using Polarity Thinking's Part *And* Whole matrix can easily serve as an antidote to this condition of our movement work."

> rusia n. mohiuddi
> principal, universal partnership

> You can read More Praise for <u>And</u> on page 335.

And

Making a Difference by Leveraging Polarity, Paradox or Dilemma

Volume Two: Applications

HRD PRESS

Copyright © 2021 by Barry Johnson
and Polarity Partnerships, LLC

Polarity Partnerships, LLC
Sacramento, CA
(916) 793-5400
www.PolarityPartnerships.com
info@PolarityPartnerships.com

All rights reserved. This book or any portion thereof*
may not be reproduced or used in any manner whatsoever
without the express written permission of HRD Press or
Polarity Partnerships, LLC, except for the use of brief
quotations in a book review.

*The Polarity Map® is a registered trademark of Barry
Johnson and Polarity Partnerships, LLC. Non-commercial
use of the Polarity Maps throughout this book is welcome;
commercial use encouraged with permission.

Printed in the United States of America
First Printing, 2021

ISBN 978-1-61014-459-9

HRD Press
27 Amherst Road
Amherst, MA 01002
www.HRDPress.com

Cover art by Luke Massman-Johnson

*To all the authors who have contributed
to this wonderful collection*

Thank you

To the Editor-in-Chief

Thank you for orchestrating and editing
this 42-chapter collaboration.

Shalom Bruhn

To the HRD Editor

Thank you for a final touch of clarity.

Jean Miller

For Layout, Graphics, and Cover Art

Thank you for making the graphics and text
as clean and understandable as possible.

Luke Massman-Johnson

To My Partners at Polarity Partnerships

Thank you for your sustained support
through <u>Volume One</u> and <u>Volume Two</u>.

Leslie DePol

Cliff Kayser

Susan Dupre

Peter Dupre

Bob Tauber

Love and Gratitude

Table of Contents

Introduction to *And:* Volume Two and Authors 1

Section One: Polarity Thinking™ Supports Radical Possibilities for Equity 3
Chapter 1   Reimagine Equity and Justice Through a Polarity Lens 5
Chapter 2   Black Survival: White Power and Privilege 13
Chapter 3   Contributing to a Just and Equitable World:
            Why Is This So Hard? 21
Chapter 4   Feminine *And* Masculine: For Health, Wealth, and Happiness ... 31
Chapter 5   Support *And* Challenge – for You and Me 39

Section Two: Expanded Applications of Polarity Thinking™ 46
Chapter 6   Who We Aspire To Be *And* Who We Are:
            Leveraging the Tension With a Polarity Assessment™ 47
Chapter 7   Values Come in Pairs at Natura: A Case Study From Brazil 55
Chapter 8   Polarity Thinking™ and Real Time Strategic Change 63
Chapter 9   Polarity Thinking™ and Creative Problem Solving 69
Chapter 10 Polarity Thinking™/Paradox Thinking in Business 77
Chapter 11 Interdependent Leadership: An Experiential Love Affair
            With the Earth! 85
Chapter 12 Build Your Inspired Authentic Leadership Style 93
Chapter 13 The Dynamic Engagement Model™: Leveraging Polarities
            to Build Engagement at Work and at Home 101
Chapter 14 The Pocket Paradox Tool 107
Chapter 15 Polarities and the Need for Vulnerability 113
Chapter 16 Navigating Transition With the Power of Polarity Thinking™ ... 121
Chapter 17 Demystifying Classic Assessments Through a Polarity Lens 129
Chapter 18 Key Polarities to Leverage for Successful IT Service
            Delivery in the Digital Era 137

Chapter 19	Polarities and Homelessness	145
Chapter 20	The Importance of Polarity Thinking™ in Healthcare	149
Chapter 21	Leveraging a Healthy Healing Organization (H2O) Framework Grounded in Polarity Thinking™ to Achieve Healthcare Transformation	155
Chapter 22	Applying Polarity Principles for a Healthcare IT Start-Up	163
Chapter 23	Applying Polarity Thinking™ to Increase Healthcare Leadership Capacity	171
Chapter 24	Post-COVID-19 Planning for Sustained Benefit of Transition to Distant Learning Using PACT™	179
Chapter 25	Managing Community Issues Through Polarity Thinking™	187
Chapter 26	Social Network Strategies and Polarity Thinking™: Driving Forces in Social Work	195
Chapter 27	Polarity Thinking™ to Alleviate Tensions in Community-Engaged Health Research	203
Chapter 28	Sacred Union of Masculine *And* Feminine Principles: Applying the Master Polarity to Leadership and Culture	211
Chapter 29	Polarity Thinking™: The Foundation of Evolutionary Spirituality	219
Chapter 30	Competing Visions: How Opposing, Underlying Feelings About Human Nature Lead to Political Polarization	227
Chapter 31	Institute for Polarities of Democracy: Leveraging Democratic Values and Advancing Social Change	235
Chapter 32	How Does Polarity Mapping Connect With Our Built-In Neurology?	243
Chapter 33	Polarity Thinking™ as a Catalyst for Experiential Learning	249
Chapter 34	Polarity Coaching®	257
Chapter 35	Polarities Are Generative Tensions at the Heart of Organization Evolution: A Living Systems Approach to Creating Conditions for Flourishing	263
Chapter 36	Polarity Thinking™ and Oshry's Organic Systems Framework	271
Chapter 37	Alleviating the Suffering of Paradox by Mapping Polarities	279
Chapter 38	Polarity-Based Inquiry	289
Chapter 39	Shifting From Drama to Empowerment: Using The Empowerment Dynamic* and Polarity Thinking™ to Engage Key Stakeholders	297
Chapter 40	Creating and Sustaining Virtual Teamwork Effectiveness: Final Research Report	305
Chapter 41	Polarity Thinking™ and Vertical Development	313
Chapter 42	Multarities™: Interdependencies of More Than Two	321

Themes Found in *And:* Volume Two

Volume Two is more of a resource book than a linear narrative; every chapter can be referenced by theme. The authors have identified up to three themes their chapters most directly address. One way you may find this book useful is to identify the theme(s) of greatest interest to you and focus on the chapters that include them.

Theme **Chapter**

- Consulting & Leadership   1, 2, 4-23, 25, 26, 28, 33-42
- IT & Tech   6, 18, 22
- Healthcare   19-24, 32
- Learning & Education   2, 9-12, 14, 17, 19, 24, 27, 30, 32, 34, 40, 41
- Social & Cultural   1-5, 26-29, 31, 35-39, 42
- Faith & Spiritual   3, 11, 28, 29
- Democracy & Politics   1, 4, 5, 25, 30, 31
- Methodology & Model   3, 6-10, 12-14, 17, 20-24, 26, 27, 29-42

Resources 331

Appendix A   Themes Found in *And:* Volume Two 332
Appendix B   Foundational Polarities and the Polarity Resource Portal 333
Appendix C   New Realities in *And:* Volume Two 334
More Praise for *And* 335
Blank Map for Your Duplication and Use 338

Introduction to *And: Volume Two* and Authors
Barry Johnson

And: Volume One is a foundational book for understanding what polarities are and how they work. Polarities are interdependent pairs that need each other to be successful over time. Because they are interdependent, we connect the two poles of a polarity with the word "*And.*"

One central polarity from Volume One is Claiming Power *And* Sharing Power. Volume One and Volume Two can be seen in the context of this polarity. Volume One is an example of me claiming power while Volume Two is about sharing power. In Volume One, I am talking; in Volume Two, I am joining you in listening.

About the Authors

When it came to inviting people to contribute to *And:* Volume Two – Applications, I chose those who have graduated from our two-year Polarity Mastery Program at Polarity Partnerships. They are all well-grounded in Polarity Thinking™ and represent a variety of disciplines and life experiences. They were invited to write a chapter and to invite other practitioners to co-author their chapter if they desired. I am grateful for their response and for the richness they have created.

Section One: Polarity Thinking Supports Radical Possibilities for Equity

This opening section directly addresses the polarity Dominant Culture *And* Marginalized Cultures by listening to polarity practitioners who are members of one or more marginalized groups. They are providing us with perspectives from the marginalized about how a polarity lens can be useful in addressing marginalization. This section provides a context for looking back at Volume One and looking forward to the rest of Volume Two.

Section Two: Expanded Applications of Polarity Thinking

The rest of the book provides a wide range of perspectives and experiences from an extended group of caring and creative people. Each has made a solid connection between their passion and Polarity Thinking. It is a feast of thought and experience.

I think I speak for all of the co-authors of *And:* Volume Two in hoping that you find this book useful in your own efforts to make a difference.

Enjoy, Barry

Find bio and contact info for all lead authors for each chapter at
www.polaritypartnerships.com/certified-polarity-practitioners

SECTION ONE
Polarity Thinking™ Supports Radical Possibilities for Equity

Beth Applegate, MSOD
Peter Whitt, MSW, LSW
Chandra Irvin, MDiv, MEd
Elaine Yarbrough, PhD
Lindsay Y. Burr, MS

Peace is the presence of every condition that dignifies you and me. Food, housing, education, justice, healthcare: conditions that make you think you have a future. ~ Nobel Peace Laureate Leymah Gbowee

This first section is unique in authorship and universal in application. These five chapters are placed first in this book with intention – to center those of us who write with the explicit purpose of inviting you to witness Polarity Thinking™ and its application through the work of those most impacted by inequitable power and privilege. These chapters offer Radical Possibilities for social Equity through the lens of Polarity Thinking.

Radical Possibilities for Equity also offers Support *And* Challenge to you in recognizing *your own* proximity to power and privilege. All of the authors in <u>And: Applications</u> recognize the embedded nature of social location/membership (race, class, gender, etc.) and proximity to power. Though authors may not speak directly to it, they are aware, individually and collectively, that this dynamic is a given and at play in each application of Polarity Thinking offered.

We understand that it will take courage and will to achieve Radical Possibilities for Equity. This is our collective way to offer another framework to better manage the feelings, thoughts, and behaviors that emerge as we each grapple with how racism produces and reproduces organizational, societal, and global structures of domination. It is also our desire to share Radical Possibilities for Equity by truly Seeing, therefore Loving, each and all of us.

Nationally, the COVID-19 pandemic is the most recent event to evidence in high relief the long history of racial injustices that expose the inadequacies of our health care system. Systemic failure to respond quickly, effectively, and without consideration of social location/membership, inevitably and dramatically impact the ability of all people to receive basic needs: food, education, jobs, healthcare, shelter, and safety. Polarity Thinking is one way to engage in alternative possibilities in order to create equitable systemic change processes, which advance just organizational structures and systems, promoting societal racial justice and social responsibility.

Each chapter acknowledges the presence and pitfalls of *Or*-thinking when not in partner with *And*-thinking. Each chapter also sits within the two overarching polarities Barry outlined in the introduction to <u>Volume One</u>, "All Are Loved *And* Accountable – All Are Connected *And* Each Is Unique." Understanding both of these will help all of us engage Radical Possibilities for Equity sooner and with more sustainability.

Find bios and contact info for these authors at
www.polaritypartnerships.com/certified-polarity-practitioners

Reimagine Equity and Justice Through a Polarity Lens
Beth Applegate, MSOD

Everyone is a member of numerous group identities.[1] Group identities shape how we see ourselves, and how others see us and treat us. Group identities intersect and impact our access to unearned privileges, resulting in a "system of inequity."[2] Group membership is woven throughout U.S. history and remains embedded today in our social, political, and economic reality, and informs and influences the network of relationships, policies, structures, rules, and laws among and between education, healthcare, faith-based, banking, criminal justice, and media institutions, etc.

I'm primarily located in the dominant group, because I'm white, cis-gender, financially secure, college educated, and raised in a hetero-normative all white family in a majority white community and state, shaped by white cultural norms of a small Midwestern college town. I'm also a member of the dominant group which defines normality. The dominant racial group that decides what behaviors are valuable. Whiteness[3] determines what groups are racialized, white fragility[4] prioritizes racial comfort, and white culture prefers *either/Or*-thinking.[5]

U.S. history has clearly demonstrated how white people have received the most accumulated unearned advantages because of race. As a result of the dominant norms, beliefs, structures, and practices, white people have benefited from an entire system that has adapted itself for hundreds of years and which has resulted in affirmative action for white people for hundreds of years. For example, I have accumulated unearned advantages because of my proximity to power based on my skin color. I also benefit from dominant culture, and related socio-political systems embedded in whiteness and white culture. This is the same system and conditioning that trained me *not* to see how white dominant culture operates or how it benefits me. It is also true that the dominant culture of which I'm a member at the same time contributes to othering, also known as marginalizing and oppressing of other groups.

I must stay aware that I operate from the filters imposed by my racial identity as a white person – and from the beliefs, behaviors, and assumptions of white supremacy.

---

[1] Coaston, J. referencing Crenshaw, K. As seen in *Vox*. www.vox.com/the-highlight/2019/5/20/18542843. Updated May 28, 2019
[2] Influencers in my learning/study about system of inequity: Butler, Leiderman, Jones, and Potapchuk, 2016.
[3] Influencers in my learning/study of whiteness: Alcoff, 2015; Allen,1994; Bush, 2011; Tochluk, 2010; DiAngelo, 2012; Jensen, 2006; Kivel, 2002; Metzel, 2019; Rasmussen, 2011; Kendall, 2012; Lipsitiz, 2006; Anderson, 2017; Wise, 2011; Olou, 2018; Irving, 2014.
[4] Influencer in my learning/study of white fragility: DiAngelo, 2018.
[5] Influencers in my learning/study of white culture: Okun,1999; Katz,1999; Shearer, 2002; Partee and Potapchuk, 2014.

Internalized white supremacy is defined as:

> *A complex multi-generational socialization process that teaches white people to believe, accept, and/or live out superior societal definitions of self and to fit into and live out superior societal roles. These behaviors define and normalize the race construct and its outcome: white supremacy.*[6]

The purpose of cultural equity, inclusion, and justice efforts are to challenge oppression and privilege and make visible the underlying assumptions that produce and reproduce organizational, societal, and global structures of domination. Polarity Thinking™ is one way to engage in alternative possibilities and create equitable organizational change processes, that advance just organizational structures and systems, promoting racial justice and social responsibility.

As I grew to understand the systemic nature of my dominant white culture, I learned I'm simultaneously a target of discrimination because of my gender and sexual orientation. Much like white privilege, heterosexism reinforces heterosexuality as the norm and other sexual orientations as inferior. While I represent the dominant racial group, I'm also a member of an oppressed group. Again, even though I may be the subject of discrimination based on my sexual orientation, privileging still occurs because I am white. That said, because of their membership in a racialized group, women of color who are also lesbians will experience additional oppression.[7]

For twenty-three years, I've led my independent organization development (OD) consulting practices and have worked with hundreds of organizations. As an Applied Behavioral Science practitioner-scholar, I focus on cultural equity, inclusion, and justice (CEIJ). I work at the intersection of OD theory, Dare to Lead™ (DTL) courage skills building, and applying Polarity Thinking through a racial justice lens. As one of the 700 worldwide certified facilitators, I utilize Brené Brown's research on courage, vulnerability, shame, and empathy in my work with other white people to disrupt their internalized whiteness. The most significant finding from Dr. Brown's research is that courage is a collection of four skill sets that, like Polarity Thinking, are teachable, measurable, and observable.

Through my journey, I've deepened my acceptance that polarities live in me and I live in polarities. I've deepened my understanding of the value of being able to distinguish *a problem to solve* from a *polarity to leverage*. A polarity cannot be solved. The wisdom that resides in the upside of both poles must be leveraged together for the greater good. With a polarity, it is always in the best interest for any part to take care of the whole it is within *And* any whole to take care of the parts within. You can see these long-term interests in *Figure 1,* p. 8. I'm grateful

---

[6] Crossroads Ministry. "Racial Identity Caucusing: A Strategy for Building Anti-Racist Collectives." www.seattlechildrens.org/globalassets/documents/clinics/diversity/racial-identity-caucusing.pdf. Accessed April, 2021.

[7] St. Onge, P., and Applegate, B. *Embracing Cultural Competency: A Roadmap for Nonprofit Capacity Builders.* Alliance, 2009, p. 9.

Barry has been part of my journey of the last eight years because Polarity Thinking brings tremendous value to my CEIJ work. White dominant culture reinforces *either/Or*-thinking and Polarity Thinking (*both/And*-thinking) expands possibilities as a racial justice practitioner with clients.

There are many barriers and common pitfalls in CEIJ efforts in my client-partner systems. From a Polarity Thinking perspective, many of the barriers are rooted in the need to build the client-partner capacity to differentiate a polarity to leverage from a problem to solve. Two pitfalls are rooted in using *Or*-thinking rather than *And*-thinking when working with the two polarities Barry shared in the introduction to <u>Volume One</u>, "All Are Loved *And* Accountable – All Are Connected *And* Each Is Unique."[8]

As a CEIJ practitioner, a primary focus of my work is to support clients in building a brave organizational culture. We start with identifying and operationalizing individual and organizational values into behaviors which everyone in the organization is held accountable to, onboarded for, evaluated against. In this process, we expose individual and organizational working assumptions, co-develop common language and common agreements to support building relationships, and create the conditions to disrupt white dominant culture in the organization. We then practice the new culture values and norms that are teachable, measurable, and observable, and we evaluate and rebuild policies, practices, and structures to be equitable, inclusive, and just. Throughout an organizational CEIJ initiative, I utilize Polarity Thinking to support my clients; clarify individual and organizational values; determine just structures, policies, and practices; and strengthen relationships. Supplementing *Or*-thinking with *And*-thinking supports those resisting change efforts, because there is wisdom in resistance. Recognizing and intentionally leveraging polarities serves as a catalyst to convert organizational dysfunction and inequity into more effective and just organizational structures.

As a keynote speaker and large-group conference facilitator, I use Polarity Thinking to support *And* challenge conference goers to reimagine equity and justice. Following is one example of how I have applied Polarity Thinking to make a difference in my life and as an CEIJ keynote. It is with Humility *And* Confidence that I offer it to you.

In April 2016, at the annual White Privilege Conference (WPC), I co-facilitated a day-long session titled: "Reimagining Equity and Justice Through a Polarity Lens." As a multi-racial team familiar with how polarities operate, we knew that some version of a Structural *And* Individual polarity would emerge. Leveraging this variation of polarity is a common and essential ingredient in successful CEIJ initiatives.

Early in the session we taught participants how polarities operate in multiple levels of system, and how and why it is in the long-term interest to leverage the Part *And* Whole energy dynamic.

---

[8] Johnson, Barry. *And: Making a Difference by Leveraging Polarity, Paradox or Dilemma. Volume One – Foundations.* HRD Press, 2020.

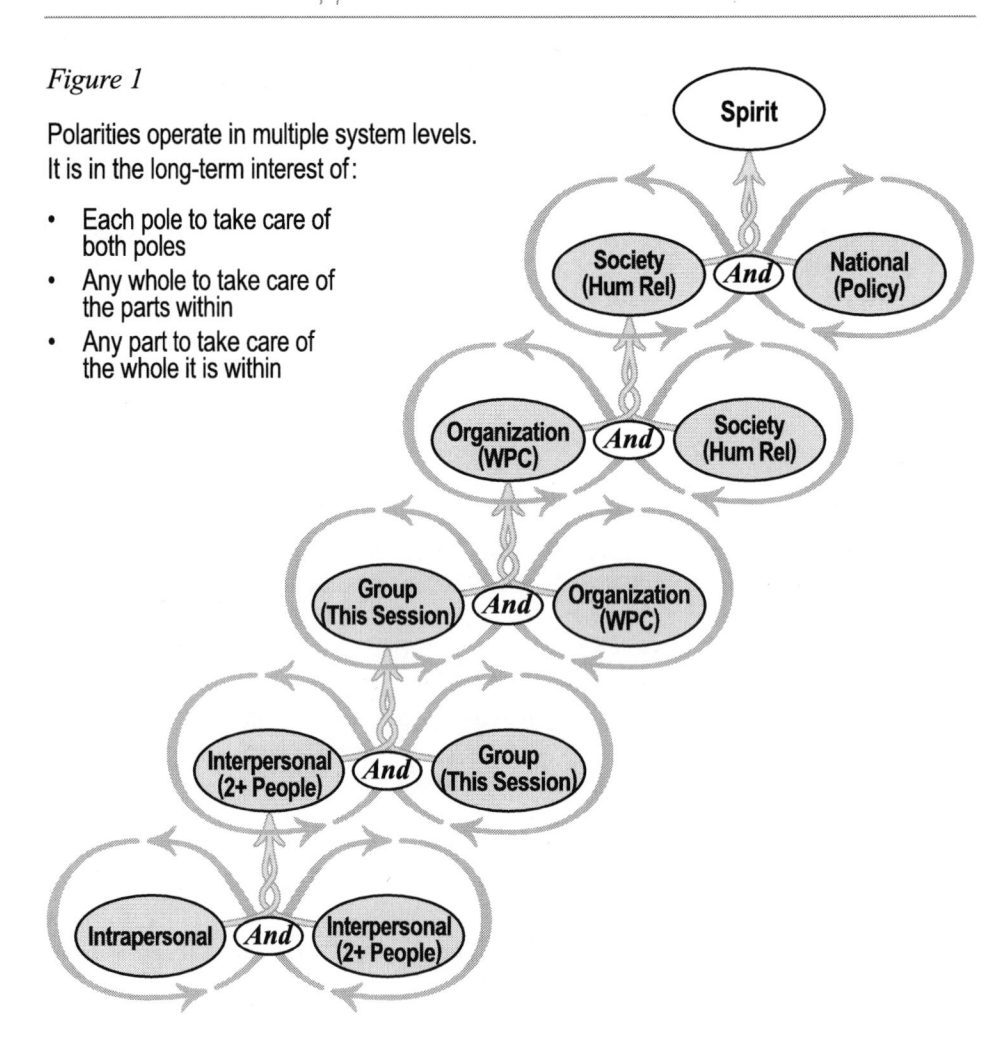

Figure 1

Polarities operate in multiple system levels. It is in the long-term interest of:

- Each pole to take care of both poles
- Any whole to take care of the parts within
- Any part to take care of the whole it is within

```
                                    Spirit
                        Society  (And)  National
                       (Hum Rel)         (Policy)
              Organization  (And)  Society
                 (WPC)            (Hum Rel)
         Group       (And)   Organization
      (This Session)             (WPC)
   Interpersonal  (And)  Group
    (2+ People)        (This Session)
Intrapersonal  (And)  Interpersonal
                       (2+ People)
```

In *Figure 1* above, we illustrated how polarities operate within the context of the White Privilege Conference (WPC), and This Session (second and third polarity set from bottom) refers to the day-long pre-conference session joined by a large number of conference attendees.

Building on a pre-session homework assignment, we asked participants to answer the following: "when confronted by the issue of white privilege, in your personal experience, what thoughts or behaviors would you like to move *from* and what thoughts or behaviors would you like to move *to?*" We then compiled the results and rewrote them as polarities to teach participants how to name their "from" and "to" poles, based on the answers to their pre-session homework assignment.

On the following page is the list of polarities (*Figure 2*) the facilitators created based on the submitted *from/to* homework assignment of 35-40 participants.

Figure 2: White Privilege Behaviors You Want to Move From ... To ...

From ...	To ...
Humility	Confidence
Intent	Impact
Honor personal boundaries	Openness
Allow others to take responsibility	Assume personal responsibility
Safety / security	Daring / untethered
Open learning	Informed sharing
Questioning the other	Questioning myself
External challenges	Personal purpose
Holding the other accountable	Patience with others
Detachment	Engagement
Rejection	Adoption
Analysis	Action
Realization of WP	Confrontation of WP
Listening	Speaking out
Independent assessments	Interdependence and unified action
Being	Doing
Knowing self	Knowing other

Figure 3 shows one assignment response within a Polarity Map®. The participant wanted to move *from* Timid statements of equality while giving deference to whites *to* Speaking Truth to Power statements that hold white people accountable. Using the *from/to* statement we looked at naming the two poles: Humility *And* Confidence were identified as possible pole names. These names can be confirmed or edited by the participant making the original statement. The advantage of putting their statement on a Polarity Map is that it helps the person appreciate that there is more to the picture. In the upper left (+A), they can fill in what they value about humility. In the lower right (-D), they can fill in what they might fear would happen if they pursued Confidence without also holding on to what they value about Humility. This more complete picture, seeing more of the polarity and more of themselves, increases the likelihood that they will in the future, as white people, be able to speak truth to power (other white people) in ways that hold all white people accountable.

Figure 3

+A Values	+C Values
	Speaking Truth to Power statements that hold white people accountable
Humility *And* Confidence
Timid statements of equality while giving deference to whites	
- B Fears	- D Fears

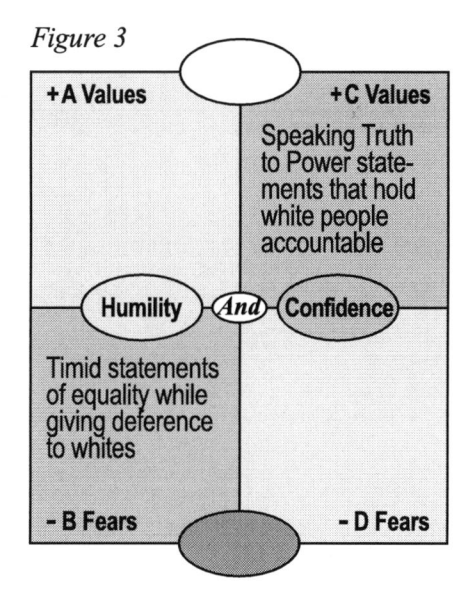

Once participants understood the *from/to* energy flow, we facilitated a group discussion which resulted in populating the four quadrants of a Humility *And* Confidence Polarity Map (like *Figure 3*). We then facilitated self-reflection, reflection in pairs, small group and full group meaning-making, and exploration processes to engage participants in asking themselves, "What does all of this say about the challenges we face when attempting to interrupt power and privilege, and the opportunities we have to interrupt white privilege and power so that we all thrive?"

To conclude the day-long session, we focused somatically, getting in touch with how the polarity energy moves externally and how it moves in and through us. We facilitated the entire group in creating a Polarity Map on the floor. As we walked through the quadrants of the map on the floor, we brainstormed content for each quadrant and put it on a large Polarity Map on the wall. The group named the poles within the greater purpose context of interrupting white privilege and power.

Another one of the ubiquitous and challenging polarities to leverage in equity, inclusion and justice initiatives, is the polarity of Impact *And* Intent – or Intent *And* Impact depending upon which is your *to/from* pole. And this answer in the case of racial equity, inclusion, and justice efforts, will be influenced based upon your racialized group identity. This map (*Figure 4*) places Impact on the left (*from*/preference) pole *And* Intent on the right (*to*/growth) pole. It was developed by Chandra G. Irvin, MDIV, M.ED, a Black mentor, colleague, and friend from the Polarity Mastery program, co-facilitator of the session described in this chapter, and contributor to this Polarity book volume.

Action Steps +A
- Listen to Impacted person – BTF
- Intent person in own words – BTF
- Is there more?
- Express regret
- Request to shift
- Dialogue for future

Early Warnings – B
- Moving to different subject before hearing from Intent person

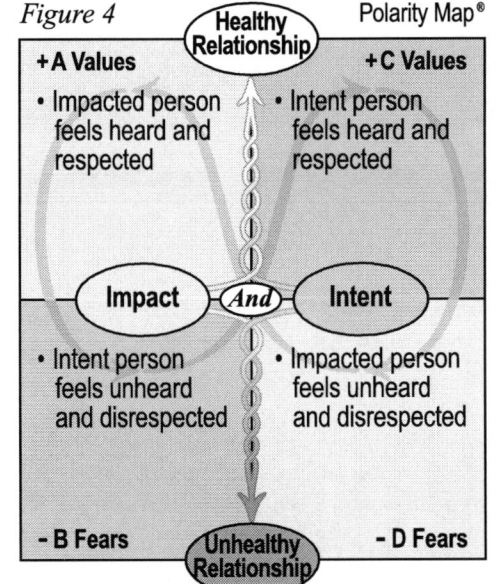

Figure 4 — Polarity Map®

Healthy Relationship

+A Values
- Impacted person feels heard and respected

+C Values
- Intent person feels heard and respected

Impact *And* Intent

- Intent person feels unheard and disrespected
- Impacted person feels unheard and disrespected

– B Fears — – D Fears

Unhealthy Relationship

Action Steps +C
- Listen to Intent person – BTF
- Impacted person in own words – BTF
- Is there more?
- Request to shift
- Dialogue for future

Early Warnings – D
- Effort by Intent person to "explain" before understanding by Impacted person

No matter what your preference poll is, the impacted person always shares the Behavior that caused the impact, along with their Thoughts and Feelings (BTF Action Steps +A) *before* moving to the Action Steps on the intent side of the map (BTF Action Steps +C). After the person holding the intent pole finishes the final step, the pair focus on the future, dialogue about how to honor intent and avoid negative impact in the future, and stay in dialogue until both feel seen, heard, and understood.

Vulnerable, courageous, and shame-free relationships with ourselves and each other across race requires a commitment to self-awareness, growth, and practice. The Impact *And* Intent Polarity Map supports both people in maintaining emotional intelligence, racial literacy, and self-mastery while at the same time also supports components of restorative justice. As my colleague Rusia Mohiuddin often states, "*At the heart of sustainable movements must be the beat of sustainable people.*" Regardless of group membership, living into the wisdom of both the Impact *And* Intent poles with integrity requires the conscious use of self. It requires us to be aware of and intentionally direct our beliefs, our emotions, our thoughts and our behaviors. Every action we take is directed by some combination of emotions and thoughts. Each is a choice point reflecting a level of mastery of the conscious use of self in service to cultural equity, inclusion, and justice. How we use ourselves in one situation may or may not be effective in another, though similar in situation. Self-mastery at the level of emotions and thought usually results from introspection, a personal practice, and often therapy, along with the understanding that our egos and minds are not who we are, or whose dictates we must follow. Rather, they are simple tools for our integrated selves to use at conscious choice.[9]

Conclusion

Every day we must strive to make choices to manage ourselves with compassion and empathy for ourselves and others. As Brené Brown says: "self-awareness and self-love matter."[10] Brown also teaches us that shame drives two messages: "I'm not good enough, and who do I think I am." We all have shame; it is universal and one of the most primitive human emotions we can experience, and we must learn how it operates and how to manage it within the context of cultural equity, inclusion, and justice efforts. Learning about our own emotional literacy and the commitment to a use of self-practice is key.[11] We cannot successfully disrupt policies, structures, rules, and laws at the systemic level, if we cannot effectively manage the discomfort, disruption, learning, unlearning, healing, relationship repair, and relationship building that is essential at the intra- and interpersonal levels (Part *And* Whole polarity).

As someone who belongs to dominant and oppressed identity groups, I have experienced the benefits of applying Polarity Thinking to myself, my relationships, and the client systems with which I consult. As a member of numerous dominant

---

[9] Seashore & Broom. OD Practitioner Program. 2005.
[10] Brown, Brené. *Dare to Lead: Brave Work, Tough Conversations, Whole Hearts.* Random House, 2018.
[11] Jamieson and Cheung-Judge, 2020; Seashore and Broom, 2005; Jamison, Auron, and Shechtman, 2017.

groups – particularly as a white person – I remain committed to leveraging the upside of the wisdom held in both upper quadrants of a Part *And* Whole Polarity Map and in the Polarity Maps within the multiple systems in which I live. I believe Arundhati Roy when she says, "Another world is not only possible, she is on her way. On a quiet day, I can hear her breathing." I'm committed to becoming a new kind of white person through owning my story and loving myself through the process of pursuing equity, inclusion, and justice within my spheres of influence.

In Mercy *And* Justice, Beth (she/her)

Find bio and contact info for author Beth Applegate at
www.polaritypartnerships.com/certified-polarity-practitioners

Black Survival:
White Power and Privilege
Peter 'Nasib' Whitt, MSW, LSW

"See me fully because I see you fully ... be a humanitarian and love beyond your oppression, but love yourself first so that you can love others. You will not lose your power." I wrote this six years ago as part of a chapter within a book titled, A Race Anthology: Dispatches and Artifacts from a Segregated City.[12]

I firmly believe that in our great country, the United States of America, leaders and powerful political agendas compete to maintain power to the neglect of sharing power; perpetuate economic wealth position, concentrate self-interests, and sustain white economic advantage. As a result, Black communities and people of color are disproportionately placed in economic disadvantage.

The greatest challenge faced by many Black people in our history was and continues to be driven by racially inequitable practices within structurally racist systems that have systematically advantaged white people over time. Government-led institutional discriminatory practices against Black people have been documented in our history for centuries. The practices have shown up as slavery, jim crow, the new jim crow (disproportionate number of Blacks and people of color in prison), discriminatory practices at the onset of public housing and bank lending toward Blacks and others, and disinvestment in urban school outcomes consistently impact Blacks and other people of color at a higher rate than whites.

Many Blacks are still alive who spent decades navigating life to avoid overt white supremacy behaviors and not die or endure physical harm as a result of appearing to have an equal voice or the same rights as stated by the Constitution. Just think, the Fair Housing Act was established in 1968. This policy was put in place to prohibit discriminatory acts by renters, municipalities, insurance companies, etc., against people based on race, religion, sex, national origin, family status, or disability. Lack of fair housing is one example among many institutional policies and practices that created inequitable conditions for Blacks across our country in disproportionate volume, that created and sustained white privilege, and that perpetuates segregated cities to this date.

I'd encourage readers to look at the work of the Race Equity Institute and authors like James Baldwin, William Julius Wilson, Tim Wise, Robin DiAngelo, Carol Anderson, Bryan Stevenson, john a. powell, and Bettina L. Love to name a few. In the body of work written by these authors and others, you can't deny the truths

---

[12] Washington, R. A. and Moulthrop, D. *A Race Anthology: Dispatches and Artifacts from a Segregated City.* GTK Press, 2016.

of racism and white privilege that have been clearly documented, shedding light on the historic and economic investment in a structure that continues to provide systemic advantages for white people and the wealthy, to the disproportionate neglect of Black people and Black communities. We must connect the dots of white power and influence. Colin Kaepernick was politicized and disenfranchised for standing up in protest of unjust policing and murder of Blacks by the police. If he were a white successful quarterback, what might have been different?

We were born into and live with the policies, practices, and political agendas that disenfranchise Black people. We live with the disproportionate and biased war on drugs campaign that imprisoned Blacks with unfair sentences for the distribution of crack cocaine in comparison to the powdered cocaine that was used primarily by white people. The war on drugs created a new biased wealth-building opportunity; companies investing in private prisons. We live with the disproportionate infection and death rate of Black people as a result of the COVID-19 pandemic based on segregated lived spaces nationally. We live with the death of George Floyd (Black man) by a police officer's knee pressed on his neck for 9:29. We live with Ahmaud Arbery, a Black jogger in a South Georgia neighborhood who was shot and killed after being tracked down by three white male citizens (one a former police officer) and killed on suspicion of being a burglar. We live with the fact that NO arrest was made for almost three months until a video emerged and civil rights lawyers were engaged and protests began. We live in white privilege.

We live with the experiences of Black and white people, as if they are the same. All people from diverse backgrounds work within organizations. It is a false expectation that people should dismiss all their lived experience to meet the mission of the organization; burying the tensions that exist due to their race and ethnicity. The transition from work to home may consist of low income or wealthy spaces, ethnically diverse or homogenous. These are a few characteristics that shape our conscious and unconscious thoughts, bias, and actions.

I have carried my tensions in organizations and so have my friends and colleagues who are Black working in majority white organizations or an organization with white accountability, like a board of directors. I wake up daily understanding that my skin color, being a Black man interfacing with white people, can provoke consistent stress. I have learned to manage that stress due to a cultivated resiliency, self-awareness, and comfort by understanding my value as a Black man, my Black voice, and a connected solidarity to uplift Black people.

Cleveland, Ohio is my birthplace. I grew up on the near east side in Garden Valley public housing and shifted to a housing development on east 75th on Woodland Avenue. Both neighborhoods were predominantly Black, low income, with limited access to economic opportunities. As a teen, my family moved to the near west side due to my mother getting a job at MetroHealth Medical Center, the city's public hospital. This began my emergence into diverse ethnicities and culture where an abundance of Latinx, whites, Black, and mixed housing coexisted.

Life has constant tension. When you spend time in a majority white space where you live, work, play, and worship, your race is always present in most things that you do; others see you before they know you due to the Blackness of your skin. Utilizing a polarity framework, what are the possibilities to survive for Black people in the midst of white space (social constructs) to uplift my Blackness, my culture, my pride in a safe and productive manner? How might I manage the pitfalls of oppressive thinking and behaviors that can result from being isolated due to my need to fit in and belong? What can I do to reduce the risk of over-focusing on proving my worth as a Black person navigating majority white spaces?

To start, I will share a few stories that may reflect Black survival within the web of white privilege and the Black Self Talk (BST) that can be stressful, challenging, and encouraging.

Story #1: Maturing in My Blackness

I got a call from a friend who had an interview for a very competitive leadership role in Cleveland, Ohio. The conversation was upbeat as my friend shared thoughts about the interview process. She went on to say her hair was braided. I paused on the other end of the phone. I said "braids hmmm." She responded by saying she did not have time to change her hair style before the interview due to recent travel. My next question was, how do you feel about that? Her reply was simple. "This is who I am, I would have normally changed my hairstyle but I am comfortable with my braids and glad I left them in." This was a powerful and affirming moment of self-assurance. It demonstrated self-confidence, comfort and pride in her Blackness.

I believe many of us have had that talk in the mirror, thoughts while driving that become the conversations running in our heads. I'd like to refer to this as *Black Self Talk* (BST) specifically due to our black skin and effort to survive in a white social construct. Here are some bullets of BST that can create stress, affirmations, and tears depending upon the lived experience as a Black person.

Black Self Talk (BST)

- Will the white people see my braided/locked hair as a display of being too Black?
- Will other Black people see my unapologetically Black expression as less professional (ghetto)?
- Maybe I should wear a more conservative look and then express myself if I get the job.
- Damn it! Why do I have to even think about this? I am Black ... not white ... my hair is different, so what?! I am qualified!

Story #2: Finding Inclusion

I was working as the Director of Community Outreach at a hospital in Cleveland, Ohio. The cafeteria was a comforting place in the hospital. Now, I must say, hunger was a great motivation to go there. However, there was something else I felt. It was a welcoming space where most of the workers were Black in comparison to other places in the hospital. In hindsight, I felt a sense of belonging. It was the head nods, high fives, and smiles. It was the consistent questions; How is it going? What's up little Whitt? You are looking good. Keep up the good work. It was words coming from other Black co-workers. While they did not know it, they inspired me and bridged that lonely space of being one of few. Upon leaving the cafeteria, I had a bit more energy in my stride. I was refueled by those small but powerful interactions.

The other part of this story is simple. My position carried the title Director within it. As stated, I found my tribe among the cafeteria staff.

Black Self Talk (BST)

- Thank God, Black people, my tribe ... amen.
- I definitely have to represent for me and my Black folk.
- Okay, remember, everyone Black is different and may not feel the same as you.
- White leadership want diversity? Here we go! Stop playing! As long as they are comfortable?

Story #3: Changing the Tone and Having a Tone

A Black professional shares her story of working in pharmaceutical sales. She has more initials behind her name than most people. Upon meeting her, it was a very casual conversation. Fast forward to my follow-up call and voicemail. I listen to the voicemail and while the name was correct, the voice did not sound like her. She sounded less Black and more white based on her dialect. She later told me, while qualified to do her job more so than many of her white colleagues, most of the physicians are white and most of the sales persons are white women. To be more effective she has learned to "code switch," sounding more white, to increase access and opportunity to fit into this white social construct and be successful.

Story #4: Speaking up Has a Cost

On the other end of this experience was a shared story of a working Black professional who expressed concerns regarding the lack of diversity within a predominantly white organization. Other Black associates agreed, and quickly let their peer know outside the meeting. Even a few white colleagues agreed. Over time, the Black professional's consistent protest and passionate communication style led to two things: The Black associates distancing themselves from their passionate Black colleagues, and/or conceding to not speak up in the meeting and eventually letting the subject become a talking point with no real action.

After hearing this story, I realized this alienation of the outspoken Black person may lead to the label of *the subordinate, angry Black person*. I do believe there is a time to unite and have white people understand the emotional isolation and lived experiences of Black people that may ignite passionate energy. It is okay if white people are uncomfortable. Yet, as white people hold power, Black people may become the target of their shame, guilt, and inability to have uncomfortable conversations on race and culture.

Black Self Talk (BST)

- Wow, everyone in here don't care ... speak up! **I can't be the only one that sees this #%$^**
- **WTF!** I get tired of having to sound white just to get my foot in the door.

- I agree with everything they are saying but I can't risk losing this job.
- Diversity ... yeah right!. They are not ready.
- These white folks will act for as long as it looks good to the public.

Most of these statements are based on a root cause; being a Black person. The BST is an important part of the narrative. I am a Black man, and the ability to feel safe when working with a white leadership team can be very challenging for Black people from multiple perspectives. No matter how effective a Black person may be in leadership, there is a consistent need to manage their Blackness and potentially their viewpoint on issues that can make white leaders uncomfortable, or that may be translated as offensive or disruptive. A white leader may welcome perspectives, yet the Black leader has to consider if they are prepared to fully disclose their Black viewpoint or to minimize their perspective to keep their job and survive.

I am suggesting that when a Black person is navigating white privilege and power, over time it can be like pushing on the gas pedal of a car with no way to stop until it is either out of gas or the engine runs hot. This level of self-management can be viewed as resiliency. I am suggesting it has become Black survival. I am suggesting this type of stress is an imbedded component of having black skin color in a white culture. It is Black survival within the social norming of our country, our history, and organizational settings, all of which mirror our national viewpoint based on dominant white culture.

In summary, the national culture of whiteness, the norms and practices that influence organizational culture and the labeling of Blackness that shapes opportunity or limits opportunity for Black people should be acknowledged and challenged. For that to happen, we need to provide a space for safe uncomfortable conversations on policies and practices that can result in a more racially equitable space. It is important that Black people find ways to better survive while white people catch up to compassion and conscious inclusion practice, and see the brilliance of why diversity can serve a greater purpose beyond their bottom financial line. Until then, Black survival in white privilege and power is required.

Survive to Thrive: Black Self Love *And* Black Collective Love

Utilizing a polarity framework, what are the possibilities to survive for Black people in the midst of white spaces (social constructs) to uplift my Blackness, my culture, my pride in a safe and productive manner? How might I manage the pitfalls of oppressive thinking and negative outcomes as I strive to fit in and be a leader within the dominant group culture.

A great possibility to better navigate and manage tensions impacting Black people navigating white social constructs effectively is to see the value of having both **Black Self Love (BSL)** *And* **Black Collective Love (BCL)**. Using the Polarity Map® as a tool to organize thinking and wisdom, we can look at **BSL** *And* **BCL** – one of many polarities to see and leverage – as a catalyst to navigate white power and privilege over time. (*Figure 1*, next page)

Figure 1 — Polarity Map®

Action Steps +A
- Uplift your Black voice, actions and lived experience within the U.S. and immigrant experience
- Appreciate unique artifacts, style, rituals, and heritage, etc.

Early Warnings –B
- Lack spirit of Black unity
- Distance from others with strong Black expression
- Overly competitive amongst Blacks
- Drifting from Black culture

+A Values
- Black Pride (individual)
- Black Self-Care
- Black Pride (my ancestry)

Black Self Love **And** *Black Collective Love*

- Black Self-Centered Voice
- Black Cold-Heartedness
- Black Isolation (overly competitive toward Blacks)

–B Fears

+C Values
- Black Unified Voice
- Black Compassion
- Black Global Unity

- Black Individual Voice Loss
- Black Self-Neglect
- Black Loss of Unique Ancestral History

–D Fears

Survive to Thrive ↑ / Oppressed & Diminished ↓

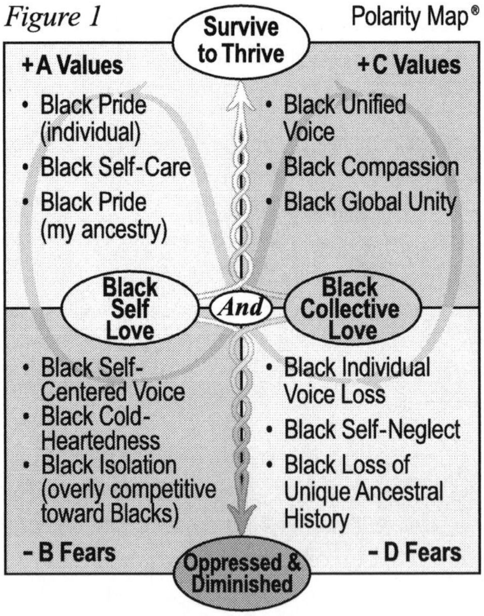

Action Steps +C
- Uplift other people's Black lived experience within the U.S. and immigrant experience
- Elevate the virtue of Black collective praise and support

Early Warnings –D
- Loosing sense of unique personal Black perspective/voice
- Distancing from my Blackness, rituals

Survive to Thrive is stated as the greater purpose statement (GPS). It is the lived Black experience and the complex outcomes that impact how one manages white privilege and power within white social constructs. Ideally, consider the GPS as a personal vision statement; a powerful and uplifting goal that allows you to aim for the galaxy and fall amongst the stars.

Seeing Black Self Love (Individual) *And* Black Collective Love (Collective)

A key step to navigating toward the GPS is by seeing value in pairs – polarities – to provide you with a full picture. For example, a typical society consists of self *And* community, one part (self/individual) of a whole (community/collective). We will start by looking at **Black Self Love (BSL)** *And* **Black Collective Love (BCL)**. Ideally, this polarity can be used to call out visionary outcomes (+A, +C Values) and potential challenges (–B, –D Fears) based on the lived Black experience as a result of white privilege and power (white social constructs). One important rule is the Polarity pair must use words/language that are positive/neutral to those using the tool.

Identifying +A, +C Values to reach your GPS (Survive to Thrive) for BSL *And* BCL

Now that you can see the polarity pair **BSL** *And* **BCL**, let us take a closer look at the values (+A, +C) of this polarity. Each of the poles and their values should promote Black men, women, and youth capacity to navigate white social constructs more effectively. Many values can be generated for each pole, of which some are seen in *Figure 1* (+A, +C Values). Our goal is to align the polarity to help you see the part and the whole. Notice the left side values are specific to the self/individual *And* the right side aligns with the community/collective.

Powerful Questions:

To be successful within the white social construct, what are the values I want to hold, and action steps I can take for **Black Self Love** *(+A Values, Action Steps +A)?*

- Black Pride (individual): My unique Black artifacts, ethnic appearance (e.g., kinky hair, style, voice)
- Black Self-Care: Rituals rooted in my Blackness (e.g., prayer, meditation, culture, food)
- Black Pride (my ancestry): Heritage, family, history of my Black lineage, and lived experience

What are the values I want to hold and action steps I can take for **Black Collective Love** *to be successful within white social constructs (+C Values, Action Steps +C)?*
- Black Unified Voice: Uplifting other people's Blackness/culture and collective shared and lived experience
- Black Compassion toward other Blacks: Collective praise and support across diversity within and toward all Black communities
- Black Global Unity: Collective share of U.S. Black experiences and of people of color beyond the United States of America

Powerful Questions:

What happens when a person over-focuses on one pole to the neglect of the other pole over a period to time? Why might this occur? A person/entity may not see the need to act on the missing pole due to a fear of change, a fear of the other pole, and/or a potential blind spot and selfish benefit.

If I over-focus on **Black Self Love** *to the neglect of* **Black Collective Love**, *what are potential negative outcomes and what are the early warning signs that might show up* (-B Fears, Early Warnings -B)?
- Black Self-Centered Voice: Distant from other Blacks, lack spirit of unity
- Black Cold-Heartedness: No concern for other Blacks
- Black Isolation: Disconnect from other Black heritage, overly competitive (e.g., my lineage is more authentic than yours.)

If I over-focus on **Black Collective Love** *to the neglect of* **Black Self Love**, *what are potential negative outcomes and what are early warning signs that might show up* (-D Fears, Early Warnings -D)?
- Black Individual Voice Loss: Lose my unique personal Black perspective/voice
- Black Self-Neglect: Distancing from unique Black rituals used to care for self
- Black Loss of Unique Ancestral History

It is important to pay attention to the values we hold tight that have been instilled in us by our parents, history, media, and white projections onto Black people and culture. Being oppressed and the desperate need to belong can cause us to lose sight of our Blackness and beauty due to the need for approval within white constructs and white etiquette.

Implications for Practicing Inclusion Within Teams and Organizations

We have not seen sustainable practices within organizational culture addressing racial equity. Racial Affinity Groups (RAG) become the practice of sustained segregation within organizations. This sense of belonging is great, yet the interdependent value of integration disrupts the current white construct, prohibiting the cross-pollination of RAG to have tough, deliberate conversations to promote racial equity at both the vertical (top leaders) and horizontal (across departments) levels.

This type of separation sustains the white power and privilege at best. It mirrors the national culture within the organizational culture. As we look at john a. powell's work on targeted universalism in his book titled, <u>Racing To Justice; Transforming Our Conception Of Self And Others To Build A Society Of Inclusion,</u>[13] he calls out the need for both universal policies and practices which also include targeted approaches that provide inclusive practice addressing the unique needs of difference within groups. This could be mapped as a polarity: Targeted Policies and Practices *And* Universal Policies and Practices, with the GPS of Inclusive Culture.

For example, the unique need of racial inclusion at the vertical axis (top leaders) is needed within organizations. This may require organizations to redefine the "right fit," and their unique pipeline and ongoing support of Targeted Policies and Practices, while still sustaining Universal Policies and Practices of inclusion that encompasses gender, disabilities, and LGBTQI+. The power of white privilege often overlooks the value of targeted practices specific to racial inclusion; the results of which sustains and promotes the use of universalism as the source to address equity and inclusion. This practice is the blind spot that ultimately sustains inequities, white advantage, and privilege.

The courageous white leaders in white social constructs can leverage the work of john a. powell as one source. This tension mirrors the work and use of polarities, and is a key source and tool for racial inclusion that can tackle the most uncomfortable space as a part of group norming. This is not done without vision, will, courage, commitment, and co-conspirators.

I believe this work requires co-conspirators. I have leveraged the word co-conspirator that Bettina L. Love emphasizes in her book titled, <u>We Want To Do More Than Survive; Abolitionist Teaching and the Pursuit of Educational Freedom</u>.[14] Co-conspirators are trained; prepared to see the value of racial inclusion without fear of losing power and privilege within, and external to, their allegiance and group.

Recognizing the utility of polarities as a tool for inclusion by leveraging a *both/And* practice are critical steps toward racial equity in the politics, workplace, and communities. Recognizing the unjust and oppressive results that have impacted Black lives historically, both in the U.S. and globally at the hand of white privilege and power, requires our Black communities to pay close attention to our **Black Self Love** *And* **Black Collective Love** to ensure we continue to reach back and pull forward as we collectively strive in being unapologetically Black.

About Peter Whitt ~ www.polaritypartnerships.com/certified-polarity-practitioners

---

[13] powell, john a. *Racing to Justice: Transforming Our Conceptions of Self and Other to Build an Inclusive Society.* Indiana University Press, 2012.

[14] Love, Bettina L. *We Want To Do More Than Survive; Abolitionist Teaching and the Pursuit of Educational Freedom.* Beacon Press, 2019.

Contributing to a Just and Equitable World: Why Is This So Hard?

Chandra Irvin, MDiv, MEd

For over 30 years, I've had the opportunity to work with people who have fought the 'isms' – racism, sexism, ethnocentrism, classism, religious oppression, heterosexism, trans-oppression, ableism, and ageism. These people are my friends and colleagues who have chosen as their greater purpose to contribute to a more just and equitable world. Because they fight for equity and justice on behalf of others, I call them "Champions." Yet, Champions know they cannot do this work alone. They need partners; those who also seek to contribute to a more equitable and just world. I call these potential partners "Seekers" because, by their own admission, they haven't contributed enough, and they seek to do more.

Champions and Seekers: equally important in the quest, they both have chosen as their greater purpose contributing to a more just and equitable world. Their situations and experiences differ. Yet, in this pursuit they both reach a point where they hit the wall and wonder, "Why is this so hard?" Although I am sure there are many answers to this question, this essay will explore what I believe is one root cause for the difficulty Champions and Seekers experience.

Champions

Champions I've worked with have been leaders, managers, consultants, and volunteers. They have worked in the corporate, education, government, religious, and non-profit sectors. They are talented, skilled, and thoughtful, and their commitment to social transformation (evidenced by equity and justice for all) is one I share.

Champions are the ones who convene allies and skeptics to examine and challenge 'isms' in our society. They are the practitioners who seek to work out possible solutions and decide on best ways to proceed. They develop action plans and ways to measure progress. They help identify people to do the work, and monitor and evaluate progress. Champions facilitate creative and meaningful solutions to challenging issues and are rewarded with some positive movement. Then, suddenly, without warning, they hit a brick wall.

The so-called "commitments" by colleagues in the fight for equality and justice start to wane. That strategic plan that was months and months in planning gets cancelled. Then comes the unexpected surprise of finding a "woke"[15] colleague – whom they thought they could count on – napping right when their help is needed to advance the cause of social justice. When Champions take stock of their

---

[15] In the common vernacular of today, the term "woke" means a state of being alert to injustice in society.

personal investments and disappointments and compare them to the successes of those who perpetuate inequity and injustice, they wearily ask themselves, "Why is this so hard?" What else do I need to do to move us forward?

Seekers

Seekers desire to do more than they have done to eradicate inequity and injustice and take steps to prepare to do more. They attend training sessions, seminars, and conferences; read books and look at documentaries to deepen their understanding of social justice issues. They engage with and listen to those who are impacted by injustices and might even partner with truth tellers who challenge their complicity with systems of oppression. They secure mentors and allies who encourage them to stick with their commitment to equity and justice. Still, when internal conflicts arise and what Seekers want to do requires sacrifices they are not prepared to make, the Seeker's resolve wavers. The following anecdote highlights this tension.

We were nearing the end of a group session called, "Talking Race."[16] Lesa, the only one who had not spoken, began to tear up as she shared an incident that occurred when she, a white woman, had taken three black teens shopping. She had noticed the teens were being followed and asked store employees, "Is there some reason you are following my friends?" "Oh, you know, they are teenagers," came the reply. "No, I don't know," Lesa contested, "I've been in this store with white teenagers and no one followed them!" She sat forlorn after recounting the scene. Then with a tone of encouragement, a member of our group said, "You did a great thing by challenging those employees who were following the boys." "I haven't done enough," Lesa rejoined, through tears and a look of utter self-disgust, "I just haven't done enough."

Lesa's response revealed an inner struggle that had been brought on by events outside the store incident. Hers was an ongoing tension between wanting, but not being prepared, to do more to dismantle structures of racism. Witnessing her struggle, the familiar question came to mind, "Why is this so hard?"

Why Is This So Hard?

Over the years, in a number of venues, I have invited Champions and Seekers to explore this question through a polarity lens. The following reflects those experiences and what I've discovered.

I had gathered a group of 30 Champions and Seekers to examine issues of social transformation. I asked for a volunteer to answer two questions. Joshua, one of the Champions, came forward.

---

[16] The mission of Spalding University includes a commitment to "promote peace and justice." In support of this mission, the Community for Peace and Spiritual Renewal offers several interventions to deepen understanding of injustices and personal commitment to do something about them. One of those interventions is a bi-weekly experience called, "Talking Race." This incident took place during one of those sessions and is shared here with permission.

Chandra: Joshua, how would you describe our current social political environment and our progress toward social transformation?

Joshua: I describe the current environment as callous toward those who suffer injustice, caustic, and slow to change. As an advocate for equity and justice, I find the environment and the challenge terribly burdensome and tiring.

I wrote down "burdensome and tiring" and asked others about their experience. They described their frustrations with short-term fixes that yielded little results.

Chandra: Joshua, from your perspective, is this a problem that needs to be solved?

Joshua: Yes, absolutely. (Other participants agreed, so I continued.)

Chandra: So what are we solving for? (Participants discussed this then agreed they were solving for Social Transformation that is evidenced by Equity and Justice for All. If the transformation did not lead to equity and justice for all, it was not the kind of social transformation they were working toward. This became their greater purpose statement.)

Moving to an exercise, I asked participants to individually reflect on how they personally pursued that greater purpose. I asked them to choose between multiple pairs of alternatives similar to those in *Figure 1* below (e.g., 1 or 4, 2 or 5, etc.).

Figure 1

As a Champion or Seeker in the current environment, which are you most likely to focus on ...		
1. Understanding and honoring your personal purpose, gifts, and the Sacred Source of your gifts	Or	4. Understanding societal systems that perpetuate inequity and oppression and root causes
2. Developing and presenting the business and moral case for pursuing equity and justice	Or	5. Cultivating spiritual values and disciplines that ground you for the pursuit of equity and justice
3. Clarifying within self what and how you should contribute	Or	6. Using external input to determine what and how you should contribute

Each alternative pair represented two different ways to contribute to the greater purpose. One way (represented by items 2, 4, 6) involves *taking actions* to achieve and measure progress toward Social Transformation. The focus is on what we do. I called this the Transactional Approach. The other way (represented by items 1, 3, 5) involves *ensuring internal readiness* to sustain commitment to Social Transformation. The focus is on who we are. I called this the Transcendent Approach.

After participants chose between each alternative, I asked them to publicly reveal their choices by moving to the side of the room that represented each of their choices as alternatives were called out. As they moved, three things became clear.

1. Though all participants aspired toward the greater purpose, *Social Transformation evidenced by Equity and Justice for All*, their approaches were different.

2. While participants occasionally experienced tension when choosing between alternatives, most participants were quite certain their approach was the superior way to achieve the greater purpose of Social Transformation. For instance, Sam argued forcefully that "standing up for change" was far superior to "sitting around cultivating spiritual disciplines." Janice countered, "Spiritual disciplines help me sustain the long-term commitment needed in the fight for equity."

3. As a whole, the group was more likely to focus on transactions than transcendence. In other words, pursuing *external remedies* to inequity and injustice (#s 2, 4, 6) took priority over *ensuring internal readiness* to gain and sustain personal commitment to the work (#s 1, 3, 5).

The Nature and Benefits of Focusing on Transactions and External Remedies

Transactions are about "doing" and external remedies to inequities and injustices. In polarity pairs (*Figure 2*), the transactional approach is characterized by such actions as:

Figure 2: Transactional Polarities

Identifying Needs	And	Cultivating External Resources
Understanding External Realities	And	Acting to Address External Realities
Developing Methods	And	Developing Measures
Challenging Power Systems	And	Collaborating With Others

After briefly describing the transactional approach, I asked the group about benefits of focusing on transactions and external remedies. They agreed one could:

- Better understand societal issues and needs through exposure to external environment
- Contribute in ways that matter to others
- Test personal readiness by engaging in equity and justice work
- Gain allies to help challenge systems of inequity and injustice

The conversation continued.

> *Joshua, with some reservation:* I know why I feel so tired and burdened. Advocating for equity and justice is mental and emotional work with unrelenting demands. I also get why some people don't change. They don't want equity or justice. They want to retain dominance and power. What I don't get are the people I've worked with who say they are committed to equity and justice, who go to all the training, read all the books, make all the commitments, then fade when it's time to stand, and conjure convenient rationales for their complicity with oppressive systems.

Joshua's words reminded me of Martin Luther King, Jr.'s "Letter From Birmingham Jail," written in response to the white clergy who had suggested in an editorial that King should have more patience in his fight for justice.

Sam chimed in: Yeah, just last week a colleague apologized to me because she didn't speak up for the Asian candidate even though she knew he was better prepared for the job than the white male who got it. 'Why are you telling me,' I asked her. Do you know what she said? 'Because I feel really bad now.' I just walked away. What?! Did she expect me to make her feel better?

Chandra: Maybe she did feel better admitting the truth to you, Sam; but that's not enough, is it?

Group's resounding response: No!

Larry: I've been one of those people. Standing up to my homophobic cousins is my challenge. I know what to do. Doing it is another thing.

Chandra: You're right, Larry – doing is another thing. Not only that, doing is just one thing. Being is the other. We often ask ourselves, 'What am I going to do?' An appropriate accompanying question might be 'Who am I going to be in this situation? Will I be true to myself and my values? Will I be content to be content while others suffer bigotry and oppression?'

I've heard versions of Larry's story enough times to believe, as individuals and a society, we would benefit by paying closer attention to sages like Harriett Tubman, Martin Luther King, Jr., Howard Thurman, and Sarah and Angelina Grimke. Their words and practices tutor us to understand that Transactions *And* Transcendence go together. They are interdependent values and we need both of them over time if we are to achieve Social Transformation Evidenced by Equity and Justice.

The Nature and Benefits of Focusing on Transcendence and Internal Readiness

The nature of transcendence is to go beyond the limits of real and perceived barriers. What we may not see in the busyness of our transactions, we may discover when we retreat from external demands and reflect on and renew our commitment to the meaning of our lives and our life purpose. In polarity pairs (*Figure 3*), transcendence is characterized by such experiences as:

Figure 3: Transcendence Polarities

Exploring Our Fears	*And*	Developing Courage
Discerning Our Purpose	*And*	Cultivating Spiritual Disciplines
Clarifying Our Motives	*And*	Establishing Our Mindset
Anchoring Our Commitments	*And*	Being Liberated To Be Self

Such inward-facing experiences require honesty and, though it may be the last thing we want to fit into a busy schedule, time for reflection. For if we approach transcendence in haste, our experience will be shallow and meaningless. Paradoxically, to really engage transcendence, we must slow down in order to go fast. Questions like those on the next page require time to examine and answer. Nevertheless, could it be that slowing down to find our meaning prepares us to take and sustain meaningful actions?

Who am I? What am I really for? To what or whom am I ultimately committed? Do my behaviors advance or undermine my ultimate commitment? How will I bring my authentic self to this work? What have been my greatest barriers to this? How does my need for approval influence my decisions? Whose approval is most important? How is the need for approval strengthening or undermining the cause to which I am ultimately committed? What spiritual values and disciplines[17] must I practice in order to withstand external difficulties and ensure my mental, emotional, and spiritual readiness for equity and justice work?

I believe transcendent questions like these open the way to explore Life and our interconnectedness as humans, to listen within, and hear the vast sacred wisdom beyond us. They alert us to disagreements among the members of our internal community – i.e., heart, mind, soul, and will – and prompt us to seek their "unanimous agreement" to commit or not commit, to act or not act. I believe these are the types of questions Seekers need to answer as they attempt to contribute to a more just and equitable world. They are also the kind of questions Champions might find useful to guide and support Seekers who are trying to do more. As we examine and answer these types of questions, it becomes possible to:

- Understand personal fears, purpose, gifts, and the Sacred Source of personal gifts
- Contribute personal gifts in ways that energize self
- Develop spiritual values/disciplines to anchor and guide contributions
- Align and strengthen internal community to withstand opposition

However, transcendent questions are often brushed over, neglected, or overlooked altogether.

The Costs of Over-Focusing on Transactions and External Remedies

It is not enough to focus on transcendence for a season and then stop. Transcendence quietly demands ongoing attention. Why? Because an over-focus on doing can be our undoing. When our urgency to exact remedies is not backed by an unfailing commitment and an ongoing readiness to deliver on well-conceived plans, we are likely to:

- Work at cross-purposes with our values, our gifts, and the Source of our gifts
- Grow weary and waver because of an overwhelming desire for others' approval
- Lack courage and direction without spiritual values and disciplines as anchors
- Experience internal conflict leading to shallow contributions and collusion with injustice

For all the good that it offers, "doing" can be our undoing if we are not internally ready to resolutely stand for equity and justice. In the end, we will have failed to

---

[17] For instance spiritual values might include patience, connectedness, generosity, curiosity, humility, gentleness, etc. Spiritual disciplines might include such practices as mindfulness, generous listening, honest self-reflection, attentiveness/seeing, reverence, hospitality, prayer, etc.

contribute to equity and justice. The remedy is not to turn toward more doing, but to turn internally towards transcendence.

The Costs of Over-Focusing on Transcendence and Internal Readiness

Nevertheless, the benefits of focusing on internal readiness are futile if they are not accompanied by actions and external remedies. Without external exposure and engagement, we will:

- Have a false or limited understanding of external needs and resources
- Not know how to contribute in ways that matter to others
- Have done little more than verbalize commitment to undo inequity and injustice
- Lose support of external community as resources to help do the work

Again, we will have failed to contribute to equity and justice.

My Point of View

Our tendency towards "doing" is baked into us and our culture as the answer to all questions. To the question, "What do you want to be when you grow up?" one little girl responded confidently, "Me!" Smiling and wanting to correct the little girl's understanding, the adult corrected, "Of course, but what do you want to *do*?"

Through acculturation, most of us have learned to respond to problems with action. Plan more, quantify more, do more, measure more. Then, if in our doing we are successful, we showcase what we have done. If we are not, we double down to figure out what else we need to do.

Identifying the external problem, finding remedies, and taking action are important elements of problem solving and can help us "Contribute to a More Equitable and Just World." However, the chronic and persistent issues of oppression, inequity, and injustice indicate our normative responses are not enough.

The challenges of equity and justice are multidimensional, complex, and yes, hard. Why is this work so hard? I believe it is because we have individually and collectively underutilized the power of transcendence and its role in making the world more equitable and just. For while it is true that external remedies and transactions (what we do) impact who we are and our internal readiness to be authentic agents of equity and justice, it is also true that our ability to effectively transact, or carry out, our external remedies depends on our commitment, internal readiness, and ability to transcend both internal and external barriers which invariably arise when we attempt to advance equity and justice.

What We Do We Become. What We Become We Do

We generally acknowledge that the inner person (who we are) impacts the outer person (what we do). For instance, if we develop internal discipline, we will demonstrate external discipline. If we are spiritually and emotionally unbridled within ourselves, we will lack discipline when engaging with others. What we may

Figure 4

Action Steps

What actions will you take, when and with whom, to gain and maintain the benefits described in the "+A" quadrant?

-
-
-
-

Early Warnings

What measurable indicators will let you know you are beginning to experience the negative results described in the "-B" quadrant?

-
-
-
-

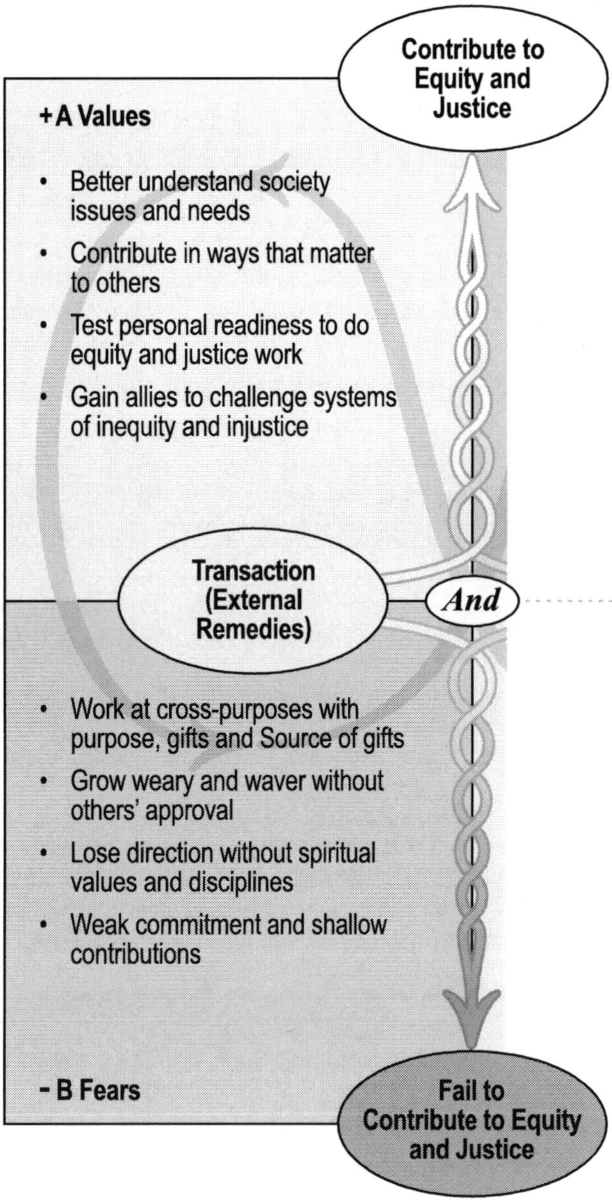

Contribute to Equity and Justice

+A Values

- Better understand society issues and needs
- Contribute in ways that matter to others
- Test personal readiness to do equity and justice work
- Gain allies to challenge systems of inequity and injustice

Transaction (External Remedies) *And*

- Work at cross-purposes with purpose, gifts and Source of gifts
- Grow weary and waver without others' approval
- Lose direction without spiritual values and disciplines
- Weak commitment and shallow contributions

- B Fears

Fail to Contribute to Equity and Justice

Chapter 3: Irvin

Polarity Map®

Contribute to Equity and Justice

+C Values

- Understand personal fears, purpose, gifts, and Source of personal gifts
- Contribute gifts in ways that energize self
- Develop spiritual values, disciplines and anchors
- Gain internal strength to resist opposition

Transcendence (Internal Readiness)

And

- Have a false or limited understanding of external needs
- Don't contribute in ways that matter to others
- Verbalize commitment without action
- Lose support of allies in external community

Fail to Contribute to Equity and Justice

− D Fears

Action Steps

What actions will you take, when and with whom, to gain and maintain the benefits described in the "+C" quadrant?

-
-
-
-

Early Warnings

What measurable indicators will let you know you are beginning to experience the negative results described in the "-D" quadrant?

-
-
-
-

forget is that, because nature does not respect the outer over the inner or the inner over the outer, the opposite is also true. The outer person (what we do) impacts the inner person (who we are).

This principle is true for good or bad. So, when we consistently seek deeper understanding of others, we open the way to more deeply understand ourselves; if we sow peace, we become peacemakers; when we sow discord, we become discordant within ourselves; when we repeatedly avoid the realities of others, we blind ourselves to our own realities; when we repeatedly collude with inequity and injustice, we become purveyors of oppression and abuse. When what we do consistently undermines who we believe ourselves to be at our core, we become at our core what we consistently do, no matter how much we declare ourselves to be otherwise.

If we are to do better, we must be better. If we are to be better, we must do better. What must we do? Champions and Seekers in my experience agree, we must manage the Transcendent *And* Transactional polarity.

Note To Reader

Understanding and appreciating the interdependent relationship between Transcendence *And* Transactions is important. However, this knowledge alone is likely to be insufficient for the Equity and Justice journey. The Polarity Map® (*Figure 4*, pp. 28 - 29) is provided to aid your journey. The content of the map reflects what is described in this chapter. There are also two sets of Action Steps and Early Warnings intentionally left open for your unique input. Follow the prompts within these quadrants to complete each section. These can be both new actions inspired by this chapter, and can include actions you may have already been taking in your life.

Your personal power comes from taking the Action Steps you have laid out. Should you find you are not getting the results you desire and the Early Warnings of either pole begin to manifest, review the Action Steps on the opposite pole to see if you are following them. If you are, rewrite them so they are stronger and you feel the results more powerfully. For your ongoing map work, feel free to print copies of the blank Polarity Map from the back of this book.

You can do this. We can do this. Together we can contribute to a more Just and Equitable world. For support in completing the map or coaching to manage this polarity, please connect with me.

Find bio and contact info for author Chandra Irvin at
www.polaritypartnerships.com/certified-polarity-practitioners

Feminine *And* Masculine:
For Health, Wealth, and Happiness

Elaine Yarbrough, PhD
Lindsay Y. Burr, MS

Some polarities, like Activity *And* Rest, affect us all. To thrive, we must leverage both so we're not chronically exhausted, allowing for only an occasional nap. Another fundamental polarity is Feminine *And* Masculine, Yin *And* Yang – basic life energies. We need both poles to achieve the greater purpose of health, wealth, and happiness and to avoid the deeper fears of disease, disparity, despair, and toxicity. Even though we may personally aspire to both, our culture values the Masculine over the Feminine. To make matters worse, when the favored group has privilege (automatically assumed to be better/smarter/deserving) and the devalued group has chronic low power (little to no voice or value), the imbalance is worse and the correction, more difficult.

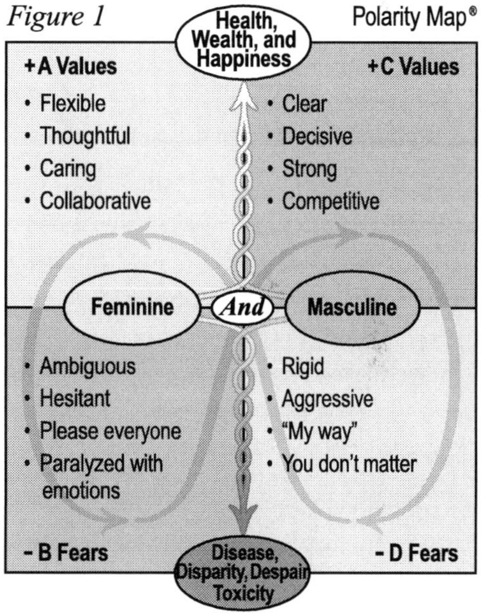

In virtually every global culture there is an over-focus on the Masculine and a trivialization of the Feminine. Clarity and decisiveness are valued; rigidity and aggression over-tolerated; flexibility and thoughtfulness, undermined; ambiguity and hesitancy, feared.[18] Eventually of course, we reap the downsides of both. (See loop in *Figure 1*.) Rigidity is met with ambiguity; aggression with hesitancy. For example, war becomes the answer, coupled with hesitation to argue against it, exemplified by the U.S. Congress' vote to invade Iraq in 2003.

Figure 1 — Polarity Map®

Health, Wealth, and Happiness

+A Values
- Flexible
- Thoughtful
- Caring
- Collaborative

+C Values
- Clear
- Decisive
- Strong
- Competitive

Feminine *And* Masculine

- B Fears
- Ambiguous
- Hesitant
- Please everyone
- Paralyzed with emotions

- D Fears
- Rigid
- Aggressive
- "My way"
- You don't matter

Disease, Disparity, Despair, Toxicity

Polarity Thinking™ theory and tools help us benefit from *both* Feminine *And* Masculine for powerful personal, social, and global results. All gender expressions have Feminine and Masculine qualities. However, by virtue of our bodies, hormones, and socialization, males and male-identified carry more masculine traits; females and female-identified,

---

[18] The first two qualities in each quadrant of the Polarity Map® are from *And: Making A Difference by Leveraging Polarity, Paradox, or Dilemma. Volume 1 – Foundations* by Barry Jonson, HRD Press, 2020, Chapter 31.

more feminine traits. Men, therefore, are valued and paid more, seen as real leaders, and are in charge of decisions in most areas of everyone's lives.

Warning Signs: Over-Focus on the Masculine

Since women are 51% of the population, how are our voices silenced?[19] NOTE: The silencing acts bulleted here are also seen in *Figure 3,* p.35, as Early Warnings (EW-D).

- The power group (men) **control meaning**. Clear and decisive (*Figure 1* +C) are good, but when over-tolerated, rigidity and aggressiveness (-D) exist indefinitely without correction. The impact of this dynamic is that women who are thoughtful and flexible (+A) are perceived as hesitant and ambivalent (-B); and when taking on the masculine traits of clear and decisive (+C), they are labeled emotional and reactive (-B, -D). Women are disempowered no matter what quadrant they enact![20]

- **Toxic** masculinity is reflected in mass shootings, sexual harassment, and abuse; "my way" and you don't matter (*Figure 1* -D). The #MeToo movement is an attempted correction.

- 'Male' is perceived as **leader**. Consider *Figure 2* polarities to see how 'masculine' and 'leadership' are conflated.[21] Leaders are often defined by Candor (saying what needs to be said), their Confidence, and being in Control.

Figure 2

Feminine	*And*	Masculine
Diplomacy	*And*	Candor
Humility	*And*	Confidence
Other	*And*	Self
Empowerment	*And*	Control

- Women are **compensated less** than men for the same work which, when combined with paying higher prices for such things as cars and insurance, means women (and children) are the largest group in **poverty**.[22]

- There are few women **role models,** making it difficult for girls and women to imagine success.[23]

- Women are **isolated** from each other, blame themselves for discriminatory patterns – *I must have brought it on myself* – thus feel unable to confront the system.

- **Unconscious bias** of women results in:
    o Being slotted into support roles of the organizations, thus being less prepared for promotion.
    o Proving self over and over again.

---

[19] See yearly reports by McKinsey & Company, "Women in the Workplace" 2016, 2017, 2018, 2019.
[20] For a longer explanation see Barry Johnson, *And: Making a Difference by Leveraging Polarity, Paradox or Dilemma. Volume One – Foundations.* Human Resources Press, 2020, Chapter 31.
[21] See *Build Your Authentic Inspired Leadership Style* by Lindsay Y. Burr, Chapter 12 in this volume.
[22] Women account for 70% of those in poverty. "Empowering women and girls for the benefit of our people and planet" by Paul Polman. LinkedIn, March 8, 2020.
[23] Ibid.

- o Having men's work rated higher when it is exactly the same work as women.[24]
- o Enduring micro-aggressions such as constant interruption (five times more than men) and having their ideas ignored but applauded when offered by men.
- o Losing visibility when men report women's work or claim it as their own.

- **Appraisal** systems are not used uniformly for women and men. Hundreds of women are told to smile more if they want to be successful and deemed uncommitted to work when they must also tend to family.

- Women senior leaders suffer **sacrifices** rarely experienced by men. Almost all are single, have no children, or in rare cases have a stay-at-home spouse.

- Most professional women have full time jobs at home and work, leading to chronic **exhaustion**.

- Women are left out of the succession **pipeline**, a key reason for non-promotion.

When Women Succeed in Spite of the Barriers, Other Damaging Patterns Emerge

- Women's accomplishments are **reframed**. A dramatic example is the first women's team to ascend Annapurna in 1978 led by Arlene Blum.[25] Male climbers criticized her for using Sherpa and 'letting' two women die. Hypocritical, since men used more Sherpa and suffered one death for every summit on Annapurna.[26]

- With success, **men are competent, women are lucky**. In attribution research studies, homogenous groups are asked to memorize a list of numbers. Men, when told they did very badly, respond "It was a stupid assignment." Women, "We're not very good at math and could have tried harder." Men, when told they did well, respond "We're good at math." Women, "We were lucky." Both patterns retain the gender power imbalance.

Correction to the Upsides of the Feminine: Benefits

- **Health:** As of this writing, the world is in the grip of the COVID-19 virus. Notice the yearnings for connection and touch and the behaviors needed for health: collaboration, caring, and flexibility in how we live. Notice the consequent health of Mother Earth: clearer skies and water. We have been forced to correct to the Feminine.

- **Happiness:** When mama's happy, everyone's happy. Studies show that men, who are in a happy, healthy relationship make more money, have more sex, live longer, suffer less chronic illness, and have less cognitive impairment in their later years.[27]

---

[24] When Hewlett Packard removed names from resumes, 50% more women were considered for positions. See also Harvard University Kennedy School, Women and Public Policy, for additional studies.
[25] Blum, Arlene. *Annapurna: A Woman's Place*. Random House, 1980.
[26] "American Women's Himalayan Expedition." Wikipedia, June 22, 2019.
[27] Gottman, J. et al. *The Man's Guide to Women*. Rachel Carlton Abrams, 2016.

- **Leadership and Capacity:**

    ... individuals and organizations that leverage polarities well outperform those that do not .... I have found that women, on average, more readily see and leverage polarities better than men .... If we were to assess the ability to leverage polarities as an essential leadership capacity, we would have more ... (women leaders). ~ Barry Johnson[28]

    Traditional masculine leadership behaviors of control, corrective action, and individualistic decision-making are the least critical for future success. Those most needed are intellectual stimulation, which men and women apply in equal measure, and five other traits (inspiration, participative decision-making, setting expectations and rewards, people development, and role modeling) which women apply more frequently by huge margins.[29] National women leaders are also recognized as being the most effective at managing the pandemic with the qualities of truth, use of technology, decisiveness, and love.[30]

- **Financial Performance:** A global study demonstrated a link between the presence of women in corporate management teams and positive financial performance.[31] Further, parity for women has huge global economic possibilities. As much as $28 million could be added to global annual GDP by 2025 with women in the workforce, compensated like men.[32]

- **Social Change:** When women are key decision-makers, communities and families benefit.[33] Swanee Hunt has worked in more than 60 countries and measures dramatic social improvement, with significant female leadership, in almost every measurable category of stabilization.[34]

- **Peace and Security:** The prevalence of violence against women in a country is a predictor of a national predilection toward terrorism and civil conflict.[35] That's why 83 countries created national action plans on women, peace, and security.

    The structure of the relationship between the two halves of humanity is the basis for the political order of every nation, and if that order allows autocracy, violence, and extortion, a nation will arc in those directions as well. ~ Valerie M. Hudson[36]

---

[28] Johnson, Barry. *And: Making a Difference by Leveraging Polarity, Paradox or Dilemma. Volume One – Foundations.* HRD Press. 2020. Chapter 31.
[29] Catalino, N., Marnane, K. *When Women Lead, Workplaces Should Listen.* McKinsey & Company, 2019.
[30] Whittenburg-Cox, Avivah. "What Do Countries with the Best Coronavirus Responses Have in Common? Women Leaders." ForbesWomen, April 13, 2020.
[31] McKinsey & Company. *Women in the Workplace.* 2007.
[32] Woetzel, Jonathan et al. "How advancing women's equality can add $12 trillion to global growth." McKinsey Global Institute, September 2015 Report.
[33] See the achievements of women in Congress www.wcpinst.org/our-work/the-womens-caucus.
[34] Hunt, Swanee. "What happens when women rule." CNN Opinion, June 8, 2019.
[35] The U.N. Security Council Resolution 1325 asserts that peace is inextricably linked with gender equality.
[36] Hudson, Valerie M. "What You Do to Your Women, You Do to Your Nation." New York Times, March 6, 2020.

- **Talent:** We cannot quantify what is invisible. We can, however, see examples of female talent that has been lost and found. Consider *Hidden Figures* by Margot Lee Shetterly[37] which focuses on Katherine Johnson, Mary Jackson, and Dorothy Vaughan, African-American women who were essential to the success of early spaceflight.

Warning Signs: Over-Focus on the Feminine

Polarity Thinking reminds us that, even though we need a correction to the Feminine, we need to be vigilant about an over-focus on that pole (*Figure 3*, EW -B). In some nonprofit organizations for which we have consulted, for example, decisions are halted until everyone is pleased, making daily processes difficult. In these cases, correction to the masculine is warranted so both poles can be leveraged.

Action Steps

Lessons learned from leading gender and inclusion organizational development projects for 35 years in 30 countries, along with research on best practices, suggest the following Action Steps (AS +A, AS +C) for leveraging Feminine *And* Masculine.

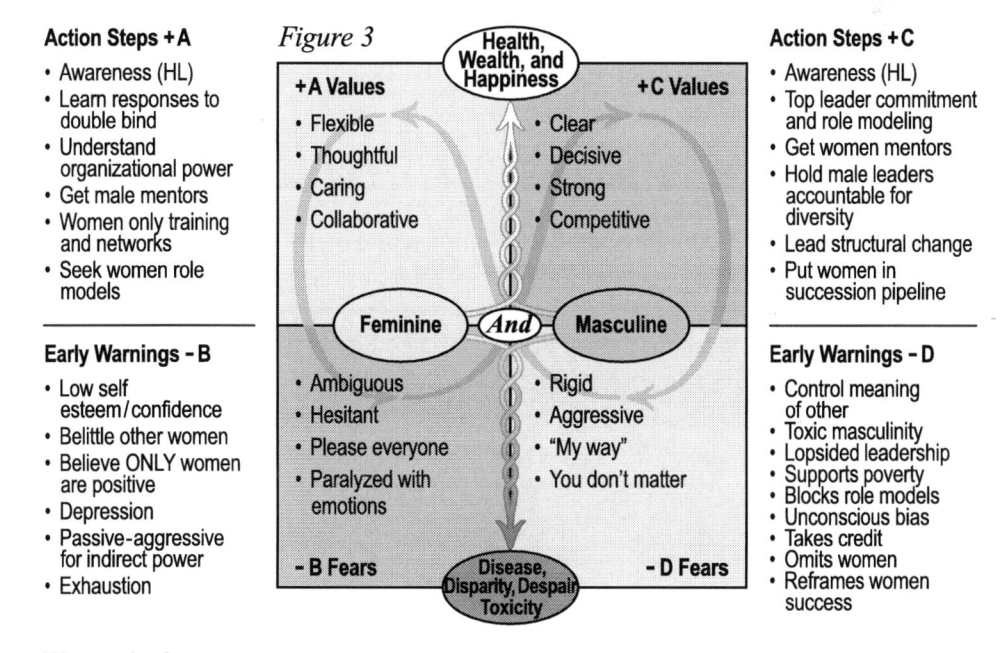

Figure 3

Action Steps +A	+A Values	+C Values	Action Steps +C
• Awareness (HL) • Learn responses to double bind • Understand organizational power • Get male mentors • Women only training and networks • Seek women role models	• Flexible • Thoughtful • Caring • Collaborative	• Clear • Decisive • Strong • Competitive	• Awareness (HL) • Top leader commitment and role modeling • Get women mentors • Hold male leaders accountable for diversity • Lead structural change • Put women in succession pipeline
Early Warnings -B	Feminine *And* Masculine		**Early Warnings -D**
• Low self esteem/confidence • Belittle other women • Believe ONLY women are positive • Depression • Passive-aggressive for indirect power • Exhaustion	• Ambiguous • Hesitant • Please everyone • Paralyzed with emotions	• Rigid • Aggressive • "My way" • You don't matter	• Control meaning of other • Toxic masculinity • Lopsided leadership • Supports poverty • Blocks role models • Unconscious bias • Takes credit • Omits women • Reframes women success

Top: Health, Wealth, and Happiness
Bottom: Disease, Disparity, Despair, Toxicity
- B Fears / - D Fears

Women's Awareness

There are many designs and interventions for gender equity. Key ingredients, which can be used personally and professionally, for women include:

---

[37] Lee Shetterly, Margot. *Hidden Figures: The American Dream and the Untold Story of the Black Women Mathematicians Who Helped Win the Space Race.* Harper Collins Publishers, 2016.

- Women, especially in their professional lives, can be stuck in over-emphasizing the Masculine because we have emulated men for credibility. So, women often hear any description of the downside of the masculine as "male bashing." In personal lives, women often over-focus on the Feminine, reaping the downside of that pole as well. Both issues are more easily addressed when using Polarity Thinking since women can see and value both poles.

- Women need to know their own history to gain courage and esteem. Do we know the stories of women in our own families? Their courage and resilience? Do we know how women have fought for our rights historically? Our **role models** need to be uncovered.

- Senior leaders in organizations can be **role models** as they transparently describe their journeys: aspirations, risk-taking, mentors, supporters, barriers and ways around them, and management of family and work.

- Most important is the **role model** of our own lives. When women learn the prototypic woman's journey, they know they are not alone. With that catalyst, women consider their own lives, and their persistence, resilience, and heroism are revealed. They also increase awareness of the life-destroying messages about being a 'woman.' Lesbian and bisexual women are good resources; often they are less restricted by traditional female messages.

- **A walk through the quadrants** of Feminine *And* Masculine, filling in the qualities of the upsides and downsides of the poles, allows women to see the whole picture.

- Because there is a **double standard** for women and men, women need to know how to respond to judgments. For example, if a man says, "You sure are emotional," a response can be "I AM very concerned about the impact of this decision." Or "You're just being bossy," a response could be "I have expertise on this subject and know it's necessary for positive results."

- Women can lower their fear of using the Feminine when they understand organizational power, including: knowledge of the organizational culture and how to frame their communication; support of mentors and sponsors; participation in activities that are visible; and up-to-date alternatives by staying current in networks, developing women's networks, and being financially solvent enough to weather the storms of inevitable organizational changes.

- When fear is reduced and esteem increased, women can envision the impact they want to have in their lives and are more open to hearing the Men's Journey that includes their restrictions as well as privilege. In this way, better relationships are possible.

Men's Awareness

Some key ingredients for men include:

- Description of leaders and friends/family they admire.

- Knowledge of the Woman's Journey from women's stories at work and home and from historical data about barriers to women's success and satisfaction.

- Reflection on the impact of sexism in their own families. "Would you want your daughter to work here?"

- A walk through the Feminine *And* Masculine polarity to explore benefits of both. GenX and Millennial men are helpful here as they talk openly about the restrictions they feel striving to embody the traditional Masculine. They want to be different kinds of fathers, husbands, and friends from previous generations. Gay and bisexual men are often good resources for teaching heterosexual men to leverage the polarity.

- Often, we use the 'Getting Unstuck' process so men are reassured masculine qualities are highly valued and that they need not automatically go to the downside of the feminine which it seems they greatly fear.[38]

Organizational Change[39]

- **Women's Support of Each Other:** In the early 1990s, we began helping women in a dozen countries form networks where they check reality with each other, clarify their goals, seek encouragement, and learn strategies to open professional pathways for each other.

- **Leadership and Performance for Diversity and Inclusion:** It is important to have women visible in top leadership and also have senior leaders drive diversity and inclusion. The commitment to diversity and inclusion of senior-level leadership has increased. However, only half of employees perceive their commitment. Further, managers under 30 are more likely than older employees to see the biases that undermine those intentions.[40] Hence, there needs to be a safe, transparent feedback loop to upper leadership about the realities at mid- and lower-level to enhance commitment throughout the organization.

- **Structural Change:** When companies have the right **foundations for change**, they can make diversity and inclusion 'just the way we do business.' Those include:

---

[38] Johnson, Barry. *And: Making a Difference by Leveraging Polarity, Paradox or Dilemma. Volume One – Foundations.* HRD Press, 2020, Chapter 13.

[39] A wonderful resource for action steps is *Inclusion Nudges Guidebook: Practical Techniques for Changing Behavior, Culture and Systems to Mitigate Unconscious Bias and Create Inclusive Organizations, Edition 2* by Tinna Nielsen and Lisa Kepinski. CreateSpace Independent Publishing Platform, April 2020.

[40] Huang, J., et al. "Women in the Workplace 2019". McKinsey & Company, 2019. https://wiw-report.s3.amazonaws.com/Women_in_the_Workplace_2019.pdf.

- Clear goals for hiring, promoting, and using business partners (e.g., Goldman Sachs refuses to finance organizations who have no women on their boards).
- Work practices that support the lives of women who are still the primary caretakers of children and family.
- Accountability for all managers to build capacity and provide access to the managerial pipeline for women[41,42]

- **Allies:** Women need men mentors to interpret masculine culture, to speak up when others may undermine women, and to open opportunities. Men need women mentors to teach them about the strengths of women as well as the barriers in women's lives that block personal and professional development.

Summary

The health of our relationships, organizations, and world depends a great deal on our willingness and ability to leverage the Feminine *And* Masculine. In this way power is balanced between the poles, truth can be told, reconciliation achieved, and a satisfied, productive future realized.

Find bio and contact info for authors Elaine Yarbrough and Lindsay Y. Burr at www.polaritypartnerships.com/certified-polarity-practitioners

---

[41] The key obstacle for women moving into senior leadership is lack of accessibility to the succession pipeline: See Huang, J., et al. "Women in the Workplace 2019". McKinsey & Company, 2019. https://wiw-report.s3.amazonaws.com/Women_in_the_Workplace_2019.pdf.

[42] See Vision 2020, Equality in Sight, a national campaign for gender equality composed of 102-member congress of women dedicated to building capacity and access to leadership in the current decade. https://drexel.edu/vision2020.

Support And Challenge – for You and Me
Beth Applegate, MSOD

Historically, pandemics have forced humans to break with the past and [re]-imagine their world anew. This is no different. It is a portal, a gateway between one world and the next. We can choose to walk through it, dragging the carcasses of our prejudice and hatred, our avarice, our data banks and dead ideas, our dead rivers, and smoky skies behind us. Or we can walk through lightly, with little luggage, ready to imagine another world. And ready to fight for it. ~ Arundhati Roy[43]

I want to express my gratitude to Barry Johnson, for his generosity, steadfast encouragement, and his invitation to contribute to this two-book volume. Utilizing Polarity Thinking™ requires me to re-center my core values, clarify my purpose, and assess my principles of engagement based on my behavior in relationships with myself and others. I do this so that I may be of service to the greater good as we work together in a multiracial liberatory movement. Our colleagueship has profoundly influenced me as I seek to continuously improve my use of self[44] in service to my relationships with others and racial justice.

As part of my responsibility-taking practice, I feel compelled to share the polarities most alive in me at this moment – five months into the COVID-19 pandemic, 100 days before the 2020 U.S. Presidential election, and four hundred years into a national mindset, culture and interlocking systems of white superiority ideology. My goal in this chapter is to use a polarity lens to Support *And* Challenge other self-identified antiracist white people to reckon with the question:

> *Are you in right relationship with yourself, and are you in right relationship with other white people as we seek to build a multiracial liberation movement?*

Barry outlined two polarities in his introduction in <u>Volume One</u>: "All Are Loved *And* All Are Accountable, and Each Is Unique *And* All Are Connected."[45] These two polarities are essential to being in right relationship moving forward. Achieving racial equity and liberation will require each of us to transform our relationships to ourselves and each other as a part of the many components of ongoing work required to reimagine just systems as we walk through the portal to Arundhati Roy's "another world."

---

[43] Roy, Arundhati. "The Pandemic is a Portal." Financial Times, April 2020
[44] Influencers in my learning/study about use of self: Jamieson and Cheung-Judge, 2020; Seashore and Broom, 2005; Jamison, Auron and Shechtman, 2017.
[45] Johnson, Barry. *And: Making a Difference by Leveraging Polarity, Paradox or Dilemma. Volume One – Foundations.* HRD Press, 2020.

Polarity Thinking helps to augment *either/Or* thinking with *both/And* thinking so that we can expand the possibilities in our multiracial liberation movement. It supports us to see the full picture when faced with challenges that seem to lead in two different directions. Polarities are unsolvable, unavoidable, indestructible, and unstoppable. Each polarity is a powerful energy system that, once we incorporate, we can learn to leverage to achieve positive change.

Consider, for example, a few polarities. Which one is more important? Racial Justice (disrupting white supremacy systems, structures, policies, laws, and creating new just ones, etc.) *Or* Racial Healing (doing the essential inner healing and emotional literacy and racial identity work to cultivate a solid sense of self and healthy relationship to self and other); Intention *Or* Impact; Individual Focus *Or* Institutional Focus; Mercy *Or* Justice; Freedom for the Part *Or* Equity among the parts within the Whole? Framing any of these polarities as problems to solve creates damaging false binary choices and too often fruitless human interactions. Societies that create systems based on false choices can lead to enormous inequities. Up until now, claiming power without sharing power led to abuse of power. Abundance for some without basics for all has led to gross inequality. Justice without Mercy led to an excessive number of laws and excessively harsh consequences. Now connect them with *And*. Radical possibilities for equity expand in that change alone.

For decades, approaches to power, racism, privilege, equity, inclusion, and justice have been and continue to be too often framed solely as problems to solve instead of a mixture of problems and dilemmas/paradoxes/tensions which we must live with and in. Too often, problem-solving approaches devolve into narrowmindedness and dualistic thinking characterized by using shame and blame of self and other. Using only problem-solving (*Or*-thinking) methods unconsciously perpetuates our society's structures, contributes to dysfunctional relationships, and ineffective and harmful intra- and interpersonal behaviors.

On an intrapersonal level, *either/Or*-thinking magnifies the false good/bad separation within ourselves, activates internal dissonance, and diminishes consciousness-raising, instead creating aversion toward ourselves which can result in damaging our relationships with others. As interpersonal relationships further devolve, polarized camps often emerge, paradoxically holding and advancing the false binary choice – you are *either* with me/us *Or* against me/us. These vicious cycles have not, and do not support us to be in right relationship with yourself or support us in strengthening authentic relationships necessary to build a racially just society. In fact, our aversion can lead to an increased inability to "own" our shortcomings because of the fear of dire consequences from our peers, and self-preservation against shame and blame.

What we cannot own about ourselves results in identifying an "other," a "not me" on whom to project all our shortcomings. Those in or with proximity to power can declare their projections as reality. Notice how unowned projections help legitimate claiming power over those on whom we project in the first place. Any effort to address systemic white supremacy that does not explicitly include *And*-thinking will be radically undermined by the absence of *And*-thinking. *Or*-thinking, alone, is not up to the job. In fact, *Or*-thinking is a fundamental source of systematic white supremacy in the first place. There are plenty of things happening in the world in which we have been and continue to be very cruel to each other. Looking for an "evil source" is an understandable but misguided way to perpetuate the cruelty.

In this sociopolitical cultural moment (summer 2020), there is an amplification of a dominate white culture narrative – the quest for an evil source. It is important to recognize, "There is no evil source. No subgroup of our humanity is inherently evil. Pursuing one 'Good' (upside of a polarity) to the neglect of its interdependent 'Good' (another upside), leads to 'Evil' (the inevitable downside of the over-focused 'Good')."[46] A polarity lens allows us to understand a source of systemic racism without blaming/condemning ourselves or a subgroup (white people) as inherently evil, and without condoning or denying the existence of systemic white supremacy culture. As Pema Chödrön reminds us: "Peace between countries must rest on the solid foundation of love between individuals."[47]

As Barry writes in <u>Volume One</u>, this moment requires us to Claim Power *And* Share Power; behave with Mercy *And* Justice, so that we can co-create **new** just systems that create Abundance for Some *And* Basics for All. For us to co-create these systems and generate radical possibilities for equity, I want to Support *And* Challenge you in embracing our part within this multiracial liberation movement.

Figure 1 summarizes, on a Polarity Map®, the focus of this chapter. I encourage you to walk through this with me. I Support myself by affirming that I am loved as I am, and I Support others by loving them as they are (+A). I Challenge myself by acknowledging my mistakes and learning from them. I Challenge others by letting them know the impact of their mistakes (+C). Support without Challenge leads to harmful mistakes that go unchallenged (-B). Challenge alone leads to being defined by mistakes (-D). Each downside is dehumanizing, whether I am doing it to myself or to someone else, and undermines the pursuit of justice/Strong Relationship in the name of justice/Strong Relationship!

Figure 1 — Polarity Map®

Strong Relationships

+A Values
I am loved as I am, and I support others by loving them as they are.

+C Values
I acknowledge and learn from my mistakes. I let others know the impact of their mistakes.

Support *And* Challenge

- B Fears
My mistakes and their impact go unchallenged. I do not challenge the mistakes and impact of others.

- D Fears
My mistakes define me, and I define others by their mistakes.

Poor Relationships

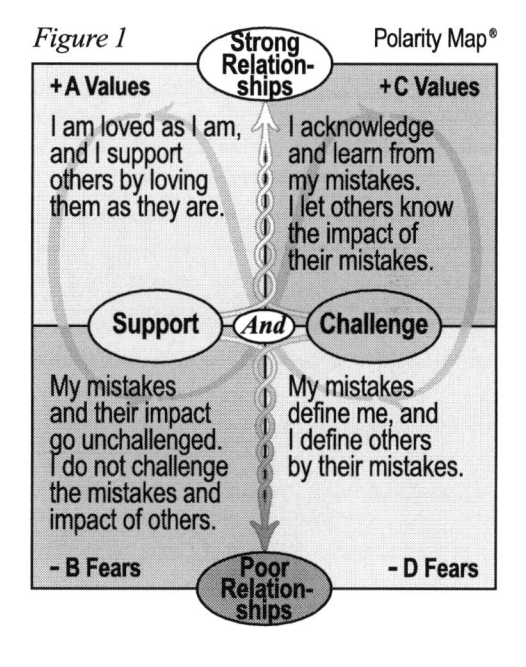

[46] Johnson, Barry. *And: Making a Difference by Leveraging Polarity, Paradox or Dilemma. Volume One – Foundations*. HRD Press, 2020.
[47] Chödrön, Pema. Quoting Mahatma Gandhi. 2017.

My social location based on my social group membership (race, class, gender, etc.) determines my proximity to privilege and power, and my roles and responsibilities are different than my Black, Indigenous, People Of Color (BIPOC) colleagues based on their social location. In a piece coauthored by racial justice practitioners entitled, "Accountability in a Time of Justice," authentic relationships are described as the "ways we treat, respect and honor both ourselves and each other based in an acknowledgement of our essential interdependence."[48] Rev. angel Williams Kyodo describes being in right relationship this way: "Radical Dharma is insurgence rooted in love, and all that love of self and others implies. It takes self-liberation to its necessary end by moving beyond transformation to transcend dominant social norms and deliver us into collective freedom."[49]

Rightfully so, following the public murder by police of George Floyd,[50] Black, Indigenous, People of Color have increased their expectations for responsibility-taking by all anti-racist white people, especially those who are monetarily benefiting as consultants, authors, and trainers, etc., from efforts to build a more just and equitable world. BIPOC are calling on anti-racist white people to dismantle white dominant culture in ourselves, organizations and society. This responsibility-taking takes root by being in right relationship with one another, as well as making commitments to build political power with other white anti-racists through national networks like Showing Up for Racial Justice (SURJ).[51] White anti-racists need to educate, organize, and mobilize into collective action towards a liberatory agenda set by the Black liberation movement that embodies the polarity Claiming Power *And* Sharing Power. The expectations of BIPOC are fluid as the movements of white anti-racist actions generate critique and additional expectations for continued responsibility-taking. For instance, it is encouraging and informative that in June and July of 2020, 400,000 individual white people discovered SURJ and began accessing support for their personal transformation to fortify themselves for collective action and to grow this work in white communities across the country. It is in seeing that we can all leverage Taking Power *And* Sharing Power.

Each day, new calls from BIPOC colleagues coupled with anti-racist white preemptive apologies within national racial justice/racial healing arenas are being discussed among colleagues and posted on social media. With each situation, there are opportunities across race to center relationships when harm has been done. There are lessons to be learned, and adjustments to be made to continue to transform and deepen our responsibility-taking behaviors – choice points and harm reduction actions when we damage our relationships with BIPOC colleagues/friends.

---

[48] Logan, Johnson, and Okun. www.dismantlingracism.org/uploads/4/3/5/7/43579015/accountability.jjo.drworks.pdf. 2008.

[49] Williams, Rev. angel Kyodo; Owens, Lama Rod; Syedullah, Jasmine. *Radical Dharma: Talking Race, Love and Liberation*. North Atlantic Books. 2016.

[50] Hill, E.; Tiefenthäler, A.; Triebert, C.; Jordan, D.; Willis, H.; Stein, R. "How George Floyd Was Killed in Police Custody." The New York Times. Updated July 28, 2020.

[51] SURJ's role as part of a multi-racial movement is to undermine white support for white supremacy and to help build a racially-just society. www.showingupforracialjustice.org.

It is critical in this evolutionary moment for anti-racist white people to listen to the critique of how we are doing ourselves, both in relationship to BIPOC colleagues, as well as to other anti-racist white people. White anti-racists must commit to change our relationships to ourselves and each other – from a transactional and compassionless approach to one that Supports *And* Challenges us to find courage in our similarities and solidarity in our differences – in service to racial equity and justice and our humanity. It is well past time for white anti-racists to increase our emotional, political, and racial literacy skills; normalize that mistakes will be made, and refocus our energy and build our skill sets in service to what happens after a mistake is made. Most importantly, we must be even more resilient and courageous as we continue to deepen our responsibility-taking and repair actions as white anti-racists collectively. We must Support *And* Challenge one another to build a more nuanced understanding of our role in cross race spaces, based on our proximity to power in each situation, be prepared to name harm when we witness it, and back that witnessing up with the skill sets involved in repairing relationships harmed by our or others' internalized white supremacy. We must increase our self-awareness, live into our core values, and center the person we believe we may have harmed. It is also important not to assume harm has been done without checking that out directly. Otherwise acting on our unchecked assumptions may re-center ourselves rather than our amends.

From a Polarity Thinking perspective, many white anti-racists need to stay resilient in our daily practice to differentiate a polarity to leverage from a problem to solve. This barrier, or pitfall, is inextricably linked to our habitual, unconscious use of *Or*-thinking rather than *And*-thinking. It is ongoing work to recognize the early warning signs (sooner) in our thinking, feeling, and behaviors, and take the action steps to course correct when we discover, once again, that we are over-focusing on the wisdom in one pole to the neglect of the wisdom in the other pole. In each moment, we can notice where our attention and resulting behaviors and actions have been focused and how we need to leverage the other pole. Practicing Polarity Thinking anchors white anti-racists in aligning with our core values, Supports *And* Challenges us to embrace the complexity of our proximity to power, and encourages us to be in right relationship with other white anti-racists without othering and shaming white colleagues/friends as they grow. As you reflect on the Support *And* Challenge polarity, I urge you to use the blank map offered on the last page of this book to assess if you are in right relationship with yourself, and if you are in right relationship with other white people as we seek to build a multiracial liberation movement.

In my own responsibility-taking, Polarity Thinking also Supports *And* Challenges me to cultivate a practice that keeps me more intentional in my action taking, and more embodied and connected to my best self. Holding the contradictions embedded in a paradox helps me recognize the stereotypes and fears in me: underneath why I "other" white anti-racists who are in different lanes on the racial justice highway from me, and why I abandon myself and other white anti-racists because of my own socially conditioned internalized perfectionism. It makes visible more quickly to me the downsides of my own position that I am ignoring, and this supports me in being more open to the humanity of other white people in building our connections and interdependent relationships.

I am clear that when I beat up on my white people for being newer drivers on the "racial justice freeway," I am NOT HELPING. Like me, most anti-racist white people want to do the right things, and we say and do the wrong things because this is a lifelong education process to unlearn all the things we were taught and are reinforced in our daily lives. This daily practice of making choices to be in relationship with my feelings and thoughts with compassion and empathy for myself and others, has resulted in me feeling more embodied, grounded, and in touch with my best self. Understanding how shame operates in me and how to manage it in myself supports me moving beyond being stuck at an intellectual understanding of the definition of white fragility without the tools and skill sets to be able to hold the discomfort in myself and in others in service to healthy relationships. It is a complex dance to tease out what part of me is shaming me about my internalized white supremacy from being shamed by another white person. If I shame myself, and blame others for shaming me, or if I shame other white people, this will only serve to keep myself and other white people stuck in a vicious cycle of self-flagellation and re-centering ourselves, our thoughts, and feelings.

As those of us who have an anti-racist personal practice know, it is a hell of a lot easier simply to espouse my values (integrity and courage) and become over focused on my fears about the complexity and messiness of my own humanity than it is to practice standing in my core values daily, in relationship to myself and in relationship with other white people. I will not kid you, working with polarities has been and continues to be filled with discomfort and painful revelations about what I have absorbed of the white supremacy culture in the United States. Though uncomfortable, I choose courage over maintaining my comfort moment by moment, by fully seeing my behaviors and actions in all of my relationships, and through showing up for myself with self-compassion. This is the only way I will be able to sustain showing up for other white people in compassion for their humanity.

In recognition that we are All Loved *And* All Accountable, that we are Each Unique *And* All Connected, I will Support *And* Challenge you and other self-identified anti-racist white people by asking again:

> *Are you in right relationship with yourself, and are you in right relationship with other white people as we seek to build a multiracial liberation movement?*

Conclusion

Throughout the five chapters in this opening section, coauthors offered a series of polarities to Support *And* Challenge readers to center your proximity to privilege and power, based on your social group membership (race, class, gender, etc.). We offer this as a primer for situating the remaining polarity application chapters of

Volume Two. While following authors may not directly speak to social membership and proximity to power, Barry and all authors understand that our social location and proximity to power individually and collectively is a given and at play in each application of Polarity Thinking offered. As Chandra noted, "if we are to do better, we must know better." Peter cautions readers that until we do better, "Black survival in white privilege and power is required." Elaine and Lindsay urge readers to address the relationship to power through better leveraging of the Feminine *And* Masculine poles. I offered an example of how I apply Polarity Thinking to my practice to stay in authentic relationship with myself and with other white anti-racist people. Together, this is how we are preparing to walk through the portal Arundhati Roy describes "... ready to imagine another world. And ready to fight for it." We hope to have Challenged *And* Supported your reimagining equity and justice through a polarity lens, and shared how you can start to apply a Polarity lens in your spheres of influence. And to remind you proximity to power is a given in each chapter ahead. Onward!

In Humility *And* Confidence, Beth

Find bio and contact info for author Beth Applegate at
www.polaritypartnerships.com/certified-polarity-practitioners

SECTION TWO

Expanded Applications of Polarity Thinking™

Polarities are everywhere! Because of this reality, we find a great diversity of disciplines and settings in which these bright and caring authors have applied Polarity Thinking®. Our hope is that reading about these applications supports you in applying Polarity Thinking to your personal and professional lives. Whatever you are doing, there will be polarities at play. The question is if and when it might be useful to intentionally leverage a few for your own benefit *And* the benefit of others.

Important Acknowledgement

Cliff has been sharing Polarity Thinking around the world and has been very inclusive of those he has worked with by inviting them to join him in sharing their work and wisdom. This collaboration is reflected in eight chapters, culminating in the final chapter which introduces us to a world of possibilities by expanding from "polarities" to "multarities."

Watch for Cliff in future books. He appears to be just getting started.

~ Barry

Who We Aspire to Be *And* Who We Are: Leveraging the Tension With a Polarity Assessment™

Leslie DePol, MSHROD

The Polarity Assessment™,[52] Reduces the Distortion Inherent in Traditional Assessments and Provides a More Accurate and Complete Picture of Reality[53]

Most assessments come from an *either/Or* mindset that sits on a single-line continuum. On one end sits the "problem" or undesirable result or characteristic. On the other end sits the "solution" or desired result or characteristic. This type of *either/Or* assessment measures where a person, team, or organization sits on this *either/Or* continuum. For example, as shown in *Figure 1*, a leader is assessed in terms of their ability to be *flexible* rather than *rigid*. The result affirms and rewards a leader's ability to be *flexible*.

Let's examine this approach and result more carefully by comparing the results of two hypothetical leaders: "Trish Tight" runs a tight ship and sets clear expectations and parameters for others to follow. "Larry Loose," on the other hand, values his ability to be flexible in responding to rapid changes and emerging circumstances. On the *either/Or* single-line continuum of *Figure 1*, Larry Loose is likely to receive a more *positive* score than Trish Tight because of his tendency to respond flexibly. This result reinforces the notion that Larry is the more effective leader.

Figure 1

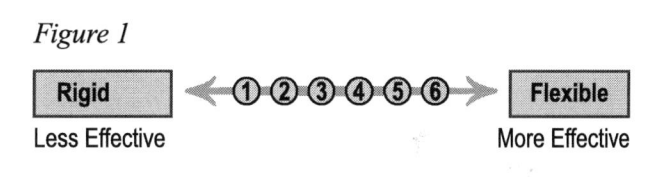

Rigid	← ① ② ③ ④ ⑤ ⑥ →	Flexible
Less Effective		More Effective

On the other hand, if both leaders were being assessed using *Figure 2*, it is likely that Trish Tight would receive a more positive score than Larry Loose because of her tendency to provide clear direction. The implication in this result is that Trish Tight is the more effective leader.

Figure 2

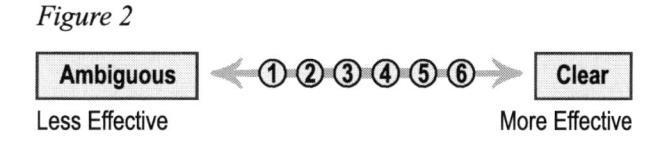

Ambiguous	← ① ② ③ ④ ⑤ ⑥ →	Clear
Less Effective		More Effective

Upon closer examination, we can see how this *either/Or* approach to assessing a leader's effectiveness might not be helpful and could be outright misleading. *Figure 1* gives Larry Loose a misleadingly positive score while giving Trish Tight

---

[52] The Polarity Assessment™. www.polaritypartnerships.com/our-impact. 2020.
[53] This opening section of my chapter summarizes "Appendix A" (DePol, L.) in Barry Johnson's *And: Making a Difference by Leveraging Polarity, Paradox or Dilemma. Volume One – Foundations*. HRD Press, 2020..

a misleadingly negative score. *Figure 2* gives Trish the misleading positive score while giving Larry the misleading negative score. In both cases, the leaders are misinformed because each assessment item is measured on an *either/Or* continuum.

Figure 3 shows the same characteristics being assessed on a Polarity-based, both/And continuum. The two characteristics of Clarity *And* Flexibility are measured as a pair of interdependent competencies that support each other and the ultimate goal of being an effective leader. This Polarity-based approach to assessing gives us a more accurate and complete picture of leader effectiveness: Larry Loose learns how his bias toward being flexible could make him seem wishy-washy and ineffective if he is unable to express himself with clarity. Trish Tight learns how her value around clarity could lead to her being experienced as being rigid if her fears about being ambiguous keep her from developing complementary strengths related to flexibility.

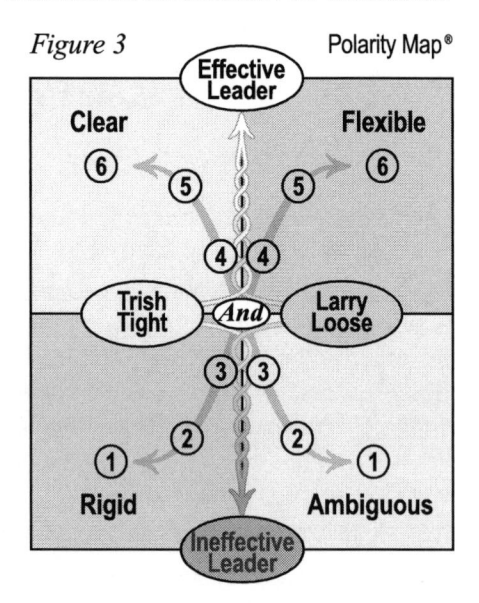

Figure 3 highlights how a *"Both-And"* Polarity-based assessment corrects a potentially misleading and distorted performance picture that can result from a traditional, *"Either-Or"* single-line continuum assessment. Polarity-based, *both/And* assessments help us to see the reality that an effective leader needs to be *both* Clear *And* Flexible, depending on the context. The Polarity Assessment is uniquely designed to assess the natural interdependency that often exists among leader competencies, cultural values, and strategic objectives. Whenever you are dealing with an interdependent pair, a Polarity-based Assessment will give you a more accurate and complete picture to guide and support your learning and development.

The Polarity Assessment Process Supports Both People *And* Performance

In an easy to follow, 5-Step **SMALL Process**™, you can **See** your interdependent competencies, values, and objectives and **Map** your desired results associated with them. Your Polarity Map® then provides the basis to **Assess** how frequently key stakeholders are experiencing the upsides and downsides associated with your most strategic dilemmas. This feedback loop supports your ability to **Learn** what conditions are supporting and/or undermining your ability to **Leverage** these natural tensions to work *for* you, rather than *against* you. Polarity Assessment results inform the development of more effective and sustainable actions to maximize upsides. Early warnings signal the need to course correct in order to minimize your experience of downsides. This SMALL Process ultimately supports achieving your greater purpose with increased speed and sustainability.

Customization Leverages Thought Leader Expertise *And* Client Expertise

The Polarity Assessment was intentionally designed to create more synergy between thought leader expertise *And* client expertise. Traditional assessments lean heavily into thought leader expertise. They help clients discover and explore what they don't know. The good ones build a compelling case for why a particular set of values, objectives, and/or competencies should be better understood and measured. This instrument may help interpret the assessment results and sometimes make recommendations for how to improve performance.

External expertise is very helpful, but it is only part of what a client needs to better understand their reality and how to improve it. Customizable Polarity Assessments include the benefits of traditional approaches to assessing and transcend their limits by supporting clients in measuring what is most important to them based on their internal expertise and unique realities.

How Do Clients Discern What is Most Important for Them to Measure?

To begin with, it would be a mistake to undervalue a client's rich leader and organization development history. Polarities play well with others; they're not another "flavor-of-the-month" that requires previous development work to be cast aside. In fact most Polarity Assessments integrate principles and objectives from a variety of methodologies and tools clients have invested in, yielding even more value from those investments. The customizable nature of the Polarity Assessment helps clients maintain a clear continuity of focus while evolving and adopting new mindsets and behaviors. This reinforces and helps sustain positive momentum in a leader's and organization's development journey.

What other sources do clients draw from in deciding what is most important for them to measure? Vision, strategy, traditional and aspirational cultural values, leader competencies, and key performance indicators are all rich places to *start with the desired end in mind.*

Starting with their end in mind, a leader at a large utility company was looking at how to sustain their proud history of ranking in the top quartile of JD Powers' Customer Service Index. Recent cost-cutting efforts combined with a strong operational focus on customer satisfaction had contributed to employees feeling as if their needs had fallen to the bottom of a long list of business-focused priorities. The VP of Customer Service understood that a continued focus on customers to the neglect of employees was a recipe for losing valuable employees *And* customer satisfaction. In consultation with Tamara Sicard of Partnership Advantage, they moved into this tension with a *both/And* mindset and methodology.

Using a Polarity Assessment to engage people and learn more, they measured how frequently they were achieving desired results for People *And* Performance in their top three strategic imperatives of customer satisfaction, cost, and reliability. Stakeholder feedback was reviewed by all levels of leadership, including Front-line Supervisors, Directors, and the Vice President. Assessment data, coupled with a qualitative meaning-making process, led to agreements on supporting the Division culture over the next two years by strengthening the connection between their leadership development efforts and their desired business results.

Assessing what we value is worth the effort because experience and research have proven that we get more of what we measure. When we see and map polarities, we get shifts in mindsets. When we assess and learn from an assessment process, it can lead to more robust insights that help shift our behavior – a key to actually leveraging the natural tensions in polarities to work *for* us, rather than *against* us.

Polarities Commonly Assessed by Clients

In choosing the polarities and examples to highlight in this chapter, I reached out to a representative sampling of practitioners and clients and asked them to share:

- Key dilemmas the Polarity Assessment helped you and/or your organization leverage better immediately *And* over time
- Specific conditions, examples, and/or anecdotes where the Polarity Assessment contributed to navigating the tension(s) more effectively

1. Continuity *And* Transformation

Every polarity, paradox, or dilemma is better understood and leveraged within the context of what needs to stay the same *And* what needs to change (Stability *And* Change). It is no surprise this universal polarity is one that clients and practitioners report as omnipresent and chock-full of opportunities and challenges! In unpacking this with clients, I start by challenging a single-minded focus on what needs to change. I often repeat a phrase coined by my friend, mentor, and colleague, Robert Jacobs, "*If you want radical change, you better have radical stability.*"

This paradoxical and powerful reframing of change work to include a focus on stability is foundational to our overall process, *The Polarity Approach to Continuity And Transformation.* Leverage it well, and it can make you. Leverage it poorly, and it will break you. We have witnessed some best practices in leveraging Continuity *And* Change in the technology sector. CIOs and people leading technology-driven change efforts are frequently early and enthusiastic adopters of a polarity mindset. Mary Sheffield, Managing Director at Accenture, championed a polarity-based change management approach in their Workday® Practice to differentiate their implementation methodology and outcomes from their competition. The Workday Change Management Team identified clear outcomes and recommended actions associated with dilemmas commonly underlying technology implementations. (See *Figure 4.*) By assessing their clients' strengths and vulnerabilities related to these polarities, Accenture and their clients are able to be more strategic in the deployment of support and resources to get a faster and more sustainable ROI on their Workday implementations.

2. Unique Identity & Interests of the Part(s) *And* Shared Identity & Interests of the Whole

As Barry Johnson has so profoundly illustrated, "It is always in the best interests of the parts to care for the interests of the whole *And* It is always in the best interests of the whole to care for the parts."

Figure 4: Strategic Polarities in Workday® Implementations

Polarities			Outcomes in IT
Centralize	*And*	Decentralize	Efficient and effective performance
Desire to Stay the Same	*And*	Desire to Change	Organization brings the best of its past and present into its desired future
Directing	*And*	Empowering	We make timely and correct decisions for our business
Directive BPR	*And*	Participative BPR	Efficient business processes
Horizontal	*And*	Vertical	Healthy matrix organization
Information Security	*And*	Information Sharing	Secure and responsible sharing of information
Manual Processes	*And*	Automated Processes	Utilize the best processes for our organization
New Technology	*And*	Existing Operations	Build our new solution while maintaining existing operations
On-Site Support	*And*	Remote Support	Project team support is reliable and responsive to our needs

Indeed, engaging key stakeholders in seeing complex realities and possibilities and enabling them to take actions that benefit Each *And* All could be seen as the heart and soul of all organization development work. In a world of increasing complexity and interdependence, this is no small effort even in the smallest of systems, but a Polarity mindset combined with a Polarity Assessment is a great place to start. Every effort to better understand and support an individual, family, team, department, organization, community, nation, or the planet must factor in our unique and shared realities.

The online Polarity Assessment can reach an unlimited number of stakeholders with relatively little effort and expense. Its filtering capabilities help illuminate the unique experiences of a given individual or group within the context of a purpose and desired outcomes shared by all. Quantitative data informs a qualitative process to better discern conditions that support and undermine People *And* Performance.

The Center for Character-based Leadership has worked deeply and broadly with a leading professional services firm to leverage the predictable tension between leaders focusing on the goals of their regional teams while also prioritizing time and energy to further organization-wide objectives. The firm rejected the limits of asking leaders to choose one versus the other and instead embraced this interdependent tension as an opportunity to transcend the limits of *either* by choosing *both*. With the help of a Polarity mindset and a Polarity Assessment, they identified clear desired outcomes across a number of critical dimensions to improve *both* Regional/Solution Set Leadership *And* Enterprise Leadership:

- Compensation & Rewards (Local Results *And* Organization-wide Results)
- Resource Allocation (Decentralized Expenditures *And* Centralized Expenditures)
- Talent Allocation (Protected *And* Shared)

- Customer Relationship (Protected *And* Shared)
- Business Development (Local *And* Global)
- Strategic Objectives (Autonomy *And* Alignment)

*Figure 5: Comparison by Region**

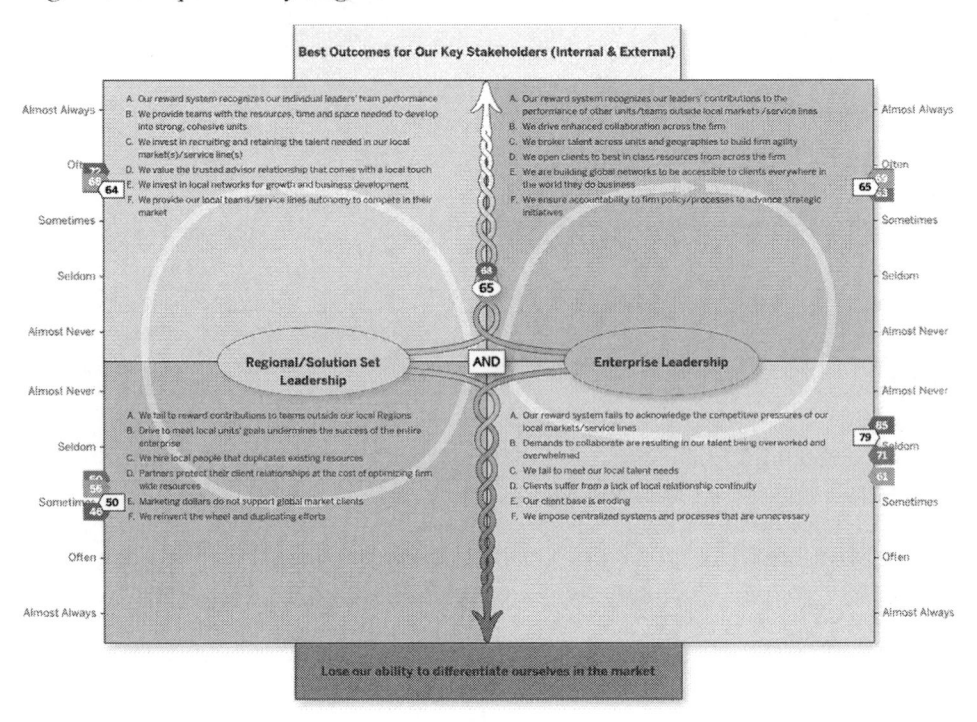

*Results displayed are representational, not actual.

The Polarity Map in *Figure 5* was assessed by 130 of the firm's top leaders and illustrates how a complex, interdependent business reality can be better grasped and understood through a polarity lens. The firm reported that their Assessment process elevated the conversation and energized the commitment to hold the embedded tensions that emerge from taking care of business locally while thinking and behaving on behalf the enterprise. As one participant put it,

> *Offices with a diverse market footprint from major metros to small markets require a level of decentralized leadership & autonomy And (not Or) we need to improve using the full power of the firm talent and capabilities. There is great value in both and we need the tension to balance and strengthen our strategy. So, my big move? Embrace the tension. Appreciate the power of the local office as well as the power of the firm as a whole and use this tension to make sure that neither one has the right to derail the journey we are on.*

The Polarity Assessment's user-controlled reporting capabilities enable comparisons across any and all parts of the system (level, function, location, etc.). *Figure 6* demonstrates how comparisons by region uncover best practices (higher scores, longer bars) and vulnerabilities (lower scores, shorter bars).

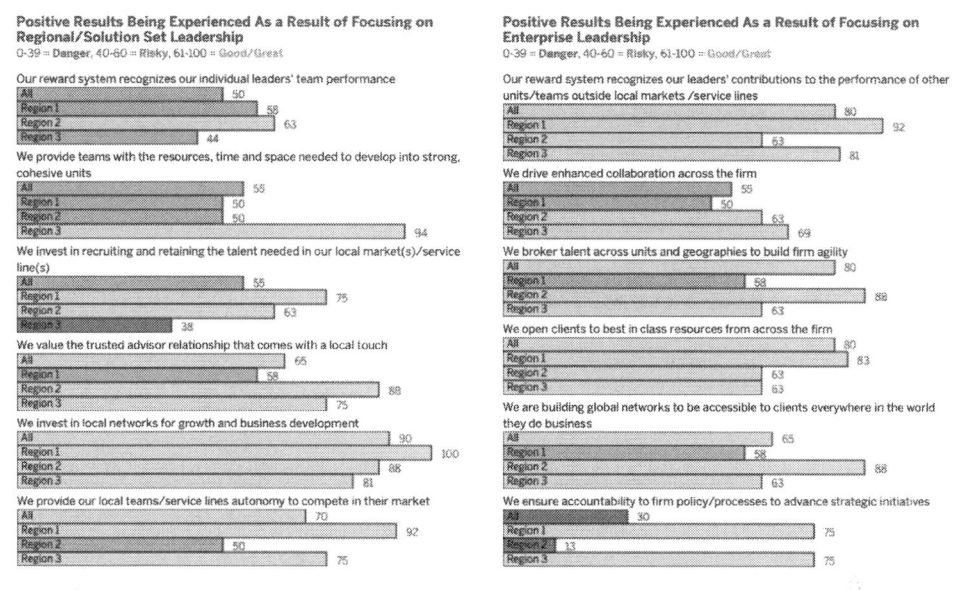

Figure 6: Comparison by Region*

Positive Results Being Experienced As a Result of Focusing on Regional/Solution Set Leadership
0-39 = Danger, 40-60 = Risky, 61-100 = Good/Great

Our reward system recognizes our individual leaders' team performance
- All: 50
- Region 1: 58
- Region 2: 63
- Region 3: 44

We provide teams with the resources, time and space needed to develop into strong, cohesive units
- All: 55
- Region 1: 50
- Region 2: 50
- Region 3: 94

We invest in recruiting and retaining the talent needed in our local market(s)/service line(s)
- All: 55
- Region 1: 75
- Region 2: 63
- Region 3: 38

We value the trusted advisor relationship that comes with a local touch
- All: 65
- Region 1: 58
- Region 2: 88
- Region 3: 75

We invest in local networks for growth and business development
- All: 90
- Region 1: 100
- Region 2: 88
- Region 3: 81

We provide our local teams/service lines autonomy to compete in their market
- All: 70
- Region 1: 92
- Region 2: 50
- Region 3: 75

Positive Results Being Experienced As a Result of Focusing on Enterprise Leadership
0-39 = Danger, 40-60 = Risky, 61-100 = Good/Great

Our reward system recognizes our leaders' contributions to the performance of other units/teams outside local markets /service lines
- All: 80
- Region 1: 92
- Region 2: 63
- Region 3: 81

We drive enhanced collaboration across the firm
- All: 55
- Region 1: 50
- Region 2: 63
- Region 3: 69

We broker talent across units and geographies to build firm agility
- All: 80
- Region 1: 58
- Region 2: 88
- Region 3: 63

We open clients to best in class resources from across the firm
- All: 80
- Region 1: 83
- Region 2: 63
- Region 3: 63

We are building global networks to be accessible to clients everywhere in the world they do business
- All: 65
- Region 1: 58
- Region 2: 88
- Region 3: 63

We ensure accountability to firm policy/processes to advance strategic initiatives
- All: 30
- Region 1: 75
- Region 2: 13
- Region 3: 75

*Results displayed are representational, not actual.

3. Support *And* Accountability

A great example of a system working deep below the surface of an ongoing culture transformation was in a K-12 school that partnered with the Center for Creative Leadership (CCL). The school had made a significant investment in building the core competencies of its leaders, including empathetic listening, greater communication, and more effective coaching. The head of the school now wanted a way for people to better understand the interdependencies among these core competencies, as well as to solicit feedback to better appreciate the impact on people who were on the receiving end of their efforts to be better leaders.

Michael DePass and Marin Burton, senior faculty in CCL's Societal Advancement Group, understood how Polarity Thinking and polarity tools could support a conversation among leaders around the tension between the school's culture of support and the need to hold one another accountable. They partnered with the school's Leadership Team to co-design and co-lead a school-wide Polarity-based Assessment process.

Given the school's historic strengths in creating a culture of support, the Leadership Team believed the opportunity to move from "*Good*" to "*Great*" would be leveraged by a deliberate lean into accountability. This shift in focus surfaced some understandable trepidation. Fortunately, a courageous head of school's openness and authenticity, a fully engaged Leadership Team, and a *both/And* mindset gave the entire school greater ease in leaning into a less developed core competency. Assessment data also confirmed the Leadership Team's instincts that people wanted and needed more accountability and gave them explicit permission to take on this developmental journey.

What Are the Internal Tensions I Need to Leverage to Support a Successful Assessment Process?

Thinking back on the stories I've heard since we launched our online Assessment, without exception the very best process and outcomes have come from individuals, teams, and organizations that whole-heartedly embraced a desire to both validate their reality *And* were willing to challenge their assumptions about that reality.

Before engaging in an assessment process, ask yourself, *"Can I see and value my intention And Can I see and value the impact I have on others?"* We are naturally more familiar with our own intentions, generated as they are from our "insides," before showing up in part through our behavior that gets seen and experienced by others on the "outside." When confronted with a negative or different experience of us than we intended, we seek solace in our reality that it wasn't our intention to hurt, anger, overlook, etc. But it is also true that if we focus *solely* on our intention and fail to understand and accept some responsibility for the impact we have had regardless of our intention, this solace will be shallow and short lived. At best, the potential positive outcomes associated with our good intentions will be undermined, and at worst the potential negative outcomes stemming from our unintended impact will become more exaggerated. This is because both Intention *And* Impact matter. It is only through considering both separately and in relationship to one another that we can manifest our best intentions *And* optimize the positive impact we want to achieve. An exercise for effectively addressing this polarity when someone's positive intent has a negative impact is described in Chapter 1, p. 10.

Safety *And* Vulnerability Through the Lens of Power

I'll conclude this chapter with the undeniable relationship that exists between a healthy power dynamic and our ability to feel secure enough to share our strengths and vulnerabilities in an assessment process. Barry has taught us to appreciate that, generally speaking, individuals and systems that leverage polarities better also know something about the benefits of Claiming Power *And* Sharing Power.

The more power I hold, the safer I feel opening up about and advocating for my realities, and the more permission I have to challenge others' assumptions about their realities. In a complimentary sense, the more power I am willing to share, the more authentic I can be about the vulnerabilities of my positions, and the more open I am to other people's realities filling in my gaps and strengthening my vulnerabilities. I give others the power to influence me/us and shape my/our reality.

If you are embarking on a deep and rigorous development journey, you will be engaging the tension that exists between Who You Aspire to Be *And* Who You Are. Holding this tension well requires a great deal of commitment and compassion for yourself and others. Polarity Thinking and the Polarity Assessment increase your capacity to leverage this tension by helping you and others see and appreciate more of the whole reality so you can attain and sustain your highest aspirations.

About Leslie DePol ~ www.polaritypartnerships.com/certified-polarity-practitioners

Values Come in Pairs at Natura: A Case Study From Brazil

Beena Sharma

This is a story about a great organization in Brazil called Natura. Since 1969, Natura's explicit, stated reason for being has been to create and sell products and services that promote the harmonious relationship of the individual with oneself, with others, and with nature. Natura & Co. is now the world's largest Certified B Corporation,[54] signifying its commitment to creating long-term value for all stakeholders and the environment, not just its shareholders. For decades, Natura has been intentionally value driven. Over the years, leaders in the organization co-created and communicated its "essence" in terms of beliefs to guide everyday actions and attitudes.

Culture and Engagement Project

This story describes a significant step in Natura's organizational development efforts during the years 2009-2011. This initiative was the Culture and Engagement project. In 2009, a cross-functional group of 260 employees engaged in dialogues focused on the culture of the organization, reflecting on the joys and pains of their past and the present experience. Simultaneously, a Core Group – comprised of the founders of the company, the members of the executive committee, and the leadership team – came together to reflect on reconsidering the values that would drive the preferred culture going forward. The core group members incorporated the output of the culture dialogues from the cross-functional group and reframed the "value drivers" for the organization. Here is how they were described, after 18 months of deep consideration. (See *Figure 1*.)

Figure 1

Value Drivers
Doing Things Well
Commitment To Truth
Continuous Improvement
Caring Relationships
Innovation
Sustainable Development
Pleasure and Happiness

It is a testament to the learning orientation of Natura that the Culture and Engagement project was one of many concurrent interventions. As a consultant to many different projects, I had the opportunity to introduce Polarity Thinking™ to diverse groups involved in various initiatives. In my experience, most aspects of organizational life can benefit from supplementing critical and/or creative thinking with Polarity Thinking. It is inevitable that wherever thinking, interpretation, and meaning making are involved, polarities show up. This is because we cannot help but

---

[54] Certified B (Benefit) Corporations are businesses that meet the highest standards of verified social and environmental performance, public transparency, and legal accountability to balance profit and purpose.

reveal both unconscious inclinations and conscious preferences when we respond to personal and professional problems and dilemmas. Investigating values and culture are no exception.

How Polarities Show up in Organizational Culture

An organization may strongly advocate an "accountability" culture, stated as a core value. When this is reiterated and employees are continuously invited to be more accountable, to keep commitments and focus on driving results, it is easy for them to understand that making mistakes and taking risks is not okay. Trying something new or different is seen as a threat to achieving results. Over time, the value of experimentation then goes underground, as it is not honored, but feared and disowned rather than valued. Thus, a strong accountability-driven culture can push the value of risk-taking into the "shadow" and create a risk-averse – even fearful – culture.

However, accountability and risk-taking are interdependent values that are both necessary and need to be embraced for a thriving culture. Choosing one over the other is inherently unsustainable over time, and *will* lead to some downsides experienced by those living in the system. On the other hand, it's easy to imagine that an organization whose core values are risk taking and experimentation can drive the interdependent value of "responsibility" into the shadow. In this case, the organizational culture may be described as lacking in responsibility or accountability. In both these cases, regardless of which value is preferred, the larger system is vulnerable to a lack of integration, and its potential for longer-term success is compromised.

I have just described the polarity dynamic as it manifests in the culture of an organization. All polarities contain two equally important points of view in which each point of view has inherent wisdom, but neither tells the whole story. The interesting thing about polarities is that the dynamics are *predictable*. We can predict the consequences of over-focusing on only one pole of an interdependent pair. Taking one pole or one point of view as the complete picture or "the whole truth" translates into an inability to transcend the current position and limits further growth. This inability to find the wisdom or benefit in what is excluded can lead to "developmental arrest" both in individuals and organizations. Therefore, supporting individuals and systems to move toward more inclusive *both/And*-thinking can facilitate vertical development,[55] and transcend the tensions created by an *either/Or* mindset.

Organizations that articulate and disseminate their core values consciously and explicitly in pairs tend to foster a more cohesive and congruent culture.

Back to Natura

When my client, the VP of HR, Strategy and Sustainability, shared with me the work that was being undertaken on redefining Natura values, I suggested examining Natura's values from a polarity lens. He was immediately responsive to and in agreement with the idea, being very familiar with the polarity dynamic. He asked

---

[55] See Chapter 41 to learn about how working with polarities can facilitate vertical development.

me to wait until the value drivers had been articulated. He assured me he would allow me the opportunity to refine the output and enrich the outcomes by exploring values in pairs. When the list was ready, he invited me to support the team leader of the Culture project.

I now had the organizational support to integrate Polarity Thinking with the values exploration. This would involve exploring each value driver and identifying its interdependent pair necessary for creating an integral, sustainable culture. If an interdependent value was not on the list, it had to be identified.

At this point, I suggested we invite Barry Johnson to visit Natura, and with my client's enthusiastic approval we set a date to deliver a workshop on Polarity Thinking and Values for key HR leaders. I talked to Barry on my return to the U.S. and shared with him Natura's list of value drivers. Needless to say, he was excited to work with Natura to help them rework their values in pairs.

Thinking Through Values in Pairs

We loved hosting Barry for a couple of days at Natura's beautiful Cajamar campus on the outskirts of Sao Paulo. Barry and I worked with the HR team on the first day of his visit. Barry and I led another session with the senior leadership of the organization and a group of high potential leaders the next day. The purpose was to orient senior leaders to Polarity Thinking and establish the significance of values in pairs, so they would be able to receive and appreciate the output of the HR group.

By the end of our workshop with the HR leaders, participants had generated a list of polarities in connection with their value drivers (next page, *Figure 2*). The process included the following:

- Adding, not subtracting. Participants were asked to look at the original value they had created and consider, "what might be another important value to pay attention to in order to keep this value from becoming problematic for us in the future?" The original value was to be retained and respected.

- Connecting, not separating. They were asked to see how one value they had was interdependent with another value they also had, but they had earlier seen as a "separate and independent" value.

With the polarity perspective and seeing values in pairs, the group was able to identify the missing values and to see and appreciate any interdependent values within their list. The project lead was quite excited with the group's work and satisfied with our output. She was sensing the completion of a long process and pleased with the enhanced understanding of values using the polarity framework. She was ready to take these interdependent pairs and present them to the Core Group as a second level, more nuanced description of the value drivers considered salient for Natura's future.

Figure 2: Natura Value Pairs (generated November 2010)

Values in Pairs		
Defend What You Believe	*And*	Recognize the Difference in the Other
Doing Things Together	*And*	Being Protagonistic
Continuously Questioning	*And*	Celebrating Success
Self-Commitment	*And*	Commitment to Other
Following Through on Your Commitment	*And*	Being Inventive
Supportive	*And*	Questioning
Quality of Relationships	*And*	Productivity
Strive to Do Better Always	*And*	Recognize Your Limitations
Innovation	*And*	Tradition
Learning	*And*	High Performance
Individual Wants/Needs	*And*	Organization Wants/Needs
Commitment to Truth	*And*	Caring Relationships
Idealism	*And*	Realism
Long Run	*And*	Short Run
Face Daily Challenges	*And*	Keep Humor, Lightness

The Work Feels Incomplete

Despite the seeming success, I was quiet at first in that meeting, sitting with some disquiet. The polarities had been named based on the best understanding from the perspective of Human Resources. I believed that the HR perspective was not necessarily representative of the whole organization, and therefore the process was incomplete. I felt we needed to include others' observations. From the conversations among the participants that day, I could hear the polarities being explored more conceptually. For example, conceptually, the value pair of "innovation" with its interdependent pole "tradition" appears logical, as certainly innovation and tradition can be in tension with each other.

However, the pain the organization was feeling (in my experience of it) was around a lack of *discipline* (not a difficulty with tradition). I had heard many complaints during the culture dialogues that there were too many last-minute changes in the project plans to accommodate new ideas. Deadlines were not taken seriously because creative exploration was more important. Many employees struggled with the fact that individuals and teams often failed to keep to the project schedules, sacrificing project completion for innovation. Thus, I did not see that the HR participants adequately connected to the felt experiences of those swimming every day in the waters of the *operating* culture. They had not reflected deeply enough to relate the value pair discussions to the occurrence of the pain that most people were experiencing. The fact that employees were having informal conversations in corridors about this issue (as a result of the focus on innovation) was an indication that the value of *discipline* had gone underground. It had become a shadow aspect of its culture. Innovation was desired and supported. Delivering on commitments as planned came in the way of that desired value (as it would, from an *either/Or* mindset). From what I was hearing, the polarity that was more *relevant* to their operating culture was Innovation *And* Discipline, not Innovation *And* Tradition as conceptualized by the HR group.

This is important. The polarities significant in a culture need to relate to the real joys and sorrows of individuals living in that culture every day. It is quite easy to name a polarity in the abstract. However, this can lead to a superficial process and create a false sense of adequacy. Identifying the poles that need to be embraced based on *felt experience* will allow for optimal impact when taking actions to shift the culture and heal the difficulty.

I proposed another last step in the process. I imagined that it would be revealing to process the value drivers with a "max-mix"[56] group. The max-mix group would be a microcosm of the company, with individuals representing as many diverse perspectives as possible. We could invite the group to share their experience of how the privileged values impacted the everyday culture. They could inquire into how the neglected or shadow values caused organizational pain. This, I anticipated, would help us capture the "pulse polarities" – those that gave us a read of the real cultural temperature of the organization. This activity would also give us a chance to validate (or not) items on the list created by HR members.

After some reluctance and hesitation due to Christmas approaching, along with resource considerations and other constraints, my client agreed to take on the recommended last step. We were now ready to put our finger on the pulse of the organization and take another reading.

Two weeks later, I was on another long flight out to Sao Paulo. Twenty-two employees showed up for a two-day working session. We explored the concept of polarities and reviewed the value drivers co-created by different groups in Natura. I set up a series of questions for participative inquiry. The inquiry led to attendees sharing their stories and recounting their hopes and the ideal expectations, starting from the time an employee considered joining Natura. They talked about their first day at work, their first year of work, through to their full tenure with the organization until the present day. They identified the consistent organizational values as experienced by everyone in the group, and those aspects that all were disappointed about. The process involved individual reflection as well as small and large group work to review each core value and arrive at the most significant polarity that was experienced as *culture-defining*. This helped create a deep, shared understanding of the pride they carried as well as the anguish experienced in the culture. Next, they paid attention to the values that were in the shadow or neglected, which in turn had led to cultural distress.

This is interesting. If you now look at two of the values drivers in the original list: Commitment to Truth and Caring Relationships, you will note they were listed as

---

[56] Max-mix is short for "maximum mix" of perspectives in an organization. This concept comes from the large scale interactive process (LSIP) developed by Kathleen Dannemiller and Associates in the early 80s. LSIP is a technology to enact enterprise-wide participative change through structured whole-system dialogues.

separate, *independent* values. Because they were not seen as an interdependent pair, they were held in tension *against* each other. In this company, Caring Relationships "won" the war. Natura was known as an organization where leaders really cared about their relationships; however, this was jeopardized if a leader had something disconfirming to say. And rather than hurt others, leaders often refrained from sharing what they really thought. This meant they did not challenge each other easily or give constructive feedback. (The HR group had identified the same interdependent value pair as well.) This is how the max-mix participants expressed their pain:

- *We are afraid to hurt people.*
- *We are worried that people won't like us if we speak honestly.*
- *We do not have a trusting environment.*
- *We don't like to challenge or hold people accountable.*
- *We listen too much to everything everyone has to say; too many politics.*
- *We go for consensus and don't stand for ourselves.*

Seeing this tension as a polarity that needed to be integrated was liberating. And revealing. And relieving. Now, for the first time, it was possible for leaders to envision doing *both*. It raised an empowering, cathartic, *developmental*[57] question. "How will I care for relationships *And* speak my truth?"

By the end of our two days together, we identified eight polarities that were critical for the organization to intentionally leverage in order to actualize a more integral, coherent, congruent culture.

One polarity that emerged in this group was stunning in its potential for making a real difference to their felt culture. It tapped into a central nerve that had caused rippling pain, because it related to its very essence as an organization. For decades, Sustainable Development (a value driver) had been at the heart of Natura's continuous development efforts. Forest conservation, waste reduction, climate protection, fair trade practice, and supporting neighborhood talent development were all forefront initiatives and commitments. Yet a deep pain welled up related to this value, which was felt by every single person in the max-mix room. While the employees experienced an abundance and generosity of resources, they were deeply pained with the "wasteful" culture they observed. This is what they said:

- *We are leaders in social and environmental responsibility, yet we waste a lot.*
- *It pains me to see half-drunk bottles of water, wasted food, excess use of paper.*
- *We waste time, we don't learn from our mistakes, we do re-work, we overlap our roles – we waste resources in so many ways.*
- *We are very generous as a company; we believe in investing resources, and yet it is shocking how much we waste.*

---

[57] I call this question "developmental" because *both/And*-thinking is a marker of vertical development, and represents the capacity to grasp greater complexity than *either/Or-thinking*. See Chapter 41.

Even as a consultant, I had gotten a taste of this wastefulness. I had lost count of the number of times I was kept waiting to meet with someone I had an appointment with. And I was being paid for each minute I waited, every minute a waste.

It had been a long-felt complaint that Natura failed to conserve its resources *internally* while advocating sustainability and conservation *outside* the organization. Natura was well-known for its generosity and spending on internal organizational development and yet there were visible signs of waste – of money, resources, time and more. This dialogue thus revealed the polarity of "Abundance of resources *And* Optimization (conservation) of resources." It opened up the real possibility of *conscious conservation*. People could stop complaining or feel conflicted about the waste; they could start taking responsibility for reducing waste in day-to-day internal operations in addition to the superlative success with functional waste management (recycled packaging for example).

Getting There!

Figure 3: Value Drivers and Their Related Polarities

Values Drivers	Polarities		
• Commitment To Truth • Caring Relationships	Being Caring/Respectful	*And*	Being Truthful
• Continuous Improvement • Doing Things Well • Sustainable Development	High Performance	*And*	Hands-on Learning, Learning From Mistakes
• Doing Things Well	Doing	*And*	Planning
• Continuous Improvement • Sustainable Development • Innovation	Philosophical, Ideal	*And*	Pragmatic, Real
• Innovation • Caring Relationships	Being A Protagonist, Individual Excellence	*And*	Being Collaborative, Team Excellence
• Innovation • Doing Things Well	Creativity, Flexibility, Change	*And*	Discipline, Keeping Commitments
• Sustainable Development	Abundant Resources	*And*	Optimizing Resources
• Pleasure and Happiness • Doing Things Well	Striving, Always Reaching Further	*And*	Celebrating, Appreciating
• Sustainable Development • Doing Things Well	Centralizing	*And*	Autonomy

Figure 3 is the final list, based on the group's output of eight polarities presented to the senior leadership team. Over a series of dialogues, the initial list was refined in two ways. First, one polarity was added; Centralizing *And* Autonomy. This polarity was felt to be more salient at the most strategic level of the organization. Second, each value pair was related to the value driver it impacted. This was a useful addition since some value pairs impacted more than one value driver. For example, leveraging the polarity of High Performance *And* Learning would support three value drivers: Continues Improvement, Doing Things Well, and Sustainable Development.

Taking It Forward

Once the co-creation work was complete, I supported Natura in delivering Engagement Workshops to 1,200 of its leaders over the following year. The top 20% of the organization participated in a four-day engagement process designed for alignment and congruence. The first segment involved leaders diving deep into their personal values and mission. In the second segment, leaders re-aligned with the emergent organizational vision, mission, and value drivers. In the third segment, they learned about the polarity perspective and dwelt on the nine key polarities that the organization was committed to managing better, for a more harmonious and energized culture. Each group of 30 leaders created Polarity Maps® for the nine polarities, identifying action steps and early warning signs to help them be intentional and more effective at leveraging them.

The feedback most heard was the "relief" participants felt during this process of realizing that they didn't have to choose one or the other. There were two noteworthy (almost momentous in a quiet way) unanticipated positive impacts on another front.

One was around the tension some leaders felt between their individual values and the organization's values. Many leaders felt overwhelmed by the aspirational values of the organization that they did not necessarily hold personally. The lesson they gleaned through Polarity Thinking was that they could value and embody both their own and the organization's perspective because an *either/Or* holding was unsustainable for the individual as well as the organization. The second impact was related to a whole community of employees feeling that they were being seen and valued explicitly. Being innovative and market-driven as a company, the production side of the organization that held the pragmatic, process-driven side of the house had long felt undervalued. They did not feel seen or owned by the organization to be as valuable as the design and market functions. With the commitment to the polarity of "Innovation *And* Discipline," they felt their contribution was now highly regarded. Indeed, "seeing is relieving." The more we can see and the more we can include, the more energy we generate for further evolution.

This is a brief outline of a profound experiment and experience for all involved. I hope this case study serves as a credible and viable illustration of a very versatile tool that helps us work with the inherent and natural tensions that all individuals and systems grapple with knowingly and unknowingly. Organizational cultures can reveal how values, when privileged without their interdependent pair, create shadow aspects and dysfunctions. These difficulties can be addressed and healed by seeing the polarities at play and understanding how they work.

Find bio and contact info for author Beena Sharma at
www.polaritypartnerships.com/certified-polarity-practitioners

Polarity Thinking™ and Real Time Strategic Change™
Robert 'Jake' Jacobs

The Stories

I was first introduced to Polarity Thinking™ in 1994 at the National Organization Development Network conference in Orlando, Florida. My business partner Frank McKeown and I were hosting a post-conference session on Real Time Strategic Change™ (RTSC), an approach I had documented in a book by the same name.[58] Little did I know that the gentleman sitting in the back of the room smiling at me through to the morning break was going to have such a profound impact on my life and work.

You see, throughout the morning I had spent time emphasizing how important the six principles were that form the foundation of all Real Time Strategic Change work (I may have even used the term "inviolate" – the passion of youth!). And as important as these six principles were, so was the flexibility with which you could apply them: culture change, work design, strategy development and implementation, team building efforts of 10 or 1,000, etc. In a multitude of applications, the principles would serve you equally well.

By the time this man introduced himself as Barry Johnson (a consultant with whom we had a common client, Fay Kandarian, who had been trying to get us connected for a while), I was more than a little curious. I was thinking, "What does this guy know that I don't that has him smiling like a Cheshire cat during my impassioned speech?" So, I asked him, "Why the big grin?" He answered, "You've been talking about polarities for the past two hours and didn't even know it. Polarities are my work in the world."[59] Now he had my attention. As Barry tells the story, he called his wife Dana at the break and told her he was going back to school as a way of saying he was going to be learning from me. What I know for certain is that I've been doing the learning. Barry's passion and wisdom about Polarity Thinking have influenced every aspect of my work and life ever since that first conversation.

The focus of polarity work has always been two-fold – the client in front of you and the planet as a whole. It is increasingly difficult to find a change practitioner anywhere in the world that is not familiar with the concept and practice of Polarity Thinking. Another constant in the world of polarities has been a continual exploration of the boundaries of the phenomena. How does it apply in the realm of politics? How can it help us better understand our history that we may create a more

---

[58] Jacobs, Robert W. *Real Time Strategic Change*. Berrett-Koehler, 1994
[59] Johnson, Barry. *And: Making a Difference by Leveraging Polarity, Paradox or Dilemma. Volume One – Foundations*. HRD Press, 2020.

fulfilling future for all? How can we, in Barry's mentor Jack Gibbs' words, *see each other more completely and find ways into loving each other regardless of the past.* These questions and entertaining planetary impact are as much about Polarity Thinking as the map and principles. It's a big field with room for everyone to play.

I remember many "polarity stories" about applications, lessons learned, and even humbling experiences. (Ever hang onto a pole a bit longer than serves the Greater Purpose Statement?) I recall the earliest large group Polarity Assessment™,[60] that Barry, Leslie DePol, and I did with the Department of Defense. The group identified a short list of key polarities they needed to leverage more effectively. Then we made massive Polarity Maps®. I mean really big "cover the side wall of a big room" size maps. Next out came the sticky dots and up they went on the giant maps, each individual completing their own assessment of how well these polarities were being leveraged. We connected the center points around that imaginary infinity loop outlined by the dots. Standing back from the charts you could see a perfect scatter plot diagram outlining the group's assessment of each polarity. Crude compared to the current online assessment? Yeah. Another step toward its creation? Definitely.

In the early days of the Polarity Assessment, Leslie and I were working with the National Health Service in the United Kingdom. We were consulting with local health authorities, helping them prepare for upcoming performance reviews. The online assessment was in its infancy yet already functional. Participants completed questionnaires before the working sessions. We created results maps for them to analyze and better understand how they were leveraging a handful of key polarities. Of course, the assessment was not possible without the scoring. However, we came up with another insight that made the assessment work well: the analysis question, "What evidence do you see in your organization that explains these results?" The evidence was there – they had said so themselves in the assessment survey. What was missing was a way to ground the assessment results in their daily experience in the organization. Steady and consistent progress was being made to what is now a web-based instrument being used the world over.

I have completely integrated my Real Time Strategic Change practice with Polarity Thinking. Each of the six principles underlying the RTSC approach is now defined as one of six key polarities that need to be leveraged well for sustained success. In Barry's terms, they are a multarity.[61] Poorly leverage any of the principles and over time you will poorly leverage all of them. Real Time Strategic Change is an approach to creating your future, faster – the results you aspire to achieve are accomplished faster and more sustainably than you ever believed possible. The key to the approach's effectiveness lies in seeing the work through a polarity lens.

Real Time Strategic Change: Polarity Thinking in Action

In response to the challenges anticipated over the coming ten years, the Board of Directors of the Ann Arbor Transit Authority (AATA) decided to use a collaborative

---

[60] The Polarity Assessment™, www.politypartnerships.com/our-impact. 2020.
[61] See Chapter 42, "Multarities™: Interdependencies of More Than Two" by Cliff Kayser.

effort to create and implement an ambitious strategy. This plan would have to respond to the growing needs of the many diverse communities needing public transportation that surrounded the city. The University of Michigan, based in Ann Arbor, was growing and needed a coordinated transportation system for students and faculty outside the campus. The suburbs around Ann Arbor were growing and needed commuter service, and there was need for direct service to the airport. The challenge for AATA: how to maintain excellent on-time, customer-oriented services and respond to the myriad demands to expand for rapid growth.

The Approach

AATA chose Real Time Strategic Change as their approach. It provides a path for people to collaboratively envision and actively create their preferred futures faster and more sustainably because it's about both strategic planning *And* strategic doing. Think of it this way: It shortens the cycle time between the poles of planning and implementation until they become one and the same.

RTSC events have brought together as many as 2,000 people where they make decisions and take actions during a single meeting – all in real time. But unlike other large group processes, RTSC is not just about events. The work is guided by six polarities (the same principles we described after that morning break was over at that OD Net post-conference) that can be used to successfully drive change without any large group meetings. It adapts to the needs of the organization. We like to say "RTSC plays well with others." Follow-through is not an issue as it is with many change approaches. Some commitments to do business in better ways are acted on immediately; others as soon as possible.

The Work

A Core Team, comprised of a microcosm of AATA employees, was charged with guiding the effort. This team included a board member, senior executive, mechanic, driver, route guide coordinator, financial analyst, and marketing director.

Employees from all parts of the company were involved through cross-functional task teams and large group meetings in a process that included:

- Building a shared base of strategic information using data gathering meetings with key external stakeholders, tools and methods to better understand the existing and desired internal cultures, and how those cultures fit with the emerging strategic direction.

- Creating a shared vision generated during a highly interactive working session attended by all AATA employees. During the session, they explored potential strategic scenarios for the organization's future and their roles in making these visions a reality.

- Developing clear overall organization and department strategies, based on data gathered and the organization's existing and needed core competencies.

- Aligning and Developing Leadership through supporting the board and senior leaders in working together effectively, making smart decisions quickly and reaching agreement on the proposed mission, vision, goals, objectives, and action plans.

- Organization-Wide Congruence through developing the skills, knowledge, and experience for all employees, supported by organizational structures, processes, and systems, to translate the strategy into daily work.

- A process to revisit progress and make necessary course corrections.

The Results

Within the first year, AATA had increased ridership by five percent, expanded service inside the city and out to suburbs, tested an innovative free-pass program for downtown workers, and strengthened its partnership with the local University of Michigan campus bus system.

Long-term results over 5 years included:

- Reduced operating costs; 17% lower than similar companies.

- 95% of the community saw public transportation as a valuable service.

- 44% increase in services offered.

- A Federal Transportation Association certificate of excellence in 2007.

- The AirRide service received the award for Exemplary Innovation at the Transportation Riders United (TRU) 2013 Regional Transit Awards.

- Increased ridership; received national recognition as fourth in the nation for ridership growth in 2012.

- Launch of private-public partnership providing Ann Arbor to Detroit Airport first public transportation shuttle; ridership in year one exceeded projections, resulting in a $300,000 reduction in cost to the contracted provider.

- Launched construction for a LEED certified transit center with state-of-the-art 21st century design.

- The annual number of riders has increased by more than 50% since 2004, while AATA productivity has improved by 43% over eight years.

Integration of the Six RTSC Principles

The six Real Time Strategic Change Principles were AATA's guide throughout their strategic journey. The more they lived them, the faster change happened and the longer gains made have been sustained over time. Note the Polarities each Principle is leveraging in *Figure 1*.

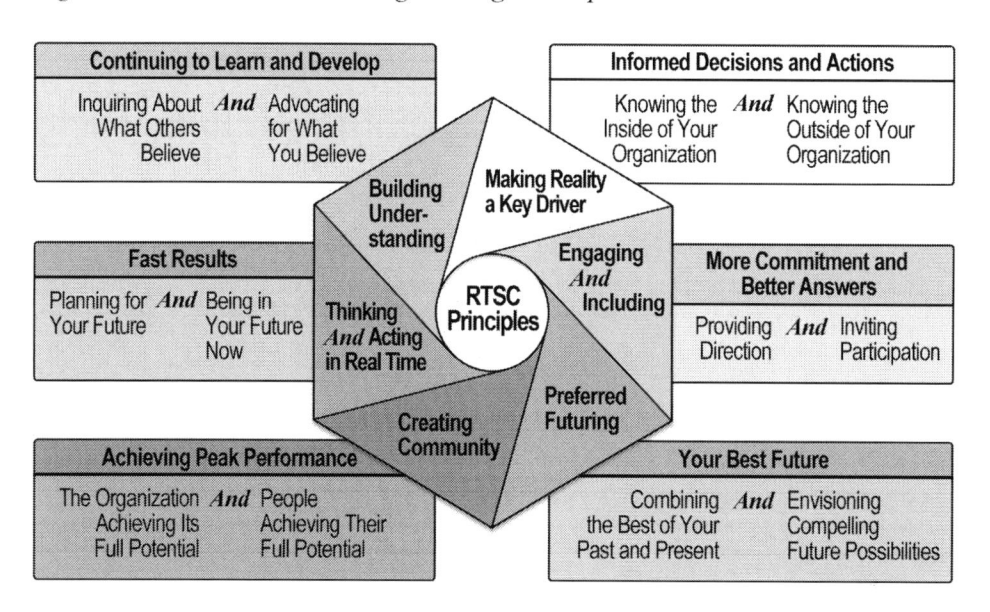

Figure 1: The Six Real Time Strategic Change Principles

Continuing to Learn and Develop	Informed Decisions and Actions
Inquiring About *And* Advocating What Others Believe / for What You Believe	Knowing the *And* Knowing the Inside of Your Organization / Outside of Your Organization

Fast Results	More Commitment and Better Answers
Planning for *And* Being in Your Future / Your Future Now	Providing *And* Inviting Direction / Participation

Achieving Peak Performance	Your Best Future
The Organization *And* People Achieving Its Full Potential / Achieving Their Full Potential	Combining *And* Envisioning the Best of Your Past and Present / Compelling Future Possibilities

RTSC Principles:
- Building Understanding
- Making Reality a Key Driver
- Engaging *And* Including
- Preferred Futuring
- Creating Community
- Thinking *And* Acting in Real Time

Making Reality A Key Driver

Know both the inside and outside of your organization in order to make informed decisions and take strategic actions.

For example, senior leaders ensured that the transit experts considered the organization's internal culture in developing the master plan. Equally important were the dozens of public meetings and industry research that informed the plan.

Engaging *And* Including

Provide clear direction when needed while inviting participation.

The board provided clear direction in defining the work that needed to be done during the meeting when they set the scope for the project. Then they and others involved every member of the organization and many key stakeholders in shaping the strategies and action plans.

Preferred Futuring

Include the best of your past and present in creating a compelling vision for your future.

The AATA vision included growing to become a regional transportation organization while retaining its best practices and remaining true to its culture.

Creating Community

Focus on the achievement of the organization as a whole, while also finding ways to support individuals in achieving their full potential.

People throughout AATA care deeply and take great pride in the very best services they can each provide. This energy was channeled into a "we're all in this together" approach that continued to build trust and momentum for the entire organization to be the best it can be.

Thinking *And* Acting in Real Time

Be in your future and plan for it at the same time. Live in your preferred future as if it were already happening in real time.

At the start of their strategic planning process, people in AATA and their key stakeholders immediately began working together in new and better ways. Mechanics and drivers partnered with board members and senior executives on the Core Team, all having equal say in guiding this effort.

Building Understanding

Stand up for what you believe in and be curious about what others think in order to continue to learn and develop – individually, in your teams, and as an entire organization.

Students and staff at the University of Michigan, customers, and employees from all over the organization had different points of view on AATA's future direction. Politicians, citizens, and other transportation organizations across the region had their own desires of what should be included. This RTSC principle ensured that all stakeholders shared their diverse perspectives so that decisions and actions came from the broadest and deepest possible understanding of the issues. The Real Time Strategic Change principles provided AATA with firm, predictable ground to stand on, enabling the organization to successfully navigate its way through to creating its continually evolving preferred future, faster and more sustainably.

Conclusion

Polarities just are. We experience them because we exist. You can choose to leverage them – or they will leverage you. Make them a part of your practice and you'll be better for it. So will all the people with whom you live, work and play.

Find bio and contact info for author Robert 'Jake' Jacobs at
www.polaritypartnerships.com/certified-polarity-practitioners

Polarity Thinking™ *and Creative Problem Solving*

Elizabeth Monroe-Cook, PhD

Over a lifetime of work in psychology, qualitative research, creativity, and group facilitation, I have found two theories that illuminate particularly well a couple of critical intuitive practices for building individual and group success: Creative Problem Solving (CPS) and Polarity Thinking™. Each theory has useful elements when applied to both old and new problems or situations, and each approach brings awareness of and structure to thought processes that are sometimes hidden, unrecognized, or even stunted. A description of CPS is included in this chapter, along with an examination of the power of combining it with Polarity Thinking. Treating CPS and Polarity Thinking as an interdependent pair produces outcomes that are more robust than what either one – at times – can do on its own.

Introduction to Creative Problem Solving (CPS)

When introduced to the principles of deliberate creative thinking, many people find CPS not only a necessary but also an exciting expansion of thinking processes. The CPS process requires a balance over time, encouraging people to be *both* critical and analytical (convergent thinking) *And* to think openly, in freewheeling and non-linear ways (divergent thinking) in order to find new ways of solving problems and addressing or capitalizing on challenges. Being able to name this holistic creative thinking process, to practice it, and to access it on demand when needed (escaping from standard or typical responses) is a direct and efficient path to innovation. Creativity is the essential operation; innovation is the result.

Defining CPS

"Creative" means production of ideas or options that are both new and useful (when faced with novel situations). "Problem" is broadly defined, meaning a gap between what someone has now and what they want. "Solving" refers to taking action or implementing the result or results of the CPS process.[62] Some people in the creativity community have been critical of the word "problem" because it may be interpreted to mean only something negative. In response, others add the concepts of positive challenges or opportunities under this umbrella word.

CPS History

The history of the CPS process is long and storied. Alex Osborn began working on what he called "deliberate creativity" in the 1940s, recognizing that creativity is an innate human capacity, yet not something always recognized as such nor being used as needed (he faulted education). Osborn is typically known for his

---

[62] Puccio, G. J., Murdock, M. C., Mance, M. *Creative Leadership: Skills that Drive Change.* Sage Publications, 2007.

development and use of the tool called brainstorming. To him, creativity is a capacity that can be improved: "The most direct way to develop creativity is by *practicing* creativity – by actually thinking up solutions to problems (1953)."[63] Osborn, a businessman, joined with Sidney Parnes, an academic, in doing research in the 1950s demonstrating that CPS training enhanced individuals' creative thinking skills. Parnes and another academic contributor, Ruth Noller, generated, delivered, and tested the college curriculum of CPS in the 1970s.

The CPS model or process has been the subject of a great deal of development and research over time, resulting in many modifications or new descriptions of its elements. Some people have striven to simplify the steps or use simple language. Others have worked to illustrate the complexity involved, or have given different emphasis to a stage. Practitioners have also made refinements through direct experiences applying the model. Nonetheless, the essential components of the early work are found or can be traced in today's versions. The intuitive basis in observable human behavior makes it an applicable theory people easily recognize and can manifest in explicit ways. In simple terms, the process itself has the following major pieces or elements:

- Identify a general goal (context, vision, situation)
- Gather or identify relevant information
- Define a specific challenge question or statement
- Generate ideas to address the challenge
- Select, refine, and develop the best option or options
- Plan and take action (implement)

Each of these steps is accomplished through first, *diverging* (generating many ideas) and then *converging* (narrowing the set of ideas and making a selection). Note well that this polarity, Diverge *And* Converge, is as fundamental to CPS as the Inhale *And* Exhale polarity is to breathing. The founders and practitioners of CPS emphasize the importance of separating these two types of thinking, just as inhaling and exhaling are done separately. To attempt to diverge and converge at the same time is said to be equivalent to attempting to drive with one foot on the gas pedal and the other on the brake.

Importantly, research and direct experience have shown that CPS can be taught and learned using proven principles and techniques. The scope and applicability of CPS are central aspects of it, as described by Puccio, Murdock and Mance.[64]

> *Creative Problem Solving is a comprehensive cognitive and affective system built on our natural creative processes that deliberately ignites creative thinking and, as a result, generates creative solutions and change. The CPS process has a dual function: thinking AND doing.*

---

[63] Osborn, Alex. F. *Applied Imagination: Principles and Procedures of Creative Problem-Solving* (3rd Edition). Scribner, 1963.
[64] Puccio, G. J., Murdock, M. C., Mance, M. *Creative Leadership: Skills that Drive Change.* Sage Publications, 2007.

The benefits of using this process seem obvious in circumstances in which people feel stuck in patterns, less able to bring new thinking forward, or desire to fulfill an exciting dream or prospect.

At the same time, one can also see how overemphasizing the use of CPS, particularly the divergent side, can result in creativity for creativity's sake. This unpleasant side effect leads to unfulfilling and un-implementable ideas. Criticism of brainstorming usually is related to just listing ideas without eventual evaluation and action planning. The fault lies in seeking more and more ideas without applying the best principles of critical thinking in selecting and developing ideas. Another issue can be over-valuing innovation and revolution when, in many cases, adaptation and evolution would be the "blue ribbon" approach.

The key to successful use of CPS is expanding thinking and possibility. Its foundational premise was to generate more alternatives, getting out of "either-or" boxes, as noted by Sidney Parnes:

> *Too many of our decisions are habit-bound, straight-jacketed by imaginary boxes* [referring to *either/Or* decisions]. ... *Too often, we examine what merely* **exists,** *choose the least of available evils, and act accordingly. But how can you know what you* **should** *do until you know all that you* **might** *do? ... When you make* **creative** *decisions, you avoid putting yourself in the "either-or" box by: first, speculating on what "might be" from a variety of viewpoints; then sensing and anticipating all conceivable consequences or repercussions of the variety of actions contemplated; finally choosing and developing the best alternative – in full awareness.*[65]

This general goal of using a process to expand thinking, possibility, inclusion and best alternatives is also deeply embedded in the Polarity Thinking approach. Thus, we come to an understanding of the power and opportunities of using them together.

Polarities of CPS

By now it should be obvious that easily observable polarities abound in the CPS framework and practice, starting with the ever-present Diverge *And* Converge. Other polarities that are prevalent in the process and practice of CPS include those listed in *Figure 1*.

Figure 1: Polarities of CPS

Novelty	And	Utility
Vision	And	Reality
Stability	And	Change
(What Exists	And	What Might Be)
Tradition	And	Modernity
Depth	And	Breadth
Ideas	And	Action
(Thinking	And	Doing)
(What Might Be	And	What Will Be)
Imagination	And	Logic
Simplicity	And	Complexity
Cognition	And	Emotion
Acceptance	And	Resistance
Play	And	Purpose
Freedom	And	Guidance
(Flexibility	And	Structure)

---

[65] Parnes, Sidney J. *The Magic of Your Mind.* The Creative Education Foundation, 1981.

Deciding When to Use CPS and Polarity Thinking

As noted earlier, it is possible but inappropriate to assume that creativity (and innovation) is always needed. To discern whether or not to apply the CPS process, the "3 I's" as criteria for CPS are recommended:

- Importance: The situation is meaningful, provoking, or exciting to the individual or group.
- Influence: It is within the person's or group's ability to decide or primarily influence.
- Innovation is needed: A solution is unknown to the individual or group – a new and useful result is needed or wanted.

As has been established in other works, the use of Polarity Thinking is not always warranted either. With one modification, the "3 I's" criteria also apply to Polarity Thinking:

- Importance: As before
- Influence: As before
- Interdependence: The problem, challenge, or opportunity contains at least one set of interdependent factors to be addressed in order to succeed.

When both the need for Innovation and for recognizing Interdependence are present, using the combination of CPS and Polarity Thinking is especially meaningful.

Additional Parallels Between CPS and Polarity Thinking

One can already see that parallel features and strengths are found in both of these approaches. The fundamental goal of expanding our thinking, and the criteria for when to use them have already been put forward. Additional shared characteristics are listed below, showing that both models have:

- A "process," a particular method of doing something, generally involving a number of steps or operations.[66]
- Reliance on an intuitive base, some kind of universal human capacity. Once introduced, people can generally quickly relate to the concepts and operations of their processes.
- Cognitive or cerebral elements, and affective or emotional aspects.
- Linear and learnable steps, and the flexibility to move between the different steps as needed.
- A need for their users to be aware of their own thinking processes and to be able to communicate about their experiences and the phases of the process they are using.
- Wide applicability in a nearly infinite set of circumstances and the potential to supplement other models easily.
- A particular *mindset* as a condition for success (e.g., openness to newness, tolerating ambiguity to a degree, modest but sincere hopefulness about achieving productive outcomes, acceptance of flexible thinking, and a desire and commitment to put something into action).

---

[66] Puccio, G. J., Murdock, M. C., Mance, M. *Creative Leadership: Skills that Drive Change.* Sage Publications, 2007.

- A set of *tools* to use during their process steps (e.g., questions to ask, suggested activities, the Polarity Map® itself, and techniques to encourage divergent thinking and convergent thinking).
- Modifications to the model over time through feedback from theorists and users.
- Particular utility in complex situations.

Finally, users of both of these approaches develop better outcomes and stronger thinking-and-doing *skills* through regular practice over time. In fact, consistent use alters one's worldview and becomes "unconscious competence"[67] or second nature.

The Case for Combining Approaches

Both CPS and Polarity Thinking can be and are used regularly as individual, standalone processes. A lot of good results have been achieved doing so. However, on their own, certain flaws can emerge. CPS is great for identifying new and useful things that can be done, but many anecdotes among practitioners and facilitators exist about how frustrating it can be when a seemingly creative solution (or solutions) has been identified, but the client individual, team, or organization fails to follow through as they encounter resistance from others.

Polarity Thinking maps can often be created, but then not followed through on in circumstances in which the map elements are too repetitious of easily known factors, have not included enough variables, the action steps included in the maps do not represent anything new, or they lack people's commitment. Filling in the map elements can fall prey to early brain "dumps," also known as same-old, same-old ideas or solutions. Polarity Mapping can lead to substantial awareness of interdependence, but not be inspiring enough in the direction of motivating actions or innovation.

What does each approach have to offer the other? Polarity Thinking helps the CPS practitioner in the clarification stage to assess whether the challenge is really a one-off problem to solve or a polarity to leverage over time. In Polarity Thinking, resistance is treated with respect and inclusion. Rather than setting up or allowing an individual or organization to identify resistance as something to ignore or overcome, Polarity Thinking encourages the exploration and use of resistance to build a more robust set of creative solutions to a challenge. Applying Polarity Thinking allows for creativity and innovation on a whole picture, not just part of it.

The following Polarity Map (*Figure 2*) is an initial attempt to illustrate the interdependence of the two approaches. Note: HL means high leverage action step; it applies to both sides. CPS, particularly the key dynamic of divergent thinking to generate a long list of options and then converging on the strongest and most novel ideas, keeps Polarity Mapping open and generative. Having a more freewheeling approach to filling in the areas of the map produces not only the awareness of interdependence, but also fresh looks at current situations and possible actions to take. In CPS terms, the upsides in particular can become individual challenge statements for divergence and convergence when generating action steps and early warnings.

---

[67] Broadwell, Martin M. *Teaching for Learning (XVI)*. The Gospel Guardian, 1969.

Figure 1

Action Steps

- Slow down to speed up (HL)
- As we assess our situation (Clarify), ask ourselves, "Do we need innovation for our outcomes?"
- Use CPS process steps, especially Diverge-Converge

Early Warnings

- Feelings of a rush to judgment because some viewpoints are missing
- Continued resistance to action steps because they're non-inclusive

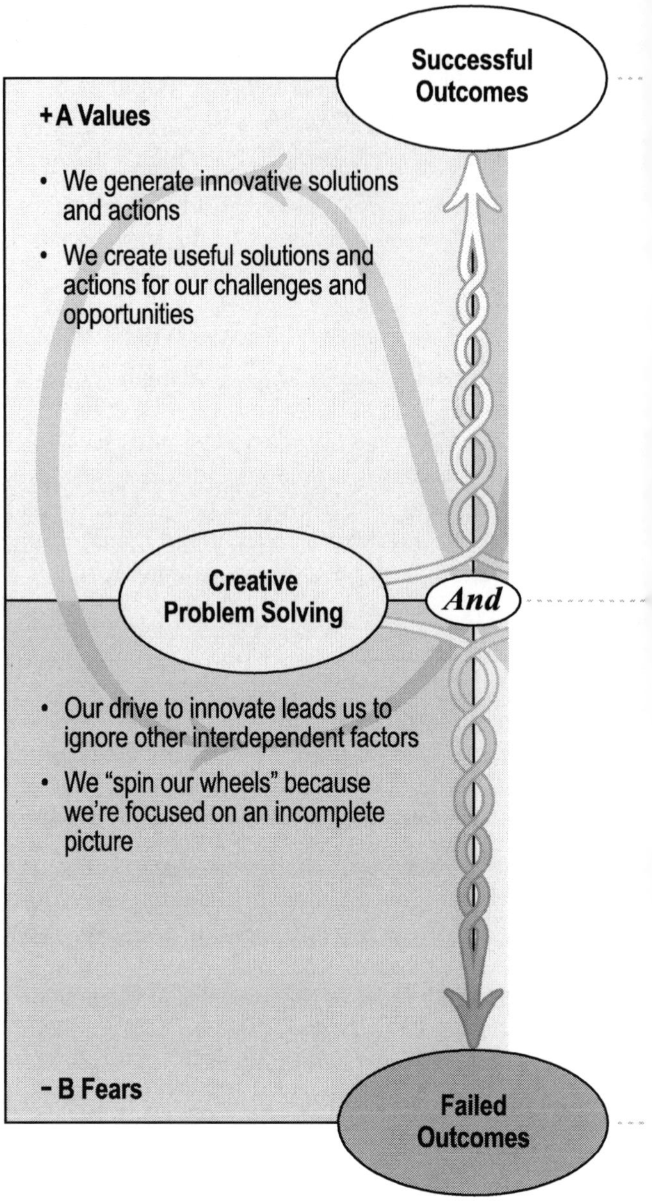

+A Values

- We generate innovative solutions and actions
- We create useful solutions and actions for our challenges and opportunities

Creative Problem Solving *And*

- Our drive to innovate leads us to ignore other interdependent factors
- We "spin our wheels" because we're focused on an incomplete picture

− B Fears

Successful Outcomes

Failed Outcomes

Chapter 9: Monroe-Cook

Polarity Map®

Successful Outcomes

+C Values

- We work on the whole picture, including interdependent factors
- We include multiple viewpoints in our solutions and actions

And

Polarity Thinking

- Our drive for awareness of interdependent factors leads us to ignore the need for creativity
- We "spin our wheels" because we're focused on first-level ideas

− D Fears

Failed Outcomes

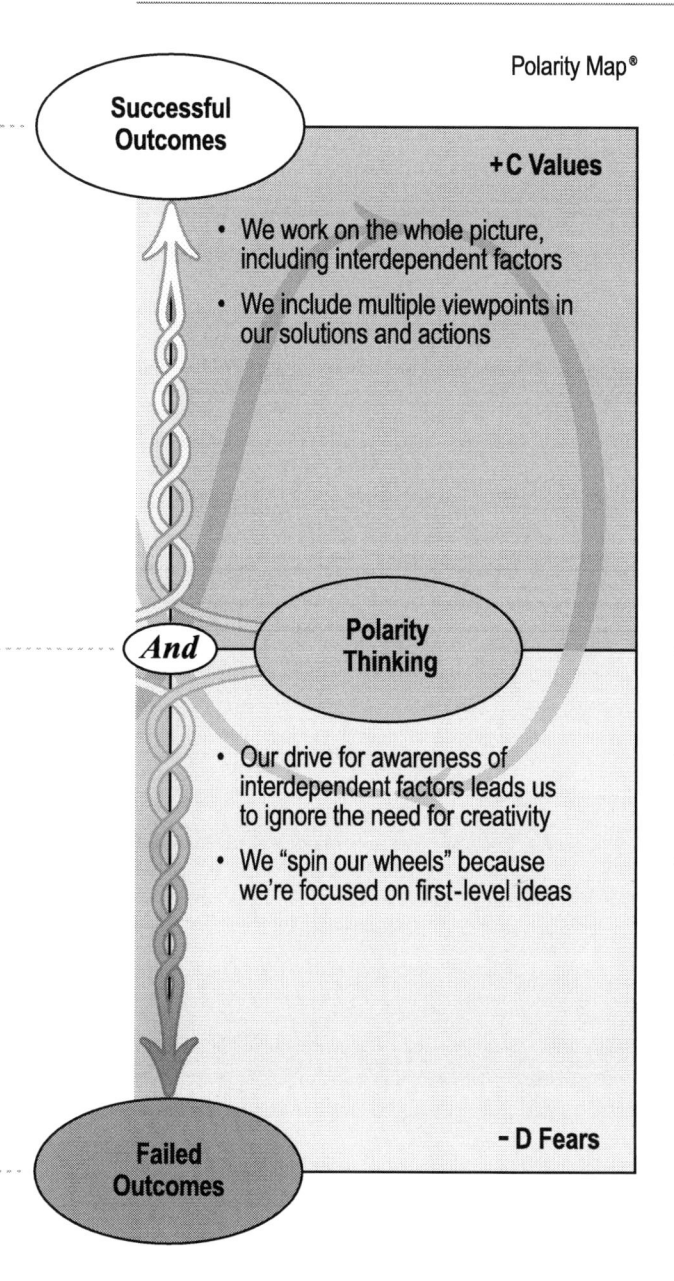

Action Steps

- Slow down to speed up (HL)
- As we assess our situation (Clarify), ask ourselves, "is it a problem to solve or a polarity to leverage?"
- Use polarity mapping process steps, especially identifying the poles

Early Warnings

- Feelings of a rush to judgment because ideas have not been explored
- Continued resistance to action steps because they're boring

75

The Yin-Yang of CPS *And* Polarity Thinking

Thinking of CPS *And* Polarity Thinking as interdependent (a polarity themselves), is not only good for deliberate use of them in combination, but also a good reminder when using the approaches singly. In the classic yin-yang symbol, each half contains a contrasting dot that signifies the presence of the other half within. All CPS processes contain polarities (e.g., Diverge *And* Converge) and all Polarity Thinking processes contain problems to solve (e.g., Action Steps).

Therefore, even when using CPS on its own for a one-off problem, it is still useful to pay attention to the underlying polarities, like Play *And* Purpose, Depth *And* Breadth, and Acceptance *And* Resistance. When using Polarity Thinking on its own, it is important to make longer lists of ideas than needed (diverge) for all of the Map's elements before selecting the ideas (converge) that will ultimately populate the Map. For example, in a group, making large pages for brainstorming possibilities (e.g., with self-stick notes) available is one way to ensure that mapping a polarity is as expansive as possible before evaluating and narrowing down the options, and transferring the final selections to a more traditional Polarity Map. The time invested in the initial brainstorming is well worth it for ensuring that a map will be well thought through, representative of multiple viewpoints, and motivating.

The partnership of CPS *And* Polarity Thinking is a beautiful marriage of vision, values, and skills. Having access to the upsides of both approaches is a treasure to be shared with all practitioners, clients, and users. This introduction is offered with both Humility about what can still be learned about this particular interdependence, *And* Confidence about its meaningfulness.

For more CPS information, seek out the Creative Education Foundation (established by Osborn & Parnes, 1954), its conference, the Creative Problem Solving Institute (CPSI), and its *Journal of Creative Behavior*. Also note the International Center for Studies in Creativity at SUNY Buffalo State.

Find bio and contact info for author Elizabeth Monroe-Cook at www.polaritypartnerships.com/certified-polarity-practitioners

Polarity Thinking™/Paradox Thinking in Business
Deborah Schroeder-Saulnier, DMgt

The elements of a system may themselves be systems, and every system may be part of a larger system.[68] ~ Russell Ackoff

Any business plans you make or actions you take are done within a universe affected by economics, politics, operational/technical factors, and social interactions. Inside of that universe is the pervasive culture of your own organization. Never lose sight of these contextual factors as you implement the process of applying paradox thinking to your problem-solving.

Creating Market Advantages

Companies that have a keen understanding of their context will naturally see new market opportunities as they emerge. In my work with the Chicago Region at IPC the Hospitalist Company (IPC), it became clear in conversations with the Executive Director that a new opportunity was taking shape for the company because of market shifts. If the company chose to exploit it, leadership would be faced with managing a significant paradox in order to drive future growth.

IPC "is on the leading edge of a growing U.S. trend toward hospitalist specialization," according to the Hoover's analysis of the company by Anne Law.[69] IPC provides more than 1,400 hospitalists in 28 states and backs up the physicians with management services. Hospitalists are health care providers who traditionally have focused on inpatient care and services:

> The hospitalists professional society, the Society of Hospital Medicine (SHM), has defined *hospitalist* as a physician whose primary professional focus (clinical, teaching, research, or administration) is general inpatient care. A hospitalist may be an employee of a hospital or HMO, a contractor, or a private practitioner. About 75 percent of hospitalists are general internists. Hospital-based primary care physicians alleviate general practitioners from the need to make daily rounds to visit hospitalized patients. Several studies have shown significant decreases in hospital costs and in length of hospital stays under the hospitalist system, with no decline in quality of care or patient satisfaction. Some academic medical centers have adopted hospitalist models for inpatient care and teaching.[70]

---

[68] Ackoff, Russell L. "Science in the Systems Age: Beyond IE, OR and MS." Operations Research, 1973, Vol. 21, p. 664.

[69] Law, Anne. "IPC-The Hospitalist Company, Inc.-Quick Report." Hoover's, March 6, 2013.

[70] Hospitalist. (n.d.) *Farlex Partner Medical Dictionary*. (2012). Accessed June 15, 2020 from www.thefreedictionary.com/hospitalist.

Until 2013, IPC's growth strategy primarily involved three types of activities. The first was expanding its services to new institutions in areas where it already operated. The second aspect of the growth strategy involved recruiting and training additional hospitalists. The third was moving into new regions.

In early 2013, company senior executives determined that IPC faced another major – and highly time-sensitive – growth opportunity related to the "traditional" definition of hospitalist. In fact, they decided to redefine it to enter an emerging market. Senior executives in the Chicago Region knew that their ability to take advantage of the significant new opportunity depended a great deal on a shared understanding of options and actions company-wide. They took the plunge into paradox thinking with the intent of bringing the process to the Chicago Region staff and the Practice Group Leaders (PGL) Council, the key leaders of each practice in the Chicago Region.

The growth opportunity was summed up in the paradox Acute (core focus) *And* Post-Acute (new focus). Post-acute is the medical term describing the care a patient receives after discharge from a hospital. It can involve a rehabilitation facility, assisted living, skilled nursing, and so on, and it can serve patients of any age – from newborns with special medical needs to elderly patients recovering after a hospitalization.

The triad of senior executives who first worked with me to capture the paradox and model all aspects of it are quite different in terms of thinking preferences. It was interesting to see how the strengths and predispositions of each actually complemented each other as we developed the original map for Acute *And* Post-Acute.

Please note that I consider it very important for engagement of the participants to use their language rather than impose some kind of standard nomenclature on them. Yes, the model may appear rough and some of the information indiscernible to "outsiders," but it helps move the process forward – it supports a team in going operational with paradox thinking.

> Before plunging into narrative analysis of the differences and similarities between the executives' model and those of the practice leaders, consider the models they created in their team sessions by reviewing the two full Polarity Map® graphics on pp. 80-83: *Figure 1: Perspectives of Regional Senior Executives* and *Figure 2: Perspectives of PGL Council*

The three teams worked on their models independently, yet the convergence of input is so interesting. Despite the differences in word choice, the positive and negative outcomes, action steps, and metrics are remarkably similar. The teams were close on citing how to go about achieving positive outcomes and what kind of numbers and results they needed to stay aware of that would signal over-focus on one part of the paradox at the neglect of the other. The most significant difference in style of expression – but not salient content – comes from the PGL Council, who are practice leaders; that is, they are physicians operating in clinical environments.

Key commonalities include the strategies to hire and retain talent, to maintain and increase the number of facilities where IPC provides services, and to manage provider relationships. Corresponding metrics appear in all three models; for example, failure to retain talent is seen in the number of resignations. This kind of compatibility is far more than a coincidence. It's a reflection of clear communication from leadership of hospitalist opportunities in the Chicago marketplace.

Ultimately, the first actions taken that correspond to those listed to support Acute included adjusting the way that new physicians are hired, reconfiguring their compensation packages, and implementing new measures to retain current doctors. They took complementary actions listed to become competitive in the Post-Acute arena. The process of both implementing action steps and keeping an eye on metrics continues as IPC Chicago pursues new ventures in the Post-Acute market.

IPC's Chicago Region operates in two contexts: The greater Chicago area and its own national organization. The different teams who built the models focused squarely on the Aim and the Miss related to their region and what they needed to do to exploit their opportunity to move into an emerging area of business; that is, Post-Acute. Not every region of IPC faced the same opportunity to move into Post-Acute in the near-term, however, so IPC's national leadership needed to manage the paradox of "Centralized *And* Decentralized," allowing Chicago to take initiative some other regions were not taking. They needed to balance making decisions out of corporate office, while ensuring autonomy for IPC Chicago so it could extend its services to a Post-Acute market that was clearly growing.

The Hoover's analysis spotlights another paradox faced by the national organization that national leadership is balancing well, that is, Acquisitions *And* Organic Growth: "In addition to its main growth strategy of acquiring existing practice groups in new markets, IPC strives to offer its services to new institutions in areas where it already operates."[71]

Nested in this set of objectives is IPC's acknowledgement that administrative and clinical leadership need to be balanced in order to meet customers' requirements in this ever-changing world of healthcare. In other words, Business *And* Patient Care have to have equal billing for the company to achieve its Aim.

Respect the context wherein you operate and the culture that enables you to thrive in that context. If your group is part of a larger organization, make it clear to your national/global leadership why your context demands that you exploit or avoid specific market opportunities.

---

[71] Law, Anne. "IPC-The Hospitalist Company, Inc.- Quick Report." Hoover's, March 6, 2013.

Figure 1: Perspectives of Regional Senior Executives

Action Steps

- Attract right staff/talent continually
- Find the business
- Adjust compensation model
- Adjust schedule
- Ensure company differentiation
- Ensure connectivity of clinicians

+A Values

- Recruiting talent
- Improved compensation
- Lifestyle
- Consistency (happy)
- Flexibility

Extreme Growth

Acute

And

Early Warnings / Metrics

- #Resignations
- #Problem docs
- #Encounters (revenue)
- Overall business numbers

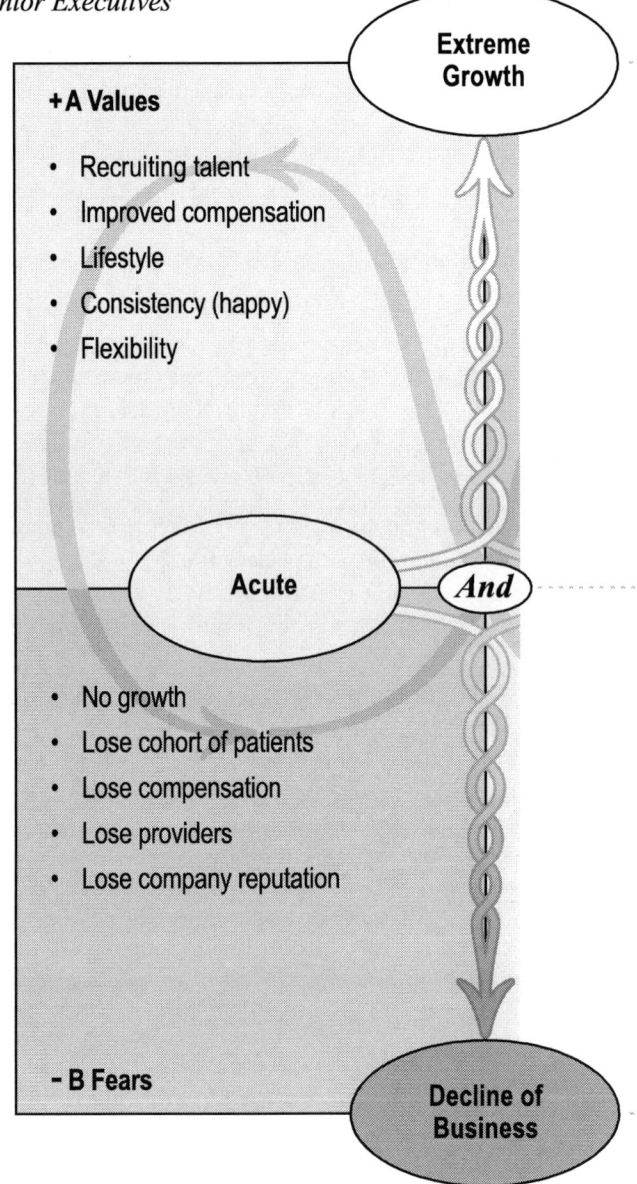

- No growth
- Lose cohort of patients
- Lose compensation
- Lose providers
- Lose company reputation

− B Fears

Decline of Business

Chapter 10: Schroeder–Saulnier

Polarity Map®

Extreme Growth

+C Values

- Recruiting talent
- Improved compensation
- Lifestyle
- Increased business opps as a result of market demand
- Sleep (supported by mid-levels)

And — **Post-Acute**

- Lose "core book" competency
- Lose providers as there would be less appeal to health plans
- Lose company reputation

− D Fears

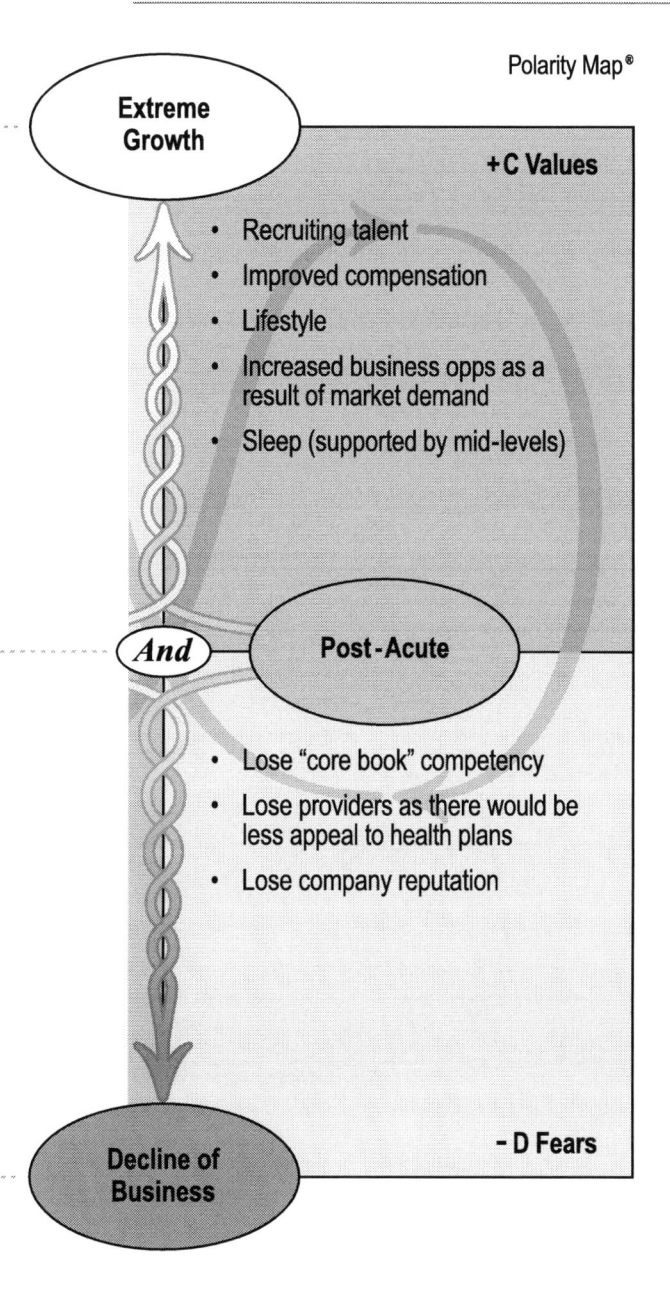

Decline of Business

Action Steps

- Meetings with urgent care MDs
- Hire the right staff/talent
- Create/shape culture for post-acute
- CEO to focus more heavily on post-acute
- Ensure company differentiation
- Ensure connectivity of clinicians

Early Warnings / Metrics

- #Business opportunities taken by competitors
- #Buildings
- #Attractions

Figure 2: Perspectives of PGL Council

Action Steps

- Staffing (we need enough; need the right staffing, need to retain staff, need to look at models/be creative)
- Definitive strategy to maintain, grow
- Differentiators (answering the phones, presence, quality, etc.)
- Engagement (get partners involved; need to be engaged)
- Leadership (common vision)

Early Warnings / Metrics

- #Volume (revenue $ decrease)
- #Hospitals (start hiring on their own; emergence of competition)
- #Resignations (increase)
- #Referrals from post-acute (decrease)

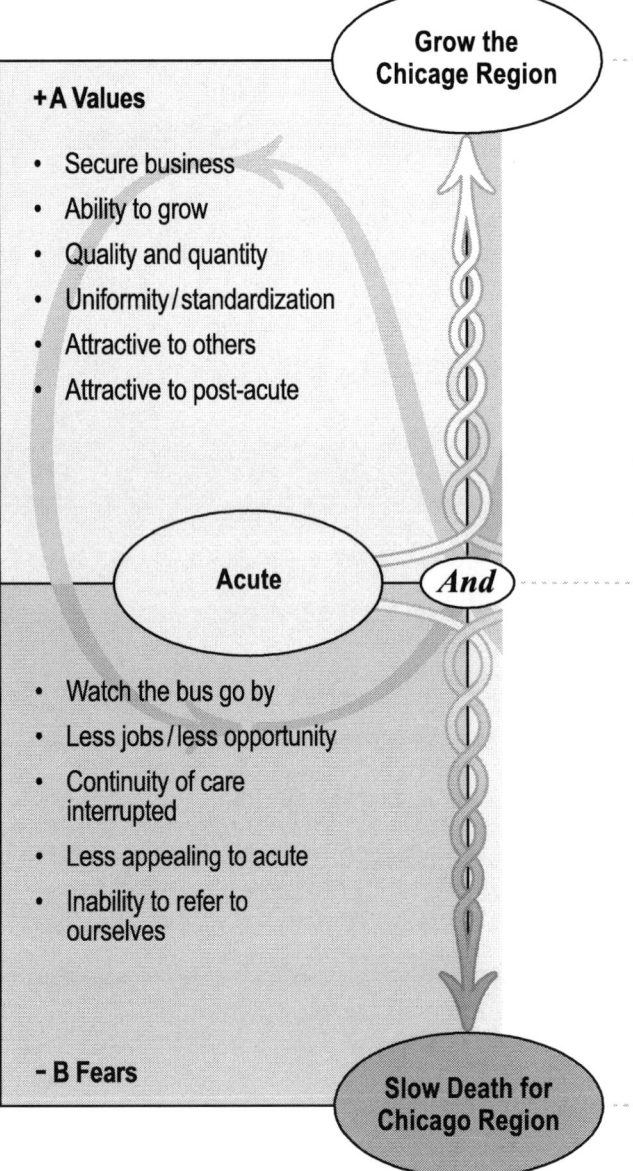

+A Values

- Secure business
- Ability to grow
- Quality and quantity
- Uniformity/standardization
- Attractive to others
- Attractive to post-acute

Acute

- Watch the bus go by
- Less jobs/less opportunity
- Continuity of care interrupted
- Less appealing to acute
- Inability to refer to ourselves

−B Fears

Grow the Chicage Region

And

Slow Death for Chicago Region

Chapter 10: Schroeder–Saulnier

Grow the Chicago Region

+ C Values

- Recruiting talent
- Improved compensation
- Lifestyle
- Increased business opps as a result of market demand
- Sleep (supported by mid-levels)

And

Post-Acute

- Wouldn't be honest
- Less referrals
- Less volume of patients
- Less appeal to payers

− D Fears

Slow Death for Chicago Region

Action Steps

- Look at "presence" in both. Need to sustain.
- Have everyone learn the "recipe" as we grow in other buildings. Mentoring on IPC Way is a good approach for this.
- Staffing
- Act fast before competition sees
- Look at models / be creative

Early Warnings / Metrics

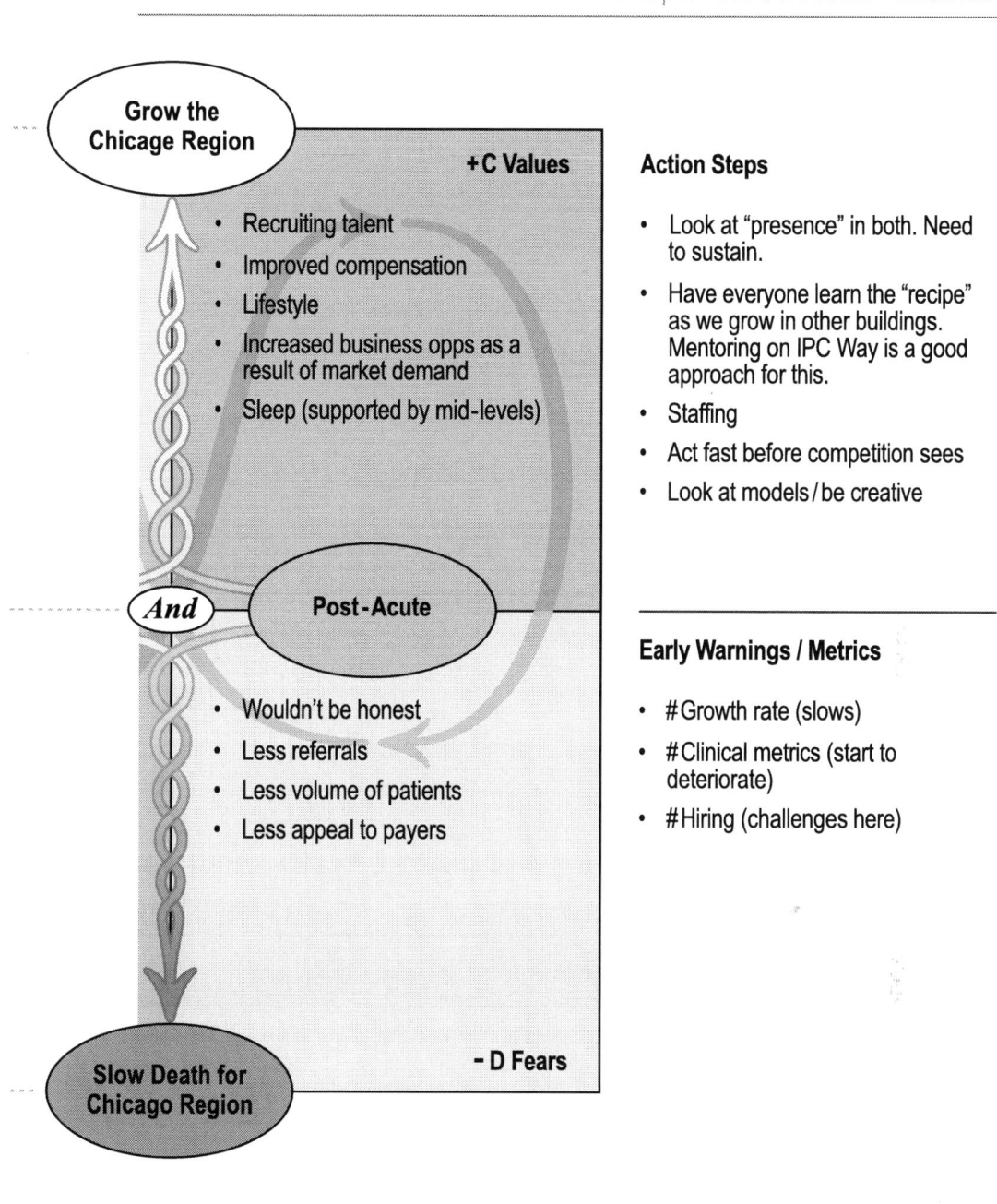

- # Growth rate (slows)
- # Clinical metrics (start to deteriorate)
- # Hiring (challenges here)

Find bio and contact info for author Deborah Schroeder-Saulnier at
www.polaritypartnerships.com/certified-polarity-practitioners

Interdependent Leadership:
An Experiential Love Affair With the Earth!
Peter Dupre, BS, MEd

Now I see the secret of making the best person; it is to grow in the open air and eat and sleep with the earth. ~ Walt Whitman

Interdependent Leadership begins with "seeing," seeing *humans* as a *part* of a much greater *whole,* as *part* of this beautiful Earth, that is more than us, that is *More-Than-Human*. Photography has always helped me do that. I share one image from our old mountain farm of a sculpture depicting my parents in a wild state. It expresses the wholesome beauty of our fuller nature. I hope as you read you create your own images in your mind that help you remember rich life experiences with Nature. It is in this remembering that we begin the journey that is at the heart of what we will explore.

Our Journey into the More-Than-Human, Interdependent Earth

I'm an "outside" dog. Growing up in the woods above the Ohio River, in a small college town, I spent my requisite 10,000 hours in the wilds by the time I was nine. From this earliest time, the wilderness was a part of my family. It is from this lifelong experiential love affair with the Earth that I share how leadership has become lost, and a vision for re-finding our way – for redemption. I speak for those who, though speaking, are not heard in the clamor of human activity.

I discovered my work early in life. In 1967, I was attending a Teen Lab in Bethel, Maine, and after a few days of this T-Group for faculty kids, I suggested we could keep the process going while climbing Mount Washington. With some nervousness everyone agreed to give it a try. The next day we launched early, in the dark, to explore Human Nature, in Nature. While climbing a beautiful peak, at 14, I knew that this was my thing; that I would lead people into the wild.

My credentials for being a voice for our relationship with Nature, for this vital life-giving partnership, for our interdependence, come from a seeming disability. Growing up dyslexic, and with ADHD, I couldn't do a regular life. I had to escape from the classroom to my "real world," the world of the wild. Here I could see the workings, it all made sense, like being on a Disney ride and realizing that inside the Matterhorn were all these invisible things making it happen.

From my youth to the present, in some form or fashion, I've led experiences that help people connect with themselves and with Nature. Using experiential learning methods, we went on adventuresome journeys designed to help us relate to others and the wilderness. Exploring Human Nature, in partnership with Nature, has been my craft and my passion. I have chosen to name this enchanting polarity Human *And* More-Than-Human. This expresses our larger self; our true identity.

I'm in the field of Leadership Development, and I've had the opportunity to work with many of the finest Executive Training Programs around the globe. I've been trying to help leaders leverage the Human *And* More-Than-Human polarity, yet sadly we continue to fail. *We have lost our way*! The trap is, we think of leadership as a strictly Human enterprise. Leadership is equally More-Than-Human and we must relate once again to the part of ourselves, and others, that is integral to the natural world. Through every learning journey, I endeavored to have leaders experience this interdependency; how we are part of the Earth, and how it is part of us.

Mapping the Territory

In his book Becoming Animal, ecological philosopher David Abram voices the importance of reclaiming our wild intelligence and reconnecting with what he described as the "more-than-human."[72] Mark Wallace, in When God Was A Bird, reveals that the world's religions, especially indigenous forms, were once full of the mythical marriage between Humans and Nature.[73] Whether the sciences, arts, or humanities, there are many voices for the natural world. Yet the hum of commerce and the clatter of human society drown them out.

Life speaking pairs abound in Nature. Birth *And* Death, Day *And* Night, Equilibrium *And* Disequilibrium, Human *And* More-Than-Human; the list goes on and on. Fortunately, for our understanding, they behave in similar ways. All interdependencies have individuating energy, pushing away, making a boundary, a repulsion, and at the same time they all have opposite forces that attract, create partnerships, bring them together, and build relationships. These forces that push apart and hold together are part of the mystery of interdependence, and show up in every polarity.

As we Humans push away from the More-Than-Human, an opposite and equal force holds us together, making a whole. Yes, we Humans are unique in all of Nature, and yet we are in relationship, in partnership, with all that is around us. There is ultimately no divorcing from this interdependent reality; we are married to the More-Than-Human.

---

[72] Abram, Dr. David. *Becoming Animal*. Pantheon Books, 2010.
[73] Wallace, Dr. Mark. *When God Was A Bird*. Fordham University Press, 2018.

Leaders who see only the Human pole, and who are blind to the More-Than-Human, don't see the whole reality. The Leadership Development Field has failed to present this fuller picture. They are lost. The infinity loop, *Figure 1*, suggests we are in the negative result of over focusing on the Human and neglecting More-Than-Human. Ironically, we are now living in the damage, the dual-downside, of this ongoing vicious cycle.

Figure 1

I want to explore with you what it means for leaders to be Human *And* More-Than-Human, and leverage the best of both. My goal is to help us, and other leaders, see the neglected More-Than-Human world, to journey into it, and come back into a courtship with it. I want us to be re-enchanted, and to experience the love and beauty of the More-Than-Human! As we cycle back to our Humanness, I hope we can tell a new story of our relationship with the Earth, and for us to be leaders of this life-giving partnership. This relationship, though philosophical, even spiritual, is also deeply practical, and without it we remain lost.

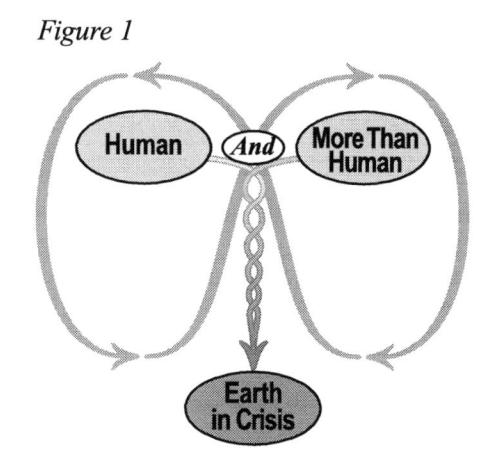

Calibrating Our Internal Compass

Exploring the ancient question, "Who are we?" orients us to the world. Our answers have always formed our reality and motivated our actions. Early in our history, we believed that we were members of a larger family composed of all living things. We believed that animals and other parts of the natural world were relatives. Over time, we tried to divorce from these creatures around us. We intentionally moved from a sense of belonging to a sense of independence, of being distinct, different, separate from, and holding power over the world.

This separation from Nature began thousands of years ago as we transitioned from hunting and gathering to agriculture. Language, logic, organized religion, the scientific revolution, the steam engine, and urbanization each separated us further. This slow human divorcing from the More-Than-Human world, this leaving home that continues on, is now the subject of great concern. How do we lead when our compass does not tell the truth?

Getting Lost

The Human story is often that we are drifters. This myth about humans roaming, but not quite belonging, is an age-old tale. It has endured and been loved because it portrays us as independent, separate from the land, lonely heroes. This makes for great books and movies but does not speak to the truth of who we are, the time we live in, or what is needed ahead. We are *inter*-dependent, yet this truth is obscured by our self-absorption; our human hubris.

The exclusionary clubs of "Whites Only" and "Men Only" are dying a slow death. These clubs of privilege, where leaders looked after their own kind, were commonly accepted not long ago. Looking back, it is easy to say that we disapproved. Yet today, in our self-absorbed way, the "Human Only Club" and its leaders look after their own kind, with no sense of who and what is excluded from their special society or their world-altering decision-making.

A few years ago, I went to the Native American Smithsonian Museum. A display told an ancient story of the people losing their way, of a descent into materialism and greed, and becoming separated from the essence of life. Only a few elders could remember the old "way" and it was up to them to be the guides. It is now the job of leadership to remember our partnership with Nature, to grow this relationship, and to be guides to others.

We are all "First Nation" somewhere, a place where we belong, where we have a natural affinity to the land, yet we fail to act with the wisdom it could afford us. Cultures that are rooted in the land and not always "looking for the next-best-thing," can teach us about our interdependency, our interconnection with the More-Than-Human. It is time for leaders to humbly observe, to listen, to learn from the Earth, and from those who still hold a solid connection to it. The original cosmic World Wide Web, this thing we call Nature, is the master teacher and role model of interdependence! Until we learn to see and leverage our partnership with our More-Than-Human identity, we will fail to be fully human, and will fail to effectively lead.

Lost Leaders

If we reflect on the Human *And* More-Than-Human polarity that makes up our whole world, we become aware of how much we, and our leadership, ignore the More-Than-Human pole. We are all so busy with the Human pole that we are in a Human centric sort of trance. If leadership exists to creatively respond to the challenges of the time, and serve some greater good, leadership has almost completely ignored the More-Than-Human and its stakeholders.

Ironically, Human interdependence with the More-Than-Human is so immediate, so complete, and so vast that it becomes invisible; hidden in plain sight, yet always operating the ride behind the scenes. Humans, in our arrogance, have imagined ourselves special, separate, independent, merely "using" the world for our benefit. Leadership Development largely mimics, or echoes, this worldview. We develop our Emotional Intelligence (EQ) to more effectively lead human enterprises. When we measure our EQ, we assess our relationship with ourselves and with other humans, with no awareness of our relationship with Nature, with the land, the woods, or with animals. This omission in EQ Testing is a glaring example of our not seeing or valuing the whole picture. We have missed that a nurturing reciprocal relationship with Nature is essential to our emotional intelligence. This is the trap we are in. Nowhere in Leadership Development do we look at our relationship with the More-Than-Human world.

An exhaustive search of books, articles, programs, and Ted Talks will reveal that the focus is all about people, the Human pole. As for the More-Than-Human, you could look far and wide to find scant mention. In our leadership programs, we may take a reflective walk or use an outdoor classroom for a team exercise yet fail to truly value our leadership responsibility to that world. We do 360-degree assessments without any thought of the More-Than-Human world. We take advantage of the re-energizing properties of Nature, but fail to offer anything in return. This lack of reciprocity reflects the attitude of the industry, and our society as a whole. We are glad to take from it yet have no thought of what we might give.

The field of Leadership Development has many successes to be proud of, however it has failed to serve the More-Than-Human world. Almost all of our training concentrates on the Human end of this polarity. Under this leadership, Human activity and organization have become destructively self-serving. This "Human Only Club" is not only unsustainable; it leaves us impoverished, cut off from the very source of our existence.

A leading business journal recently featured an article on the importance of worshiping "speed." Really, of all the things we might worship!? Interestingly, only when we slow and quiet ourselves can we truly come into relationship with Nature. Contrary to worshiping speed, most leaders develop and become more effective when they pause, they listen, and they see more clearly. However our training for executives must be fast and furious and overfilled. We too have caught the disease!

Regardless of what we call this More-Than-Human world, we do in fact work for it, with it, in it, and through it. Our Human hubris has us making Nature a thing, a thing that is over there, while we are over here. Sure we love to visit it, we sing songs and write poetry about its beauty, and we go on vacation in it, but we don't make it central to our leadership, and we do not proclaim it as a most important stakeholder. In a hundred years, this disregard for our essential other half will be viewed as our failure of leadership.

Seeing Our Way

Long ago my mentor Joe Nold, President of Outward Bound, shared with me that, "learning wasn't learning until brought into a social context!" What constitutes this social context? I challenge us to imagine the whole of life, even what we call inanimate, as our social context. This is a bigger stretch than you might realize, as we have such a Human-centric habit. In focusing on only half, we miss our interdependency, the essential partner we have sidelined. These interdependencies are here, but first we need to see them.

Our consumer culture has us making our "bucket list" – all the grandest places, places over there, places for someday – while what we need is right here, right now. In Alice Walker's book The Color Purple, the young girl says, "I think it pisses God off if you walk by the color purple in a field and don't notice it!"[74] The

---

[74] Walker, Alice. *The Color Purple*. Harcourt, 1982.

relationship with Nature is as simple and basic as appreciating colors, or savoring a cool glass of water after mowing the lawn. Each day we can work on this union through seeing, through attention, through appreciation, and through living fully in the interdependency.

The general "Principle of Threes" says we have only three minutes to breathe (inhale and hold it to test this principle), three hours to stay warm in the cold, three days to drink water in the heat, and three weeks to eat food, before we begin dying. We could add that it only takes three seconds to wake up, to see, to appreciate. Exploring polarities – the world's many partnerships – is a wonderful way of reconnecting, of paying attention. Their simplicity, elegance, and reliability turn everyday interdependent pairs into an endless graduate school of learning. Paying attention to these pairs is both a meditation and an act of love. When noticing interdependencies in twos, threes, and fours, you are seeing the workings inside the ride. In these times of being awake, you are finally with your fuller self; you are Human *And* More-Than-Human!

Discovering Fire

Immersing ourselves in the More-Than-Human, the world of the wild, sparks a fire, and two things occur. First, we wake up once again to the bounty and beauty around us. Second, we feel our animal-ness, our biological aliveness, our deep memories, and our belonging. When we reclaim being an animal, we experience a relationship with the land and become more alive. This frees us from our cultural hypnosis. We all, in our own way, have had experiences of this, holding a pet, or walking in the woods. Let's notice these moments, these little love affairs.

Why would it be important for a leader to access this place? First, is the sheer joy and creative energy it brings. Leaders need this. Also if, as Jerry Useem's Atlantic article "Power Causes Brain Damage" suggests, the more our positions separate us, which damages our brains, the more important it is that we rejoin and reconnect.[75] These moments heal the brain damage and soul damage that civilization causes us every day. By rejoining the More-Than-Human world daily, we humbly enter an ecosystem where we have no positional power. This is a very alive, awake, and healing place for leaders who have been important, perhaps too important, and it undoes the damage of human hubris.

We have spent so much time becoming civilized that we have a lot of catching up to do in our relationship with Nature. Ten thousand years ago, an average human would have been quite developed in their intelligence surrounding Nature. In this realm they would be much smarter than us. They would have known intimately the cycles of plant growth and the habits of animals. For us, learning to be in concert with the More-Than-Human natural world does not require rigorous survival training. We simply need to grow the relationship, little by little, like tending a fire, to learn again who we are, and redevelop our intelligence with Nature. This

---

[75] Useem, B.S. Jerry. "Power Causes Brain Damage." Atlantic Magazine, July 2017.

is reciprocity, this is what we need to learn, this is the essence of Vertical Development, of EQ, of Influence, and of Resiliency. This reciprocity, and the state of aliveness it brings us into, is the heart of leadership.

The lessons of interdependence are the key to our survival, to our health, to our joy, and to effectively leading into the unknown. When we express being Human *And* More-Than-Human, in harmony, we create an upward cycle towards being fully alive. Our leadership needs the spirit of this reciprocal relationship. Without it, we are blind to reality, which is dangerous for leaders and followers alike.

The Journey Home

We think leadership is for people, for human systems. I looked out the window at a flock of ravens and think whimsically, "There are my people!" I still take an avid interest in the Human end of this polarity, but my call is towards the More-Than-Human. This step into the wild, a journey of becoming uncivilized, of being Animal once again, is the partnership Humans desperately need. We must once again feel the aliveness, the awareness, and the awake-ness of being with this interdependence. From seeing and being in this reality, we can lead the way.

Every day, in small ways, we live and lead in the most marvelous and unimaginable place, the Earth! Here we are, Human *And* More-Than-Human. Here we are in the interdependence. Here we are with our family. This is our home. Expressed in harmony, the Human *And* More-Than-Human is a whole, an integrity, creating a virtuous cycle towards being fully alive. As leaders, it is up to us to remember, to invite others with us, and head home. Leading this journey is now one of the most important and urgent challenge Humans face. Let's not let Earth down in this time of need: let's be its partner, let us be its hero! Our happiness, our joy, our survival, and our leadership depend on it.

Find bio and contact info for author Peter Dupre at
www.polaritypartnerships.com/certified-polarity-practitioners

Build Your Inspired Authentic Leadership Style
Lindsay Y. Burr, MS

Introduction

In the modern era of Volatility, Uncertainty, Complexity and Ambiguity (often called VUCA), we need inspired, authentic leaders who can solve problems and leverage polarities. We have limited ourselves thus far by equating leadership with masculinity and, by extension, being male. In reality no sex or gender is inherently better at leadership. What *is* required for inspired leadership is the internal integration of Feminine *And* Masculine which is held by all genders.[76]

Polarity Thinking™ is an excellent lens through which to plan integration. The Greater Purpose Statement (GPS) is "Authentic and Inspired Leadership" and the deeper fear perhaps "Failed, Dangerous Leadership." Most generic leadership trainings focus only on masculine traits to achieve that goal and ignore feminine traits that support excellent leadership. Trainings also ignore the unique strengths of each person for a genuinely authentic style.[77] The purpose here is to encourage integration of the Feminine *And* Masculine including each person's uniqueness for the kind of great leadership we so desperately need.

Historical Context

Feminine *And* Masculine need to be more fully understood. While acknowledging that femininity and masculinity are social constructs, we also find that, historically, the traits have been universally understood in certain ways. Most religions include stories that describe the sacred feminine and the sacred masculine which are not linked to biological femaleness and maleness. Most ancient cultures celebrate them separately, and some celebrate them together. These intuitive and broader definitions are the ones to which this chapter refers. It cannot be emphasized enough that all of us have both sets of traits and, when combined with each person's personality and background, produce a truly authentic style with unique strengths.

Current Context of Feminine *And* Masculine: Unconscious Bias

For at least two thousand years, Masculinity has been identified as the dominant energy of leadership and has been linked to men themselves. Most religions rely on males as the conduit of the divine. Most presidents and monarchs have been men. Most CEOs of Fortune 500 companies have been men. We have a default view that masculine traits *are* leadership traits. Often, successful women mimic

---

[76] Jim Collins describes Level 5 Leadership; the poles integrated for great leadership are Yin and Yang. See: Collins, Jim. *From Good to Great.* HarperCollins, 2001.

[77] The systemic issues that support or force leaders to act in certain ways are not addressed in this chapter. See Chapter 4, "Masculine and Feminine for Health, Wealth, and Happiness".

male traits since they are seen as weak when using feminine traits, a situation that further perpetuates the expectations of masculine-energy leadership. Men and women are equally hamstrung by this point of view.

Leadership activities are also gendered. For example, it is expected that men will focus on task; and women, on relationships. Men are expected to be straightforward; and women, diplomatic. Even though individual leaders may defy these expectations – you may know men who prefer diplomacy or women who are direct – as a group, men are expected to be direct and women to be diplomatic.

Societal views of other leadership polarities illuminate the confusion of leadership and masculinity. Feminine traits are on the left side, and traditional Masculine traits, on the right in *Figure 1*.

Figure 1

Feminine	*And*	Masculine
Learner	And	Expert
Diplomacy	And	Candor
Humility	And	Confidence
Other	And	Self
Relationship	And	Task
Empowerment	And	Control
Reflective Decision-making	And	Quick Decision-making
Feeling	And	Thinking
Collaboration	And	Individual Action
Participative	And	Directive
Support	And	Challenge

When individuals look at leadership polarities intellectually, they often say that both poles are valuable. But internal resistance increases when it becomes obvious a pole is 'gendered.' Leaders want to be all of these traits but will choose Expert, Candor, Confidence, Self, Task, Control, Quick Decision-Making, Thinking, Individual Action, Directive, and Challenge, aligning with cultural expectations and unconscious bias.

To compound the unconscious bias, girls and women are socialized to have feminine traits; boys and men, masculine traits. Furthermore, boys and men who exhibit the feminine traits are punished (emotive becomes sissy), and girls and women who exhibit masculine traits are excluded and/or assigned the downside of the masculine (confident becomes bossy). Brené Brown's book <u>Daring Greatly</u>[78] outlined ample research about how, for men, it is less of a put-down to be called an asshole than it is to be called "pussy." When women stand their ground, they are immediately labeled a bitch. If they are collaborative, taking in multiple points of view, they are weak. In both cases, women are perceived in the downside of both poles. There is no way for women to be seen in the upside of either pole without interrupting the unconscious bias.

We know from polarity dynamics that by choosing only one pole, the downside of that pole is the inevitable outcome. So, by choosing only masculine as the leadership pole, the inevitable result is aggressive, domineering, and bullying behaviors

---

[78] Brown, Brené. *Daring Greatly: How the Courage to Be Vulnerable Transforms the Way We Live, Love, Parent and Lead.* Gotham Books, 2012.

that are over-tolerated by organizations and society. In addition, we not only lose the positive values of the masculine (driven, goal-oriented, individual contribution) but also lose the upside of the feminine (thoughtful, reflective, collaborative). A vicious downward cycle is created. An over-tolerated masculine pole, aggressive bullying, interacts with the downsides of the feminine, hesitant and ambiguous. The cycle means that a person or a system will whip back and forth between aggression and hesitancy.

Even when we know the outcome of over-focusing on one pole, the unconscious bias toward leadership and masculinity is so strong that organizations will consistently and reiteratively tolerate and excuse destructive behaviors because leaders are so fearful of being seen as indecisive doormats.

Choosing to integrate both poles is essential to get back the upsides of the poles. If a leader chooses one side, as Polarity Thinking would predict, that will lead into the downside of *both* poles. Ultimately that leader will follow a vicious cycle until the result is the deeper fear "Failed, Dangerous Leadership."

Polarity Thinking Provides Answers

To create healthy systems, Polarity Thinking plots the path of change.[79] When in the downside of one pole, the correction is to the upside of the other pole, in this case the Feminine. When the Feminine is incorporated *And* the Masculine honored, we have the opportunity to gain the benefits of both poles.

Application: Two Exercises

Two exercises can assist you in building your authentic, inspired leadership style that reflects the upsides of Feminine *And* Masculine and leadership qualities associated with each.

Exercise 1 is a 'values sort' where you choose poles you tend to prefer and, by definition, ones on which you may need work. Again, notice that all the leadership polarities align under Feminine *And* Masculine.

First, in *Figure 2*, check the pole you prefer in each polarity pair. Reminder: every person has all of these. *Push to identify your preferred leadership tendencies, not aspirations.*

Figure 2

Feminine	Masculine
Learner	Expert
Diplomacy	Candor
Humility	Confidence
Other	Self
Relationship	Task
Empowerment	Control
Reflective Decision-making	Quick Decision-making
Feeling	Thinking
Collaboration	Individual Action
Participative	Directive
Support	Challenge

---

[79] Research indicates that organizations that leverage polarities do better than ones that do not. See: Johnson, Barry. *And: Making a Difference by Leveraging Polarity, Paradox or Dilemma. Volume One – Foundations*. HRD Press, 2020.

Action Steps +A   *Figure 3*   Polarity Map®   **Action Steps +C**

+A Values   GPS   +C Values

Preferred Poles   *And*   Stretch Poles

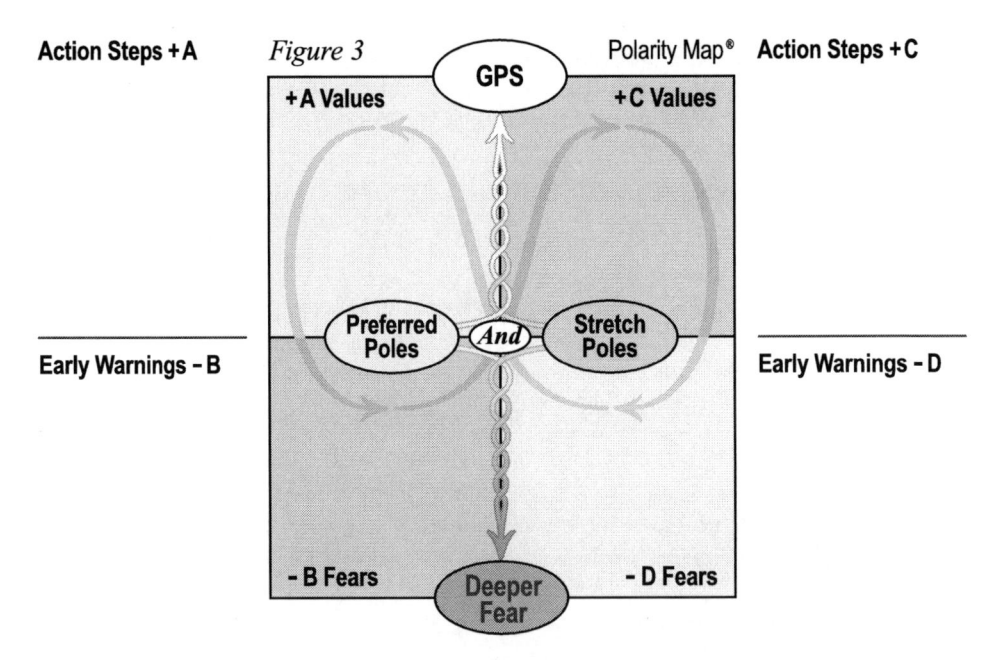

Early Warnings - B   **Early Warnings - D**

- B Fears   Deeper Fear   - D Fears

Next, use *Figure 3* above and the instructions below to build your leadership map:

1. Write all your preferred pole names from *Figure 2* in the upper left (+A Values).
2. Write your less preferred pole names from *Figure 2* in the upper right (+C Values).
3. In the lower left (-B Fears) and lower right (-D Fears), write what becomes of the chosen qualities when each is overdone (e.g., "Expert" (Value) becomes "Arrogant" (Fear), "Learner" (Value) becomes "Clueless" (Fear)).
4. Assess how well you are managing this polarity. (Assessment Map *Figure 4*)

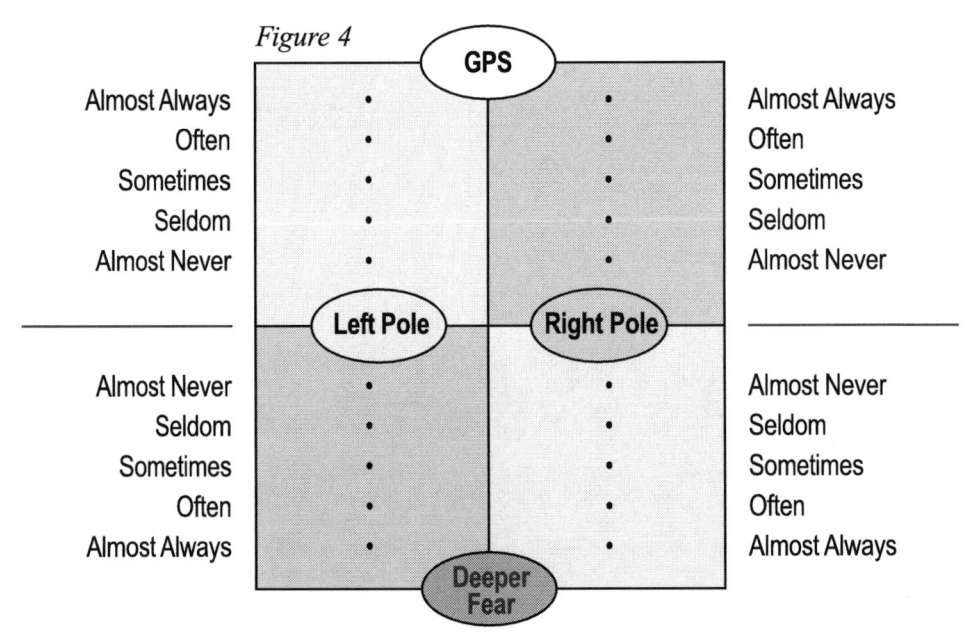

Figure 4

GPS

Almost Always	•	•	Almost Always
Often	•	•	Often
Sometimes	•	•	Sometimes
Seldom	•	•	Seldom
Almost Never	•	•	Almost Never

Left Pole   Right Pole

Almost Never	•	•	Almost Never
Seldom	•	•	Seldom
Sometimes	•	•	Sometimes
Often	•	•	Often
Almost Always	•	•	Almost Always

Deeper Fear

In *Figure 4*, circle the dot that corresponds to *Almost Never, Seldom, Sometimes, Often or Almost Always* as you ask yourself, cumulatively, how often am I ...

- getting the benefit of the upside of the Left pole: *Figure 3* (+A Values)?
- getting the benefit of the upside of the Right pole: *Figure 3* (+C Values)?
- experiencing the downside of the Left pole: *Figure 3* (-B Fears)?
- experiencing the downside of the Right pole: *Figure 3* (-D Fears)?

In addition to assessing the cumulative nature of each quadrant, you can also ask yourself about the individual polarities, using the average to determine your experience in each quadrant.

Example: Let's use the polarity Confidence *And* Humility from *Figure 1*:

- How often do I experience the benefits of the upside of Confidence? How often do I feel confident? How often do I feel self-assured and notice my expertise? (Select your corresponding dot)
- How often do I experience the downside of Confidence? How often do people tell me I am arrogant? (Select your dot)
- How often do I experience the upside of Humility? How often do I ask people questions? How often do I notice I leave space for people to work at their own pace? (Select your dot)
- How often do I experience the downside of Humility? How often do I feel like a doormat? How often do I notice I am holding back my voice when I know I should be speaking my mind? (Select your dot)

Having selected your corresponding dots (Almost Always, Often, Sometimes, Seldom, or Almost Never) on the Assessment Map for each quadrant, now draw your infinity loop connecting those dots.

Assessing and drawing your infinity loop is incredibly important. It helps you see where you are getting the benefits, where you have room to grow and stretch and where you may need to flag your behavior to get less of the downsides.

5. Moving back to *Figure 3*, fill in a GPS. It might be "Inspired Leadership" or it might be something that embodies your vision of your best leader self like "Leading the Parade."
6. Fill in the deeper fear. It might be "Failed Leadership" or "Ridiculed or Berated When I Call Myself a Leader." This is a powerful fear or difficult outcome, something scary and worth avoiding.
7. Develop Action Steps to maintain the benefit from your preferred poles. It is likely to include things you are already doing.
8. Develop Action Steps to nudge yourself to step into the poles that are your less preferred ones. These can be little nudges. They do not have to be drastic changes. E.g.: take a goal then half it, then half it again and that is likely the first step/nudge you need.

9. Develop Early Warnings for your preferred poles. These should be things you are *willing to have happen*, not just things you have become accustomed to tolerating. They need to be *early* warnings, not *too late* warnings.

10. Develop Early Warnings for your less preferred poles. These can be *later than you'd like*. Chances are that you rush back to your preferred poles at the first sign you are getting any downside of your less preferred poles. Give yourself a little time and space to try on these new attributes. It will be a little awkward at first. That's ok. It is worth it.

11. Take Action by supporting other people's individual expressions of leadership. Your authentic leadership is not theirs, and theirs is not yours. Support your network.

Now you have a fully mapped polarity that can guide your personal leadership development and integrates the values of a truly inspirational leader. *Note: This process can be used to map, assess and operationalize any polarity.*

Exercise 2 is a map with aspects of leadership written in sentences that you can use to assess yourself, develop action steps to enhance the upsides of both poles, and specify early warnings to alert you to an over-focus on one pole.

In this exercise, respond to a partially populated Polarity Map®: the poles, GPS, Deeper Fear and inner quadrants. If there are words that don't resonate with you, feel free to change them but keep the spirit of the quadrant intact.

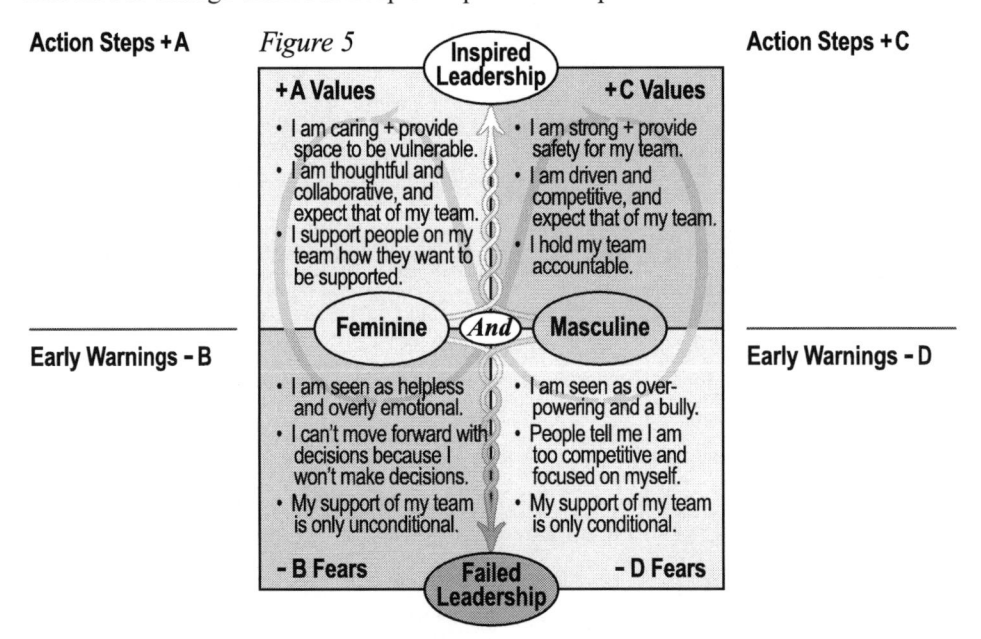

Action Steps +A   *Figure 5*   **Action Steps +C**

+A Values — Inspired Leadership — +C Values
• I am caring + provide space to be vulnerable. • I am thoughtful and collaborative, and expect that of my team. • I support people on my team how they want to be supported.	• I am strong + provide safety for my team. • I am driven and competitive, and expect that of my team. • I hold my team accountable.
Feminine *And* **Masculine**
• I am seen as helpless and overly emotional. • I can't move forward with decisions because I won't make decisions. • My support of my team is only unconditional.	• I am seen as overpowering and a bully. • People tell me I am too competitive and focused on myself. • My support of my team is only conditional.
− B Fears — Failed Leadership — − D Fears

Early Warnings − B   **Early Warnings − D**

Assess how often you experience the cumulative nature of each quadrant. Mark your dots on the following *Figure 6* Assessment Map, then connect your dots to see how well you are currently balancing the *Figure 5* Feminine *And* Masculine polarity. *Detailed instructions included in previous Exercise 1, step 4, p. 96.*

Figure 6

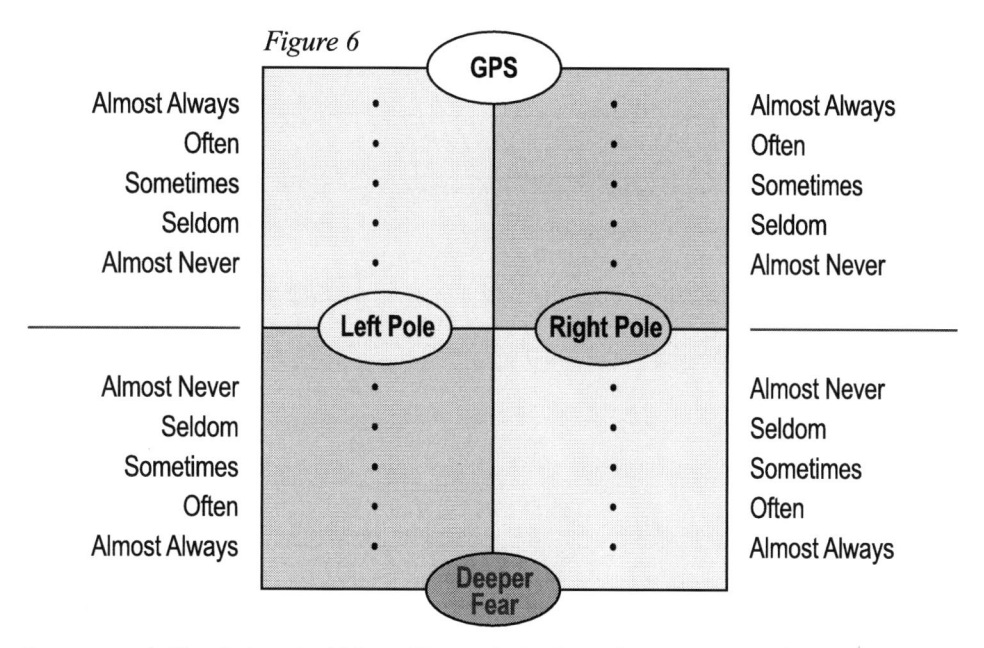

```
                    GPS
Almost Always   ·         ·    Almost Always
Often           ·         ·    Often
Sometimes       ·         ·    Sometimes
Seldom          ·         ·    Seldom
Almost Never    ·         ·    Almost Never
─────────── Left Pole ─ Right Pole ───────────
Almost Never    ·         ·    Almost Never
Seldom          ·         ·    Seldom
Sometimes       ·         ·    Sometimes
Often           ·         ·    Often
Almost Always   ·         ·    Almost Always
                  Deeper
                   Fear
```

Leverage th Feminine *And* Masculine polarity by using steps 7-10 from Exercise 1 to develop your Action Steps and Early Warnings for *Figure 5*.

Take action by supporting other people's individual expressions of leadership.

Conclusion

When only masculine traits are valued on a global scale, we see the ultimate slide into toxic masculinity and war. Furthermore, we devalue those who embody the non-preferred pole. Women are devalued and become the objects of projection. Their physical presence is seen as superfluous, and their points of view are rejected. Men who present as feminine are ridiculed. Gay men are the object of hatred and violence. Gay women, who are not the object of male gaze, are dismissed. Trans-men and trans-women are subjected to discrimination and hate crimes. All fear for their lives in many situations knowing that toxic masculinity is over-tolerated and men's perspectives will always be believed.

Seeing Feminine *And* Masculine as a polarity helps give the world a path toward equality that spans race, location, leadership and communities. Integrating Feminine *And* Masculine traits is a critical component for improving the globe. In addition to creating more tolerance and equity, their integration provides an opportunity to have more sustainable solutions. Choosing to value Feminine *And* Masculine leadership traits is an act each of us can do in order to create the ripple effect of equality throughout our families, businesses, communities, and world. Not only that, it is also good business and ensures the efficient and effective full use of the talents of all.

Find bio and contact info for author Lindsay Y. Burr at
www.polaritypartnerships.com/certified-polarity-practitioners

The Dynamic Engagement Model™: Leveraging Polarities to Build Engagement at Work and at Home

Laura Mendelow, MAOD, PCC

A Rocky Start to a New Job

Meet Brendon. Brendon is an experienced leader in a highly sophisticated, fast-paced Data Analytics organization. He launched his own start-up company in the early 2000s and sold it for a large profit in 2005. Soon after, he was asked to join a highly reputable company to oversee one of their divisions with approximately 1,000 employees. He inherited a team of managers who were competent and experienced and, from their perspective, self-managing just fine before Brendon came on board. After about three months on the job, Brendon's manager quickly realized that Brandon could use some support to help him acclimate to the organization and to his team. I was then hired to work with him as his Executive Coach.

During our initial conversations, Brendon explained what he was seeing and hearing. He began explaining his frustrations around a "lack of interaction." Brendon shared that there was so much silence – little to no dialogue – during team meetings that he would often end them early. He sensed the team might be feeling resentful that the company had hired him from the outside, when perhaps one of the team members was eager for the promotion. Lastly, he assessed that his direct reports were doing the bare minimum to get the job done. There didn't seem to be any excitement around his fresh new ideas and no commitment to support a new vision.

Figure 1: Dynamic Engagement Model™

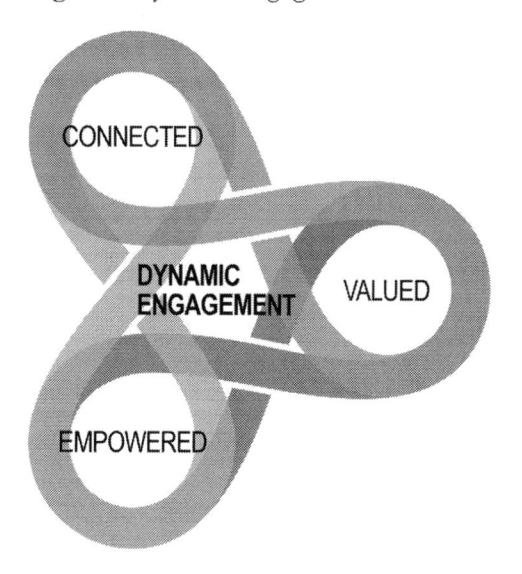

On the surface, each of these issues may seem like an individual *problem to solve*, but in reality, they are inter-related. All of these issues are elements of engagement. However, it may not seem obvious until you look beneath the surface to understand the core needs of the team members and the leader.

I introduced Brendon to the Dynamic Engagement Model™ (*Figure 1*). This model represents a "Multarity™," or a polarity with more than two poles, that identifies the three core psychological needs of all humans. People want to feel **Connected**, **Valued**, and **Empowered**. When these three psychological needs are leveraged well, people (regardless of age) will feel more engaged and fulfilled.

From a leadership perspective, it's important to remember that these three needs are true for the leader and for the team members. However, the intention of the Dynamic Engagement Model is designed to offer a framework for leaders to help them build a culture of engagement for their teams. We all know that leaders are not able to change how people feel. In other words, if someone is a disgruntled employee, no one can *make* that person feel engaged. That person has to choose to feel engaged. How then does the leader influence engagement? The leader sets the tone for the group and has influence over the *culture* of the team. The leader also has influence over behaviors that are tolerated, establishes ground rules, creates forums to have safe, open dialogue, and can role model the behaviors they want the team to repeat. My approach in working with leaders is to leverage the Dynamic Engagement Model to help them create a culture of engagement where team members feel Connected, Valued, and Empowered.

In the center of this multarity lies the greater purpose – an engaged workforce. Each of the poles (Connected, Valued, and Empowered) has upsides and downsides. In other words, it is possible for a leader to over focus on connection, value, or empowerment. For example, if a leader over-focuses on wanting to connect with others and build relationships, the leader may end up being conflict avoidant so as to not damage relationships. If a leader over-focuses on valuing the strengths of others, individuals may not receive honest feedback on how to improve. Lastly, if a leader allows for the team to take full control over decisions, the team may go off the rails and become misaligned to the organization's vision. A leader's role then is to be mindful of how they're addressing the needs of others and ensuring that they are maximizing the upsides and minimizing the downsides. *Figure 2* lists

Figure 2: Dynamic Engagement Model™

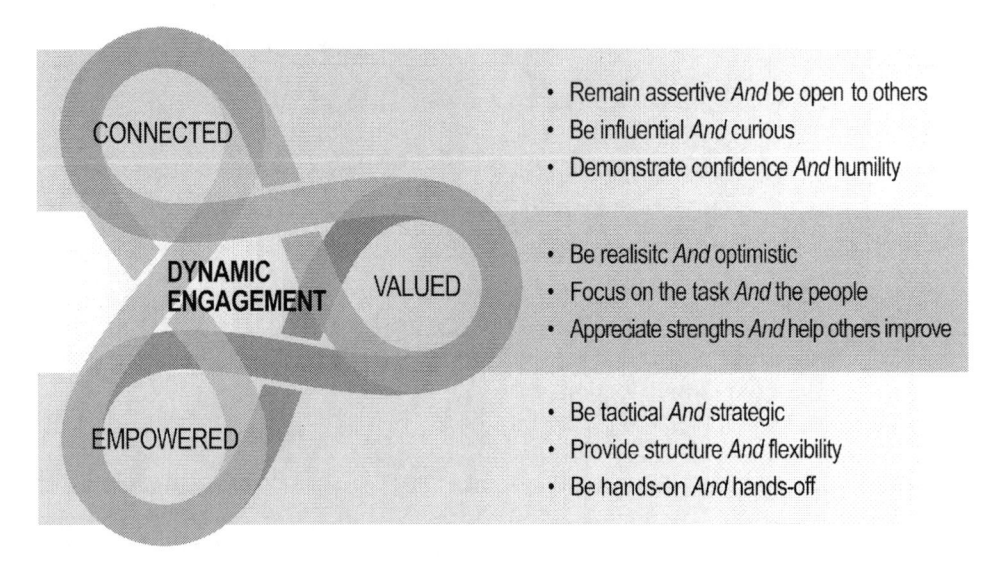

CONNECTED
- Remain assertive *And* be open to others
- Be influential *And* curious
- Demonstrate confidence *And* humility

DYNAMIC ENGAGEMENT — **VALUED**
- Be realisitc *And* optimistic
- Focus on the task *And* the people
- Appreciate strengths *And* help others improve

EMPOWERED
- Be tactical *And* strategic
- Provide structure *And* flexibility
- Be hands-on *And* hands-off

supporting polarities that effective leaders navigate for the greater purpose of building a culture of engagement within their teams.

Looking Beneath the Surface

After meeting with Brendon and conducting interviews with his peers, subordinates, and superiors, we then analyzed the data through the lens of the Dynamic Engagement Model. For each of the issues presented, here's what we uncovered beneath the surface.

- **Disconnected:** The team members felt that Brendon joined the team with his agenda and was not interested in listening to anyone else's ideas. They viewed him as somewhat aloof and wanting to be the "hero" for the division. The team didn't feel that Brendon honored what was working nor did he spend any time asking about their perspectives or the history of the division.

- **Devalued:** The team at first provided ideas and opinions about improvements, but Brendon dismissed these ideas because, in the past, he had seen those ideas fail. After a few weeks of the same pattern, the team stopped offering their ideas. They didn't feel that Brendon valued any of their expertise or perspectives, so they stopped contributing to the conversation.

- **Disempowered:** Through the interview discussions, it also became clear that the team felt micromanaged. No one felt empowered. They were, after all, running the division on their own before Brendon took over the position, so they felt they knew how to manage a division. Brendon would question every process, every decision that the managers made, and asked to be copied on all communications. The team felt deflated.

In a nutshell, Brendon was still operating as an entrepreneur, drawing on the approach that had helped him to be successful in the past. That, however, was not the right methodology for this role, team, and organization. He was hired because of his innovative ideas, his compelling vision, and his passion for the work. Brendon agreed that there was great potential in combining his innovative thought leadership with the high performing team, but he had trouble finding the right strategy.

Taking a Deeper Dive into Connection

After gaining a better understanding of the team's core needs, Brendon felt that the most pressing issue was around connection. He knew that if the team wasn't gelling and didn't buy into the vision, they were not going to be successful. Therefore, we co-created a Polarity Map® with the greater purpose of building connection to uncover the patterns that he was experiencing.

Brendon's entrepreneurial spirit led him to approach his team with passion and confidence: it was up to him to inspire the team towards a new vision. From Brendon's perspective, "*Either* I push my vision and we succeed *Or* the team leads and we fail." If they continued down the current path, they would likely fail. After all, this was the reason he was hired to begin with. The problem he was facing, though, was that his team was not on board. There was much resistance.

After mapping out the problem on a Polarity Map (*Figure 3*), Brendon began to see his problem differently and more completely. The data from the interviews with his colleagues revealed that the team did appreciate his innovative ideas (+A) however, they were primarily experiencing the downsides of this behavior (-B). In other words, Brendon over-focused on his ideas to the neglect of inquiring about others' ideas.

Brendon acknowledged that he was tapping into the downside of this pole; however, he didn't see a viable alternative approach. The alternative in Brendon's mind was to stop leading the team, let the team implement their ideas, or continue down the same path and fail. I explained that I heard this alternative as the downside of the right pole (-D) – which was still unnamed – and I agreed that stepping back completely would not help the team or the organization. I asked, "What do you think is keeping you on this pole?" Brendon opened up and revealed that he valued his team, but sometimes felt inferior to them because they were extremely intelligent. The underlying fear was that they might discover that Brendon may not be as smart as they thought. If Brendon didn't share his "brilliant" ideas, the team might see him as a weak leader (-D). As a result, Brendon's fear was pushing him to lean even more into his own ideas (-B) to prove to others just how smart he was.

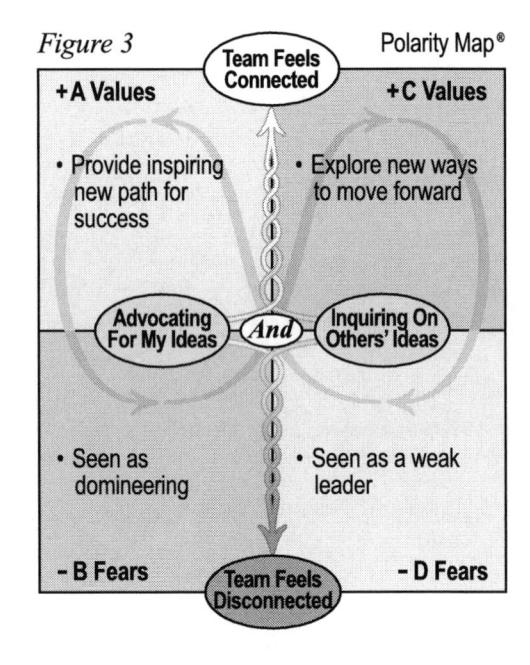

Figure 3 — Polarity Map®

- **+A Values**
  - Provide inspiring new path for success
- **+C Values**
  - Explore new ways to move forward

Team Feels Connected

Advocating For My Ideas *And* Inquiring On Others' Ideas

- **-B Fears**
  - Seen as domineering
- **-D Fears**
  - Seen as a weak leader

Team Feels Disconnected

This was a big breakthrough for Brendon. He could now see how his good intentions of leading the team were actually being overused and getting in the way of connection, rather than building connection. At this point he knew he needed to help shape a vision for the team and he also needed to leverage the expertise and ideas from his team (+C). How could he do this? Essentially, the question he asked himself was, "How could he get the best out of his team and how could they get the best out of him?" We then brainstormed ways to structure the conversation to create space for open dialogue without expectations that the ideas on the table were the ideas that would be approved. This safe space for conversation put Brendon at ease, and the team appreciated the dialogue. Finally, their ideas were being heard and acknowledged. It's important to note that Brendon knew how to solicit others' ideas; it wasn't that he lacked this skill. Rather, he was stuck in an *"either/Or"* mindset and once he could see new possibilities, he was welcoming to their ideas, and the team strengthened their connection.

This was an example of how we explored Brandon's team's core needs around Connection. Throughout the coaching discussion, we continued to leverage the model by analyzing his team needs of feeling Valued and Empowered. As a result Brendon identified several strategies that all contributed to enhancing engagement on his team.

Building a Culture of Engagement

The Dynamic Engagement Model™ helps leaders to engage with staff by offering sets of behaviors within the three primary psychological needs that are common to all humans. It is a tool to help leaders leverage well the polarities that support the three primary needs, to optimize each situation. This creates a sustainable culture of engagement in the workplace. The model is dynamic (ever-changing) and situated in the leader's unique context and as such, there is no "right" way of leading. Working collaboratively with leaders to surface hidden assumptions and shed light on blind spots, this approach can help teams feel more Connected, Valued, and Empowered.

Find bio and contact info for author Laura Mendelow at
www.polaritypartnerships.com/certified-polarity-practitioners

The Pocket Pardox Tool

Patrick Masterson, MSOD
Ann Caton Linares, MSOD, ACC

Practitioners of polarities and paradox often find ourselves supporting teams and leaders who are stuck. We might be mid-stream in a coaching session and realize that the client has become so exasperated with a colleague that they have turned that colleague into a caricature: a one-dimensional dragon to be vanquished. The goals of the client are now at risk because they cannot advance work with a critical stakeholder. Or we might be in a team meeting, fully focused on the task at hand, when we notice an undercurrent of toxic beliefs or behaviors at odds with the stated goals of the team. The way the team is working is undermining its own vision and values. It has become trapped in a dungeon of its own making.

When teams and leaders are stuck, they are unable to name, reframe, and effectively manage the tensions at play within themselves and their systems. How can we help leaders get unstuck when we don't have the luxury of weeks of data gathering? How can we help clients define and manage the dynamics at play when all we have is one coaching session, one team meeting, one moment? The pocket paradox tool is designed to help practitioners deploy polarities quickly and with maximum impact.

Pocket Paradox Tool: Leadership Application

The pocket paradox tool can be used when supporting a leader who is stuck and facing the limitations of what they already know. For instance, the leader has thoroughly villainized someone who works above, beside – or worse – below them. Or the leader has arrived at a new level of responsibility and organizational scope, and is perplexed that their core values, ethics, and leadership habits are no longer achieving the desired results. In these moments, you can ask the client to take out a sheet of paper and give them the following instructions.

1. Turn the paper so that it is more wide than tall (landscape). Draw three columns.

2. Label the first column (1) **Points of Pride/Characteristics**

    In this column, write down three points of pride about yourself. For example, if you consider honesty a point of pride, you might write: "genuine."

3. Label the second column (2) **Personal Opposite**

    In this column, write a personal opposite for each point of pride. These are not necessarily the opposite values that you would find listed in a dictionary, but rather what you personally would call the opposite of that point of pride. So, if you wrote down "genuine" in the first column, a personal opposite might be "fake" or "liar" instead of "dishonest." It's how you would describe the opposite in a free-flowing conversation with a close friend.

4. Finally, label the last column (3) **Positive Reframe**

   In this column, write down a positive reframe for each personal opposite. For instance, the positive reframe for "fake" might be "intentional" or "adaptable."

5. Once completed, you have a key polarity for the leader to manage. The poles come from columns 1 and 3. In this case, "Genuine *And* Adaptable."

6. Pro tip: The middle column represents the results of the potential overuse or downside of column 3. In this case, if I over-use "adaptable" to the neglect of "genuine," then I might be seen as a liar or as someone who is fake.

The challenge to the practitioner, of course, often comes in the positive reframe. A leader may be tempted to reframe the personal opposite into something that others value or regard as positive – but that they themselves do not truly value or regard as positive. For them to become unstuck, they need help identifying what is personally of value to them in the other pole and why. The more stuck the leader is, the harder it will be for them to reframe, and the longer you will stay in this part of the exercise.

Leadership Client Example

The language in the instructions above came from a real coaching client. We walked through each of the steps in the tool, and the client was easily able to come up with a positive reframe for each point of pride – except "fake." The leader was stuck and kept saying, "I can't think of how fake can be positive." The breakthrough came when he was reflecting on the necessity of speaking differently to different audiences. He was able to make the connection that others may not be fake or insincere, but that they may be trying to connect to different audiences as best as they could (*Figure 1*).

Figure 1: Leadership Application

Points of Pride/ Characteristics	Personal Opposite	Positive Reframe
Genuine	Fake	Adaptable
Loyal	Out for self	Self-invested
Approachable	Not personable	Focused

When asked how this point of pride shaped his treatment of others, he responded, "Oh, sometimes I label others as fake in my head. That could be impacting how I work with them. I need to really reconsider this." That was the shift in mindset. In the moment, the leader could now see his existing mindset, the limitations of it, a new mindset, and a new set of choices and behaviors. Once both poles are named, the leader's mindset becomes available for examination, a new mindset becomes accessible, and the situation can be more effectively managed. It is valuable to note that even if something is not a preferred pole, it still lives within you or near you, and you are able to access it as a resource.[R121, 80]

---

[80] "Realities", e.g.[R121], are principles that apply to all polarities and multarities. See Appendix C.

Pocket Paradox Tool: Team or Whole System Application

The pocket paradox tool can also be used when a team or organization needs to level up developmentally. It may be that an enterprise-wide technology effort is underway that will require new behaviors, or a leader is seeing long-term culture change begin to backslide. In our experience, the teams and organizations with the strongest lived values are often in most need of this type of exercise. In these cases and others, the team or system needs to explicitly name the driving forces that have been implicit, unsaid, or driven underground. When you see these dynamics at play, you can ask the team as individuals or in small groups to complete the exercise, as modified below, using sheets of paper or easel charts.

1. Turn the paper so that it more wide than tall (landscape). Draw three columns.

2. Label the first column (1) [Team/Organization] **Points of Pride/Characteristics**

   In this column, write down three points of pride for this team or organization. For example, if the team considers careful stewardship of resources a point of pride, you would write: "stewardship."

3. Label the second column (2) **Team Opposite** (Note: we often still use the phrase "Personal Opposite," even at the group level, while explaining that we mean personal/specific to the team or group.)

   In this column, write a team opposite for each point of pride. This is not necessarily the opposite value that you would find listed in a dictionary, but rather what the team would call the opposite of that point of pride. So, if you wrote down "stewardship" in the first column, a team opposite might be "reckless" or "wasteful" instead of "spending." It's how you would describe the opposite in a free-flowing conversation with a trusted teammate.

4. Finally, label the last column (3) **Positive Reframe**

   In this column, write down a positive reframe for each team opposite. For instance, the positive reframe for "wasteful" might be "iterating" or "innovation," using a word that would be considered desirable or positive.

5. Once completed, you have a key polarity for this team to manage. The poles come from columns 1 and 3. In this case, "Stewardship *And* Innovation."

6. Pro tip: The middle column represents the result of the potential overuse or downside of column 3. In this case, if I over-use "innovation" to the neglect of "stewardship," then the team might be seen as wasteful or reckless.

There are at least two considerations to keep in mind during a team or system application. First, if you are working at the organizational level, someone will ask this question when populating the first column: "Do you want our real characteristics and points of pride, or do you want the things executives say about what they want the company to be – the values listed on our website?" In this case, you want the true points of pride, which may turn out to be one and the same as espoused values, because these will be deeply felt principles or strengths that may be seen as endangered or at risk.

Second, the challenge for the practitioner will again come from the positive reframe. The practitioner may need to push the team through several iterations in order to reframe the opposite into something that truly is of value to them. If they simply parrot the party line or echo executive soundbites that are not compelling to them, they will not open up new possibilities for action. In our experience, groups at the top, middle, and bottom of organizations are able to come up with the point of pride and the personal opposite quickly and with poignancy.

Team Client Example

The language in the instructions above came from a client offsite with a large division in a 14,000-person organization. All levels of the organization were in the room, including senior leadership, middle management, and front-line individual contributors. The division had become known throughout the enterprise for their stewardship of resources, exceptional commitment to high standards of operations, and a high level of technical expertise. However, internally there was a growing dynamic of us versus them between the newer, largely younger employees and the tenured, largely older employees.

At the offsite, we walked them through the instructions generating *Figure 2*.

Figure 2: Team Application

Points of Pride/ Characteristics	Personal Opposite	Positive Reframe
Stewardship	Wasteful	Innovative
Excellence	Low quality	Learning
Respect for experience	Rude/entitled	Different styles

The newer employees were able to name the personal opposites with ease, although the risk to naming those qualities was real. The positive reframes were perhaps equally risky. The tenured employees were now being asked to openly talk about the actual value that had been brought to the system by people labeled "wasteful, low quality, or entitled" who presumably were in the room. It takes risk, courage and vulnerability to name and hold a pole in a system where that pole is not valued.[R122]

This process allowed the organization to openly name fault lines between generations and styles, and more importantly the cost they were paying by not attending to these dynamics as polarities. The costs were very high. They needed to innovate; they could not simply rest on their laurels. They had an aging leadership circle and needed to support a culture of learning if they were going to grow. They needed to be inclusive of different styles or they would be a one-hit wonder, with the division unable to sustain itself in the years to come. They needed to accomplish all of these things, while still valuing what gave them their competitive edge: stewardship, excellence, and respect for experience. If they continued to pit their points of pride against their fears of the other pole, they were not going to make it to the next phase of their development as a division.

Pocket Paradox Tool: Powerful Follow-Up Questions and Activities

Although the examples included in this chapter focus on leadership and organization applications, follow-up questions at multiple levels can help deepen the learning and expand choices after a client completes the pocket paradox tool. We offer a few adaptable questions here.

Intra-personal

- What is your inner dialogue around points of pride and their opposites?
- What is the impact of calling yourself _____ [column 2] when you're not _____ [column 1]?

Inter-personal

- Is there anyone you label as _____ [column 2]? How do you want to shift that relationship?
- If you aren't able to accept _____ [column 2] in yourself, you are going to have a hard time managing and dealing with it in others. To what extent do some of your trouble spots relate to your listed issues in column 2?

Team/Whole System

- What happens to individuals here who aren't _____ [column 1]? What happens when individuals, teams, or initiatives are labeled _____ [column 2]?
- What is it costing the team or company if it can't value and capitalize on _____ [column 3]?

All Levels

- Map polarities: _____ [column 1] *And* _____ [column 3]

Origins and Impact of the Tool

The pocket paradox tool owes intellectual debt to our mentor Edie Seashore, who was a giant in the field of organization development. It builds on a 3-column model that she used to bring greater awareness and choice to our belief systems. We expanded the model for a polarity application.

This tool, like much in our field of polarities, has both simplicity and depth. It can be worked on the back of a napkin in a 10-minute conversation with a leader, and it can be mined for gems and lead to breakthroughs in large group, whole system work. For practitioners seeing polarities emerge in real time, the tool offers an intuitive way to get data on the table, redefine dynamics, expand choice and generate energy for more powerful action.

Find bio and contact info for author Patrick Masterson at
www.polaritypartnerships.com/certified-polarity-practitioners

Polarities and the Need for Vulnerability
Kelly Lewis, PCC

Becoming a skillful polarity navigator is hard. Helping others to do that is really, really hard. The easier and more straightforward part of navigating polarities is learning how they work and helping people map them – what we "do" as practitioners. The more tumultuous and challenging part of staying with the contradiction is discovering and integrating self-knowledge – who we "be" as practitioners. As many of us know, this type of learning is anything but straightforward, usually a bit messy, and often scary. It entails self-awareness, loving acceptance, and courageous action. It requires us to explore how our well-established preferences and habitual patterns might be undermining the results we seek. It challenges us to be both expert and learner, stepping out of our comfort zone to grow and expand, just as we ask our clients to do.

Navigating polarities is *both* a doing *And* a being practice – one that necessitates the head and the heart. Standing in that tension can feel like we are standing in a fire. It demands the capacity to be with our own discomfort and the discomfort of others. It suggests that we can grow into something that requires bigger capacity, more risk, and more compassion. In this way, it can be truly transformational.

Along my path of becoming, I realized I was neglecting the being and the heart part of the pair. I had a strong preference for doing and approached these interdependent pairs from my head. But then, out of the blue, life offered me the opportunity to step out of the comfort of my preferred pole into something that felt uncomfortable and unknown. It was challenging, brutal at times, but I found that when I mustered up enough courage to do so, I couldn't help but connect to myself, the situation, and the people in it more fully. It was beautiful and it illuminated how I had so often sacrificed this connection simply because it required me to expand my capacity for discomfort. It required vulnerability. And it was worth it.

This chapter outlines my personal journey and how I have applied it while coaching clients. My hope is that both new and veteran polarity practitioners will consider the essential role our hearts (and our heads) play in helping others develop a polarity practice. Perhaps sharing my personal experience with this practice will support (and challenge) your process of becoming. As you read this chapter, I invite you to consider a few questions:[81]

- What is your relationship to the Doing::Being, Head::Heart polarities?
- Which pole do you naturally hold? How strong is your attachment to it?
- What is at risk if you don't navigate this polarity more effectively?

---

[81] Emerson, Brian and Lewis, Kelly. *Navigating Polarities: Using Both/And Thinking to Lead Transformation.* Paradoxical Press, 2019, p. 138.

Discovering the Need

I was in the midst of facilitating a leadership development program when a text from my older sister, Lisa, came through telling me to call her ASAP. My sister had accompanied my mom to a doctor's appointment earlier that day. I gave Lisa a call. Her voice was shaky. I could feel myself bracing. She told me our mom had been diagnosed with bulbar ALS, a debilitating and unpredictable disease with no cure. I sat down, speechless, knowing that everything had just changed. My first reaction was to hide in the comfort of the work I love with clients I had fallen in love with. Yet deep down, I knew I needed to go and be with my mom and sisters. Despite my impulse, I chose being uncomfortable that afternoon. We sat with silence, the unknown, and some hard questions to which we had no answers.

As the weeks went on and my happy place of being energized by possibilities was nowhere to be found, I was on the search for comfort. Looking back now, I can see I was "Suffering Paradox."[82] The energy of a polarity had me. I swung like Tarzan back and forth from Embracing Hope to Embracing Reality. I clung to my preferred pole of Hope and resisted the Reality of the situation. I learned how my optimism relied on me being able to make everything "better." In my mom's case, there was no better, an extremely painful reality to accept. The fact that there was "no better" sobered me up from my naïveté – one of the overuses of my preferred pole. With awareness on my side and the loving support of my cohort (fatefully, three months prior to my mom's diagnosis I had begun the two-year Polarity Mastery Program), I began to allow it all in.

I greeted Reality, the truth of the interdependent pair, and my relationship to it. I could see my attachment to Possibility and my fear of losing my optimistic outlook. Humbled by how much of my identity was attached to "betterment," I watched my ego kick and scream as I loosened my tight grip on this protective strategy. At the end of the day, I chose love over fear. I stepped into the vulnerability rather than away from it, opening up rather than armoring up, and to my surprise discovered a more expansive space that lived between Hope::Reality. I called it Faith. This space included both poles and excluded neither. It was a place where Hope could accept and withstand Reality and Reality had a buoyant texture to it. It consisted of a kind of knowing that didn't need to know for certain and yet didn't dismiss knowledge either. It was sustained by awareness and deep acceptance and had the capacity of the human heart on its side.

Acceptance is a loving act done with an open heart. Like awareness, acceptance is experienced when we bring our full attention to the moment and sit with a deep trust of what is. Asking questions like these, without judgment, can help with acceptance:[83]

---

[82] Emerson, Brian. *Navigating Organizational Paradox with Polarity Mapping*. PhD diss., Fielding University, 2013.

[83] Emerson, Brian and Lewis, Kelly. *Navigating Polarities*. Paradoxical Press, 2019, p.138.

- In what ways have the benefits of my preferred pole made me successful and/or comfortable?
- What are the real impacts of the overuses on this situation and those involved?
- How have the overuses resulted from my desire to get the benefits I value?

Poignantly, my mom's last weekend on earth was also the last weekend of our mastery program. Instead of graduating with my cohort, I graduated with my mom in her home. Our dance with one of life's greatest paradoxes, Life/Death, and my struggle with the polarity of Hope::Reality illuminated for me that acceptance is the end of separation, the end of two and the opening to one. It taught me how to participate in, rather than separate from, the interdependent nature of the polarity dynamic. Acceptance facilitated my ability to withstand the fire, and vulnerability accelerated my ability to accept.

Applying the Learning

As I emerged from one of the most beautifully grueling, richly rewarding, and sweetest gifts of my lifetime, I was exhausted, relieved, grateful, heavy with grief, and really curious. I wondered how my struggles navigating paradoxical tensions were similar to and different from what my clients were experiencing. I was curious to explore how my learning might be useful to my clients on their journey. I wanted to examine how vulnerability played with Barry Johnson's work and how it influenced what my clients did when they encountered a polarity.

I was many months into a coaching relationship with a 40-something CEO. His executive team considered him a "deeply caring, extremely smart problem solver with a strong desire to be the best leader he can be; solid in decisiveness and thoughtful, he needs to work on being more present, less anticipatory, and more trusting of his people." Our work together had centered on his desire to be more intentional in his leadership and feel less on the defense. One particular day, Jordan immediately told me about an earlier conversation with a colleague. His voice quickened and his breathing became shallow as he blurted out, "He caught me off guard and I hate being caught off guard." I learned the two things that Jordan valued most that day – predictability and stability. Jordan did not like surprises and "spent a lot of time and energy anticipating responses so he would never be caught off guard."

I had introduced Jordan to polarities earlier in our relationship. He appreciated the concept of paradoxical tensions and quickly saw the value of a *both/And* mindset in his organization, leadership, and personal life. Like many of my clients, despite Jordan's most valiant efforts, he often slipped back into an *either/Or* mindset and treated the polarities he encountered as a problem to solve. I brought the polarity of Structure::Flexibility to Jordan's attention and asked him if he wanted to look at the situation using this lens. He was grateful for the reminder and a bit humbled that he wasn't able to see this dynamic himself. I reminded him that "seeing" is one of the most difficult yet most important aspects of working with polarities. After all, we can't change what we can't see. As we wrapped up our conversation, I wondered what might be at risk for Jordan if he loosened his grip on predictability to make room for finding unexpected solutions to some of the organization's problems.

Later that week, a dear friend and colleague sent me a link to one of Krista Tippett's On Being podcasts. It was an interview with Brené Brown called "Strong Back, Soft Front, Wild Heart."[84] They were discussing how to move beyond the crises of our lives. It felt serendipitous given my experience with my mom. I listened to the podcast that evening and about fell out of the bathtub when Brené Brown talked about the correlation between our ability to stand in the "tension of the and" and our capacity for discomfort. She suggested our need for *either/Or* is driven by our fear of the vulnerability required by *both/And*. Her words completely resonated with my own experience and what I was now noticing in my clients. What a moment of complete clarity – vulnerability not only played with Barry's work, I could see how it stood at the center of it. (See [R122] in Appendix C)

I heard something else that evening that gave me a moment of pause. Brown spoke about "strong back, soft front, wild heart" as a practice of integration – the opposite of living in a world of false binaries. One of her teachers, Roshi Joan Halifax, says that far too often our professed strength comes from fear, not love. Instead of having a strong back, we have an armored front shielding a weak spine. If we strengthen our back and develop a spine that is flexible yet sturdy, we can risk having a front that stays open and curious. The mark of a wild heart is being able to live within the discomfort of these paradoxical tensions without giving into the comfort of the *either/Or*.[85] Was that what I had experienced – a practice of integration, a wild heart, showing up in our vulnerability and our courage – when I'd discovered the space in between Hope::Reality?

The dots were connecting and generating more curiosity. I sensed this practice of integration would be useful as my clients encountered polarities, and I knew from experience it was going to require emotional capacity and mindful attention. I couldn't wait until my next coaching conversation with Jordan. We had agreed to work the polarity of Structure::Flexibility. I had a hunch we needed to engage his heart as he made sense of his relationship to this interdependent pair. I decided to keep the map operating as a framework in the background. We explored each quadrant using coaching questions and recent 360-degree feedback. Here's how it went:

- **Benefits of Structure** (his preferred pole): I asked Jordan to imagine he'd just walked into a conference room and people didn't know he was there. He hears people saying, "Jordan spends a lot of time independently considering all options. He can anticipate the next question and what people are thinking." Jordan was sitting across from me absolutely beaming. His smile was bright and his chest proud. I asked him how it felt to hear this. He said it felt "delightfully affirming" and that he could "hear this every day and it wouldn't be too much." I encouraged him to hold onto this feeling and we moved on.

- **Overuses of Flexibility** (his less preferred pole): I asked Jordan to imagine he'd just jumped on a conference call but his executive team didn't know he was

---

[84] Brown, Brené. *Strong Back, Soft Front, Wild Heart*. RadioPublic, On Being with Krista Tippett, 2018, Feb. 8.
[85] Brown, Brené. *Dare to Lead: Brave Work, Tough Conversations, Whole Hearts*. Random House, 2018, p. 90.

there. He hears the team saying, "Jordan was caught completely off guard on our investor call this morning. He had no idea how to answer Carol's question and completely missed her point. It wasn't good." Jordan's fists were balled up and he looked like he was ready to throw a punch. He said, "I hate how this feels and hate it when I put myself in this situation. This feels just like it did a couple of weeks ago." I let that land and we both sat with the intensity of this emotion.

- **Overuses of Structure** (his preferred pole): I asked him to recall his recent 360-degree feedback. "One of Jordan's overused strengths is he thinks so much about the conversation before it happens it can feel pre-meditated. When the direction of the conversation doesn't align with what he is thinking, he gets locked into his way of seeing the situation. It really gets in the way of his listening and collaborative problem solving." Jordan looked at me and said, "Wow. I feel a little silly. I never realized that my value of predictability could result in my defensiveness and rigidity." I affirmed his new awareness and offered that it doesn't have to be this way.

- **Benefits of Flexibility** (his less preferred pole): I told Jordan to imagine it is a year from now and we gather 360-degree feedback from his team again. This time they say, "Jordan is truly listening to me from my perspective. He brings ideas to the table and is open to finding creative and unexpected solutions to our biggest challenges." Jordan's voice sounded hopeful. "This would be great to hear but I might get taken advantage of if I do that. I am not willing to give up my ability to anticipate to become more adaptable." I knew this voice. It was the voice of vulnerability. Jordan was assuming he had to give up what he valued the most. It wasn't that Jordan didn't want to be adaptable; he was afraid of losing predictability.

We were now outside the boundaries of the Polarity Map® and inside the heart of the conversation. We got curious about the vulnerability we'd stumbled upon as he considered becoming more flexible, and we wrapped up that day by exploring a practice of integration, something I now call the Transformational Third Way in my book, Navigating Polarities.[86] I said to Jordan, "What if you don't have to let go of predictability? What if you could loosen up your grip on it so you can expand and make more room for adaptability? What would that be like?" It was a relief to Jordan when he realized I wasn't asking him to give up a part of how he saw himself in order to become something someone else wanted him to be.

Over the months ahead, Jordan slipped in and out of an *either/Or* mindset and swung from flexibility to structure and back again as he encountered the risk of "losing control" – the fear he sometimes struggled to face as he worked to embrace both poles and eliminate neither. Like many of my other clients, he started to appreciate this could be a practice of many years and that he'd make many mistakes before he learned how to do it. Some exercises, practices, and experiments that helped Jordan increase his capacity for vulnerability included:

---

[86] Emerson, Brian and Lewis, Kelly. *Navigating Polarities*. Paradoxical Press, 2019, p.31.

- **Putting it in perspective:** Ask yourself: Is it really scary or does it just feel scary? Usually the step we need to take isn't actually as scary as it is in our heads. Fear is typically divorced from any concrete or immediate danger. It feels scarier than it actually is. It is typically about something that might happen, not something that is happening now.[87]

- **Expanding what you can see:** Ask yourself, What is true? And, What is also true? Remove the judgment and practice being with all that is true – what is easy for you to see and what requires a harder, deeper look.

- **Accepting how you feel:** Feelings, especially the uncomfortable ones, are often avoided, numbed, or resisted. Focus your attention on the feeling. Watch it without identifying with it. Accept that it is there. No need to think about it, judge it, or analyze it. Know that the feeling isn't who you are. Don't make an identity for yourself out of it (I am _____). Stay present and continue to be the observer of what is happening inside of you.[88] As the sensations of these feelings become familiar, the capacity for vulnerability increases.

- **Bringing joy into the practice through safe-to-fail experiments:**[89] We are often most successful at sustaining a practice over time when a flywheel effect propels us into continued learning through a mixture of failure and success. Safe-to-fail experiments are small, pragmatic, within our control, and "at the edges" of our issue. Start with a direction, not a destination, to allow for learning along the way and to keep open the space for joy. The more one can hold experiments lightly, embracing the playful side of learning, the higher the likelihood of continuing to experiment, learn, and transform.

When Jordan could stay aware long enough to accept the interdependent nature of the dynamic, his vulnerability became availability, unlocking his mind and pulling his heart open to the Third Way. But when he stopped paying attention or resisted the contradiction, vulnerability collapsed into fear, pulling his heart apart and further entrenching him into his preferred pole. As time went on, Jordan found a more intuitive way of knowing that allowed him to experience the reality of *being* with both "this" and "that." Jordan also found the Third Way between Structure *And* Flexibility. He called it Attentive Openness. He learned to come back to that place again and again.

Being in the Practice

The more we prefer a pole, the more likely we are to unknowingly construct part of our identity around it. In my case that sounded like, "I make things better" and in Jordan's case it sounded like, "I know." The strong attachment to our preferred pole sets us up to feel as if we are being challenged or confronted when met with

---

[87] Tolle, Eckhart. *The Power of Now: A Guide to Spiritual Enlightenment*. New World Library; Namaste Publishing, 1999, p. 43.
[88] Ibid. p. 40-41.
[89] Berger, Jennifer G. *Three Key Ingredients to Learning From Failure*. Cultivating Leadership, Blog, 2015, July 19.

our less preferred pole. This is when we are at greatest risk of defaulting to an *either/Or* way of operating and convincing ourselves that we are right and "the other" is wrong. When we do this in a polarity situation, it leads to what Brian Emerson calls Suffering Paradox, discussed in Chapter 37, p. 279.

As I wrote about in Navigating Polarities,[90] I also came to learn a lot about the emotional capacity needed to stand in the Third Way. While grief, loss, fear, and vulnerability are part of the common ground of humanity, they are ground many of us were never taught how to stand on. It was a humbling discovery, one that continues to serve as a reminder that I must be attentive to expanding my own emotional capacity and be adept at wading into these emotional waters with my clients. Finding ways to help others understand the natural tendency to pull away from discomfort and name what feels risky about being with *both* "this" *And* "that" is important. So important, in fact, we developed the Polarity Navigator, a sense-making tool that builds on the Polarity Map, to allow for the exploration of the reintegration of the poles and the vulnerability it takes to stand in the tension of paradox, two topics that are vital to the conversation about polarities. Without this exploration, our fear of the opposite downsides or losing a part of our identity can keep us from operating from *both/And*.

Think back to the Doing::Being and Head::Heart polarity we began with. I encourage you to consider these two questions:

- What part of your identity might be constructed from the upsides of your preferred pole of Doing::Being or Head::Heart?
- How might the fear of losing that keep you from embodying both?

No matter what you chose to call it – standing in the tension of the *And*, standing in the fire, operating from the Third Way – *both/And* is an internal shift through which our basic identities are reconstituted. This kind of transformation requires our active engagement. It is an invitation to feel the fear and do it anyway. We can't think our way through it. It isn't a strategic plan or a map we execute. It is a practice that requires a strong back (courage), a soft front (open-ended willingness to be vulnerable), and a wild heart (not giving into the certainty and comfort of *either/Or*).

Find bio and contact info for author Kelly Lewis at
www.polaritypartnerships.com/certified-polarity-practitioners

---

[90] Emerson, Brian and Lewis, Kelly. *Navigating Polarities*. Paradoxical Press, 2019, p. 45.

Navigating Transition With the Power of Polarity Thinking™
Susan Walker-Morgan, GPCC, ACC, BCC, MPOD

Several years ago, my daughter invited me to run a half marathon with her. My immediate response: I'm not a runner! To support my case, I cited how long it had been since I'd last run for the sake of running – 35 years. I added to this argument protestations of my age, my lack of knowledge about training, and (I thought this was the linchpin) how I would only serve to slow her down. Despite these swift, well-formed arguments, she insisted it would be a great experience to share together. That opportunity – to honor her request, engaging in an experience she was passionate about – was enough for me to change my "no" to a scary, yet unequivocal "yes."

Training. I Googled how to train for a half-marathon. I downloaded guides for daily runs, supplemental exercises, food choices, and rest. I was ready to start training. I began with a two-mile run. On paper, that sounded easy enough. Real life was a very different story. One mile out and back from my front door, I struggled. Just half a mile in, the scary part of my "yes" was confirmed. I was out of breath, running with leaden legs. Back home, hydrated and physically recovered, I reminded myself I was not only training to increase my capacity as a runner, I was increasing my capacity as a mother, willing to forego my desire to bail on this running deal for the greater goal of connecting with my daughter in a new way.

The difficulty of that first run was real and metaphorical throughout my training. I was transitioning physically and emotionally. I had naïvely thought my training would allow me to steadily increase my mileage with ease; I expected to discover a new-found love of running. Instead, I wavered between days of anticipation, running with energy, and feeling demotivated, sluggish, questioning the sanity of my "yes." Likewise, I was reminded that the transition from being my daughter's teacher and guide to becoming her student had begun the day she was born and would continue throughout our lives. Running offered me the opportunity to learn from and lean on her. On joint training runs, she reminded me of my breathing, my posture, and encouraged my flagging spirit. At times, I accepted her advice and support with gratitude and grace. Other times, I snapped impatiently with frustration. This wasn't a straight, flat course we were on with incremental improvement. We were running the highs and lows the terrain Northeast Ohio has to offer, inside and out.

In the midst of this training regimen, I was a student of Barry Johnson's in the study of Polarity Management.[91] I recognized this pursuit with my daughter contained several Polarities to be leveraged – Activity *And* Rest, Novice *And* Expert, Individual *And* Team, with the most alive being the polarity of Task *And* Relationship while

---

[91] Johnson, Barry. *Polarity Management: Identifying and Managing Unsolvable Problems.* HRD Press, 1996.

continuing my transition as a runner (task) and a mother (relationship). Polarity Management made explicit what implicit experience was teaching me. There is an energy that flows between and connects two seemingly disparate goals, in this case, completing the task *And* building relationship.

Four months after my first training run, we completed that race. Throughout those 13.1 miles, the polarity of Task *And* Relationship was present. Immense effort flowed into exchanges of encouragement and praise, laughter to the point of tears, miles passing with effort and ease. At mile 13, a sideline spectator promised us the finish line was just down the hill. We crossed that line, clasped hands held high, my daughter laughing, me crying, living the transition of our relationship from adult/child to adult/adult. That transition continues.

Training for that race wasn't a linear transition; it was a process of receiving feedback from my body, adjusting, and going for the next run. The relationship my daughter and I share continues to transition as we each mature and change, discovering new patterns of relating and connecting. Finishing that half-marathon was one of the hardest missions I've accomplished, physically. Living in transition with my daughter is one of the sweetest gifts we continue to enjoy.

Transitions. They can be exciting. They can be difficult. They always contain an element of confusion and uncertainty. We typically consider them to be a linear experience. What if they're not? What if, instead of moving from one experience to the next, we view the ending *And* beginning inextricably linked with energy flowing between the two. And what if moving on and never looking back, or attempting to always recreate the past, is actually what prevents us from gaining all that we have available to us for new beginnings?

Transition is one large polarity, connecting ending *And* beginning. This word order is deliberate because paradoxically enough, "Transition begins with the ending."[92] Considering transition through the lens of Polarity Thinking™, specifically as a back and forth experience, allows us to flow between the ending and all it has to teach us *And* the new beginning with its promise of possibilities. We move from a linear experience into the dynamic, effectual stance of flow.

Transitions come in all shapes, sizes, and timeframes. A new job, birth, death, even preparing to run a half-marathon, are all transitions between different experiences. There are always several Polarities to be leveraged within any transition. While leveraging the Ending *And* Beginning poles we've identified on a specific Polarity Map®, it is helpful to ask three critical questions: What do I want to bring forward? What do I want to leave behind? What do I want to create new? Using these questions and developing action tasks while navigating transition is the difference between getting stuck in the downside of either pole and moving between the poles with agility.

Following are three scenarios, one within a large, established organization, another with a fledgling startup, and one from an individual perspective. Each speaks to Polarity Thinking and the importance of *And* in the midst of the transition.

---

[92] Bridges, William. *Transitions: Making Sense of Life's Changes. Revised 25th Anniversary Edition.* Da Capo Lifelong Books, 2004.

Established Organization

A Fortune 500 Company where I was hired as a consultant was preparing to take a radical step toward a successful future. Over 50% of their top 250 leaders were "home-grown." These leaders had advanced in the organization from front line staff positions. This internal advancement was a tremendous asset in terms of retaining institutional knowledge and understanding the grass roots of the business, but there was concern it was also a liability. There was tension mounting between these home-grown leaders and those who had been hired with more schooling and experience outside the organization. Were the employees-now-leaders current enough about best practices in business development? Were they willing to embrace innovative ideas from "outsiders?" Would the organization lose its established track record of success by embracing new ways of thinking? How could new leadership learn from those with years of experience?

While I was not schooled in Polarity Management at the time of this engagement, it is unmistakable the impact Polarity Thinking[93] brought to their transition. How do we keep the Institutional Knowledge alive – flowing freely through the organization *And* embrace Innovative Thinking? The organization needed to understand what *And* might look like rather than a forced choice based in "*Or*."

Working with senior human resources leadership, we established a leadership development program that engaged these leaders in leveraging the Institutional Knowledge within their ranks *And* embraced Innovative Thinking. Our goal was to advance a strong organization through empowered employees, while providing service to its customers and communities. The Greater Purpose Statement is labeled Vibrant Organization. Failure to leverage the poles of Institutional Knowledge *And* Innovative Thinking, could lead to a Declining Organization out of touch with its employees, the market, and the communities it served – the Deeper Fear (*Figure 1*).

A 10-month development program was designed to mine the expertise in the room (Institutional Knowledge), and provide training in alternative business models, effective leadership styles, and strategic planning (Innovative Thinking). Each month, mixed cohorts from across the organization convened for one day of training and engagement in emotional intelligence, team building, strategic and financial planning, marketing, and business development. Each cohort was also charged with identifying and developing a business plan for an initiative of their choosing to be presented to Executive Leadership.

Start on the upside of the Institutional Knowledge pole. Valuable information resided in the leaders who had advanced from front-line positions. This knowledge needed to be integrated throughout the organization. Inherent wisdom was disseminated through the monthly engagements. Leveraging only this pole of Institutional Knowledge risked being stuck in outdated processes and procedures, repeating ineffective patterns of communication and planning, and resistance to innovation.

---

[93] Johnson, Barry. *And: Making a Difference by Leveraging Polarity, Paradox or Dilemma. Volume One – Foundations.* HRD Press, 2020.

Figure 1 — Polarity Map®

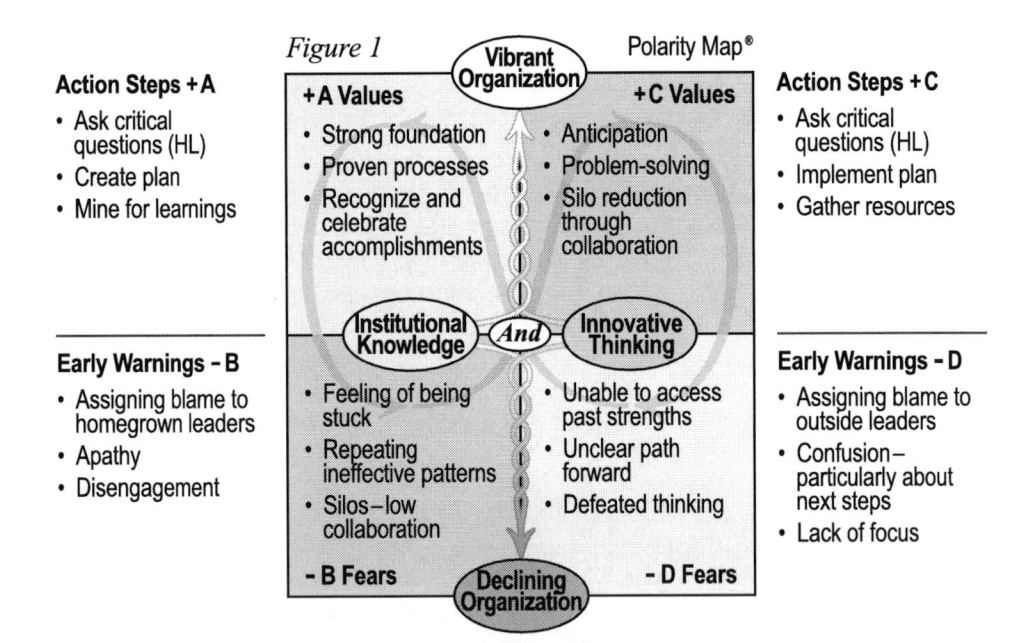

Action Steps +A	+A Values	+C Values	Action Steps +C
• Ask critical questions (HL) • Create plan • Mine for learnings	• Strong foundation • Proven processes • Recognize and celebrate accomplishments	• Anticipation • Problem-solving • Silo reduction through collaboration	• Ask critical questions (HL) • Implement plan • Gather resources
Early Warnings − B	**− B**	**− D**	**Early Warnings − D**
• Assigning blame to homegrown leaders • Apathy • Disengagement	• Feeling of being stuck • Repeating ineffective patterns • Silos – low collaboration	• Unable to access past strengths • Unclear path forward • Defeated thinking	• Assigning blame to outside leaders • Confusion – particularly about next steps • Lack of focus

Upper pole: **Vibrant Organization**. Left pole: **Institutional Knowledge** *And* Right pole: **Innovative Thinking**. Lower pole: **Declining Organization**. − B Fears / − D Fears.

This pole's early warning signs of assigning blame to homegrown leaders, apathy, and disengagement is what spurred senior leadership to reach out for assistance. Silos between departments lead to ineffective processes, causing employees and customers to complain. Action Steps within the design of the development program included building opportunities for seasoned employees to disseminate their knowledge and experience to others (business initiative project), and creating a plan for moving forward. The building opportunities ask three critical questions. What do we want to retain? What do we leave behind, either because it is no longer effective or won't serve us moving forward? What do we need to create new?

The Action Step – implementing the plan for development of all leaders – moved us to the upside of the Innovative Thinking pole. In-person collaboration between departments allowed employees to meet face-to-face, formerly known to one another exclusively through email. Previously siloed departments were sharing information critical for higher employee and customer satisfaction. Relying only upon the strength of Innovative Thinking could move the organization to its downside. When process and procedure are changed too quickly or simply for the sake of change, chaos ensues. Unclear expectations lead to disengagement and a loss of energy. Warning Signs that we were heading in this direction included assigning blame to outside leaders, confusion about current and next steps, and lack of focus. Asking the three critical questions was part of the business initiative project chosen and designed by each cohort. These initiatives inherently required each cohort to rely upon the Institutional Knowledge *And* Innovative Thinking for success, keeping the energy of the polarity flowing well.

Key benefits from this engagement: increased response to service calls, individual and team development, and continued viability in the communities served. Institutional Knowledge *And* Innovative Thinking remain alive and continue to be leveraged well.

Fledgling Start-Up

The second example exhibits how polarities and transitions are inherent in all organizations, regardless of size, ranking, or longevity. A tech start-up I'm working with is building a hiring platform committed to making a difference for organizations and candidates in tech developer hiring. They envision a process in which the candidate and the employer are able to access projects built by the candidate, showcasing their skill and their propensity for working well within a team environment. They believe the difference they can make in the recruitment world is to design a forum to showcasing skill *And* collaborative ability.

As they transitioned from being a group of friends with a good idea, to an organization with a vision *And* mission, they wanted to be intentional about the creation of their culture. What do we need to consider as we create our product *And* our culture? What will ensure the culture we are creating is effective in developing our product *And* our people? Exploring these questions with them moved us into a discussion of Polarity Thinking. Recognizing they were already living their culture, we identified several polarities in place. Once identified, the six employees fleshed out how they wanted to enculturate each polarity to build their business.

Audacious *And* Conservative. For them, Audacious means doing the impossible, confronting the status quo, going further, higher, and faster; taking risks to make unprecedented change. Conservative means understanding the realistic boundaries of company, mission, and team; placing focus on responsibilities and efficiency.

Empowering *And* Critical. Fostering just, equitable treatment of human evaluations; promoting confidence and courage within workforces needed to be balanced with framing ideas in context of their implemented states. Providing relevant, realistic, and productive feedback to ideas past the initial stage of development.

Flexible *And* Structured. Novel approaches, agile development, and disruptive ways of thinking; infinite variability between current position and goal poised with following defined roles in a common, collaborative approach toward goals; acknowledging roles and responsibilities and acting accordingly.

Innovative *And* Stable. A novel way to think and to do; advancing knowledge and capability with advanced, original methods, decisions, and structures juxtaposed with finding middle ground; maintaining inertia; acknowledging maintenance in relationship to success.

Collaborative *And* Autonomous. Working as a team toward a collectively held goal, bound by a mutually defined mission; defining team roles and dynamics while taking ownership, accountability, and authority for decisions; taking independent initiative.

Identifying polarities inherent in their own development clarified the polarities their hiring managers and candidates were navigating. This clarification informed their discussions with clients and users for the improvement of their platform. Knowing the polarities at play in their own organizational development was beneficial to internal and external evolution.

Individual Perspective

A third transition is individual. I write it in honor of all of us who have started a project with gusto, only to find ourselves stalled and stuck in the throes of uncertainty and frustration. In December of 2019, Barry Johnson asked if I'd be interested in submitting a chapter for this book. I was thrilled. I've found Polarity Thinking to be instrumental in my life personally and professionally. Yes, I was in! I was ready to transition from student to contributor (*Figure 2* maps my journey).

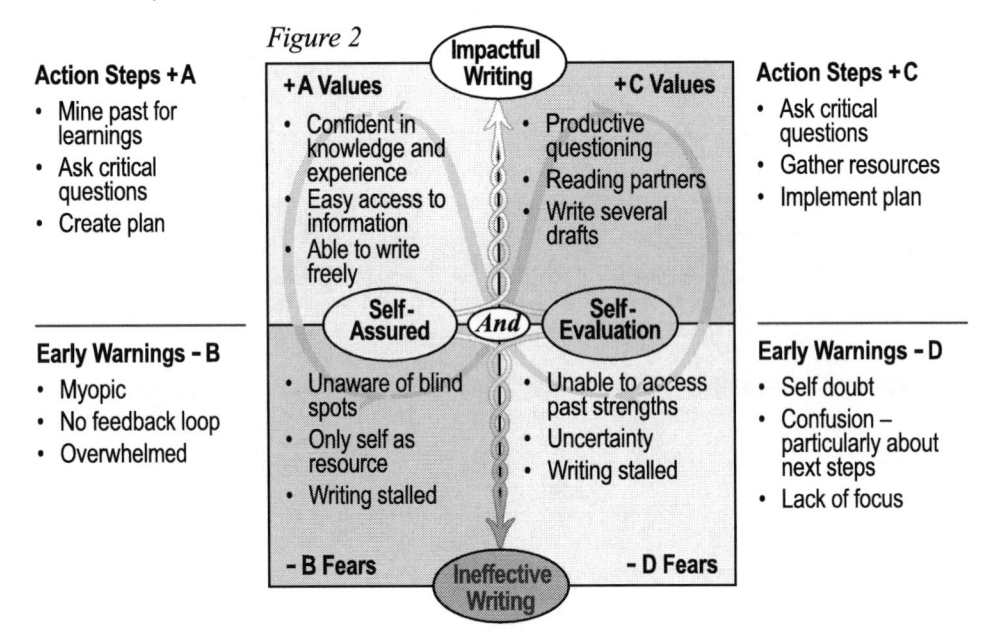

Figure 2

Action Steps +A	+A Values	Impactful Writing	+C Values	Action Steps +C
• Mine past for learnings • Ask critical questions • Create plan	• Confident in knowledge and experience • Easy access to information • Able to write freely	Self-Assured *And* Self-Evaluation	• Productive questioning • Reading partners • Write several drafts	• Ask critical questions • Gather resources • Implement plan
Early Warnings -B				Early Warnings -D
• Myopic • No feedback loop • Overwhelmed	• Unaware of blind spots • Only self as resource • Writing stalled		• Unable to access past strengths • Uncertainty • Writing stalled	• Self doubt • Confusion – particularly about next steps • Lack of focus
	- B Fears	Ineffective Writing	- D Fears	

I started to review the materials from the training I'd attended with Barry and other Polarity Master teachers and students. I perused files of clients with whom I'd used Polarity Management. Myriad coaching sessions highlighted the difference Polarity Management had made for clients navigating a plethora of polarities. Preparation increased my excitement and energy for writing. I felt resourced and well prepared. I was on the upside of Self Assured. I started writing. I wrote and rewrote, with a growing sense of frustration at my inability to articulate well what had made such a difference in my life and the lives of my clients.

Anxiety-fueled negative self-talk took over. What was I thinking??? What do I have to contribute to the Polarity Management community that hadn't been illustrated more adeptly by the experts who taught me? I had the certificate and plaque of Polarity Mastery Graduate. What I didn't have was the self-assurance I was worthy of the title.

Fortunately, that spiral was interrupted by an appointment with my coach. I talked through the imposter syndrome these questions told me I was feeling. We reviewed several engagements in which I'd used Polarity Management with clients. I went back to basics. Here, the Polarity Map and the three critical questions were helpful. What did I want to retain and bring forward? My knowledge, stories of the impact of Polarities, and the transitions they had informed. What did I need to let go? This answer was a result of answering the first question. By reviewing success, the self-doubt of the imposter syndrome began to fade. My strength of understanding polarities was evident in the work. What did I want to create new? Using that coaching engagement to assess my knowledge base and remember examples fueled creative ideas and generated a first draft. I was back to the upside of Self-Assurance. With the draft complete, I needed a larger perspective than my own. I reached out to colleagues and one of my sons, an English major and writer, for feedback.

Feedback is an invaluable resource; I needed to assess its value for myself. I wanted this work to represent the wisdom I'd received from a mentor I respected, as well as my experience putting that knowledge to practice. I continued to read through the feedback, cleaned up some files on my computer, set my office in order, allowing the external order I was creating to align the internal order of my thoughts. I was also aware that I had so many perspectives, I was uncertain how to integrate them into a cohesive body of work that still contained my voice and those of my clients. I reread through edits and suggestions with the question in mind – does this serve the idea of Doing Good through leveraging Polarities? Filtering with that question in mind guided which feedback to integrate and which to let go.

I've cycled through this polarity several times throughout the writing process. Each cycle, the specific details of the experience are different and the value of Polarity Thinking grows. When my thoughts are clouding, energy is waning, and writing is stalling, I recognize it for the warning sign it is. I'm moving into the downside of one of the poles of this transition from student to contributor. I have the tools I need to follow the energy of the Polarity to the Upside of the opposite pole. My mantra – Keep the energy flowing.

Training for a race, working with organizations, writing – all are unique transitions, and all can be understood more fully through Polarity Thinking. Polarities are always with us. Transition a constant. They both live in us and we in them. Whether we find transitions to be exhilarating, terrifying, or somewhere on that spectrum, we have assistance for the journey when we recognize and leverage the Polarities they hold.

> Find bio and contact info for author Susan Walker-Morgan at
> www.polaritypartnerships.com/certified-polarity-practitioners

Demystifying Classic Assessments Through a Polarity Lens

Sandy Carter, PhD, MSW, PCC
John Fraser, MBA, ACC
Cliff Kayser, MSHR, MSOD, PCC

As management consultants and coaches, we are trained to utilize a variety of leadership assessments designed to enhance self-awareness, growth, and development in our work with individuals, teams, and organizations. More often than not, in a competitive market, it is the client's request for proposal and resulting contract, not the consultant/coach preference, that dictates the specific assessment chosen for a given engagement.

The multiple leadership theories and associated assessments discussed in this chapter require familiarity through education/certification and delivery experience to successfully integrate the assessment nuances into practice. Due to this steep learning curve, it becomes challenging for professionals to debrief, educate, and coach clients to results across a variety of assessments.

In addition to the vast diversity in assessment models and formats, we see added complexity when considering the divergent perspectives various experts bring to the process. Leadership/executive coaches, consultants, mentors, and therapists are examples of professionals typically utilizing assessments to expand their clients' developmental strategies.

It is useful to understand the distinct differences amongst these various professions. Though there is some overlap, each professional is unique in their focus. The International Coaching Federation defines coaching as *"Partnering with clients in a thought-provoking and creative process that inspires them to maximize their personal and professional potential."*[94]

Consultants are generally hired to translate their particular technical expertise into problem diagnosis and solution delivery. A mentor provides wisdom and guidance, typically based on their own professional experience. In contrast, a therapist is highly trained in specific skills to address underlying emotional and psychological dysfunction and pain.

A common denominator throughout this broad spectrum of helping professionals is that success depends on the practitioner's ability to evolve trust and initiate meaningful conversations that are centered on competencies such as active listening, powerful questioning, and direct feedback. Given the diversity of both classic assessment formats and service provider roles within their professional

---

[94] ICF. coachfederation.org/faqs?fwp_faqs_search=define. Accessed July 17, 2020.

community, it would add value to identify language and an interpretive model that translates across multiple assessments and simplifies the process. Unfortunately, management theory authors and assessment designers offer little support in this area. However, if we shift our perspective from a singular focus to examining the tensions – polarities – that exist in the "whole," this opens up innovative and creative pathways for framing and discussing critical similarities and differences among assessments. A polarity lens demystifies the "now what?", which is left unanswered by the client behavior strategy development steps of classic assessments.

Polarities, often known as paradoxes, dilemmas, and tensions, are not new and have been recognized as challenging since ancient times. They are a fundamental part of life and, if acknowledged and leveraged, are a key to wellbeing and success. Polarities are opposing interdependent pairs representing conflicting points of view, both being correct. More than just opposites, polarity implies differences that are interconnected and interdependent wholes. Looking at life through a polarity lens allows the observer to see not half, but the entire picture. Recognizing the upsides of both poles allows avoidance of being forced into making false choices. This is *both/And*-thinking, as distinct from *either/Or*-thinking, and facilitates society's ability to focus on *both* mercy *And* justice, the leader's ability to focus on *both* relationships *And* task, and the athlete to focus on *both* rest *And* exercise.

The classic assessments considered in this chapter – Myers-Briggs Type Indicator (MBTI),[95] Thomas-Kilmann Conflict Mode Instrument (TKI),[96] Blake and Mouton's Managerial Grid (B/M),[97] Leadership Circle Profile (LCP)[98] – all exemplify polarities inherent in their parent models. These models, however, do not explicitly identify the contradictions or polarities present. Therefore, opportunities for intentionally using their innate wisdom, or leveraging them, as part of the developmental process are limited or non-existent. Yet, polarities are fundamental to the structural design of the models; thus, underscoring their necessity when identifying complex constructs related to personality, conflict management, team development, leadership styles, and so on.

Successful client conversations associated with each of the classic assessments discussed in this chapter are both validated and supplemented by Polarity Partnerships' SMALL Process™: Seeing the relevant polarities, Mapping these polarities, Assessing and Learning how effectively the polarities are utilized, and strategically Leveraging these polarities (PACT™). More specifically, the recommended solution (if not explicitly stated) in all cases is essentially a version of Barry Johnson's process for "getting unstuck" by implementing specifically identified polarity leveraging strategies.[99]

---

[95] Myers, I. B. "The Myers-Briggs Type Indicator Manual". Princeton, NJ: Educational Testing Service, 1962.
[96] Thomas, K. W. and Kilmann, R. *Thomas-Kilmann Conflict Mode Instrument.* CCP, Inc. 2007
[97] Blake, R. R. and Mouton, J.S. *The Managerial Grid: Key Orientations for Achieving Production Through People.* Gulf Publishing Company, 1964.
[98] Anderson, Bob. The Leadership Circle. www.leadershipcircle.com/en/home. Accessed July 13, 2020.
[99] Johnson, Barry. *And: Making a Difference by Leveraging Polarity, Paradox or Dilemma. Volume One – Foundations.* HRD Press, 2020, Chapter 13, "Paradoxical Change and Getting Unstuck," pp. 99-105.

Polarity Thinking™,[100] is a meta-theory with the structural capacity to encompass a multitude of management and leadership theories within the model. In the end, the solution always rests in identifying the two poles of the tension – the polarity – and ultimately leveraging both poles to maximize the "upsides" and to minimize the "downsides" of each. There will always be a "getting unstuck" discussion because humans have a preferred pole, which is over-emphasized to the neglect of the less preferred pole. Preferences arise from a combination of our values and fears. We defend what we value and try to avoid what we fear. So, we judge based on assumptions we hold related to the side we are favoring. The more strongly we are attached to one side, the more challenging it is to see anything positive about the other side. When we only see a portion of the whole picture, we eventually get the negative effects or downsides of both sides, as we have limited or narrowed our mindset.

It is critical that the inevitable "getting unstuck" coaching conversation not be a lecture or telling session. Rather, it is ideally a series of powerful coaching questions allowing the client to: claim their *values* (more preferred pole), acknowledge their *fears* (less favored pole) without retribution, explore the potential "upsides" of their *fears* pole (while, importantly, not losing their *values* pole), and obtain the client's identified greater-good goal. The beauty is that this conversation is relevant for every polarity (tension, paradox, dichotomy, or dilemma) embedded in all classic assessments.

Classic Assessment Models and the Polarity Framework

Myers-Briggs Type Indicator (MBTI) assesses psychological preferences based on how individuals direct their energy, perceive the world and their surroundings, make decisions, and live in the world. This assessment has four primary dichotomies (polarities): Introversion/Extraversion, Sensing/Intuition, Thinking/Feeling, and Judging/Perceiving. Final assessment results indicate a preference toward one or the other dichotomy pole. For example, individuals are typed as *either* introversion *Or* extraversion. In other words, results are framed using a single-line continuum, and what is not explicitly addressed is the inherent tension and the dynamic energy flow within the polarity of *both* introversion *And* extraversion.

Some clients score deep into the continuum, indicating a clear and strong preference for one or the other pole, and are comfortable with their resulting type designation. However, by examining their type through a polarity lens, these clients could gain powerful insights available through understanding their potential aversion to their interdependent pole. Clients who are more moderate on the continuum indicate they *feel* the pressure of a *both/And* pull. In this case, the coaching conversation shifts to "context" and how the client can most effectively manage the tensions between embracing extroversion energy at times, and at other times drawing on their introversion preference.

To build on the multifaceted nature of type and further clarify the differences between the four dichotomies, the Step II MBTI instrument[101] was introduced.

---

[100] Johnson, Barry. *And: Making a Difference by Leveraging Polarity, Paradox or Dilemma. Volume One – Foundations.* HRD Press, 2020.
[101] Myers, P.B. and Myers, K.D. *MBTI® Step II™ Manual Supplement.* CCP, Inc., 2011.

Including five "facets" (polarities) for each of the four MBTI dichotomies allowing greater type preference clarity. When appropriately coached using these constructs, clients recognize the dynamic process between their preferred and non-preferred poles and can actively avoid "getting stuck." Although a preferred style is identified, clients see they can leverage energy flow (polarities) to achieve goals and strategies outside of their designated preferences.

Thomas-Kilmann Conflict Mode Instrument (TKI) uses two axes, assertiveness and cooperativeness, to identify five styles that individuals utilize when deciding on a course of action in a conflict situation. It is designed to help individuals identify potential overuse or underuse of any of those styles. The five styles are: Competing (assertive, uncooperative), Avoiding (unassertive, uncooperative), Accommodating (unassertive, cooperative), Collaborating (assertive, cooperative), and Compromising (intermediate assertiveness and cooperativeness). Assertiveness speaks to the degree one attempts to satisfy one's own needs, and cooperativeness is how much focus is placed on meeting the other person's needs. Understanding and managing personal styles, and the inherent tensions within the model, are essential due to their powerful impact on personal and group dynamics. Once recognized by the coach as a polarity, leveraging assertiveness *And* cooperativeness as dynamic energy from a *both/And* framework (removing the "black and white" label) opens up possibilities for transformational growth and development. Looking at the TKI through a polarity lens assists clients in identifying effective change strategies as opposed to remaining "stuck" in one style even if it is not effective.

Two additional assessments examined for this chapter are distinct bodies of work focusing on production/task *And* people/relationship with common polarity threads fundamental to leadership and organizational frameworks.

Blake Mouton Managerial Grid (B/M), also known as the Leadership Grid, is based on two behavioral dimensions: what degree of concern (1-9 scale) does a leader have for people/relationships, and how relevant (1-9 scale) does a leader view production/task achievement. In theory, how these tensions are managed will determine leader success. Too much emphasis on one to the neglect of the other will result in less effective outcomes for both people/relationships and production/task. B/M identifies five behavioral styles and through its assessment process, clients are placed specifically in one of 81 potential box options.

The five managerial/leadership styles are:
- Impoverished (1,1): Concern is low for people and low for production.
- Task Management (1,9): Concern is low for people and high for production.
- Middle of the Road (5,5): Middle of the four quadrants, which represents a balance between concern for people and for production – mediocre on both.
- Country Club (9,1): Concern is high for people and lowest for production.
- Team Management (9,9): Concern is high for people and high for production. In theory, this is the ideal management style and should be the ultimate goal.

It is essential that coaching focuses on implementing strategies to enhance *both* concern for people/relationships *And* concern for production/task achievement, which opens the possibility to see/visualize the dynamic flow of energy within the polarity; Concern for People *And* Concern for Production.

Returning to a polarity lens perspective and the SMALL Process framework, the client is able to shift away from an *either/Or* mindset "box/label" and move toward a fluid state. With the clarification of the polarities present, the client now has the ability to leverage them by implementing action steps, identify early warnings, and successfully maximize the upside of both poles while simultaneously minimizing each downside.

Leadership Circle Profile (LCP) is a leadership assessment that reflects the complexity of the combination of 18 highly researched competencies and 11 inner states, graphically represented on the upper and lower halves of a circle, respectively. We will focus on nine of the upper 18 competencies in our supplementing LCP with Polarity Thinking, with the assertion that this could extend to the entire profile.

The upper half of the LCP circle can be further broken down into five dimensions of which two leadership dimensions are:

- *Relating Dimension:* Caring Connection, Fosters Team Play, Collaborator, Mentoring and Developing, and Interpersonal Intelligence. This dimension lands on the left-hand side of the upper half of the circle.

- *Achieving Dimension:* Strategic Focus, Purposeful and Visionary, Achieves Results, and Decisiveness. This dimension lands on the right-hand side of the upper half of the circle.

Among the Leadership Circle assessment results is a "Relationship–Task Balance" score, which suggests the degree of balance a leader shows between the Achieving and Relating Dimensions. Additionally, the assessment points out high negative correlation coefficients – suggesting interdependencies – between the Relating (relationship) dimension and the Achieving (task) dimension. The assessment's suggested coaching strategies, that essentially emphasize one pole over the other, make no explicit mention of the tension/polarity of Achieving/task *And* Relating/relationship. Yet, when viewed through a polarity lens, as in the Blake Mouton Grid, if there is over-emphasis on *either* Achieving/task *Or* Relating/relationship pole to the neglect of the other, the polarity is not being appropriately leveraged, and the dynamic energy will shift from a virtuous cycle to a vicious cycle. Eventually, this neglect will result in deeper seated fears: being "stuck" to an even greater degree and ongoing disfunction. Only when coached through a polarity lens will the client develop awareness of the dynamic flow of energy between poles and learn to leverage the polarity, thus maximizing the upside and minimizing the downside of both poles.

The final assessment included in this summary is the Polarity Assessment™.[102] When the energy of *both/And*-thinking is harnessed, the "infinity loop" is an illustrative differentiator that shows how the energy system works in all of the

---

[102] The Polarity Assessment™. www.polaritypartnerships.com/our-impact. 2020.

referenced assessments. Recognizing and capturing this dynamic energy is critical, as it sets in motion a predictable process that supports integration, collaboration, and breakthroughs in leadership growth and development and, most importantly, provides the necessary foundation for building trusting and sustainable partnerships.

Value Added Utilizing the Polarity Assessment

As a meta-theory, Polarity Thinking with its associated Polarity Assessment is spacious enough to hold the "parts" of the various classic assessment models. The Assessment, even as a stand-alone, offers value across several dimensions including:

- Scalability: Applicable to individuals, teams, organizations, and nations
- Versatility: Honing in on specific "parts" while offering a holistic perspective
- Customization: The assessment is designed specifically for the client's needs
- Measurability: Rare consistent and highly reliable
- High validity: The assessment measures what it claims to measure

Furthermore, the Polarity Assessment offers Consistency regarding language and change strategies. This is a critical distinction, as having the ability to leverage energy flow and the dynamics for differentiation and integration across boundaries is essential in complexity management. Organizations cannot achieve high-level collaboration without accepting and actively managing paradoxes, dilemmas, and tensions. The polarity framework helps people identify the big picture – the whole picture. As previously mentioned, when problem-solving only goes in one direction, people become frustrated and end up "feeling stuck" because nothing gets resolved. When "tabled" items pile up or create conflict or people begin blaming each other, organizations are trapped with the ineffectiveness of stagnant decision-making. This is how unresolved conflict and drama creep into work environments. Working within a polarity framework allows for cooperation *And* healthy competition without pretending any one of us has all the answers. When "black and white," *either/Or*-thinking falls back, broader growth mindsets can then develop.

Barry Johnson asserts, "values come in pairs," and underscores the risks associated with favoring one's preferred pole over the inclusiveness of valuing both poles (the whole). With a singular focus on only the parts, major challenges and dysfunctionality surface. We see evidence of this in yet another classic model, the Gallup StrengthsFinder[103] assessment, as it ranks (1-34) the participant's talents that, through time and practice, can evolve into strengths. However, the premise is that effective leaders succeed on the basis of their strengths, as long as their weaknesses don't get in the way. Gallup does not explicitly discuss polarities but does refer to the "power" and "edge" (dark side) of each of their 34 strengths. Who would not be proud to have Self-Assurance as their top strength? After all, the upsides of being self-assured include self-confidence, possessing a strong inner compass, and having the ability to effectively take risks. Gallup warns, however, that the "edge" related to Self-Assurance may lead others to view the self-assured leader as

---

[103] Rath, Tom. *StrengthsFinder 2.0*. Gallup Press, 2007.

arrogant, self-righteous, over-confident, and stubborn. From a polarity perspective, this is the result of an overemphasis on the Self-Assurance pole to the neglect of the Humility pole, and thus, beautifully emphasizes Barry Johnson's point that "values come in pairs."

We have limited our discussion to five assessment models, but it is critical to reiterate that Polarity Thinking – polarities, paradoxes, dilemmas, tensions – as a meta-theory, fundamentally impacts all leadership theories and associated assessments.

Nearly all leadership workshops employ some variation of a values exercise where participants are forced to pick their top ten or five or three values from a long list of traditionally accepted values. A typical example might be Family Life, Taking Care of Others, and Empathy. Values originate from a deep belief system and are typically very significant to the individual proclaiming them and are not to be challenged!

Using a polarity lens, a professional assisting a client in value clarification supports their client in stepping back to consider their major blind spots: the upside of the missing pole, and the downside of their preferred pole. When undertaking an in-depth conversation to promote awareness, coaches educate their client, helping them to recognize the importance of letting go of an overemphasis on singular thinking in order to broaden their perspective and to hold a larger picture. In this process, the client "sees" the power of *both/And*-thinking and quickly recognizes too much focus on one pole leads to unsatisfactory results overall. Seeing the value examples listed above through a polarity lens, one sees the importance of focusing on Family Life *And* Work Life, Taking Care of Others *And* Taking Care of Self, and Empathy *And* Assertiveness.

In conclusion, it is critical for professionals to meet their obligation in service to their clients by providing them with the most effective knowledge and tools to function successfully. When leaders supplement *either/Or*-thinking with *both/And*-thinking, they are more able to create interdependent strategies. Polarities are particularly relevant in today's world as complexity, diversity, and speed of change becomes our new normal reality.

As Barry Johnson indicates, when you look through a polarity lens, "Instead of contradicting each other's view, the task is to supplement each other's view in order to see the whole picture. Each has key pieces to the puzzle. Paradoxically, opposition becomes a resource."[104] It is our contention that classic assessments and the polarity model complement one another. When leadership professionals are intentional in cultivating the polarities embedded within classic assessments, they become demystified and consequently, simplified, and the work with our clients is greatly enriched.

> Find info for authors Sandy Carter, John Fraser, and Cliff Kayser at
> www.polaritypartnerships.com/certified-polarity-practitioners

---

[104] Johnson, Barry. *Polarity Management: Identifying and Managing Unsolvable Problems.* HRD Press, 1996.

Key Polarities to Leverage for Successful IT Service Delivery in the Digital Era

Karen McCague

I've spent half of my professional career working in the field of Information Technology as an internal IT service provider for large corporations in multiple industries. I've found that the tensions that arise for internal IT organizations are much the same regardless of the industry vertical you are operating in. Just when you think a problem or challenge is unique to your IT organization, there you see it humorized in a Dilbert cartoon!

Some of the tensions within IT, and within the IT ecosystem, are timeless and some have recently manifested with the shift into the digital era where technology is everywhere and is used by nearly everyone, every day. In today's technology-driven environment, automation and digitalization are essential for most businesses and organizations to stay competitive, connected, and agile. Ironically, the increased dependence of businesses, organizations, and individuals on technology is threatening the very existence of the traditional IT organization. As technology proliferates and becomes part of everyday living at work and at home, business units and individuals are bringing their own technology solutions and service providers to the workplace, often bypassing the IT department altogether. This practice is known as shadow IT and it introduces some interesting dilemmas into many businesses and organizations.

Another major shift that today's IT organization must adapt to is the growth and complexity of the IT ecosystem. The IT organization no longer simply builds and manages technology; it must also build and manage a myriad of relationships within the IT ecosystem in order to successfully connect and deliver technology services to the businesses that it supports.

This chapter explores the tensions that these digital era shifts have brought to the workplace and presents three case studies that exemplify how Polarity Thinking™,[105] can be applied for successful IT service delivery and IT organization relevancy.

The IT Ecosystem

The IT ecosystem is a large, complex network of firms and organizations that drive the delivery of IT products and services to support automated business processes and transactions. In today's digital era, the CIO is no longer just responsible for

---

[105] Johnson, Barry. *And: Making a Difference by Leveraging Polarity, Paradox or Dilemma. Volume One – Foundations.* HRD Press, 2020.

leading the IT department. They are also responsible for managing relationships within an ecosystem comprised of three types of participants:

- **Consumers:** The customers and end-users of technology within the organization
- **Producers:** The technology makers and managers, including both internal and external product and service providers
- **Influencers:** The key stakeholders within the business that have an increasing voice over the direction and role of IT

The boundaries among participants in the IT ecosystem are becoming less defined. For IT organizations to remain relevant, they need to skillfully navigate, manage, and span these boundaries. This approach is different from how IT has operated in the past, where the primary focus was on technology and where technology was procured, built, and managed exclusively by IT.

Figure 1

Key IT Leadership Polarities		
Technology Alignment	And	Business Alignment
Technical Skill Sets	And	People Skill Sets
Short-Term Solutions	And	Longer-Term Strategy
Information Security	And	Information Flow
Task (Managing Systems and Services)	And	Relationship (Managing the Players in the IT Ecosystem)

While the mission of the IT organization continues to be enabling business and organization objectives through technology, the role of the IT organization and the CIO has evolved from technology provider to product and service broker. As such, today's successful CIO must leverage these key polarities (*Figure 1*):

Case Study #1: The Shadow IT Dilemma

I managed the IT Workforce Services team for a large media and entertainment company with the mission of enabling an engaged, productive, and collaborative workforce. As the Digital era evolved, consumer-grade technologies and cloud-based services proliferated. End-users became more technology savvy, were presented with many options outside of the internal IT department offerings, and at times bypassed the IT organization by building or bringing in solutions that better suited their needs and preferences; a practice dubbed "Shadow IT" by the IT industry.

Shadow IT was a growing problem and causing a great deal of tension between IT and the business we supported. While some considered the practice to be an important source of business productivity and innovation, shadow IT solutions were not in line with organizational requirements for control, documentation, security, reliability, support, etc., and introduced additional cost, risk, and complexity into the company's computing environment.

There was much debate and dissention within the IT department and the company's executive team about what to do about the shadow IT situation. Information security advocates wanted to shut down the practice completely. Information flow advocates appreciated that the business units could react more quickly and precisely to specific business needs and opportunities by bringing in their own solutions rather than "making do" with only what IT provided.

I was tasked with coming up with a department position and strategy. Recognizing this tension as a polarity to manage, I gathered a team, and we created a Polarity Map® (*Figure 2*, pp. 140-141) including Action Steps and Early Warnings to develop a *both/And* strategy and execution plan that leveraged the use of *both* IT-Provisioned Standards *And* Customer-Driven Solutions for effective IT service delivery. The Greater Purpose Statement of this polarity is "An engaged, productive and collaborative workforce supported by IT services to achieve business objectives," summarized at the top of *Figure 2* as Effective IT and Workforce. The Deeper Fear is "Ineffective service delivery not connected to business requirements or outcomes," summarized in *Figure 2* as Ineffective IT and Workforce.

Please take a moment to consider the richness and value of the map, seen in full over the next two pages, reflecting the wisdom of the team using an IT ecosystem overlay to the essential Structure *And* Flexibility polarity.

Case Study #2: Leveraging the Enemy

As a female IT executive, I was frequently approached by aspiring young women in the technology field for advice and mentorship ... a role that I am honored and privileged to fulfill. One day I was having lunch with a talented young software developer from another company. She was wrestling with the problem of non-IT professionals building one-off Microsoft Access applications to support processes within their business unit. These rogue applications were often unsupported or orphaned when the employee that developed them left the company. To add insult to injury, IT was often called upon to support and manage these applications down the road without additional budget or support resources. One particular offender was a business professional in one of the business units who had a reputation with his management team for his ability to get things done. But from the software developer's perspective, something had to be done about this guy! He was stepping on her turf, diminishing the role of IT, and was developing applications using a non-standard development platform. What's more, he was getting glory and kudos for "getting things done" and she was behind-the-scenes getting his headaches to handle and messes to clean up. These rogue applications were not scalable, did not meet IT standards, and were not IT-supportable. This was a big problem!

After hearing her out, I asked her why she thought this was happening. She described a scenario of competition among the company's business units for limited IT resources, resulting in long turnaround times and the inability of IT to meet all the business units constantly changing needs and requirements.

Figure 2

Action Steps

- Be more engaged w/ the business to understand needs (HL)
- Provide a forum for the business to provide input into technology decisions (HL)
- Develop and communicate technology strategies, roadmaps, and product selection rationale to stakeholders
- Employ change management methodology to drive adoption and mitigate change fatigue
- Measure, monitor, and improve service performance, adoption, and support
- Explore and evaluate alternative technologies w/ regular frequency

Early Warnings

- Decreasing technology satisfaction survey ratings
- Low technology adoption rates
- Increase in negative feedback from Service Delivery Managers/Business Relationship Managers
- IT budget cuts
- Increased Business Unit technology spend

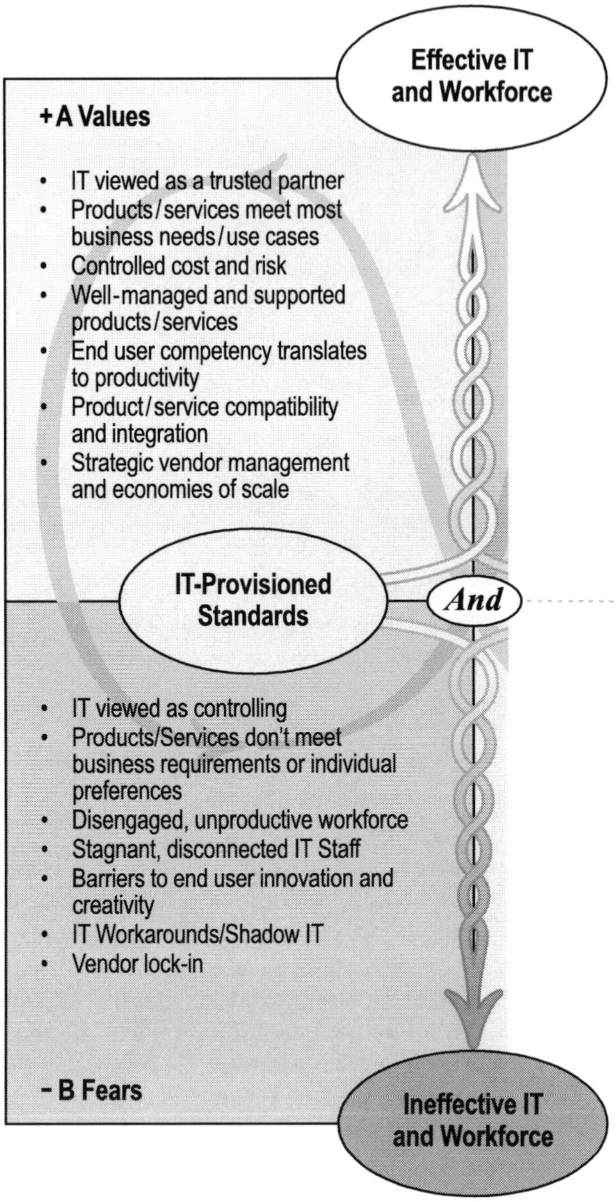

+A Values

- IT viewed as a trusted partner
- Products/services meet most business needs/use cases
- Controlled cost and risk
- Well-managed and supported products/services
- End user competency translates to productivity
- Product/service compatibility and integration
- Strategic vendor management and economies of scale

IT-Provisioned Standards

- IT viewed as controlling
- Products/Services don't meet business requirements or individual preferences
- Disengaged, unproductive workforce
- Stagnant, disconnected IT Staff
- Barriers to end user innovation and creativity
- IT Workarounds/Shadow IT
- Vendor lock-in

−B Fears

Effective IT and Workforce / *And* / *Ineffective IT and Workforce*

Chapter 18: McCague

Polarity Map®

Effective IT and Workforce

+C Values

- IT viewed as a business enabler
- Products and services meet unique business needs/wants and individual preferences
- Workforce engagement and productivity
- Self service/Support Communities
- End user innovation and creativity
- Technology agility
- Vendor versatility

And

Customer-Driven Solutions

- IT not consulted
- Product/Service redundancy
- Uncontrolled cost and risk
- Unmanaged, unsupported chaos
- Overwhelmed/confused end users
- Product/service incompatibility/disconnects
- Vendor management complexity/ineffectiveness

− D Fears

Ineffective IT and Workforce

Action Steps

- Be more engaged w/ the business to understand needs (HL)
- Provide a forum for the business to provide input into technology decisions (HL)
- Cost/benefit and risk evaluation for customer-driven solutions
- Establish a process for onboarding and operationalizing sanctioned customer–driven solutions
- Leverage power users
- Define service levels and support models to set customer expectations

Early Warnings

- Increased licensing costs
- An increase in unmanaged applications and services as measured by services like Netskope
- Increase in Support Desk cases
- Increase in Support Desk case resolution times
- Decrease in customer satisfaction (monthly Net Promoter scores)

Time to reframe things a bit ... One phase of the software development life cycle is requirements definition and analysis. This can often be a tedious, iterative, and time-consuming process between people speaking different languages; i.e., business-speak and IT-speak. I asked her to consider whether these rogue applications could serve as prototypes for future IT-developed applications. Wouldn't it make the requirements definition phase of the IT development process a whole lot easier? And doesn't it take some of the pressure off IT if the business has a solution that meets its short-term needs? Could the business unit software development efforts offer some benefit if they were managed cooperatively with IT? Once she started viewing the situation from that perspective, she became open to a *both/And* approach to dealing with it. She agreed that it was a polarity to manage rather than a problem to solve.

We met again to come up with a plan to leverage this tension between IT and the business units. After some discussion, she identified the poles in this polarity as "Empowered End-User Development" *And* "IT Professional Development."

Mapping this polarity enabled the software developer to identify a dilemma to her manager and present recommendations for managing it instead of merely complaining about a perceived problem. She was able to show how the "problem" could be leveraged as an opportunity and resource when managed strategically.

This case illustrates that building alliances with the influencers in the business units can create a dynamic between IT and the business that enables viable short-term wins for the business *And* can lay a foundation for longer-term operational efficiency. In looking at this situation through a polarity lens, the "enemy" became the ally.

Case Study #3: Merger and Acquisition

Earlier in this chapter, I spoke to the importance of building relationships within the IT ecosystem and the importance of the "Task" *And* "Relationship" polarity. Never has this been clearer to me than in merger and acquisition situations.

In 2016, my company acquired a very large commercial television network in Eastern Europe. The acquisition would more than double the size of our company. As integration plans throughout both companies were being developed, the integration of IT communications systems (email, videoconferencing, file sharing, etc.) became paramount since all other departments were dependent on the ability to effectively communicate with their overseas counterparts in the integration planning process. There were firm regulatory deadlines and business commitments to be met, so time was of the essence. We needed to get down to business and integrate our communications systems! The task of securely integrating our systems became a primary, urgent focus.

After the initial meetings between technical counterparts from both companies, it became clear that this was going to be an arduous process. The technical aspects of the integration were going to be complex. One of the biggest issues was that all their IT infrastructure was managed on-site, while most of ours was in (outsourced) cloud services. Essentially, they were where we were 10 years ago. Integration of our communications systems would require them to migrate from their in-house systems to our cloud service providers. There were a lot of legitimate reasons for the acquired company to be concerned and justify resistance including cost, regulatory, and security issues.

To add to the mix, there were also language, time zone, cultural, ego, and power distance considerations to contend with. The technical aspects of the integration were going to be hard. Navigating the non-technical aspects of this integration was going to be harder. Trust and relationship building were going to be important precursors to getting anything done. I quickly realized the need to go overseas, meet people, and build relationships, and presented my case to our IT Management team. The reaction from one of my peers was "Hell, we bought them. They'll do things our way. Just tell them what we want them to do." Fortunately, our team leader saw the value of relationship building and its importance to a smooth transition and a healthy, whole, and unified company.

Well aware of critical deadlines, we took the time and energy necessary to build trust and strong relationships with our overseas counterparts. Doing so allowed us to leverage the technical expertise of both IT teams as we moved forward, cooperatively and successfully, with integration efforts. In addition, we built bonds that remain in place today – long after many of the players moved on to other jobs and companies. What was first thought of as an arduous process turned out to be a wonderful life experience. What a different story it would have been if the acquiring company simply assumed the position of directing the acquired one!

The theme of all three of these case studies is that in today's business environment *both* technology *And* relationships are important for successful IT service delivery.

Find bio and contact info for author Karen McCague at
www.polaritypartnerships.com/certified-polarity-practitioners

Polarities and Homelessness
Tim Arnold

I sure thought that things would be a lot easier!

I had left a job that I loved running a successful training and development company to take on a new challenge that I felt was more important – leading a 40-bed homeless shelter. The shelter was still in start-up mode and full of excitement and opportunity. We were a small staff of about a dozen employees: some of them, like me, had little to no experience dealing with homelessness, some had spent much of their career in the social service world, and a few had lived the experience of homelessness themselves. Interestingly enough, as diverse as we were, we were incredibly unified on what we had identified as our core values: **Love**, **Hope**, **Fairness**, **Beauty**, and **Home** (*Figure 1*).

Figure 1: Southridge Shelter Core Values

What was baffling to me, however, was that even though we seemed unified on these core values, when it came down to how we should go about living these values out, we were incredibly divided. Someone would argue that **Fairness** meant being consistent and making sure we treated everyone equally – but then someone else would push back and say, "Wait a minute, not everyone has the same abilities. **Fairness** isn't making sure everyone gets the same thing – it's that everyone gets what they need." We were 100% aligned on our core values, yet we were becoming more and more of a polarized team each day.

An Example of Love

I mentioned that one of our core values was **Love**. Even before I started working at the shelter, I was quite involved in street outreach. It all started for me when one day I had an unexpected conversation with a guy named Wayne. Wayne spent most of his life on the streets, and it had taken a significant toll on him physically, mentally, and emotionally. Wayne also had a crippling drug addiction. On many levels, Wayne and I were quite different, yet surprisingly on many more levels we found that we were incredibly similar. Within a short amount of time, Wayne became one of my best friends and one of the biggest teachers in my life.

When I learned about Wayne's life, it became clear to me that the one thing he had never experienced in life was unconditional acceptance – love and friendship that came without strings or judgment. Something that I often took for granted in my life was that in spite of making some really bad decisions now and then, I always knew that I had friends and family in my corner. I never had to question if I would have people there for me to provide love, acceptance, and support. Seeing that this had never been the case for Wayne, I thought that if somehow I could just be there for him, regardless of how well or how poorly he did – if I could just love and support him in a way that unconditionally accepted him as a person – there might be a chance that this could give him the encouragement and confidence he needed to be able to get out of his desperate situation.

So that was my strategy in trying to "solve the problem" of Wayne's homelessness. I would be unconditionally accepting. I was going to be there for him, no matter what he had done, no matter what he did. I wasn't going anywhere. To the best of my ability, I would not judge him. I would just be there. And it worked ... for a while.

Over the course of the next few months, I saw an incredible change in Wayne's life. Not only was he able to move off the streets, but he also had new job opportunities, he began addressing his addiction issues, and he even started to reach out to estranged family members. Although this positive change could be attributed to a number of things, I definitely saw the "upside" of unconditional acceptance being lived out in Wayne's life.

However, it started to become clear that when we choose one side of a polarity to the neglect of the other, we eventually lose the things we set out to achieve, and inevitably start to experience the downside of our approach. I learned the hard way that by only caring and relating to Wayne in an unconditionally accepting way, I was actually hurting him. I was not allowing him to experience the consequences of his behavior. I was not challenging Wayne to live up to his potential. I had become an enabler, and things started to fall off the rails. In time, Wayne's progress started to slow and he started to move back into the same old patterns and behaviors that worked against his recovery.

What I began to realize – the hard way – was that the only way I could live out my greater purpose of **Love** in Wayne's life was to be able to be Unconditionally Accepting *while at the same time* holding Wayne Accountable (*Figure 2*). My preference towards unconditional acceptance (gentle love) was actually dangerous when not held in tension with accountability (tough love).

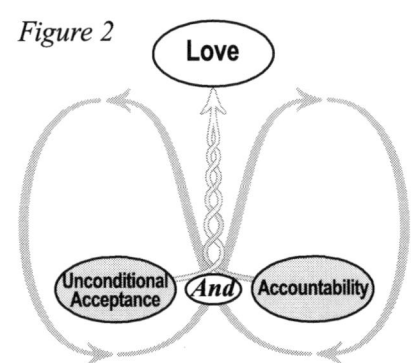

Figure 2

Seeing Is Relieving

And the tension involved in trying to support Wayne was not unique. As we dealt with more and more challenges in the shelter, it became incredibly clear to us that if we really wanted to live out our core values of **Love**, **Hope**, **Fairness**, **Beauty**, and **Home** – renamed Greater Purposes – then we needed to grasp that each of our Greater Purposes had a unique underlying polarity. We realized that if we were not able to embrace these polarities and lean into the inevitable tension that resulted from them, the words **Love**, **Hope**, **Fairness**, **Beauty**, and **Home** would never become a reality for our community. The only way we would be able to live out our vision would be to acknowledge and leverage polarities (*Figure 3*).

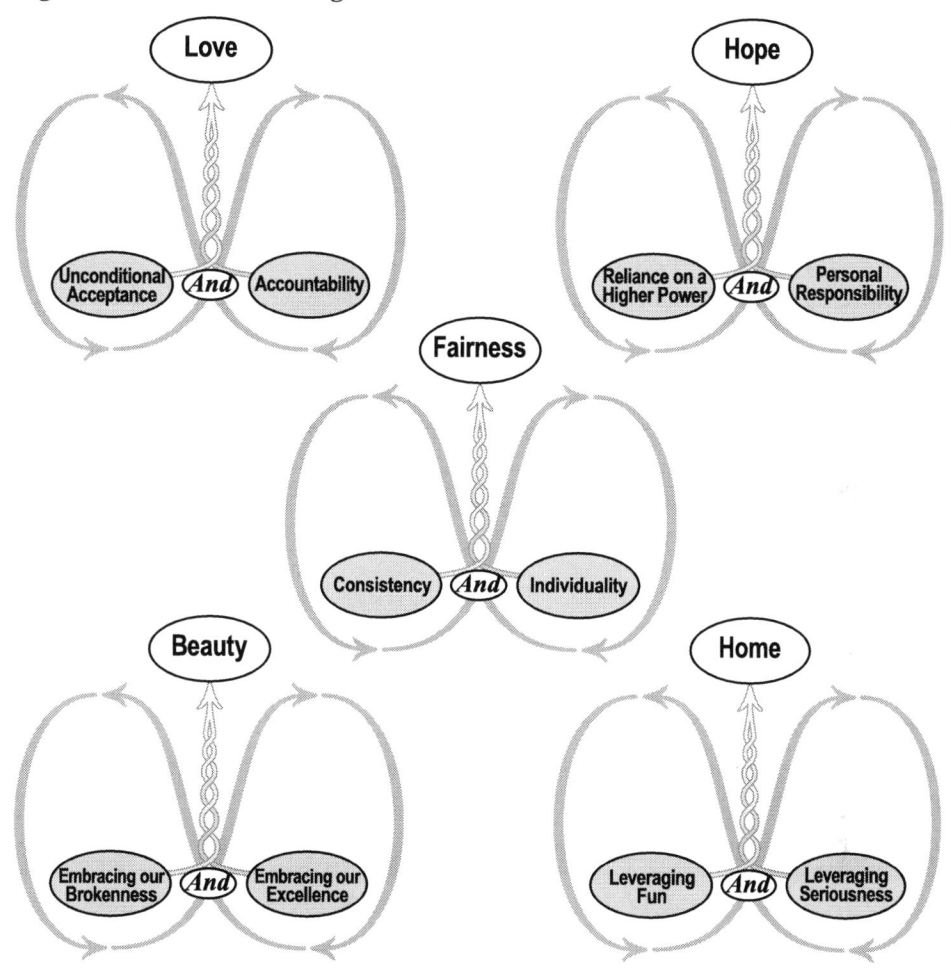

Figure 3: The Five Southridge Shelter Polarities

```
         Love                                    Hope
   Unconditional   Accountability        Reliance on a   Personal
   Acceptance  And                       Higher Power And Responsibility

                         Fairness
                  Consistency  And  Individuality

         Beauty                                  Home
   Embracing our  And  Embracing our     Leveraging  And  Leveraging
   Brokenness         Excellence          Fun              Seriousness
```

In our shelter, we found that once we identified these core polarities, seeing was relieving. We realized that it was okay that we were dealing with these ongoing tensions every day; in fact, it was important that we embraced them. Now, when we are divided about how we do things in our shelter, the identification and understanding of these key polarities provide us with a common language that helps to defuse the situation and navigate the way forward in a healthy way. It shows us that we are at odds and feeling tension for good reasons. It helps us pinpoint what we need to train our staff and volunteers in, and how these tensions need to be acknowledged and integrated into any work plans or change initiatives. Identifying and focusing on achieving healthy tension in our core polarities has allowed us to start to walk our talk.

The Five Southridge Shelter Polarities

- Unconditional Acceptance *And* Accountability in order to experience **Love**.
- Reliance on a Higher Power *And* Personal Responsibility in order to experience **Hope**.
- Consistency *And* Individuality in order to experience **Fairness**.
- Embracing *both* our Brokenness *And* Excellence in order to experience true **Beauty**.
- Leveraging Fun *And* Seriousness in order to experience **Home**.

Find bio and contact info for author Tim Arnold at
www.polaritypartnerships.com/certified-polarity-practitioners

The Importance of Polarity Thinking™ in Healthcare

Bonnie Wesorick, MSN, RN, DPNAP, FAAN
Tracy Christopherson, PhDc, MS, BAS, RRT
Michelle Troseth, MSN, RN, FNAP, FAAN

The need for Polarity Thinking™ in healthcare cannot be overstated. Those who live in the healthcare arena know the complexity of healthcare, and every day they actively engage in efforts to address the chronic issues that surround those who have committed their lives to be the healers for this humanity.

The focus of this chapter will be at the point-of-care, that is, the place where the hands of those who give care and the hands of those who receive care meet, because, in the end, what happens there determines the quality of healthcare.[106] This allows us to narrow our focus as there are hundreds of polarities in healthcare. In addition, we count on you knowing the principles and understanding the whole polarity mapping process. Therefore, we can share information in a different way that we hope can enhance your knowledge.

The best healthcare practitioners and leaders are master problem solvers. It is logical. Historically, people came into the medical care system because they had a problem and they expected us to fix it. Everyday our success is measured on the ability to diagnose and treat problems accurately. As a result, thousands of lives are saved every day through problem solving and *either/Or*-thinking. It is no wonder that the healthcare providers are such good problem solvers and are so skilled at *either/Or*-thinking. We can and should take great pride in that. It also explains why *either/Or*-thinking is embedded in the DNA of healthcare cultures and that Polarity Thinking is not a norm, nor is it spontaneous. Whenever a difficult issue arises, it is natural to think of it as a problem and take action to solve it. Yet many of the major issues that haunt those who lead and live in healthcare are not just problems to be solved, but polarities that must be leveraged. In these cases, our well-developed skills in problem solving are not enough.

The end result of a dominant problem-solving culture leads to unipolar thinking. Those who know the principles of Polarity Thinking know the unintended outcomes of focusing on one pole and neglecting the other.

> *It is this predictability that helps explain the common shadows of the healthcare cultures; chronic problems and care outcomes which are often the downsides of a pole. They persist because it was unknown that the "issue" being addressed and focused on was really one pole of a polarity.*

---

[106] Wesorick, B. "21st Century Leadership Challenge: Creating and Sustaining Healthy, Healing Work Cultures and Integrated Service at the Point of Care." Nursing Administration Quarterly, 2002, 26(5), pp. 18-32.

It is common to vigorously address the issue/problem which would appear to get better and then, over time, the desired outcomes were not sustainable.[107]

Because polarities were treated as problems to solve, *common outcomes and patterns of behaviors* were evident in our healthcare cultures. These patterns became norms and multiple settings were facing the same critical issues as they attempted to transform healthcare. For example, each setting was working diligently to reach a "Greater Purpose" such as excellence in quality, cost containment, and safety, to name only a few. However many leaders were unaware the "Greater Purpose" required leveraging fundamental polarities, such as creating the best places to give *And* receive care, decreasing the cost of care *And* enhancing the quality of care, and assuring safety for *both* those who give *And* receive care. What becomes evident is the number of polarities that must be leveraged to actually achieve those higher purposes. A few more are highlighted on the next page.

Overview of the Key Healthcare Polarities

With the help of thousands of clinicians in over 400 rural, community, and university settings, we were able to identify common culture and practice problems and demonstrate that many were in fact the early warnings or downsides of polarities. We were able to name these common polarities. In addition, we created a framework to help us determine the priority action steps to leverage these polarities.[108,109,110]

On the next page I picked the **Reality Quote** found under each Key Healthcare Polarity listed because they are common problems or issues occurring in healthcare, and even though they correlate to one pole of a polarity, they were being treated as a problem to solve. The quotes below are really *early warning signs* or evidence of the "downside" of an <u>unidentified</u> pole being over-focused on in the setting.

The **Reality Quote** captures the settings assessment of reality and represents the first pole mentioned in its Key Healthcare Polarity. The quote will always relate to the first pole mentioned in the pairing because the first pole in each of the pairs has been, historically, the pole getting the attention or primary focus in most healthcare organizations. When an issue is seen as a problem, there are many action steps taken to solve the problem. Much was being done to support the first pole. Because these issues were not recognized as a polarity, there were no action steps being taken in the organization to simultaneously support the other pole *which explains the intensity and chronicity of the downsides of the first pole.*

The **Action Step** listed below the **Reality Quote** supports the other <u>unrecognized</u> pole (the second named pole) as it relates to the quote. This information is based on actual clinical feedback from hundreds of clinical settings across the continent.

---

[107] Wesorick, B. 2016
[108] Wesorick, B., Doebbeling, B. "Lessons from the Field: The Essential Elements for Point of Care Transformation." Medical Care, 2011, 49(12 Suppl 1), S. 49-58.
[109] Wesorick, B., Shaha, S., "Guiding healthcare transformation: a next-generation, diagnostic remediation tool for leveraging polarities." Nursing Outlook, November, December, 2015, 63(6), pp. 691-702.
[110] Wesorick B. Polarity Thinking in Healthcare: the missing logic to achieve transformation. HRD press, 2016.

The action step listed is an actual one that has been implemented in settings successfully addressing this polarity. Only one is listed, but there were others. The listed one specifically relates to the expressed reality quote.

Obviously this is not an overview of the whole complete map, but a way to bring attention to a reality that exists today; polarities are often treated as a problem to solve which explains – for those who understand polarities – the presence of chronic downsides exacerbated by the lack of action steps needed to support the other pole. I hope this approach helps you become aware of a few common polarities in healthcare and the importance of Early Warnings, Downsides, and the necessity of specific Action Steps that prevent the stated downside. There is much to understand about each of the polarities below, and specific steps are needed to assure that both poles are supported in order to reach the Greater Purpose. This is just a glimpse.[111,112]

Placing Bias in Balance Within Some Key Healthcare Polarities

Technology Platform *And* Practice Platform:

Reality Quote: *Millions of dollars have been spent on the technology without improving patient care outcomes.*

This is the result of over-focusing on the Technology Platform to the neglect of the Practice Platform.

Action Step to support the Practice Platform: Provide tools and resources to assure evidence-based delivery of each discipline's scope of practice.

Patient Safety *And* Staff Safety:

Reality Quote: *Staff complain that they don't have what they need to give safe care.*

This is the result of over-focusing on Patient Safety to the neglect of Staff Safety.

Action Step to support Staff Safety: Establish interdisciplinary partnership infrastructures to facilitate coordination of care.

Routine Task Care *And* Scope of Professional Practice:

Reality Quote: *The only thing that matters around here is how much you do and how fast you get it done before your shift ends.*

This is the result of over-focusing on Task Care to the neglect of Scope of Professional Practice.

Action Step to support the Scope of Professional Practice: Provide all disciplines access to evidence-based content that facilitates delivery of their scope of practice.

---

[111] A more complete approach is described in: Wesorick B. *Polarity Thinking in Healthcare: the missing logic to achieve transformation.* HRD press, 2016.

[112] A more complete approach is described in: Wesorick, B. "Essential steps for successful implementation of the EHR to achieve sustainable, safe, quality of care." In Moumtsoglou, A., Katrina, A. (Eds). "E-health technologies and improving patient safety." Medical Information Science Reference, 2013, pp. 27-55.

Standardized Care *And* Autonomous Care:

Reality Quote: *All we do here is cookbook medicine.*

This is the result of over-focusing on Standardized Care to the neglect of Autonomous Care.

Action Step to support Autonomous Care: Provide clinical tools designed to clarify patient/family values and uniqueness in order to individualize plan of care.

Conditional Respect *And* Unconditional Respect:

Reality Quote: *This is how we do it here.*

This is the result of over-focusing on Conditional Respect to the neglect of Unconditional Respect.

Action Step to support Unconditional Respect: The being of each person is honored, and their unique story, values, and perspectives are sought.

Vertical Relationships *And* Horizontal Relationships:

Reality Quote: *There is a failure to use the collective wisdom of the team to further the purpose and direction of the organization.*

This is the result of over-focusing on Vertical Relationship to the neglect of Horizontal Relationship.

Action Step to support the Horizontal Relationship pole: Establish interdisciplinary partnership infrastructure to tap the wisdom of the team.

Patient Satisfaction *And* Staff Satisfaction:

Reality Quote: *Morale is low, and staff do not feel valued or recognized for their contributions and expertise.*

This is the result of over-focusing on Patient Satisfaction to the neglect of Staff Satisfaction.

Action Step to support Staff Satisfaction: Engage staff in decision making that improves the environment and care processes.

Change *And* Stability:

Reality Quote: *All we do is Change and our traditional patient centered values are being lost.*

This is the result of over-focusing on Change to the neglect of Stability.

Action Step to support Stability: Provide opportunities to clarify what matters most to each member of the team related to quality care.

Medical Care *And* Whole Person Care:

Reality Quote: *Our care is becoming mechanistic, impersonal, fragmented, and dehumanized.*

This is the result of over-focusing on Medical Care to the neglect of Whole Person Care.

Action Step to support Whole Person Care: Provide resources to capture the "patient's story" based on body, mind, and spirit.

Margin *And* Mission:

Reality Quote: *Cost containment is more of a concern around here than a caring and compassionate culture.*

This is the result of over-focusing on Margin to the neglect of Mission.

Action Step to support Mission: Clarify the deep values that support the mission and assure financial support to live them.

Individual Competency *And* Integrated Competency:

Reality Quote: *There is duplication, repetition and overlapping of care/services across the interdisciplinary team which is wasting time, money, and resources.*

This is the result of over-focusing on Individual Competency to the neglect of Integrated Competency.

Action Step to support Integrated Competency: Provide tools, resources, and infrastructure to enhance coordination and integration of care across the interdisciplinary team.

In Conclusion

Over the past 30 years of engaging in the transformation at the point-of-care, there are many lessons. The simplicity of Polarity Thinking is magical, but its complexity is what assures sustainability of the greater purpose. For example, each of the Action Steps mentioned above are not simple quick fixes or checklist approaches. They require vigilance and a commitment to real change within the infrastructure, cultures, and practice. Success requires the skill of Polarity Thinking becoming embedded into the DNA of the culture, as is problem solving. This work is a priority today. We have a long way to go. To achieve this goal, it became obvious we needed to provide a tool that would help leaders know how well they are leveraging the polarities in their organization.

Measures based on interdependent pairs have not been part of evaluation processes because polarities are not a part of the established formats today. Leaders in healthcare are expected to demonstrate outcomes. Achieving outcomes is not enough, they must be sustained. Well-managed polarities lead to positive, sustainable outcomes. When you know the importance of polarities, it becomes imperative that you have a way to know if you are leveraging them well.

The metrics that address problem-solving success are insufficient for addressing whether an organization is managing or leveraging polarities well. We needed a valid and reliable tool.

The good news is Barry Johnson created the PACT™,[113] and in partnership, Wesorick carried out research in healthcare to determine its reliability and validity. The importance of the tool is that it gives real time, highly reliable assessment for strengths and limitations while visualizing the current and evolving status of organizations which saves time, money, and resources. It is a next-generation, diagnostic remediation tool for leveraging polarities. The tool removes guesswork and explains why the "find-fix approach" has failed to achieve the lasting successes healthcare is struggling to achieve.[114]

We hope this perspective and brief list of common issues, correlated to common polarities that must be leveraged in healthcare, will give you hope and direction as you leverage polarities in your organizations.

> Find bio and contact info for author Bonnie Wesorick at
> www.polaritypartnerships.com/certified-polarity-practitioners

---

[113] The Polarity Assessment™. www.polaritypartnerships.com/our-impact. 2020.
[114] Wesorick, B., Shaha, S. "Guiding healthcare transformation: a next-generation, diagnostic remediation tool for leveraging polarities." Nursing Outlook, November / December, 2015, 63(6), pp. 691-702.

Leveraging a Healthy Healing Organization (H2O) Framework Grounded in Polarity Thinking™ to Achieve Healthcare Transformation

Tracy Christopherson, PhDc, MS, BAS, RRT
Michelle Troseth, MSN, RN, FNAP, FAAN
Bonnie Wesorick, MSN, RN, DPNAP, FAAN

Introduction

Ever hear the phrase: Everything has changed and nothing has changed?

As healthcare undergoes exponential change, why is it that so many of the fundamental problems we faced 30 years ago still exist today? Why is it that we are still hearing the phrase, "culture eats strategy for lunch" – and sometimes for breakfast and dinner! – whenever leaders speak of healthcare transformation? In Chapter 20, "The Importance of Polarity Thinking™ in Healthcare," p. 149, we describe the impact of only having a problem-solving mindset or unipolar approach to addressing issues resulting in unintended consequences and unsustainable outcomes. It can also impact the overall health of the work environment that healthcare practitioners and leaders work in every day.

The quest to transform healthcare and create healthy work environments has been cited in the literature and on the lips of healthcare leaders for the past 30 years. Much of this was driven by two landmark Institute of Medicine (IOM) reports that laid out significant patient safety and quality issues: "To Err is Human: Building a Safer Health System"[115] and "Crossing the Quality Chasm: A New Health System for the 21st Century."[116] Unfortunately, large-scale sustainable healthcare transformation remains elusive despite the efforts to implement the recommendations in the reports. The purpose of this chapter is to learn from the past and to shine a light on a new National Academy of Medicine (NAM) consensus report, "Taking Action Against Burnout: A Systems Approach to Professional Well-Being."[117] The opportunity before us is to apply a polarity lens to the reoccurring issues and chronic imbalances that have now created a national crisis of clinician burnout, and a call for healthy healing work environments where clinicians can thrive.

---

[115] Institute of Medicine. *To Err Is Human: Building a Safer Health System*. The National Academies Press, 2000.
[116] Institute of Medicine. *Crossing the Quality Chasm: A New Health System for the 21st Century*. The National Academies Press, 2001.
[117] National Academies of Sciences, Engineering, and Medicine (NASEM). *Taking Action Against Clinician Burnout: A Systems Approach to Professional Well-Being*. The National Academies Press, 2019.

Clinician Burnout: A National Crisis

Clinician burnout is not new, but it has now reached a state of crisis in the U.S. healthcare system. The NAM has given a clear call that we must collectively confront the clinician burnout crisis in the U.S. health system today.

In October of 2019, the NAM released the new consensus report. The report describes burnout as a syndrome characterized by high emotional exhaustion, high depersonalization, and a low sense of personal accomplishment from work. Current research indicates between 25% to 54% of U.S. nurses and physicians have substantial symptoms of burnout with escalating suicide rates. These statistics are staggering and reveal a sad reality. The changing landscape of the U.S. healthcare system and "mounting system pressures" have created intense stress and a "chronic imbalance" of job demands and job resources resulting in this new reality. The NAM committee developed the System Model of Clinician Burnout and Professional Well-Being to articulate the system aspects of clinician burnout and well-being. The model describes the interactions between system levels and identifies the work system factors that influence burnout and professional well-being. The three levels of the system model include the external environment, healthcare organization, and frontline delivery. The model also includes individual factors such as coping strategies; social support, etc. which mitigate the effects of the system factors on clinician burnout and professional well-being. While the committee recognized that research suggests both the system and individual factors are at play, there is much more emphasis on system level interventions in their recommendations.

Naturally, we are aware of the importance of seeing and leveraging the polarity (interdependent pair) of system and individual in addressing clinician burnout. The focus of this chapter is to describe how a framework-driven approach grounded in Polarity Thinking[118] can support the development and sustainability of healthy healing organizations at the system level.

Creating and Sustaining Healthy Healing Organizations (H2O)

Clinician burnout is a problem that needs to be solved but beneath the surface of the problem many polarities are in play. The authors of the NAM (2019) consensus report recommended that organizations pursue six goals in the effort to take action against clinician burnout and create healthcare systems that support professional well-being. The first goal is to create positive work environments "that prevent and reduce burnout, foster professional well-being, and support quality care."[119] Outlined within the goal are three recommendations and numerous action steps to propel organizations forward.

---

[118] Johnson, B. *Polarity Management: Identifying and Managing Unsolvable Problems.* HRD Press, 1996.
[119] National Academies of Sciences, Engineering, and Medicine (NASEM). *Taking Action Against Clinician Burnout: A Systems Approach to Professional Well-Being.* The National Academies Press, 2019, p. 9.

Why do we recommend a framework approach? Using a framework grounded in Polarity Thinking draws attention to and makes visible the interdependent pairs or polarities at play. This enables leaders to see the whole picture, take a systems thinking approach, and make advances toward sustainable outcomes.

The H2O framework was developed based on over thirty years of experience co-creating healthy healing work cultures in rural, community, and university healthcare settings across North America. Core values, partnering relationships, dialogue, and measurement form the foundation, and eight crux polarities represent the core components of the framework. The crux polarities are aligned with the recommendations included in the NAM consensus report. Leveraging these polarities provides structure and guidance in determining the necessary actions and strategies to create a sustainable healthy healing organization. Below is a description of how the components of the H2O framework align with the recommendations in the report.

Core Values

When there is a lack of alignment between the organization values and behaviors and the clinician's values, it affects the work culture, specifically: morale, energy, hope, and care delivery.[120] As noted in the NAM report, research indicates when clinicians feel there is alignment between organization and personal values, it can result in improvements in satisfaction and engagement.[121] Providing a process to seek and hear the voice of those in the organization around what matters most and achieve alignment is essential to establishing a healthy healing organization.

Partnering Relationships

Partnering relationships between clinicians and patients/families, between members of the healthcare team, and between leaders and employees in healthcare organizations are an important component in the delivery of quality care and the development of a health healing organization. Based on the NAM report, challenging and poor interpersonal relationships in the work environment contribute to burnout. Partnering relationships have the potential to serve as a support mechanism that may help limit the effects of stress and burnout. Because of the strong history of hierarchical relationships in healthcare, infrastructures and new skills relationships are needed to develop partnering relationships.

Dialogue

Effective and meaningful communication between clinicians and patients and from clinician to clinician is an important component of quality care. The ability to engage in meaningful conversations is also a fundamental skill for leveraging polarities,

---

[120] Wesorick, B & Doebbling, B. *Lessons From the Field: The Essential Elements for Point of Care Transformation.* Medical Care, 49 (12 Suppl 1), S49-58, 2011.

[121] National Academies of Sciences, Engineering, and Medicine (NASEM). *Taking Action Against Clinician Burnout: A Systems Approach to Professional Well-Being.* The National Academies, 2019, p. 100.

establishing partnering relationships, and working in teams. Providing opportunities for individuals to improve their dialogue skills is essential to leveraging the polarities that impact a healthy healing organization.

Measurement

Recommendations from the NAM committee call for the routine evaluation of the factors that contribute to burnout in the healthcare environments. In addition, an assessment of the effectiveness of interventions and use of data to guide system strategies are also recommended. The Polarity Assessment™ enables organizations to assess and monitor the leveraging of the crux polarities in the framework.[122]

Technology Platform *And* Practice Platform Polarity

The NAM report identifies the electronic health record (EHR) as a systems factor that contributes to clinician burnout. For the past decade, there has been a significant focus on establishing, developing standards for, and implementing the EHR within healthcare environments. The technology was implemented rapidly and was not designed in a way that amply supports the clinical practice of the health professions who utilize the technology. This results in excessive documentation, additional administrative burden, poor communication, and in some cases signs of dissonance and a tone of moral distress.[123] The technology platform needs to be improved but this is not a problem to solve. Equally important is the establishment of a strong clinical practice platform. The practice platform ensures that the tools, processes, and resources are in place to support a consistent, standardized practice that is safe, efficient, and of the highest quality. If organizations do not give simultaneous attention to both the improvement of the technology platform and the establishment or advancement of a consistent practice platform, sustainable improvements in the usability of the EHR will not be achieved.

Patient Experience *And* Clinician Experience Polarity

Every healthcare organization is focused on the patient experience of care and rightfully so. Patients are at the center of the mission of each healthcare organization. Since 2008 when the Triple Aim (improving the patient experience of care, improving the health of populations, and reducing the per capita cost of healthcare) was introduced as a strategy to improve the healthcare system, there has been an emphasis on improving the patient experience. With the rise in clinician burnout it became apparent that the clinician experience and patient experience are an interdependent pair. As noted in the NAM report, research indicates clinician burnout is associated with reduced patient satisfaction. Using a Polarity Thinking approach will assist healthcare leaders in seeing, monitoring, and analyzing the effects the interdependent relationship between the patient and clinician experience more effectively.

---

[122] The Polarity Assessment™. www.polaritypartnerships.com/our-impact. 2020.
[123] McBride S, Tietze M, et al. Statewide Study to Assess Nurses' Experiences With Meaningful-Use-Based Electronic Health Records. Computers, Informatics, Nursing. 2016;32(2):pp. 18-28

Individual *And* Team Competency Polarity

The care team members, including clinicians, staff, learners, patients, and families, are at the center of NAM's system model. Teamwork is also noted as a strategy to improve the work environment and balance job demands and resources. A benefit of strengthening the competency of the team is it takes the pressure off individuals having to "know all and do all," and optimizes the workload which can relieve clinician stress and anxiety. Authors of the NAM consensus report simultaneously acknowledge the need to provide resources for the purpose of professional or personal development, which can lead to individual competency. Individual competency assures that each health professional is clear on their scope of practice (professional responsibilities) and provides care that is based on the more recent evidence or research. Balancing individual *And* team competency is a crux polarity that, when leveraged, has the potential to alleviate clinician burnout. Over-focusing on establishing teams can lead to unintended negative consequences, so applying a polarity lens to team-based care enables healthcare leaders to establish effective strategies that strengthen the competency of the clinicians and at the same time, the competency of the team.

Vertical (Hierarchy) *And* Horizontal (Partnership) Relationships Polarity

In the NAM report, the recommendations call for leaders at all levels of a healthcare organization to be held accountable for creating and maintaining a "positive, healthy work environment"[124] within the scope of their leadership responsibilities. There is also a call for a formal leadership role to lead and coordinate the efforts to create and sustain professional well-being across the organization. While the development of a healthy healing work environment requires leadership and leader accountability (vertical), it also requires a partnering relationship (horizontal) with those who work in the environment. You cannot successfully mandate or use the power that comes with a formal leadership role to create and sustain a healthy work environment. Leaders have a different perspective on the realities in the organization and need the voices and perspectives of others in the organization to see the whole picture and engage in owning the outcomes. Without the engagement and support of the clinicians in the organization, the positive outcomes of professional well-being will not be sustained.

Directive *And* Participative Decision-Making Polarity

Closely associated with the call for leaders to take accountability for healthy healing work environments and professional well-being within their organizations is the call to create and sustain a culture that provides opportunities for participative decision-making across the healthcare organization. Another of the recommendations indicates the need for leaders to evaluate the impact of their decisions on job demands and resources, quality and safety of care, and burnout among clinicians,

---

[124] National Academies of Sciences, Engineering, and Medicine (NASEM). *Taking Action Against Clinician Burnout: A Systems Approach to Professional Well-Being.* The National Academies, 2019, p. 9.

and to take corrective action when needed. Leveraging the interdependent relationship between directive *And* participative decision-making is key to implementing these recommendations. It not only can support a virtuous cycle toward sustainable outcomes, but evaluation of decisions and course correction is supported by use of the Polarity Map® and Polarity Assessment.

Margin *And* Mission Polarity

This polarity is at the heart of the work system factors that impact burnout and professional well-being. The polarity supports the recommendation to bring into alignment organizational values, incentives, compensation, and reward systems as well as the recommendation mentioned previously regarding evaluation of the impact of leadership decisions.[125] In the NAM report, it is noted that clinicians feel a disconnect between their personal or professional mission and purpose to serve, and what they experience in their work environments. Clinicians want to serve patients and families and often make choices to become employees of an organization because there is alignment between the organization mission and their personal mission. This polarity is a crux polarity that must be leveraged. There is no mission without margin and no margin without mission.

Productivity *And* Relationships Polarity

As noted previously, there are recommendations within the NAM consensus report that focus on examining clinician workload and the complexity of the work done by the clinicians to optimize it and create sustainable positive outcomes. The report also indicates the importance of facilitating and improving clinician interactions, teamwork, collaboration, and communication; all of which are supported by healthy relationships. No one person can ensure or be responsible for productivity; it takes everyone on the team who is caring for an individual. In other words, clinicians rely on the relationships they have with other members of the team and the patients and family. When productivity is over-emphasized to the neglect of relationships, it can result in disjointed processes, fragmentation, and feelings of dehumanization. Leveraging this interdependent relationship can lead to shared purpose and a sense of meaning and purpose in the work, which are important elements of professional well-being.

Task *And* Scope of Practice Polarity

Workload and the complexity of the work can have an impact on burnout. In order to optimize clinician workloads, both the tasks clinicians are accountable for and accountabilities for critical thinking and decision-making associated with the professional scope of practice must be considered. Over-emphasis on the tasks can lead to efficiency without effectiveness or quality. Focus on establishing workloads that enable clinicians to deliver services based on their full scope of practice

---

[125] National Academies of Sciences, Engineering, and Medicine (NASEM). *Taking Action Against Clinician Burnout: A Systems Approach to Professional Well-Being.* The National Academies, 2019, p. 10.

and complete tasks is essential to safe, quality care. These poles both need to be strong and simultaneous actions need to be taken to effectively optimize workloads and not compromise quality care.

Conclusion

In conclusion, the call to transform the broken U.S. healthcare system is not new. Despite recommendations from national landmark reports, we have yet to see large-scale sustainable results. One reason for the lack of positive sustainable outcomes is that the interventions were designed through a problem-oriented mindset or unipolar approach to addressing the issues.

Today we have a new problem and another call for healthcare transformation. The rate of clinician burnout is alarming and has reached national crisis. A national initiative has been launched by the NAM to engage key stakeholders and address the problem. The latest NAM consensus report provides a significant and timely opportunity to address the problems and recommendations identified with a polarity mindset. One of the key recommendations the committee made was to create positive work environments. Understanding that there are many interdependent pairs or polarities within healthcare work environments, we can apply polarity-oriented action by implementing a framework grounded in Polarity Thinking and measuring the impact. In summary, the Healthy Healing Organization (H2O) framework was introduced and we reveal how its components are aligned to the NAM report including the major crux polarities to be leveraged.

> You can find more detail and discussion on the crux polarities within the H2O Framework on Healthcare's MissingLogic at www.missinglogic.com/podcast or on Apple Podcast or iTunes® and in Polarity Thinking in Healthcare: The Missing Logic to Achieve Transformation.[126]

> Find bio and contact info for author Bonnie Wesorick at www.polaritypartnerships.com/certified-polarity-practitioners

---

[126] Wesorick B. *Polarity Thinking in Healthcare: The Missing Logic to Achieve Transformation.* HRD Press, 2016.

Applying Polarity Principles for a Healthcare IT Start-Up

Petra Platzer, PhD, NBC-HWC, PCC
Cliff Kayser, MSHR, MSOD, PCC
Dave Levin, MD

Can polarity principles be successfully applied at a smaller scale and in highly dynamic environments? Chapter 38, "Polarity-Based Inquiry," p. 289, examines polarity-based inquiry at a large department of United States government. This chapter will explore how a small, healthcare IT start-up deliberately adopted and used Polarity Thinking™.[127]

The Milieu

The healthcare system in the U.S. has been undergoing significant change as a result of many factors including new reimbursement models, consumerism, and adoption of information technology. And, healthcare is a complex, fragmented, and highly regulated industry that can be resistant to change. In other words, healthcare is subject to a polarity between the need to change *And* the desire for stability.

Newly formed companies or "startups" typically face a number of challenges. They have limited resources on the journey to become profitable and self-sustaining. Statistically, the majority of new companies fail, often within the first year of operation.

A Deliberate Choice

Given the combined challenges of startups and healthcare, succeeding as a new company in healthcare can be particularly difficult. The founders of a new, healthcare IT startup which we will call "NewCo" recognized this and made a deliberate choice to focus on culture as a key strategy from the beginning. NewCo's founders had experienced the negative effects of companies that neglect culture, to the point of toxicity. They explicitly started the company to *both* catalyze innovation in health IT *And* create a healthy, sustaining workplace. Their early mantra was "build a great company and a great place to work."

While some might see investing in culture work as a distraction from "getting the real work done," the NewCo founders believed that this was the right thing to do and would confer strategic advantages. They envisioned a culture that would maximize the potential of individuals *And* teams, allowing them to recruit and retain high-caliber talent and thus, lead to sustainable high performance.

---

[127] Johnson, Barry. *And: Making a Difference by Leveraging Polarity, Paradox or Dilemma. Volume One – Foundations.* HRD Press, 2020.

Knowing What You Know and What You Don't Know

Once the choice was made to make building culture a key, the founders faced the initial challenge of how to go about this. They had prior experiences in organizations which talked about the importance of culture but failed to "walk the talk," or were widely perceived as a waste of time or counterproductive.

They knew that culture could be a powerful driver of success and recognized, as one founder said, "We have no idea how to do this." They also realized that as healthcare and IT professionals they had a natural bias toward data, science, and engineering. "Soft" approaches wouldn't cut it in such an environment. A successful approach would require a proven methodology for *both* measuring *And* managing culture.

In retrospect, these early insights about what they knew and didn't know proved to be profound. They knew culture could be a powerful lever for success broadly defined. They knew that their current culture required a somewhat rigorous, data-based approach. And they knew they did not have the experience or tools to succeed on their own. This led to the conclusion that they would have to seek outside help. Time and money are precious resources for a startup, so the decision to invest in building culture in this way was not taken lightly.

Getting Started

NewCo's founders took several initial solid steps. They talked explicitly and regularly about their belief in the importance of culture and their twin goals to *both* build a successful company *And* be a great place to work. They established the NewCo Culture Team (NCT) with diverse representation and committed executive sponsorship. The NCT would fill the role of guiding culture development: "We don't do the work; we work on how NewCo does the work." To address the gap in their own knowledge and experience, they engaged a consulting firm that promised to bring proven, measurable approaches to culture management.

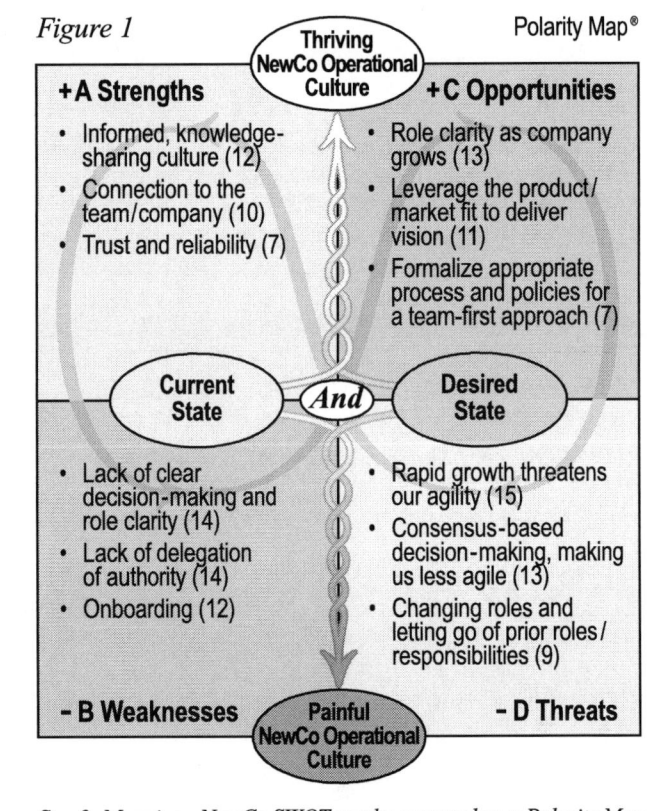

Figure 1 — Polarity Map®

Thriving NewCo Operational Culture

+A Strengths
- Informed, knowledge-sharing culture (12)
- Connection to the team/company (10)
- Trust and reliability (7)

+C Opportunities
- Role clarity as company grows (13)
- Leverage the product/market fit to deliver vision (11)
- Formalize appropriate process and policies for a team-first approach (7)

Current State *And* Desired State

−B Weaknesses
- Lack of clear decision-making and role clarity (14)
- Lack of delegation of authority (14)
- Onboarding (12)

−D Threats
- Rapid growth threatens our agility (15)
- Consensus-based decision-making, making us less agile (13)
- Changing roles and letting go of prior roles/responsibilities (9)

Painful NewCo Operational Culture

Step 2: Mapping—NewCo SWOT results captured on a Polarity Map

NCT's first steps were to assess the current status and discern where to go next. They began with a SWOT analysis. Surveyed employees chose items from lists of potential Strengths, Weaknesses, Opportunities, and Threats. The goal was to see if there was consensus on Current State *And* Desired State (*Figure 1*), and the potential high-leverage actions for both.

From SWOT to Polarity

Guided by experienced consultants,[128] the NCT came to understand that many of the key findings of the SWOT represented tensions between things that exist in a balance. In short, they began to see the polarities in their SWOT analysis. *Figure 1* on the previous page shows the SWOT results captured on a Polarity Map®.

Introducing Polarity Thinking proved over time to have multiple benefits. It provided a gateway into seeing things differently and to leveraging polarity mapping as a powerful exercise in understanding current state *And* planning for the future. A key pivot was transforming the learnings from the SWOT into a set of polarity mapping exercises. This approach built upon and extended the existing SWOT efforts and introduced and reinforced the basic concept of Polarity Thinking within NewCo. It provided a structured way to measure key aspects of NewCo's culture and to identify areas for increased focus that were critical within the NewCo environment.

In the 5-Step SMALL Process™ (Seeing, Mapping, Assessing, Learning, and Leveraging), the first steps (Seeing, Mapping), followed the original SWOT analysis. The NCT selected three Polarity Maps (Figure 2) for a company-wide survey.

Figure 2: NewCo's Three Polarity Maps

Polarity Map	Purpose	Value to NewCo
NewCo *And* Customer	Strong Organization-Customer Partnership	We are a tech-enabled services company that believes in the power of partnering and collaboration with our customers. We seek to balance serving their needs with ensuring NewCo operates efficiently and effectively.
Continuity *And* Transformation	Enduring Success	We are an agile startup that needs to preserve our core values and the things that "work" while also continuously experimenting, evolving and discarding things that no longer serve us well.
Individual *And* Team	Peak Experience and Performance	We believe peak performance comes from a balanced approach to empowering individuals and rewarding them for initiative and risk-taking while also promoting teamwork.

---

[128] SixSEED Partners. www.sixseedpartners.com.

Substantial effort was invested in customizing the question items in the off-the-shelf Polarity Maps. This process supported matching the specifics of NewCo's language and context, and provided a "container" to surface important dialogue within the NCT. The purpose and value of the selected maps was shared as part of the company-wide survey process.

Using this customized Polarity Assessment™,[129] (step three: Assessing) provided high survey participation and responses that validated the polarities selected by the NCT. The summary results (*Figure 3*) provided guidance on where to focus in the next stage of culture work and served as a baseline to measure future progress over time.

*Figure 3: NewCo Polarity Assessment, Summary Results**

Individual And Team	Continuity And Transformation	NewCo And Customer
79	64	57

Detailed results for each Polarity Map omitted for confidentiality.

Leveraging Polarity Assessment Findings

In step four (Learning), the NCT further explored the Assessment results to identify and prioritize actions to maximize the upsides and minimize the downsides of each pole. Common themes emerged, including the need for greater clarity of roles and responsibilities, a desire and need for connecting and collaborating across a diverse and scattered workforce, and more effective group problem-solving. These high-leverage actions (step five: Leveraging) became part of a specific set of follow-up activities and projects chartered with support and guidance from the culture consultants. Key action steps leveraged techniques such as the Thinking Environment (TE),[130] the Team Work Cycle (TWC),[131] and Conversational Intelligence® (CiQ®).[132]

The NCT anticipated that an "adopt, model, and spread" approach was most likely to succeed within the technically-minded NewCo. Working with their consultants, the NCT therefore "went first" and adopted this new set of meeting techniques: TE, TWC and CiQ. Practicing within NCT meetings provided a safe starting point for early adoption and validated the power of the specific techniques. Formally

---

[129] The Polarity Assessment™. www.polaritypartnerships.com/our-impact. 2020.
[130] Kline, Nancy. Adapted from :*Time to Think: Listening to Ignite the Human Mind.* London Cassell III. 2016.
[131] Mumma, F. EdD. *Team-Work & Team-Roles: What makes your team tic?*, 3rd Ed,. HRDQ. 1992.
[132] Glaser, Judith E. *Conversational Intelligence: How Great Leaders Build Trust and Get Extraordinary Results.* Bibliomotion, Inc. 2014.

piloting and integrating this action step enhanced the ability of a team to think creatively together, drawing out the best each individual had to offer, creating greater buy-in, and leading to more efficient and effective decision making. Incorporating the Team Work Cycle was an Action Step to make explicit the usually sequential phases of a work cycle: Initiation, Ideation, Elaboration, and Completion. This helped take advantage of each person's strength or style preference and raise awareness of the roles each person plays in each phase and overall task. Lastly, Conversational Intelligence® was introduced to improve awareness of three key types of conversations and practices that would assist to improve trust, integrity, empathy, and good judgement.

Buoyed by this internal success, it was time to begin to spread by engaging others at NewCo. After careful deliberation, the NewCo marketing team was recruited to test this approach as several members of the marketing team were members of the NCT.

Watching this experiment unfold was instructional. Initial reaction to the experience was mixed, with some of the marketing team openly voicing skepticism that this approach "feels weird" and they were "not sure this will make us more productive." Interestingly, over a period of weeks, as the team practiced, discussed the results and became more agile, this new meeting approach became their "new normal."

This one action step – adopting a new meeting structure – which came from focusing on the individual *And* team polarity, began to organically spread throughout other areas of NewCo. The NCT termed this new meeting structure a Creative Thinking Environment (CTE). A pivotal moment came when NewCo's Executive team recognized it was "stuck" and wanted to do things differently. Their strategic discussions were dominated by a few members leading others to feel bored, frustrated, or disengaged. This provided a logical opening to introduce the same action step of CTE to them. The "adopt, model, and spread" approach really paid off at this time since several members of the leadership group were involved in the NCT and/or the marketing team. The VP of Marketing was able to provide testimony about the value of CTE and some commentary on how his team initially responded. The executive team agreed to a trial and over a period of weeks, also became proponents of these techniques.

When recently asked, after a particularly important strategic discussion, if using the CTE format was impactful in knowing that all thoughts would be heard to improve their strategic capabilities, one leader responded, "TOTALLY agree. That was my immediate thought upon seeing the draft proposal circulated. [With CTE format], I had the confidence that I would get to say my point during my turn and I didn't have to get all 'Lord of the Flies' to get my idea out and jammed down folk's throats."

Seeing the Polarities Around Us

Introducing the idea of polarities has proven relatively straightforward. Within NewCo, those introductory conversations often sound like this:

> *Many things in life and in our work exist in balance with each other. It's not that one is good and the other is bad. Take breathing for example. Is*

inhaling better than exhaling? No. They both have upsides and downsides. What's important is that they are in balance and that we see them both.

Once people grasp this basic idea, they begin to see polarities all around them. Powerful insights occur when someone calls out a polarity or alludes to "Polarity Thinking" in the midst of discussion and debate. In a recent example, a group had gathered to discuss one customer's "excessive" technical support needs. There was an initial airing of concerns that mostly focused on what the customer was "doing wrong." Then a member suggested that this was a polarity between the needs of the customer and those of NewCo. The dynamic of the conversation quickly shifted as members began to identify NewCo's contributions to the situation.

The Power of "*And*": Defusing Tension, Changing Viewpoints, and Creating Buy-in

Embracing Polarity Thinking helps groups avoid the "Tyranny of *Or*" by supplementing "*Or*" with "*And*." This shift in thinking alone can have significant impact. The NewCo leadership team experienced this at a particularly crucial time while dealing with an important, emotionally charged issue.

NewCo had merged with a similar size and stage company and the newly combined leadership team was working through a series of critical issues. Near the top of that list was expectations for how work would be done. Pre-merger, one company had embraced a combination of a central office and some flexibility to work remotely. The other company had operated as a purely remote, virtual workforce. Flexibility and the option to work remotely were highly prized by some, while others felt coming to an office was critical to team building and efficiency. Initial discussions about how to proceed were framed as an *either/Or* and quickly became tense and emotionally laden.

The turning point came when Polarity Thinking was introduced to this group. They agreed to go through a polarity mapping exercise based on the assumption that office-based *And* remote work *both* have potential good and bad aspects, that they could exist in tension, and that the goal was to maximize the best of both for the Greater Purpose Statement of "Efficient and Effective Work Environment." This exercise was facilitated by a member of the executive team who had been exposed to the basics of polarity mapping via his work in the NCT. The group began by mapping out the upsides and downsides of each pole. The clear shift for the group came when one executive, who a week before had been adamant about remote work-only, leapt up, went to the map, and began to add items to the "upside" of having an office. Tension and emotion were drained away as the team focused on reaching consensus about actions that would maximize the upside and minimize the downside of both poles. Seeing the tension from an *And* (not just *Or*) perspective and working through it by seeing and mapping led to the NCT being asked to work on a set of activities designed to improve situational awareness, communication, and engagement across a distributed, semi-virtual workforce.

Pitfalls and Challenges

Polarity principles have proven to be powerful tools in NewCo's journey to build a great company. Unsurprisingly, it has not always been easy or consistently successful.

Startups – and other dynamic companies – are subject to constant challenges, change, and constraints on resources. An abundance of performance-oriented, high achievers face enormous pressure to "get stuff done." Working on culture as described here exists in tension with that pressure. There is great temptation to just "get on with the work," making it easy to discount the value of culture building efforts. This has required constant attention and reminders about the power of "going slow to go fast," bolstered by examples of concrete payoffs for NewCo and employees.

The general principles of Polarity Thinking are not particularly difficult to grasp. However, in practice, the tools and practices are rich, deep, and subtle. Most find it takes multiple exposures over time to begin to grasp the details. The initial complexity can be overwhelming. Having a good guide and patience are essential.

Polarity principles are not a substitute for change management. There's no getting around the basic principles and hard work of leading and managing change in an organization. As illustrated by the anecdotes above, careful attention must be paid to how an organization will adopt, model, spread, and embed polarity principles and the associated activities they generate.

Conclusion

So, can polarity principles be successfully applied at a smaller scale and in highly dynamic environments? As evidenced by NewCo's experience, they most certainly can. An intentional focus on building culture by leveraging polarities has played a key role in NewCo's successful growth, from a few co-founders with an idea to a company with 45 employees, while weathering many storms – including successfully merging with another company. The work continues as additional polarities are recognized and new opportunities to maximize the upsides are identified.

Find bio and contact info for author Cliff Kayser at
www.polaritypartnerships.com/certified-polarity-practitioners

Applying Polarity Thinking™ to Increase Healthcare Leadership Capacity

Joy Goldman, MS, PCC
Petra Platzer, PhD, NBC-HWC, PCC
Cliff Kayser, MSHR, MSOD, PCC

Healthcare Leadership's Capacity

Coaching within healthcare, particularly for physicians, has become more common and accepted since Atul Gawande, MD, published his article in the New Yorker.[133] His TED talk, "Want to get great at something? Get a coach!", has had over three million views.[134] Dr. Gawande "normalized" having a coach as a way to improve his competency as a surgeon. The goal of this kind of coaching was not to upgrade *technical* competence, but to enhance *thinking* competence as a way to improve performance. For example, Dr. Gawande noticed that to improve the performance of a procedure, he had to consider additional perspectives to his when he considered draping the patient. In order to better his outcomes, he learned the competence he was missing – to look at the whole system.

This chapter will share several examples of how applying the polarity framework became an essential tool, used by one healthcare system's leadership, to increase their capacity to manage complex and rapidly changing dynamics, at multiple levels.

One System's Leadership Landscape

A forward-thinking, eight hospital, and 1,500 provider-integrated health system, and their board, recognized that their CEO and several additional senior level, Vice President roles were planning to retire in the upcoming three to five years. While this rate of transition is not uncommon, the system is notable in their foresight to invest in developing their internal, high-potential leaders as possible successors.

Our coaching consultancy was initially approached for "succession planning" over a four-year engagement. In partnering with the system's Chief Human Resources Officer, Chief Executive Officer, Chief Operating Officer, and a Senior Vice-President, we co-designed a process to *both* challenge *and* support seven identified physician and administrative leaders to learn, think, and act at the "next level." In the early discovery and design phase, it also became apparent that for the leadership capacity of these high-potential (HiPo) leaders to elevate, we also needed to increase the systemic thinking capacity with the four executive sponsors.

---

[133] Gawande, Atul MD. "The Coach in the Operating Room." The New Yorker, October 3, 2011.
[134] Gawande, Atul MD. "Want to get great at something? Get a Coach!" TED, 2017.

Introducing Polarity Thinking™ at the Individual Level

A notable asset with this system was learning that the CEO was an avid proponent of Barry Johnson's Polarity Thinking work.[135] And, despite the CEO's previous advocacy for the polarity framework, the practice had not yet penetrated throughout the leadership tiers. Our team therefore designed a process to introduce Polarity Thinking at multiple levels and in multiple phases to seed a common language and thinking approach throughout the organization.

At the individual leader level, we began by using a Polarity Map® to organize and document the results of feedback from interviews of subordinates, peers, and supervisors. Using the poles of Continuity *And* Transformation was an effective visual for clients to see the larger context: the benefits of their leadership strengths, the risk of overusing those strengths, and what might be getting in the way of leveraging their less preferred pole.

Figure 1 on the following page is an example of organizing the wisdom generated from a leader's 360-degree assessment interview, using a Polarity Map. The polarity framework was then used in service to each leaders' developmental goals by defining high-leverage actions for the upper quadrants of each pole, as well as increasing awareness for signs of dipping too long into the downsides of either pole. This resulted in each having a broader perspective, including how to leverage current capacities and see opportunities for leadership growth. The visual learning and leveraging of their developmental strengths and opportunities increased their agility and their capacity to lead themselves and others.

Integrating Polarity Thinking at the Team Level

Polarities are based on interdependencies, which provided us a natural next step for these leaders to be open to sharing their own Polarity Maps with each other, thus navigating another key polarity – Individual *And* Team. While the system originally wanted to keep this HiPo group of leaders in separate developmental paths, our team continued to express the benefits of them learning and growing together as a cohort, which was then embraced. As the leaders began to share and explore this Polarity Thinking approach with each other, they gained greater appreciation and trust for their cohort peers who had complementary strengths and opportunities. We continued to support these leaders and their leadership capacities to work with their teams, explicitly leveraging Polarity Thinking, to focus on the necessity of leveraging the "what" of the work (tasks) with the "how" of the work (relationships). This polarity is nicely modeled in the Leadership Circle Profile,[136] which was also administered to the HiPo leaders in year two of the multi-year engagement. Together, this Task *And* Relationship framing helped these leaders shift their perspectives from reactive tendencies toward more creative leadership competencies.

---

[135] Johnson, Barry. *And: Making a Difference by Leveraging Polarity, Paradox or Dilemma. Volume One – Foundations.* HRD Press, 2020.

[136] Anderson, Bob. www.leadershipcircle.com/en/products/leadership-circle-profile. Accessed July, 2020.

Figure 1   Polarity Map®

Effective Leverage of Team

+A Values

Leader's Strengths
- Vision
- Leads-by-example
- Navigates obstacles and sees things through
- Good listener
- Communicates well, written and verbal
- Adaptive to audience

+C Values

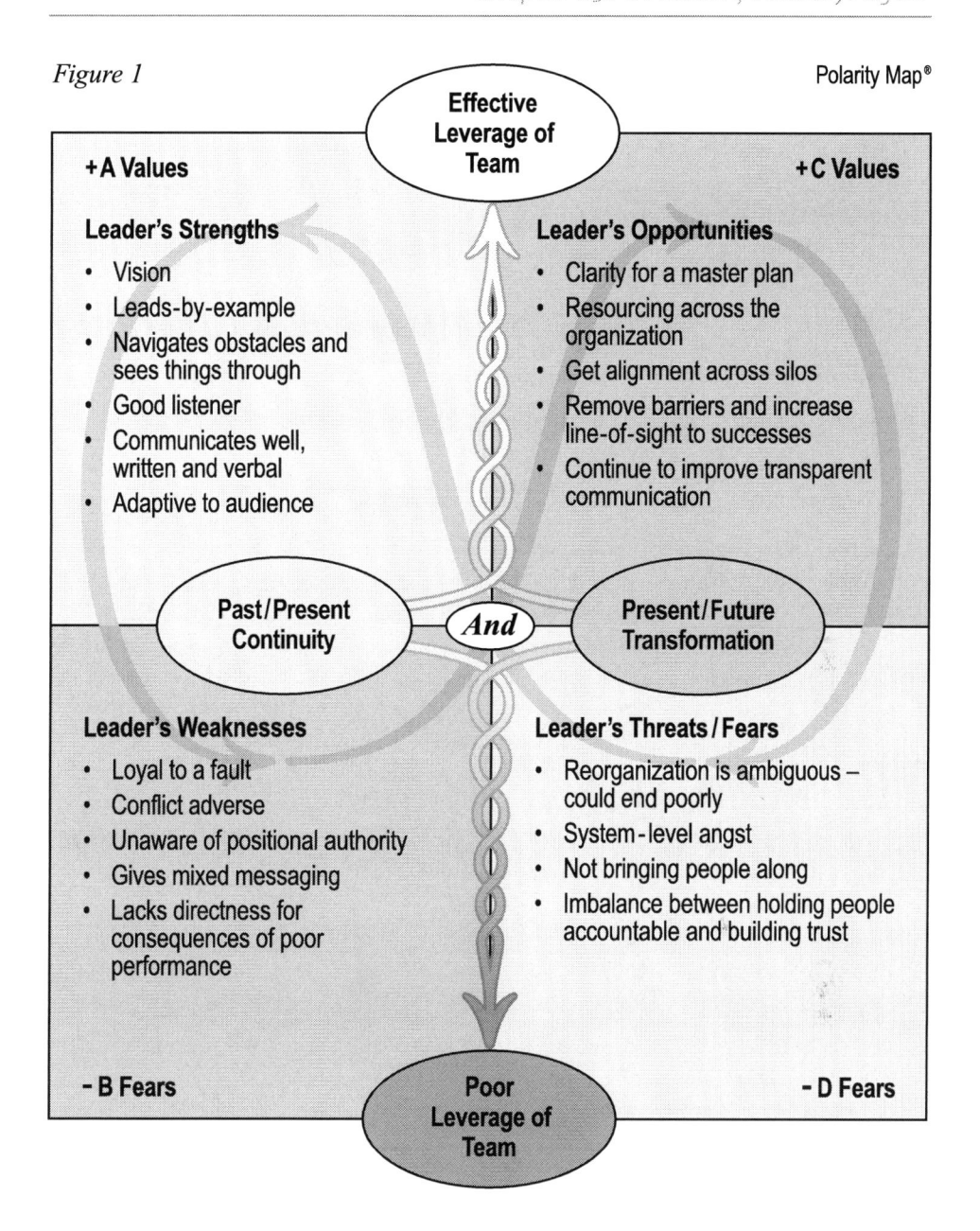

Leader's Opportunities
- Clarity for a master plan
- Resourcing across the organization
- Get alignment across silos
- Remove barriers and increase line-of-sight to successes
- Continue to improve transparent communication

Past/Present Continuity   *And*   **Present/Future Transformation**

Leader's Weaknesses
- Loyal to a fault
- Conflict adverse
- Unaware of positional authority
- Gives mixed messaging
- Lacks directness for consequences of poor performance

Leader's Threats/Fears
- Reorganization is ambiguous – could end poorly
- System-level angst
- Not bringing people along
- Imbalance between holding people accountable and building trust

−B Fears   **Poor Leverage of Team**   **−D Fears**

Having integrated the foundations of Polarity Thinking with the leader and their teams, clients reported doing less judging of others' behavior as "bad/frustrating" and appreciating more the differences and necessity for including different styles and strengths. Leaders also shared that their team meetings were more productive due to members being able to speak into possible tensions on topics by identifying potential polarities at play.

Leveraging Systemness Using Polarity Mapping

With the Polarity Thinking efforts and additional work integrating across these leaders and their teams, the resulting trust within the system allowed us to expand the polarity framework to measure systemic challenges. Working with the sponsor group and tapping into our team's systemic knowledge – gleaned during the two years of work with the HiPo cohort – we identified four critical polarity tensions, or interdependent pairs, for the system (*Figure 2*).

Figure 2

Mission	*And*	Margin
Tactical	*And*	Strategic
Centralized	*And*	Decentralized
Continuity	*And*	Transformation

The sponsors and HiPo leaders unanimously agreed these tensions were consistently causing inefficient and frustrating rework. The seesaw-like dysfunctional patterns were playing out throughout the system in the noticeable flips from one pole to another as a "solution." Using the 5-step SMALL Process™ (Seeing, Mapping, Assessing, Learning, Leveraging), we created a Polarity Assessment™,[137] to measure how well these four polarity pairs were being leveraged by the individual HiPo leaders, their respective areas, and the entire system. The two polarities providing the greatest opportunity for impact for their systemic challenges were: Centralization *And* Decentralization, and Continuity *And* Transformation. A benchmark measurement of performance helped maintain focus on action strategies in anticipation of conducting a follow-up Polarity Assessment at a future point.

Increasing Overall Leadership Capacity with Polarity Thinking

From our experience, applying Polarity Thinking to increase capacity must go beyond creating awareness. The application process takes time and practice. As capability to apply tools and skills increases, the system's capacity to address system complexity follows. Our design began with the individual leaders applying Polarity Thinking for themselves, then broadening its use to their teams, and expanding into systems level applications.

As one method to measure progress in their leadership capacity during this multi-year process, our team and the sponsors co-designed a six-week strategic simulation. The HiPo leaders were presented with an actual strategic challenge for the organization which included issues such as competitive pressures within their geographic region, possible merger and acquisition, and reengineering their existing organizational structure to drive strategic change. The HiPo leaders, who rarely worked together, were intentionally paired based on their differing styles and given limited time to mimic the real-world pressures that exist in their dynamic, rapidly changing healthcare landscape. The HiPo leader teams prepared a presentation to a mock board, consisting of the executive sponsors, and received feedback from the mock board, our team, and the entire HiPo cohort.

---

[137] The Polarity Assessment™. www.polaritypartnerships.com/our-impact. 2020.

We witnessed the HiPo leaders use the polarity framework as a key thinking approach during this simulation. Several teams created their own Polarity Maps that acknowledged and identified elements within tensions. *Figure 3* is an example of one such map that focuses on Localized *And* Centralized, with identified Values (+A, +C) and Fears (-B, -D), surrounding how to sustain a competitive market advantage (GPS) or result in unsustainable operations as a system (DF). The leaders were challenged on their strategic and systemic thinking as well as their executive presence and received feedback – and self-confidence – on how far they had progressed in their leadership capacity.

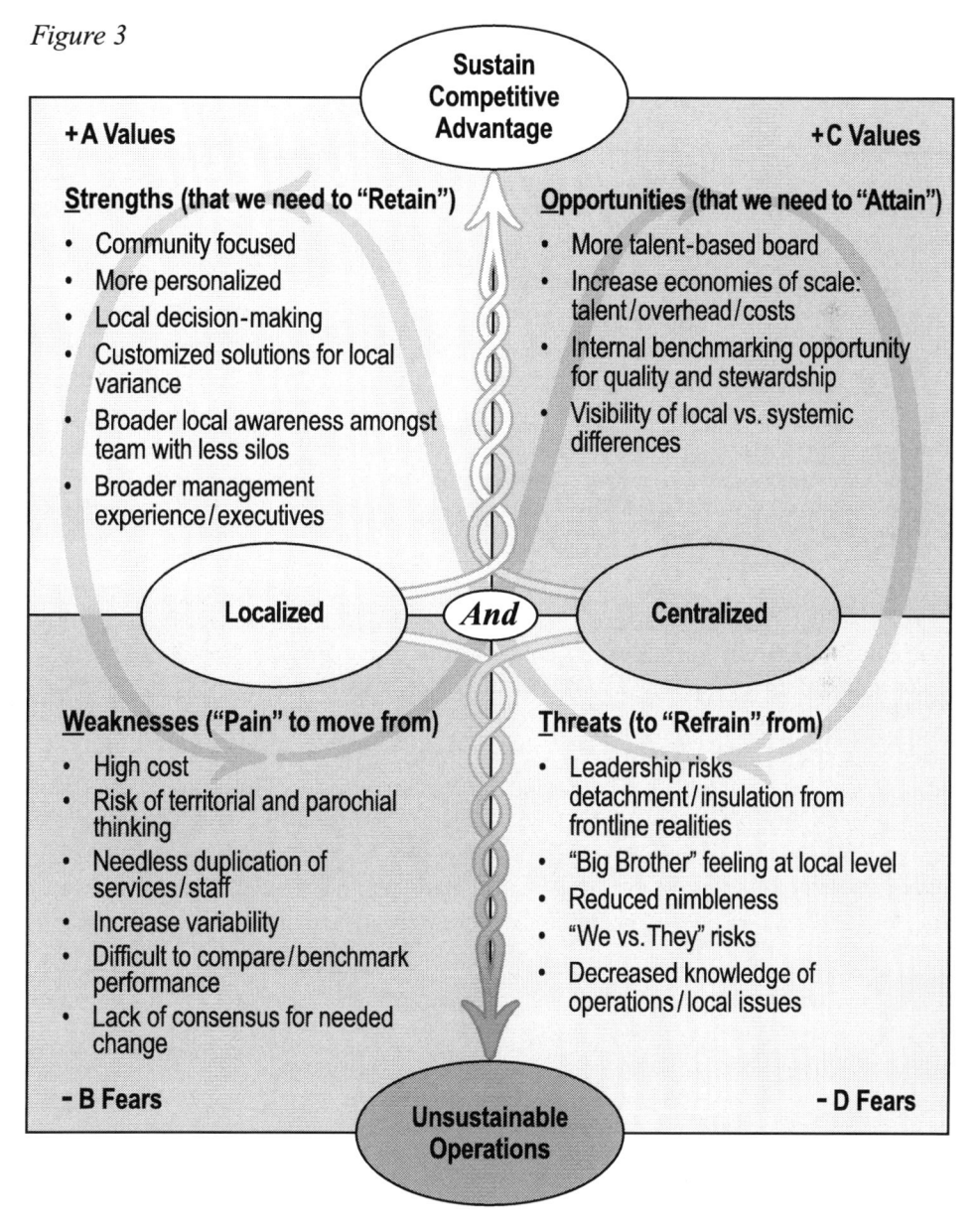

Figure 3

Sustain Competitive Advantage

+A Values

Strengths (that we need to "Retain")
- Community focused
- More personalized
- Local decision-making
- Customized solutions for local variance
- Broader local awareness amongst team with less silos
- Broader management experience/executives

Localized *And* **Centralized**

+C Values

Opportunities (that we need to "Attain")
- More talent-based board
- Increase economies of scale: talent/overhead/costs
- Internal benchmarking opportunity for quality and stewardship
- Visibility of local vs. systemic differences

Weaknesses ("Pain" to move from)
- High cost
- Risk of territorial and parochial thinking
- Needless duplication of services/staff
- Increase variability
- Difficult to compare/benchmark performance
- Lack of consensus for needed change

Threats (to "Refrain" from)
- Leadership risks detachment/insulation from frontline realities
- "Big Brother" feeling at local level
- Reduced nimbleness
- "We vs. They" risks
- Decreased knowledge of operations/local issues

- B Fears

- D Fears

Unsustainable Operations

Applying Polarity Thinking also increased the capacity for these HiPo leaders and the sponsors to navigate the earlier-than-planned retirement of the CEO, integration of a new external CEO, and a merger with another health system. We also pay tribute to the insight of these leaders who foretold the new CEO's emphasis on Regionalization *And* Systemness.

Amidst the system hiring an external CEO, several of these HiPo leaders have also gone on to assume larger roles within the organization, demonstrating their success in developing a higher degree of strategic and systemic thinking. To this day, they speak of the impact Polarity Thinking and mapping has had on their integrating "*either/Or*" problem-oriented thinking with the "*both/And*" systemic thinking required to thrive in this complex world.

Based on the noticeable impact of the work cited above, this system decided to cascade the learning to their nursing and physician leadership academies. Bringing the two audiences together was novel for them and proved to be positive in many ways. The leaders were challenged with the real work need of implementing a reduction in force. Close to 100 nursing and physician leaders mapped out the tension of implementing *challenging* strategies (holding people to performance standards) with *support* strategies (providing empathy and compassion) as seen in *Figure 4*. They were able to visually see their need to demonstrate *both* Courageously Challenging their staff *And* Supporting them as they adjusted to the loss of jobs. In addition, as the leaders physically stood in their observed preferences, they were able to have powerful dialogues around a culture that preferred relationships to some neglect of accountability/challenge. This allowed the leaders to leave the room with a shared perspective of the role they needed to play in elevating individual, team, and organizational performance.

Conclusion

We have described the use of the polarity framework and Polarity Thinking as an essential and impactful way to elevate the overall leadership capacity of healthcare leaders, their teams, and the overall system. Not only has Polarity Thinking helped leaders better manage complexity, it has helped lessen wasted energy that can contribute to unnecessary conflict and burnout. Polarity Thinking supplements traditional black and white, *either/Or*-thinking and problem-solving with capability for *both/And*-thinking and leveraging polarities. By applying both thinking competencies where and when they are needed, healthcare leaders can begin to see the larger system in operation and implement strategies to create sustainable results.

Figure 4

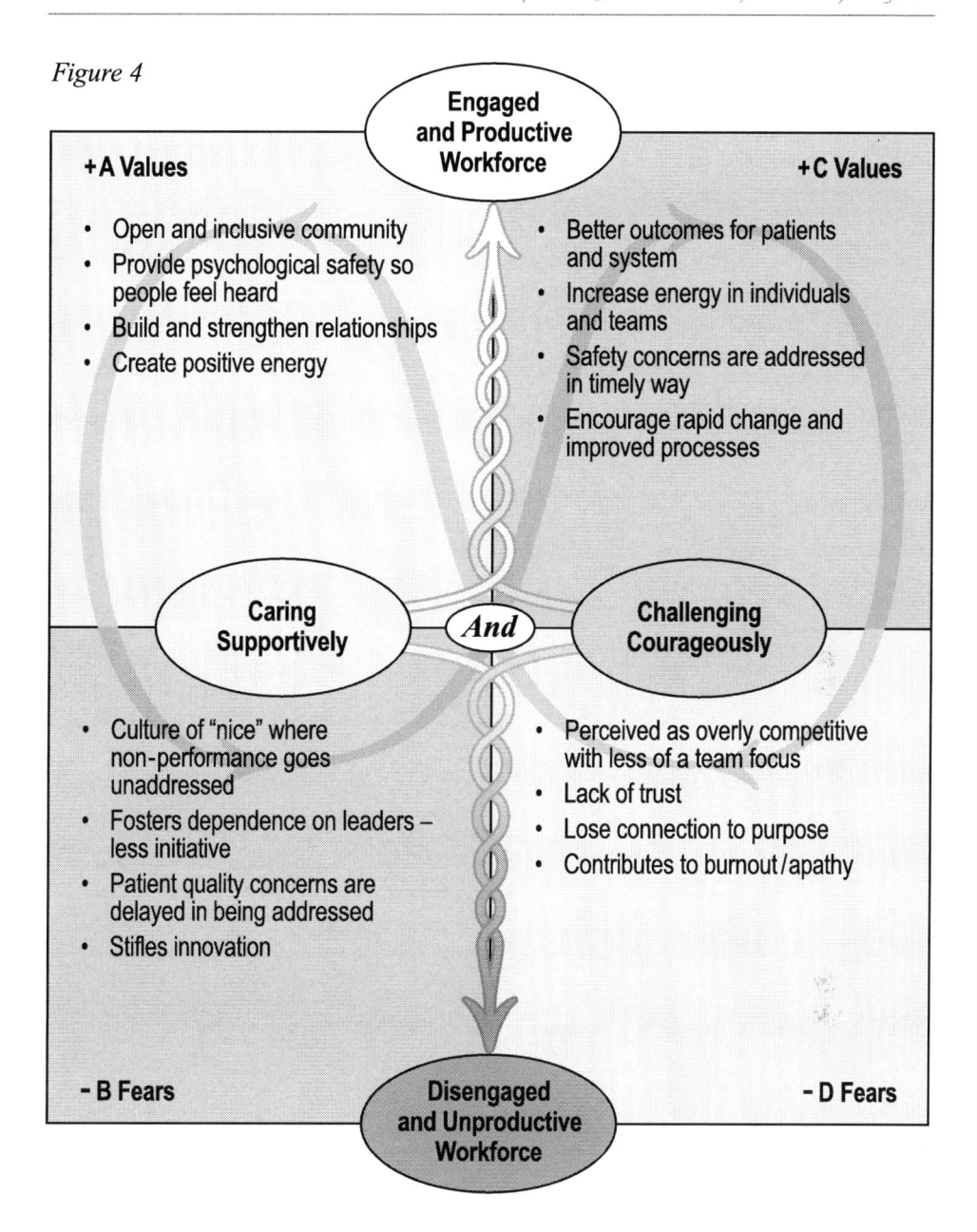

```
                    ┌─────────────┐
                    │  Engaged    │
                    │and Productive│
                    │  Workforce  │
                    └─────────────┘
+A Values                                              +C Values

• Open and inclusive community          • Better outcomes for patients
• Provide psychological safety so         and system
  people feel heard                     • Increase energy in individuals
• Build and strengthen relationships      and teams
• Create positive energy                • Safety concerns are addressed
                                          in timely way
                                        • Encourage rapid change and
                                          improved processes

        ┌──────────────┐                    ┌──────────────┐
        │    Caring    │      And           │  Challenging │
        │ Supportively │                    │ Courageously │
        └──────────────┘                    └──────────────┘

• Culture of "nice" where               • Perceived as overly competitive
  non-performance goes                    with less of a team focus
  unaddressed                           • Lack of trust
• Fosters dependence on leaders –       • Lose connection to purpose
  less initiative                       • Contributes to burnout/apathy
• Patient quality concerns are
  delayed in being addressed
• Stifles innovation


– B Fears           ┌─────────────┐              – D Fears
                    │ Disengaged  │
                    │and Unproductive│
                    │  Workforce  │
                    └─────────────┘
```

Find bio and contact info for author Cliff Kayser at
www.polaritypartnerships.com/certified-polarity-practitioners

Post-COVID-19 Planning for Sustained Benefit of Transition to Distant Learning Using PACT™

Cliff Kayser, MSHR, MSOD, PCC
Samar A. Ahmed, Msc, MD, MHPE
Mohamed H. Shehata, Msc, MD, MHPE
Mohammed A. Hassanien, Msc, MD, MHPE
Hany Waheeb, Msc, MD
Nagwa Hegazy, Msc, MD, DHPE
Noha Elrafie, Msc
Abdulmonem A. Al-Hayani, PhD
Sherif A. El Saadany, Msc, MD
Abdulrahman O. Al-Youbi, PhD

Background and Introduction

The COVID-19 pandemic forced colleges and universities globally to make shifts from traditional learning modalities that relied heavily or even exclusively on face-to-face (FF) to new and unfamiliar distance learning (DL) modalities.[138] This chapter describes how a medical education and training organization (ASU MENA FRI[139]) used the PACT™ (Polarity Approach for Continuity and Transformation) process to facilitate rapid response and planning in the early weeks of April, 2020.[140] A more detailed account of the process and outcomes described herein may be found in our qualitative study.[141]

Step 1: Seeing

In this step, key stakeholders examined the challenges and opportunities. In the process, they paid particular attention to the thinking and mindset distinction related to solving *"Or"* problems and leveraging *"And"* polarities. Development and training programs at ASU MENA FRI had previously exposed leaders to Polarity Thinking™, polarity mapping, and PACT. This enabled leaders to more rapidly

---

[138] ASU-MENA-FRI. "ASU-MENA-FRI Health Professions Education YouTube Channel." www.youtube.com/channel/UCF53wrxV2XWv8g8qkr06ntg. Accessed March 29, 2020.

[139] ASU MENA FRI refers to Ain Shams University Middle East North Africa FAIMER Regional Institute. FAIMER refers to the Foundation for the Advancement of Medical Education and Research.

[140] Samar A. Ahmed, Nagwa Nashat Hegazy, Hany W. Abdel Malak, et al. "Model for Utilizing Distance Learning post COVID-19 using (PACT)™ A Cross Sectional Qualitative Study", May 28, 2020. PREPRINT (Version 1) available at Research Square https://doi.org/10.21203/rs.3.rs-31027/v1

[141] Amin, H., Shehata, M., and Ahmed, S., 2020. "Step-by-step Guide to Create Competency-Based Assignments as an Alternative for Traditional Summative Assessment ", *MedEdPublish*, 9, [1], 120, https://doi.org/10.15694/mep.2020.000120.1

apply PACT in real-time as they responded to the real-world needs they were facing. In this particular case, by viewing FF and DL as a polarity, they could plan and respond effectively by seeing the benefits, over time, of both FF and DL. PACT helped key stakeholders in the rapid DL shift that incorporated contextual strategies to maintain as many of the unique benefits provided by FF as possible.

Step 2: Mapping

A group of 79 faculty and medical education leaders from 19 countries (mainly in the Middle East) convened for a facilitated session using the Zoom videoconference platform. This group included those who brought perspectives from different levels in the chain of command, 30% of whom were decision makers and the remainder active educators in schools of health professions. The first part of the meeting involved a short introduction to Polarity Thinking for participants who had not previously been exposed to Polarity Thinking and PACT.[142] Core definitions of terms-of-use for the session were also discussed. For example, DL was defined as, "Individual study of specially prepared learning materials, usually print and sometimes e-learning, supplemented by integrated learning resources, other learning experiences, including face-to-face teaching and practical experience, feedback on learning, and student support."[143]

To accelerate the mapping process, the facilitator divided attendees into four groups using the Zoom breakout room function. A facilitator was assigned to each of the four groups to support the development of content based on a question focusing on a particular quadrant of the FF and DL polarity. The four questions were:

Group 1 (Upside Benefits of DL): *What are the benefits that emerged from the use of DL post COVID-19?*

Group 2 (Upside Benefits of FF): *What are the benefits of FF teaching that we realized after we had to experience the post COVID-19 social distancing?*

Group 3 (Limitations of DL without FF): *What are the drawbacks that emerged from the use of DL in post COVID-19?*

Group 4 (Limitations of FF without DL): *What are the drawbacks of FF teaching that we realized after we had to experience the post COVID-19 social distancing?*

The sub-groups returned to the large group and shared the items they identified. There was an opportunity to ask questions about the content and to make suggestions to clarify or supplement content. This provided the opportunity for all in the group to gain clarity about content generated for all four quadrants in the Polarity Maps®.

As the group reviewed the content from each of the sub-groups, they began to notice several key categories or "themes" in each of four quadrant data. For example, some answers focused on "students" and others "teachers." As these theme

---

[142] Johnson, Barry. *And: Making a Difference by Leveraging Polarity, Paradox or Dilemma. Volume One—Foundations.* HRD Press, 2020.

[143] Taylor, D., Grant, J., Hamdy, H., Grant, L., Marei, H., and Venkatramana, M. 2020. "Transformation to learning from a distance." *MedEdPublish*, 9, [1], 76, https://doi.org/10.15694/mep.2020.000076.1

categories were named, they began to organize the data for the quadrants according to the themes Teacher (Faculty), Students, Curriculum, Social aspects, and Logistics. This turned out to be a significant observation for three primary reasons. First, by helping organize and simplify the large volume of content in each quadrant. Second, by facilitating a decision to create five Polarity Maps for FF and DL with specific focus on each category. Third, by supporting a more robust performance measurement in Step 3: Assessing.

A seven-person working group of medical educators took on the task of segregating the content for each of the five category themes into unique Polarity Maps. From the five category-focused Polarity Maps, this same working group began Step 3 to develop a Polarity Assessment™[144] instrument for the five Polarity Maps.

Step 3: Assessing

The seven-person subgroup refined content for each of the five category-focused Polarity Maps for DL and FF. They converted upside and downside content to survey item statements that survey respondents could answer based on a Likert scale for frequency of their experience (Almost Always, Often, Sometimes, Seldom, Almost Never). The subgroup also identified demographics they thought would be useful to capture from respondents. These demographic categories (Role, Age, and Degree of Familiarity with DL) would provide the ability to segregate results for analysis in Step 4: Learning. Before the survey launch, the subgroup piloted the survey from the perspective of the respondents and made several refinements. The survey was launched to a group of respondents connected to 79 faculty and medical education leaders.

Step 4: Learning

When the survey period closed, the large group convened online to review and analyze the results of the assessment for each of the FF and DL category-focused Polarity Maps. *Figure 1* shows the summary view of the results for all five maps. The following *Figures 2* and *3* show results for two of the five DL and FF polarities.

Figure 1: Polarity Summary

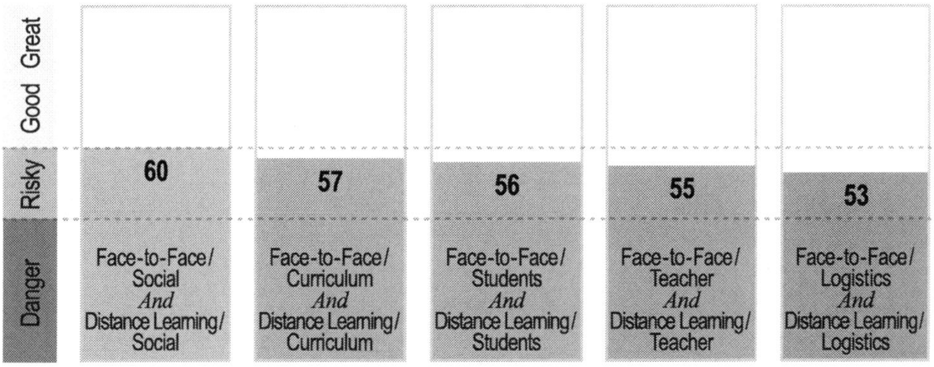
Great
Good
Risky
Danger
60
57
56
55
53
Face-to-Face/ Social *And* Distance Learning/ Social
Face-to-Face/ Curriculum *And* Distance Learning/ Curriculum
Face-to-Face/ Students *And* Distance Learning/ Students
Face-to-Face/ Teacher *And* Distance Learning/ Teacher
Face-to-Face/ Logistics *And* Distance Learning/ Logistics

[144] The Polarity Assessment™. www.polaritypartnerships.com/our-impact. 2020.

Figure 2: Sample Result, Teacher

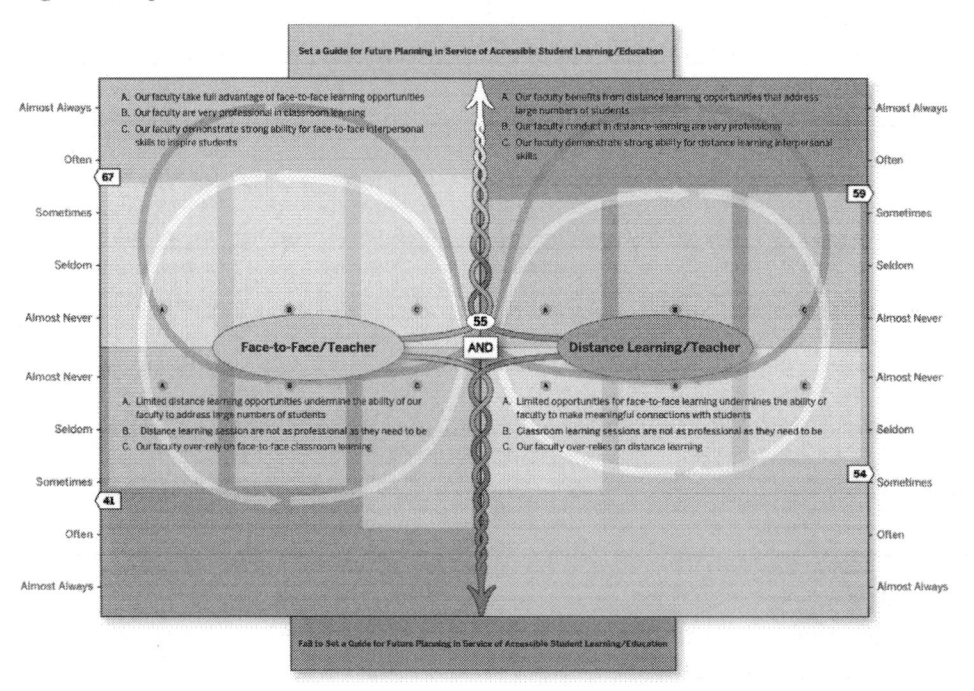

Figure 3: Sample Result, Students

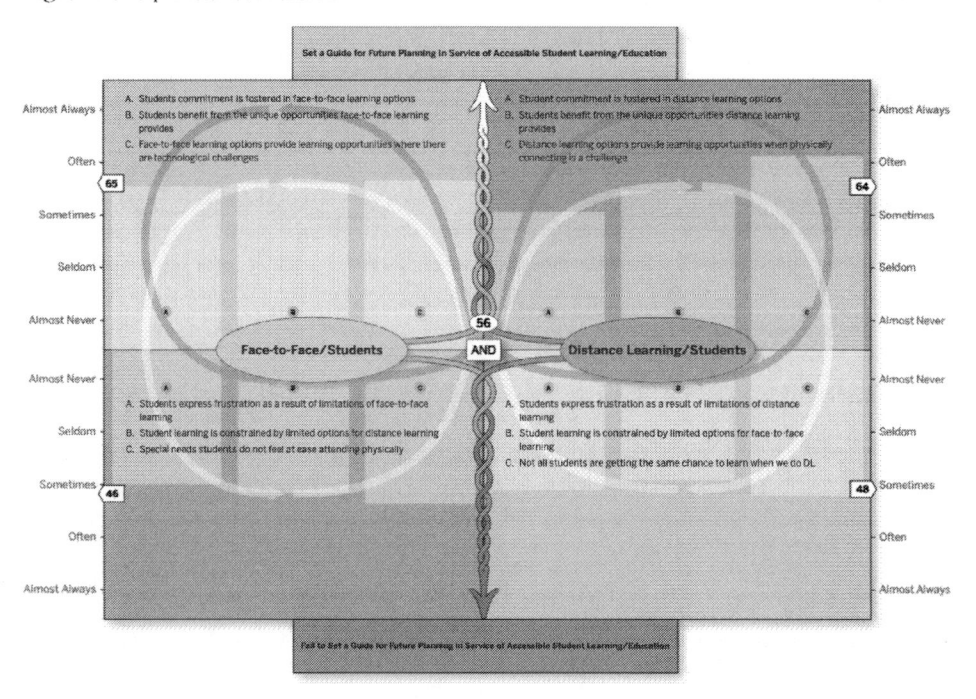

While the details and conclusions that arose in Step 4: Learning, analysis data go beyond the scope of this chapter. We will share a few key learning themes.

First, quality of the relationship between faculty and students was evidenced in the results as a high value and key factor in the learning process. Therefore, in the shift to DL, it would be necessary to examine ways to more intentionally highlight this value that had traditionally been developed in the FF learning interactions.[145] As faculty and administration rapidly embraced DL technology skills, concerted effort was needed to develop quality relationships and maintain focus on that dimension, which was critical to learning success.

Prior to the COVID-19 pandemic, the medical education in the Middle East Region struggled to adapt to DL needs, despite training investment and encouragement. In discussing this, the group speculated that applying this PACT process earlier would have supported the leveraging of DL and FF, and they would better prepared to deal with the current realities. This conclusion was reinforced by the realization of how the dialogue in the Seeing and Mapping steps had improved the speed and efficiency of Step 4: Learning, from the results of Step 3: Assessing. The process itself, which included sharing information and organizing individual and collective wisdom, illuminated important connections among teaching methods, roles, and values. The learning from one another in real-time reinforced what "professionalism" looked and sounded like and supported the emergence of integrated solutions.

Step 5: Leveraging

There was a thin line between Step 4: Learning, and Step 5: Leveraging. When Step 4: Learning connections were made, the natural tendency was to immediately begin suggesting actions in response. It took some discipline and strong facilitation to ensure the two steps were kept distinct. One supportive method the facilitator used was to say, "I'm capturing that suggestion for Leveraging, which is Step 5. For now, let's capture just what we're Learning in Step 4." When the group moved to Step 5, the facilitator shared the list of Leveraging suggestions she had captured as a way to begin the Leveraging discussion. In Step 5: Leveraging, key stakeholders identify Action Steps to maximize benefits of each pole of the polarities, and Early Warning Signs to minimize the downside limitations for each of the poles. As with previous steps, the group divided into sub-groups in an effort to accelerate this process. Each group answered a particular question related to the five Polarity Maps:

Group 1: *What are the steps you and/or your organization can take to maintain the benefits that emerged from the use of DL post COVID-19?*

Group 2: *What are the steps you and/or your organization can take to maintain the benefits that emerged from the use of FF learning?*

---

[145] Ahmed, S., Shehata, M., Hassanien, M., 2020. "Emerging Faculty Needs for Enhancing Student Engagement on a Virtual Platform." *MedEdPublish*, 9, [1], 75, https://doi.org/10.15694/mep.2020.000075.1

Group 3: *What are the Early Warning Signs that you and/or your organization should look for to avoid experiencing the drawbacks that could emerge from the overuse of DL when planning the future of your education interface?*

Group 4: *What are the Early Warning Signs that you and/or your organization should look for to avoid experiencing the drawbacks that could emerge from the overuse of FF learning when planning the future of your education interface?*

Each of the groups returned to the large group to share their ideas. The large group then asked clarifying questions, made additional suggestions, and prioritized Action Steps that were required first for other Action Steps to logically follow them.

Identifying Early Warning Signs proved to be the most difficult part of the Step 5: Leveraging. In particular, the group struggled to ensure each Early Warning Sign was measurable for the particular downside item. For example, an "increase in student complaints" is not specific enough to determine if the complaint relates to an over-focus on DL or an over-focus on FF. The group managed this challenge by adding the word "because" ("increase in student complaints because _____.") Being more specific about the complaint had the ancillary benefit of supporting the identification of a useful Action Step for the upside of the other pole of the polarity. For example, an Early Warning Sign of a student complaint about: "Students report few or no DL options available in reference to FF curriculum content" (a common result of an over-focus on FF to the neglect of DL). This FF Early Warning Sign can then be offset by an Action Step for the upside of DL such as: "FF curriculum content includes a DL supplement reference and discussion thread option for questions."

A key outcome of Step 5: Leveraging, was the sense of agency and control it provided for the leadership team and their ability to translate that to strategy plans they could communicate to their constituents. The April 2020 time period was chaotic and the number of questions about what was being done and how it related to learning was overwhelming for the group. The group embraced the tension and slowed down. In the end, they gained a sense of control and ownership of their challenges and solutions and built confidence in each step that increased the speed and ability to identify, prioritize, and move forward. Overwhelm and confusion converted to strategy plans and clear communications. It was as if the team had stepped in front of a collective mirror and took actions individually and collectively to what they had seen, which are reflected in the following comments.

What the Team Had to Say

At first I thought this would just be another time-wasting exercise ... what possibly new can it tell us that we do not already know? However, after we generated that first map, it was like a whole new world of information opened up. ~ Hany Waheeb

When my school shared information in the assessment, all I could think of was, 'what kind of exposing effect will this have on me and my school?'

When I read the results, I fell back in ease! There was very little need to hide anything because we are just part of a big body of evidence showing that we are all on the same boat and suffer from the same issues and have the very same objectives. ~ Abdelmoniem Alhiani

Prioritizing was such a relief. It instantaneously cut down so much jargon and themes just emerged like a piece of cake. One of the best investigatory tools I have ever used! ~ Mohamed Hany

I am in love with the concept and have been for years – but this was eye opening! I saw the beauty in the assessment and how much power it can generate. In no time it seemed the process and indicators from the assessment paved the pathway to understanding and planning. ~ Samar Ahmed

Conclusion

The PACT provided a real-time experience for rapid response to medical education challenges in the wake of the global pandemic crisis. While the tension between DL and FF was present prior to the COVID-19 pandemic, the crisis imposed a no-alternative solution requiring DL. The use of PACT, which includes mapping tensions using Polarity Maps and measuring performance using the Polarity Assessment, had a number of benefits for key stakeholders of medical education. First, it supported clarity and a shared reality, individually and collectively. Second, assessment results informed a strategy to leverage the tension in real-time. Third, the successful application increased the level of confidence and competence for applying this powerful methodology to other academic and medical education polarities.

Addendum

A more detailed account than was possible in this Chapter, including: Abstract, Figures, Background, Methods, Results, Discussion, and Conclusion, can be found at BMC Medical Education.

https://bmcmededuc.biomedcentral.com/articles/10.1186/s12909-020-02311-1

The authors of this paper are currently engaged in using PACT for additional research related strategy development. Please connect with Cliff Kayser if you are interested in learning about these results.

Find bio and contact info for author Cliff Kayser at
www.polaritypartnerships.com/certified-polarity-practitioners

Managing Community Issues Through Polarity Thinking™
Margaret Seidler, MPA

Charleston, South Carolina: A City Grounded in History and Tradition
2019 – A Brief Reflection

Having returned home to South Carolina in 2001, the year after meeting Barry Johnson and learning about Polarity Thinking™,[146] I made a commitment to spread the word far and wide, to all corners of the country, and most especially to this city where *either/Or* thinking had dominated the landscape for centuries.

The story begins in April 2010, with the city of Charleston Police Department, where Polarity Thinking was applied to support a relatively new Chief, Greg Mullen, in gaining support for the department's first ever strategic plan. Successful polarity work with the police led to further work with department heads across the entire city. After using Polarity Thinking within the city's internal leadership, we came out publicly to facilitate the local community in a highly visible and polarized situation. The *Late Night Activity Review* project addressed the complex issues surrounding Charleston's burgeoning nightlife area while also supporting the health of daytime businesses and the quality of life in nearby neighborhoods. We achieved resounding success in bringing unity of purpose to these differing "camps." Next, we took a bold step forward and one that we hope becomes a model for the nation.

In light of police shootings in 2014 and 2015, even one in an adjacent municipality, we watched as riots erupted across the country. In the wake of the Charleston massacre, and the death of nine parishioners, during the Bible Study at Mother Emanuel African Methodist Episcopal Church in June 2015, Chief Mullen felt an obligation to honor those who lives were taken and those who had professed forgiveness at the bond hearing for the perpetrator. With the confidence of several years of experience by city leaders and police command staff using the principles of Polarity Thinking, Chief Mullen, Jake Jacobs, Chandra Irvin, Bob Seidler, and I embarked on a groundbreaking effort to ask citizens how to Strengthen Relationships with Police; how to *both* Preserve Public Safety *And* Safeguard Individual Rights.

I want to share with you the groundwork laid over several years, because it is important to see how the multiple steps of trainings and consulting efforts developed a new-found capacity for the police within the city. From this work grew a higher level of openness in being more vulnerable with the community, which resulted in Chief Mullen taking this calculated risk of asking the public for input. The promise

---

[146] Johnson, Barry. *And: Making a Difference by Leveraging Polarity, Paradox or Dilemma. Volume One–Foundations.* HRD Press, 2020.

was to hear and honor all voices, regardless of community status, and from that input crafting a plan of action for police and citizens.

2010 – A "Chance" Encounter

All of my extended family was in Charleston when I was raised there. Community service and leadership was a core value across the male members. I also subscribed to that as the first-generation female active in the community. At this time, I headed a large committee of several Charleston single-family residential neighborhoods. With nearby high-profile crimes in the apartment communities, I called the Charleston Police Department to come address our large group and explain what actions they were taking to "fix this problem." After the meeting, the Police Lieutenant asked me where the folks from the apartment communities were, that it just seemed to be single family residents in attendance. This was a major "wake up" call to me, a professed systems thinker, and Polarity Management Mastery graduate.

It was now apparent that I had invited only *my part* of the system to the meeting; a traditional "us vs. them" approach for an issue that was complex, chronic, and much better suited to the *both/And* approach. I was seeing that "others" needed to fix the "problem" rather than an opportunity to collaborate across a whole geographic area.

I began where I had the most influence and control – with the neighborhood committee. We first expanded the committee to include apartment owners and managers. We had a community dinner where we got to know each other better and during the meeting portion, we focused on learning about polarities. Together, we drafted a Polarity Map® where our common desire for a Safe Community (Greater Purpose) could provide the solid ground to build relationships and begin the process of creating partnerships in our effort. Charleston's new police chief, Greg Mullen, was in attendance. After the session, he handed me his business card and asked if we could meet in his office at nine the next morning. This was a pivotal moment, and of course I agreed to meet.

Polarities in Policing Services

Here is what Chief Mullen said the following morning at our meeting: *I believe we have these things you call 'polarities' in law enforcement.*

Imagine my excitement when I was able to respond with a resounding "*YES.*" I further stated that polarities are ubiquitous and that the more able we are to see their existence, the better able we are to manage them.

For me, the best place to start working with a client is to find something for which they already have energy, where a polarity approach can be an enhancement. The Police Department's strategic plan was a good candidate. As a new chief, it was something Mullen had pressed hard to create. Formalizing a strategic plan and a strategic planning process would be a major shift for his officers and staff, a shift from thinking about everyday tactics to thinking about the big picture and long-term successes. As you might imagine, he ran up against predictable resistance.

We imagined that each of his five key strategic directions were actually Greater Purpose Statements (**GPS**) as listed here in *Figure 1*:

Figure 1

Enhancing Community Safety
Law Enforcement   *And*   Community Support

Creating Community Partnerships
Department's Interests   *And*   Citizens' Interests

Creating an Exceptional Workforce
Operational Commitments   *And*   Education/Training

Effective Resource Management
Take Care of What We Have   *And*   Get What We Need

Advancing Technological Efficiencies
End-Users Needs/Capabilities   *And*   Innovations

We were off to a great start. Next, we discussed the steps to engage his officers and staff in supporting a broader, new view of their roles.

Strategic Planning: Tapping Tradition to Create Change

We invited a highly diverse group of 35 police department employees – including sworn and civilian, young and old, Black, white, Hispanic – to learn about themselves individually and collectively using a polarity lens. Our mix was diverse by design. We included those who might naturally hold onto the way things had been done in the past as well as others who might naturally prefer going after new ways of doing things.

Using a time tested one-page exercise we call "The Preferences," we helped the group gain an appreciation for seeing how strengths can become weaknesses when the benefits from both poles are not present and honored over time. With solid context in place, we then applied the learning to individual leadership polarities in their day-to-day lives. I intentionally added Traditionalists *And* Pioneers to the list, having each declare their preference. Then I asked the Traditionalists to please raise their hands again and keep them up in the air. I turned to Chief Mullen and said publicly, "Chief, you seem to have a strong preference for being a Pioneer." As he nodded yes, I continued, "You see these Traditionalists? These are important in your department; honor them and hear them for the wisdom about what is working today and that you may want to hold onto while you bring about needed changes in the Department." You could see the Traditionalists, who *had* been the resistors to change, react to the news that they were not only valuable, they were necessary over time for success as a police department.

From that place of all being honored for their values, they eagerly jumped into the process of mapping Enforcement *And* Community Support, and the other Strategic Directions. The group created five high quality, initial Polarity Map drafts in just a few hours! From those maps came the Strategic Plan – a new, yet guiding force for the ensuing years.

2013 – Engaging all City Departments

As Chief Mullen's experience with Polarity Thinking in the police department began to take root, we decided to look at the ongoing tension among the more than 30 departments across the city. We conducted a similar session for the city's Executive Steering Group (ESG). Again, we entered using an existing truth; turning an *either/Or* view of My Department vs. Other Department into a heightened *both/And* awareness that would systemically lead to cooperation and collaboration. Again, the group developed a staff leadership plan based on six Greater Purpose Statements (**GPS**) with each key polarity mapped out, as listed here in *Figure 2*:

Figure 2

Robust Service Delivery
Quality of Service *And* Cost of Service

Sustainable Community
Thriving Economy *And* Beautiful Environment

Effective Public Engagement
Needs of the Community *And* Needs of the City

Effective Intergovernmental Relations
Local Focus *And* Get What We Need

Exceptional Workforce
Operational Requirements *And* Org. Development Needs

Effective Resource Management
Take Care of What We Have *And* Get What We Need

2014 – A City Polarized

With a burgeoning nightlife economy in Charleston's Central Business District, specifically Upper King Street, crowding, public safety, and quality of life issues in adjacent neighbors became contentious and polarizing. As those interests took sides in a public debate about who was right and who was wrong, then Mayor Joe Riley decided it was well worth a try to take Polarity Thinking outside of the city operations and into the public arena for addressing this complex problem.

Uniting All Sides Through a Common Greater Purpose

A 21-member Steering Group called the *Late Night Activity Review Committee* was formed with an overriding goal to ensure that those working on this nightlife activity initiative were not confrontational. Throughout the process, we engaged the committee and the public in a calm, measured exploration of public sentiment. With each step, we built greater understanding and agreement. A highly diverse group of neighborhood leaders, nightlife business owners, daytime business owners, real estate developers, and zoning board members came together because there was something each agreed they wanted at the end of the day; for "Charleston to Remain a Vibrant, Relevant, Forward-looking City," the Greater Purpose Statement they defined on their Polarity Map.

The Wisdom Resides Within

Mayor Riley told me that he wanted me to use a Polarity Thinking approach without first providing the training to the committee. He feared that it would seem too theoretical for everyday citizens. So Jake Jacobs and I abbreviated the process by asking the questions from a Polarity Map without explaining Polarity Thinking. We used the pole names, Nightlife Business *And* Diverse Business/Neighborhoods, with a Greater Purpose, "Charleston to Remain a Vibrant, Relevant Forward-Looking City."

Once the committee had created the map, the next question was, "How are we doing with managing this polarity?" We used the online Polarity Assessment ™,[147] and results for the Steering Group to see the whole picture. A pivotal element for the committee's success was that all involved felt that their voices, points of view, and concerns were heard. This inclusion honored the essential roles businesses and neighborhoods play in the city's success.

With a more complete picture of the situation and the assessment findings, the committee conducted public listening sessions and had more than 120 citizens repeat the process of answering four key questions in support of this common Greater Purpose and then suggest Action Steps for how to get the best of both poles.

The results were phenomenal. The citizens' ideas were focused on the positives of both poles in pursuit of a common Greater Purpose. With this input, the Committee crafted a set of integrated recommendations, which ended with a broad base of support across the city. Every recommendation from these previously polarized constituent groups received a unanimous vote from City Council.

2015 – Mayor Joseph P. Riley Comments to Charleston City Council

Report of the *Late Night Activity Review Committee*

> Before we begin, let's just thank them. This has been a community civic engagement/elected legislative body partnership in action. What seemed

---

[147] The Polarity Assessment™. www.polaritypartnerships.com/our-impact. 2020.

a year ago to be an intractable challenge, a group of citizens, well-led and well-facilitated, came together in a series of meetings over a period of time for this amazing American city that presents marvelous opportunities as well as challenges for this very special place we have. They have worked hard, listened and came together with amazing unanimity and recommendations. There really is no college course in civic engagement that could top this as an example of a best practice. It converted 'either/Or-thinking' to 'And'; the result is just extraordinary.

2015 – The Illumination Project

The morning of June 17, 2015, the above-the-fold front page headline in Charleston's *Post and Courier* newspaper proclaimed the success of the *Late Night Activity Review Committee's* work. That euphoria was short-lived when that evening, around 9 pm, a hate crime occurred just across the street from our Committee's public Listening Session.

Race relations nationally, especially between communities and law enforcement, had already resulted in riots across the country. If ever the Charleston Police Department needed assurance of the importance of the pole of Community Support, they saw it now. They had been consciously building relationships in the preceding years. Polarity Thinking principles and actions had prepared them to deal with this crisis both as law enforcement officers and as trusted members of the community.

Within minutes of the massacre, officers reached out to community influencers deep and wide. These were citizens with whom they had already built relationships, confidence, and trust. They shared what they knew and began the process of calling people together. In the days following the massacre, outsiders descended on Charleston with intentions to protest as a way of expressing their outrage. The community's response was to request they leave. What the community and its police officers had created together in the previous five years made an undeniable difference in the face of this unimaginable tragedy.

While not new to our discussions, in August of 2015, Chief Mullen recognized an opportunity, almost an obligation, to those whose lives were so senselessly taken, hence The *Charleston Illumination Project* was born. Our work is to Preserve Public Safety *And* Safeguard Individual Rights. The Greater Purpose Statement for this polarity was: "To further strengthen relationships between the police and the citizens they serve Grounded in Trust & Legitimacy." It provided an avenue for Charlestonians to do something positive and to move forward together. Before going public, Polarity Thinking training was provided to the most diverse group of 99 community influencers ever assembled in Charleston. Within the city of Charleston, we hosted 34 public listening sessions and engaged more than 850 citizens in dialogue about their ideas for what improvements can be made for both police and themselves as citizens. The effort brought forth more than 2,200 ideas/comments for police and citizens. From those came suggested priorities resulting in a new Strategic Plan of 86 strategies. In addition to bringing Jake Jacobs back to Charleston, we secured the special expertise of Chandra Irvin, a Master of Divinity, peace agent, and Polarity Thinking Master. With Chandra's support, we broadened our work by engaging faith communities in their places of worship, an additional way to engage large numbers of citizens, explore commonalties, learn, and pray for our community's continued success. With Jake's leadership, the project model is now starting in other cities.

2017 – Broadening the Base

We learned a lot in 2016, including seeing that a police department can serve as a portal into many parts of a community and that relationships, never previously imagined, are formed. Using this momentum, we hosted 16 Listening Sessions during the year, mostly focused on racial history in Charleston. More than 900 citizens participated. Police were always present, part of the experience, and included in our signature facilitated small group discussions. Police effectiveness has moved from the foreground since the Strategic Plan was put in place. That year, we created for our police many shared experiences to continue building relationships for community support, and all the while they continued to enforce the law to provide a safe place for all.

We were humbled to announce that the *National Law Enforcement Museum* in Washington, D.C., which opened in fall of 2018, contacted us and developed a permanent video exhibit of the *Illumination Project*.

In 2016, Police Chief Gregory G. Mullen was named by Polarity Partnerships as the first Honorary Polarity Master Practitioner. He now serves as Associate Vice President for Public Safety and Chief of Police for Clemson University.

Find bio and contact info for author Margaret Seidler at
www.polaritypartnerships.com/certified-polarity-practitioners

Social Network Strategies and Polarity Thinking™: Driving Forces in Social Work

Drs Riet Portengen MLD

There has been a missing link in the development and embedding of Social Network Strategies (SoNeStra)[148] in the practice, organizations, and policy of social work. Why do problems repeat over and over again, when we thought we had solved them each time, only to find ourselves stuck again?

In my introduction to Polarity Thinking™ in 2011, I walked the infinity loop and literally experienced the power of Polarity Thinking; it can be both/And! Polarities are an interdependent pair of two poles, often experienced as a tension, paradox, or dilemma, and are energy systems we can leverage. Polarity Thinking can also be a leverage point in a process that creates movement in seemingly unsolvable, chronic social issues, the impact of which can be robust and sustainable. What a relief; some problems can't be "solved" but the underlying tensions can be leveraged to create forward motion and positive results. This is done by seeing the issue through the lens of polarities and connecting the poles with both/And.

This chapter demonstrates how Social Network Strategies and Polarity Thinking reinforce each other in the practice of Social Work. In part, the model and language of Polarity Thinking made explicit what was implicitly embodied in SoNeStra. It also opens new perspectives. In this chapter, I describe SoNeStra, the integration of Polarity Thinking and a case study as an illustration from our practice.

Driving Forces

SoNeStra recognizes Polarity Thinking as a driving force in our social work practice in the Netherlands and Belgium. New methods built from core polarities include:

- Vulnerability *And* Strength, in a method for people with dementia or Alzheimer's
- Trust *And* Control, in a program to prevent or shorten the stay in a youth prison
- Ordinary Life *And* Professional Upbringing, in a program to build sustainable social capital for children and families with social, emotional, and pedagogical challenges

Polarity Thinking is also a driving force in creating Circularity *And* Alignment in practice, organizations, and policy. It's interesting that the same polarities show up in working with individuals, families, and communities, as with professionals, teams, organizations, and in policy. For example, Self-direction *And* Structure, Safety *And* Development Opportunities, and Part *And* Whole.

---

[148] SoNeStra stands for Social Network Strategies and is an organization in the Netherlands and a way of working that contributes to a paradigm shift in Social Work.

Family Smith:[149] A Case Study

A family consisting of a mother, father, and three children (Rose 13, Marc 10, and Sunny, 8 years old) came to the attention of Social Work (CPS).[150] Rose and Sunny's school recognized signs of neglect and abuse. Marc attended a school for children with special needs because of his mental health challenges and behavioral problems. The social worker spoke with the parents, formulated the family's request for help, set goals, and created a support plan with a multi-disciplinary team. The parents disagreed but cooperated for fear that the children would be taken from them.

After a year, the school and social worker concluded that there was no progress. Problems and discussions repeated over time while parents, including grandparents, increased their resistance to the offered professional help. The conclusion was that the parents didn't want to change and were not honest in what was really going on. But they were missing the full story. By using the threat of taking away their kids, the system set up the parents, who became very afraid of what they shared, how it was said, and whether or not they could be honest in their cooperation. Despite these fears, the parents insisted on development opportunities for their family.

Although all professionals demanded safety for and the development of the children, they argued about the solution; foster care *Or* an intensive parenting program. Some professionals believed that the children's traumas would increase by leaving them with their parents, while others believed that traumas would increase by handing them over to the foster care system.

Feeling unheard and disowned from the process, the parents refused both.

Social Network Strategies

Living World *And* System World

Social Network Strategies, SoNeStra, is a way of working that enables adults, children, families, and communities to set their own course, design their own strategy, make their own decisions, and Action Plan. They decide if, how, and which professionals they will invite to collaborate in their Action Team to make their Action Plan a success. This seems very ordinary, but becomes complicated as soon as professionals in care, welfare, and justice are involved.

Generally, professionals are used to creating a support or treatment plan for their clients. After talking with them, they design their professional strategy and make their plan in a (multi-disciplinary) team. Part of their strategy is how to motivate the client to cooperate with them, and how to involve social network members to support their plan. SoNeStra requires a paradigm shift; *individuals, families and communities design their strategy, make their Action Plan, and involve professionals to contribute* and not the other way around. This is a fundamental shift in the culture of social work. Social workers learn to fix problems and involve people

---

[149] This case study is based on a true story. All names are fictitious and some features of the situation are changed to respect the privacy of the family and its social network.
[150] Child Protection Services.

in their system. But actually, they are the ones who get involved in the living world of people. From the perspective of Polarity Thinking, it is a process from ownership of professionals towards ownership of people making decisions and plans for their own life. The system world and thus the role of professionals must support the living world of individuals and social networks. The challenge for social work is to leverage the polarity: living-world *And* system-world.

Attitude *And* Method

SoNeStra is an attitude with an intention, a philosophy, and associated professional behavior. It is also a method which includes techniques, instruments, and competencies. If the use of the method does not match with the SoNeStra attitude, or vice versa, the outcomes will be different. SoNeStra is a way of decision making, planning, and collaboration that informs every professional as they intentionally work together with individuals, families, and communities. Individuals and their significant others are the experts of their own context and life. Ownership of their problems and solutions is multifold as it strengthens the impact of professional help, leads to more sustainable results, empowers children and adults as individuals, and strengthens families, communities, and the society as a whole. SoNeStra stimulates development towards ownership *And* participation, self-direction *And* co-direction, individual accountability *And* shared responsibility (note the polarities). The SMALL Process™ of Polarity Thinking – Seeing, Mapping, Assessing, Learning, and Leveraging – has an incredible added value to make the most of any polarity.

SoNeStra aims toward sustainable solutions, self-realization, and social coherence, manifested by enabling people to activate, revitalize, and build social capital to strengthen safety and create development opportunities, continuity, and connection. By building social capital for children, we pave the way for a sustainable environment for future adults who feel seen, loved, and have a sense of belonging.

The SoNeStra Navigator

The SoNeStra Navigator (see *Figure 1,* next page) – we say the Wyber[151] – supports professionals, organizations, and policy makers in the paradigm shift toward participant ownership. The Wyber consists of four phases: the Story (1), the Network Compass (2), the Conference (3), (3a-d), and Collaboration in an Action team (4). A professional takes the role as facilitator in this process.

The vertical line represents participants (an individual and their social network) designing their own strategy. Before they do, they have to figure out the "Main Thing"; *what should our strategy be about and why should it be about that?* The outcome of this thinking defines their course within their context. The horizontal line represents the work processes and the roles of professionals as they support the Main Thing and the resulting course, strategy, and Action Plan. We start in the upper right – the wisdom organizer – involving the Story and Network Compass.

---

[151] A Wyber is a Dutch liquorice in the shape of a rhombus.

Figure 1:
SoNeStra Navigator

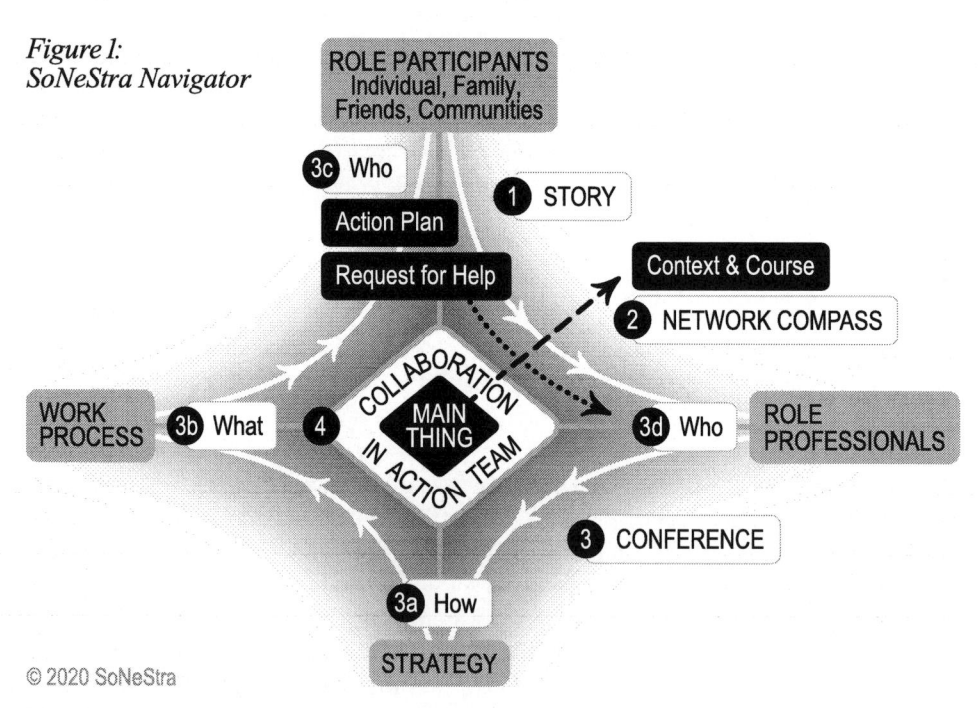

The Story (1) is all about seeing; seeing the individual and social network more completely by listening to their stories. Everyone can bring a supporter who brings their perspective. Be aware: professionals do not belong to the social network. They are part of the professional network. The facilitator supports the exploration of the social network by illustrating the Story. They encourage curiosity with powerful questions to explore and recognize all perspectives and illustrate them as parts which make up the story as a whole. Because judgements can stop curiosity and motion, the facilitator holds a space, free from judgement or the need to defend interests, and encourages acknowledging different perspectives including seeing polarities. Embedding Polarity Thinking helps participants see themselves and their world more completely allowing their wisdom about "the Main Thing" to be fully recognized.

Family Smith: Their Story

The parents asked the Social Community Team for help. The Social Worker invited family members to bring a supporter. Dad took his best friend; mom, her sister; Sunny, her grandmother (mom's side); Rose, the mother of a friend; and Marc, his grandfather (dad's side). The Social Worker wanted to facilitate the family regaining their ownership and move toward a new life inside of their context.

The family's story unfolded. The supporters added a variety of perspectives. In the illustration, everybody recognized their perspectives as a part in the whole story. It also became clear who belongs to this family; family, friends, and community. The lifeline brought, for almost everybody, new information. Grandpa was telling about his nephew John, who had almost the same challenges as Marc, but nobody recognized his special needs. Even his parents and siblings had expected more from John than he was capable of. He was severely punished to unlearn "bad" behavior. Dad became emotional; he grew up with his cousin, he always stood up for him, and he even fought when others bullied him. He was the only one his cousin felt safe with. One day CPS came in, their interventions didn't work, and John went into foster care. Dad was not allowed to stay in touch. At the age of 16, John died and the cause is still unclear.

Dad said he wanted to protect Marc against this scenario and was frightened that it was already unfolding. He also needed to protect the girls against the aggression of Marc, but how? Sometimes Marc bruised them. The parents forbid the girls to tell anyone that Marc did this. To avoid confrontations, the parents kept the girls in their room or sent them outside. By doing these things, they emphasized, they were keeping the girls safe and protecting Marc. And now, "If we can't turn the tide," Dad sobbed, "I will lose all three!" Everybody agrees that should not happen!

The facilitator held an attitude of curiosity, recognizing that not knowing is a strength and in resistance there is wisdom. With curious, nonjudgmental questions, discussions turned into conversations, accusations turned back to signals, and problems were defined as issues. Parents, children, and supporters said, "For the first time we feel heard, seen, and loved as individuals, as a family, and as a community."

The Network Compass (2) enables the person and their supporters to connect all perspectives and set their course. Every perspective contributes to a new course that matches their desires and talents, while recognizing context and challenges. A Triptych (*Figure 2*) is an instrument used to brainstorm and organize the issues behind the experienced problems. The Triptych focuses on the future based on issues in the present and integrates the polarities Self *And* Others, Self *And* Family / Social Network, along with Family / Social Network *And* Formal Support Systems.

Figure 2

Fears for the Future (Fears / Early Warnings)	**Bridge: Past / Present / Future** (Preparation for Action Steps)	**Hopes for the Future** (Greater Purpose)
Do not want to go this way! Not far in yet, but these things shouldn't happen!	A place to formulate questions to be answered so fears are dealt with and a desired future happens. They decide what information they need and who they want to invite for their Conference.	Unity of individual wishes and shared vision of what the future should look like.
What's the situation like in six months if nothing changes? How are you individually, and you in relation to your family and social network?	What problems can be solved? What issues are polarities that need leveraging? How do you, individually and collectively, map and leverage Past *And* Present, Present *And* Future for a better future?	How would you like to see the situation in six months? What do you want for yourself, and for / with your family and social network?

The Past *And* Present, Present *And* Future Polarity Maps® add sources of hope, while Past *And* Present can add concerns to the Triptych, generating other questions. The process to formulate questions can help prevent jumping from Early Warnings to accusations, while formulating Action Steps that move beyond the ineffective "doing more of the same."

The family and supporters decide – Triptych, middle column – what information is needed in order to make a plan that works for them, including inviting other members of the social network to help design an Action Plan. Note: the more participants, perspectives, and ideas, the stronger the plan.

Family Smith: Their Network Compass

In the Triptych, parents, children, and supporters connected each unique perspective. They all saw the tension and interdependency between Protection (Marc) *And* Safety (Girls). Together, they mapped Figure 3. The deepest fear – Triptych, column 1 – was that the family would fall apart; the children would disappear in the system, lose their sense of belonging, be disconnected with their roots, and would be severely traumatized. They all thoroughly agreed that this should not happen. They shared their Hope for the Future – Triptych, column 3 – that the traumas at home had to stop! They all wished for a safe place allowing healthy development for the children, opportunities for the parents to change in ways that worked for them, and to be surrounded by people to whom they belong.

Figure 3: Family and Supporters Polarity Map®

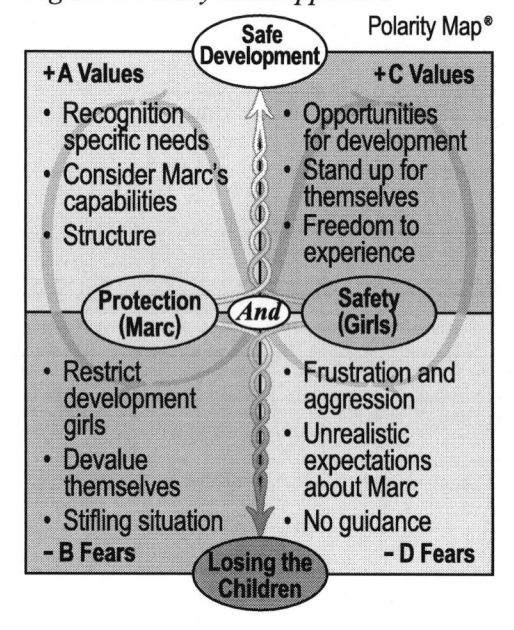

+A Values	Safe Development	+C Values
• Recognition specific needs • Consider Marc's capabilities • Structure		• Opportunities for development • Stand up for themselves • Freedom to experience
Protection (Marc)	*And*	**Safety (Girls)**
• Restrict development girls • Devalue themselves • Stifling situation		• Frustration and aggression • Unrealistic expectations about Marc • No guidance
− B Fears	Losing the Children	− D Fears

Two main questions – based on the Triptych, column 2 – and the Polarity Maps were:

- How can we (parents) fulfill the special needs of Marc and support (family and social network) the parents and the girls in this?
- How can we (parents) recuperate from this very intensive period?

They decide they need information, from a professional perspective, about the specific needs and capabilities of Marc, the requirements of CPS, and the possibilities for professional help. And Dad wanted to tell his story.

At the same time, the facilitator listened to the story of the CPS team – blaming the parents and each other – and introduced Polarity Thinking. Together they identified and mapped the polarity of Safety *And* Development; they saw the values of both, recognized the downsides of each, and noted the natural tendency to defend the safety of the children to the neglect of development opportunities (*Figure 4*, next page). They also realized how the early warnings from both poles turned into accusations against the parents.

The facilitator presented to CPS, with permission of the family, their Protection *And* Safety map (*Figure 3*). The CPS team was impressed. They permitted the family to design their Action Plan, subject to a number of conditions:

- Create learning opportunities and space for development for all children
- Work on trust with professionals and cooperate in verifying what is going on
- Protect the children's safety, including disciplining in a responsible manner

The Conference (3) is where the family, supporters and invitees gather, make decisions, and design their plan. A facilitator guides them through three phases: sharing information, private time, and presenting the Action Plan to the professionals.

Figure 4: CPS Team and Professionals

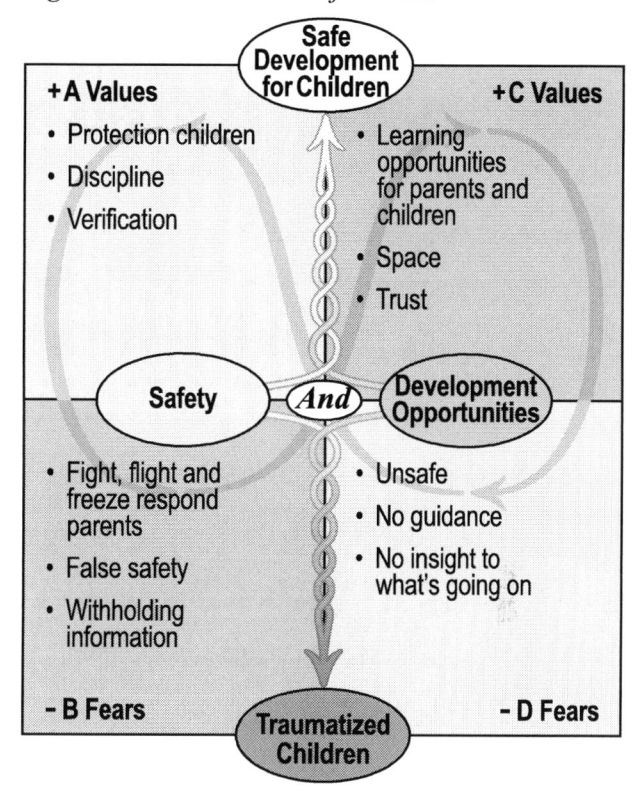

+A Values
- Protection children
- Discipline
- Verification

Safe Development for Children

+C Values
- Learning opportunities for parents and children
- Space
- Trust

Safety *And* **Development Opportunities**

- Fight, flight and freeze respond parents
- False safety
- Withholding information

- Unsafe
- No guidance
- No insight to what's going on

- B Fears

Traumatized Children

- D Fears

Family Smith: Their Conference

Two weeks later, 22 invitees from the family's social network gathered to make decisions and the Action Plan. The family and supporters share their story by presenting all the work they did; the illustrations, the Triptych, Polarity Maps, and the questions they formulated.

A psychologist explains Marc's challenges and what that means for every family member. Dad shared his deepest fear for Marc – the story of his cousin. CPS expressed their appreciation about the formulated questions, which intentionally included CPS requirements. The polarization between professionals themselves and with the family transformed into unity as they all tackled the challenge of connecting the positive values of Protection, Safety, and Development Opportunities.

In private – all professionals left the room including the facilitator – the family, supporters, and invitees were looking for answers for the questions. They brainstormed, checked reality, made decisions, and finally designed their Action Plan; how they want to deal with it, what needed to happen, what they would take on by themselves, and which professionals they would involve who could contribute to the success of their plan. They then formed their Action Team. They called the professionals back and presented their plan with great enthusiasm.

Collaboration in an Action Team (4) is a logical next step. The family and their supporters are the core of this team and invite professionals who can fulfill a specific role in their Action Plan. This is a shift from "traditional cooperation" where the "client" is invited when a professional deems it necessary, to "different collaboration" where a person, their family, and social network invite professionals to join them to work on their plan.

The Action Team guarantees the progress; they celebrate success, share concerns and fears, solve problems, leverage polarities and, if necessary, adjust the plan. The "Wyber" is the navigator and Polarity Maps help heighten awareness of early warnings, help leverage polarities, and enable learning. Professionals assist when asked and leave the Action Team when their task is done.

In these ways, individuals, families, and communities continually develop towards a learning living system. It is development through motion; working on sustainable and agile solutions by solving problems and leveraging polarities. In this process, the power of social capital grows, the individual's uniqueness and connectedness are both experienced, and the system-world supports the living-world.

Family Smith: Collaboration in an Action Team

After six weeks the Action Team gathered. All members completed the assessment of both Polarity Maps. They used the Triptych framework, but flipped the content. The first column became what they were proud of; the sources of hope. They celebrated success and honored everybody's contribution. The third column highlighted what didn't work till now; the concerns of past and present. The middle column generated questions that needed answers in order to adjust their plan. They use the Wyber again to navigate and realize continued development.

They were very proud. The parents went on a vacation, while Marc stayed with an aunt and uncle who lived on a farm. The girls went to their grandparents. One evening a week the parents enjoy their hobbies as friends and neighbors take care of the children. The parents chose a family intervention program which included individual therapy for Marc. The girls opened up, and felt safe in sharing what's going on in their family because everybody knew and understood the situation. They all experience that when you talk with others you find ways to deal with tensions that are inherent in situations like theirs. Through this work, the family and their social network, *and* the specialists developed personally and professionally.

> With gratitude to Danine Casper for all her support in creating this chapter.

> Find bio and contact info for author Riet Portengen at
> www.polaritypartnerships.com/certified-polarity-practitioners

Polarity Thinking™ *to Alleviate Tensions in Community-Engaged Health Research*

Melinda Butsch Kovacic, MPH, PhD
Theresa Baker, MS

Beginning Community-Engaged Research Partnerships

My story begins not unlike others. Enrollment into my federally-funded clinical research study was falling behind. I needed non-asthmatic, non-allergic African American children to serve as a comparison group for the numerous asthmatic children I had already enrolled. A colleague suggested I partner with a local urban community center to boost my enrollment, and introduced me to Sandy, a faculty member and center volunteer. My clinical research coordinator Sara and I met with Sandy and then visited the center with very little idea of what to expect. We had planned to have a discussion with the center's staff about our research study.

We found the center in the middle of an established urban neighborhood, lined with row houses in need of tender loving care, and limited parking. As we entered the building, we observed that it was desperately in need of renovation, but were showered with feelings of vitality in the heartwarming greeting we received. We were escorted into a musty meeting room that clearly indicated a leaky roof. I was incredibly curious about the community center and its purpose, how it had gotten in the state it was in, and what it needed. I was so distracted that I remember little of Sandy's presentation. I could feel both my tension and excitement rising. Should I mostly talk or listen? Should I focus on their needs or mine? How should I ask my questions? Was the fact that I was of another race going to affect their willingness to work with me? I tempered my talking and asked very specific questions. Who did the center serve? What were their needs? What research had they supported? What results had they been given? What research was needed in the future?

I listened to their responses. It seemed that they had been over-focusing on mission to the neglect of margin, leaving them with little funds to repair their roof. Many of the staff at the center were unpaid. They had participated in various research projects prior to our visit, but they had never received the results of any of them – a fact that shocked me. Why did they participate then? Most of their research projects had been student-led with no ongoing relationships with faculty. However, the institution regularly visited with 10-20 students at a time for service projects. Students often painted and cleaned the building while receiving valuable exposure to an organization that served lower income, minority families.

As the meeting neared the end, I asked the group if they were interested in an ongoing partnership with us to do mutually beneficial research. I asked them if I could ask the investigators of the research they had previously participated in for their results on their behalf. I also asked them about research questions they personally had. Luckily, I was interested in pursuing answers to several of their research questions. As I left that day, I decided not to ask them to help me with my ongoing research. I would find another way to finish my asthma study. Instead, I decided to focus on growing our relationship. More important than my own short-term needs were the long-term potential of a mutually beneficial partnership.

Problems to Solve *And* Tensions to Manage

One of the things I like about being a researcher is that I get the opportunity to attempt to solve a lot of problems – or at least try to. I had always enjoyed looking for the right answers or choosing what I thought were the best options between possibilities. I quickly learned that community research wasn't about solving others' problems. There were no easy problems to solve and even if there were, I knew that I wasn't the best person to solve them. From the start, I realized I needed to work with the community rather than in it, and with the center staff and people they served rather than on them. Still, I did not know how to convince them to let me. I had much to learn. From my community partners, I learned that I needed to have patience and build my relationships before initiating research. This was a very different approach than my traditionally trained colleagues who often had problems (like my deficient study recruitment) and were looking for quick solutions (working in community to get access to study participants).

Because of my community partner's honesty and modeling, I made many thoughtful decisions that helped me during those early years. Some of my decisions were even against my initial inclinations. Undeniably, they were often counter to my own training as a traditional biomedical researcher. However, as my community relationships strengthened, I realized I didn't need to abandon my early training, but rather, I could leverage what I had learned in my community work and traditional training to create a mutually beneficial research program that honored the needs and desires of my community partners and my scientific colleagues. Indeed, I later found that if I over-emphasized one approach to the neglect of the other, I personally struggled. For me, the two approaches were values that were in tension and need not be perfectly in balance. Indeed, with community-engaged research, everything is constantly changing as there are many tensions to be managed.

Common Partnership Polarities

Clinical Research *And* Community-Engaged Research

I didn't always get it right. I have had several valuable relationships that have gone awry over the years. Personally, I was doing a delicate internal dance functioning both as a clinical researcher *And* as a community-researcher. I was not always aware of underlying polarities (aka I couldn't SEE them); I commonly treated them as problems to solve. Being raised in a different environment than those living in the community that the center served meant that I had to observe and listen more than I ever had before, rather than talking and acting as an expert. Frequent communication was more important than ever. In observing other traditionally trained researchers' journeys to becoming community-engaged, I realized my experiences were not unique. In fact, there are many common tensions for those becoming community engaged including each of the highlighted polarities below.

Logic *And* Gut-Feeling

Growing up, my mother said I was all too logical. When others told silly jokes, I rarely laughed. The jokes didn't make any sense to me. As an adult, my husband says I should avoid trying to make others purposely laugh; I can rarely pull off a joke. I still try and I think humor is so useful in breaking the ice. In community research, I think over-reliance on logic and seriousness to the neglect of fun can harm relationships. In the first several years of working with my community partners, I learned to pay much more attention to how I was feeling. My gut more often than my logic helped me navigate the tensions I was experiencing. My gut told me that I should put my asthma enrollment needs aside and focus on building relationships instead. My gut has kept me from letting my frustration overcome me and often urges me to ask questions and seek support during times of challenge even when logic tells me to run or quit.

Direct *And* Participate

As a traditionally trained clinical researcher, I am asked to design, develop, initiate, maintain, analyze, and interpret studies. I am the director. In community-engaged research, I am often required to participate. I participate in community meetings, staff meetings, and one-on-one meetings. I attend parties and community events where I am rarely recognized for my contributions. In fact, my primary community partner once forgot to name me when acknowledging a long list of supporters though I clearly deserved acknowledging. She later sincerely apologized. The traditional researcher in me might have walked away in resentment, but the community researcher in me stayed and continued to contribute and participate.

Planning *And* Action

By participating consistently, I was able to better plan my work. My partners grew to respect me and because of their respect for me, I am more easily forgiven when I make mistakes. While I am a person of action, because of them, I realized I need to oscillate more slowly between planning *And* action. Because these values are in tension, I know that one will follow the other. With respectful relationships, partnership sustainability becomes possible – a greater purpose. Over the years, I have observed that partnership sustainability is a greater purpose for many community-engaged researchers, and losing valued partnerships is a one of their greatest fears.

Critical Feedback *And* Encouragement

As with any challenge, many lessons can be learned. Tensions are expected but it is how we respond to them that determines if they can be managed. Personally, I have always believed that critical feedback is necessary for success. No one is so great that they get it right the first time. I can remember working with a community partner, Sheila, to submit a small community-partnered research grant application. We met and discussed the application, and each left with a handful of tasks to do.

When we came together again and shared our work, I was surprised at how little she had progressed. Had she not understood our plan? I remember doing everything in my power to not show my frustration. I had learned from other situations like this that I had to be careful when providing my critical feedback. Encouragement was critical to helping my community partner to feel appreciated for her work. I realized she needed more help than originally thought and so we met more often to work together. It turned out that I needed her help more than I thought as well. I too misunderstood how our project could be best implemented in our target population. As a result of our collective work, our proposal was later funded.

Ensure Quality *And* Build Capacity, Deep Understanding *And* Simplicity

Sheila's involvement was critical to the empowerment drumming program for which we received funding. I wanted to both ensure quality *And* build capacity in her and two others from the community center. High quality training as drumming facilitators was vital. Also, Sheila and her colleagues would need to administer surveys to community members visiting our food pantry and to a group of homeless men at a nearby shelter. The surveys would measure the program's ability to diminish the participants' perceived stress levels, improve their feelings of well-being and overall perception of health. We chose the tools to both gain an adequate understanding of the effects of the program *And* keep it simple, given this was Sheila's and the others' first official research study. Shelia did an amazing job implementing the study, far exceeding my expectations with her data quality and understanding of our results. Our study was simple, but effective. In the end, I had greater confidence and respect in my community partners and vice versa.

Quantitative *And* Qualitative Research

One of the biggest lessons I learned early on was to begin any new relationships by first researching the people I was to be partnered with. In speaking with Alexis, the unpaid director of my partnering community center, I learned that many of the center's children saw the center as a "safe haven." While conceptually I understood what she meant, I didn't understand how it felt to need a "safe haven." I didn't think my typical quantitative survey would get me the critical information I needed. If I were to do research *with* Alexis and her typical clientele, I needed to understand their lived experiences. I really didn't know how to study their lived experiences, so I attended a lecture offered by our institution's Action Research Center. I approached the lecturer after her seminar and asked to meet. I had hit the jackpot – as she was primarily a qualitative researcher! The rest is history. She encouraged me to enroll in her community-based participatory research course and even before the course was over, I partnered with Alexis and began our first academic-community partnered research study (my first qualitative study). We used a photovoice methodology that is based in photojournalism. Participants were asked to represent their points of view or opinions by photographing scenes relevant to our research questions. We spent 14 weeks snapping photos and having discussions on our five health topics – community/environment, heart, mind, body, and soul. I walked away with a much better understanding of my partners and them of me. I also better appreciated the power of qualitative research and how it could complement my typical quantitative approaches. This appreciation led to me taking mixed methods coursework. Further, our photovoice work was published in a peer-reviewed journal[152] and is one of my most cited articles even to this day!

Data-driven *And* People-driven, Individual *And* Team

In my second year of partnering with Alexis and her community center, I was introduced to Sherman, a dynamic minister of a new, small African American church. Sherman shared some of his great ideas and I quickly jumped at the opportunity to help him offer his summer health and education festival. I would organize his health screening and education tables and he would organize the venue, entertainment, and event advertising. He would have his church members volunteer for the event and I would solicit the help of clinicians at my place of employment (a pediatric medical center associated with a university). At the start, I decided it was a great opportunity to collect health information that could provide Sherman and our other partners with a source of local data to inform new health program development and future funding applications. That first year, I was very data driven. As a result, I developed the Health Passport, a tool that could be carried by attendees to each table and used to collect screening results and survey responses. The Health Passport could then be retrieved as attendees exited the event. Undeniably, the Health Passport was a success, but I wanted to improve it. How could we make it easier for attendees and health screeners to use? How could the data be entered into a database more quickly so that our partners received the data faster?

I realized I wanted to be more people centered. To do so, my team needed to expand. I invited my colleague Theresa to work on the event with me. Theresa brought a fresh new perspective to the health passport with innovative ideas that sparked my own creativity. Leveraging the power of team allowed us to propose an electronic version of the health passport (aka ePassport) that we later successfully piloted at the event. By harnessing the skills and strengths of both the individual *And* the team, we were able to quickly and effectively take our idea from concept to realization. The ePassport was successful at producing a sustainable, high quality health event that was easy and useful for our event attendees, our screeners, and our citizen scientists. (See the following page, *Figure 1*.)[153]

Beyond my work with Sherman, growing my team was critical to my growth as a community-engaged researcher. In fact, I realized the great need for my teams to be more interdisciplinary in nature with many more perspectives from diverse community partners. I also wanted to support other traditionally trained researchers who, like me, were interested in leveraging community-engaged approaches.

---

[152] Butsch Kovacic, M., Stigler, S., Smith, A., Kidd, A., Vaughn, L. *Beginning a Partnership With Photo Voice to Explore Environmental Health and Health Inequities in Minority Communities.* International Journal of Environmental Research and Public Health. 2014, 1. 1-x manuscripts; 11(11), 11132-11151; https://doi.org/10.3390/ijerph111111132

[153] Butsch Kovacic, M. *Outliers.* TEDx UCincinnati, March 2017. www.youtube.com/watch?v=ws2p8fZnMKM

Figure 1   Polarity Map®

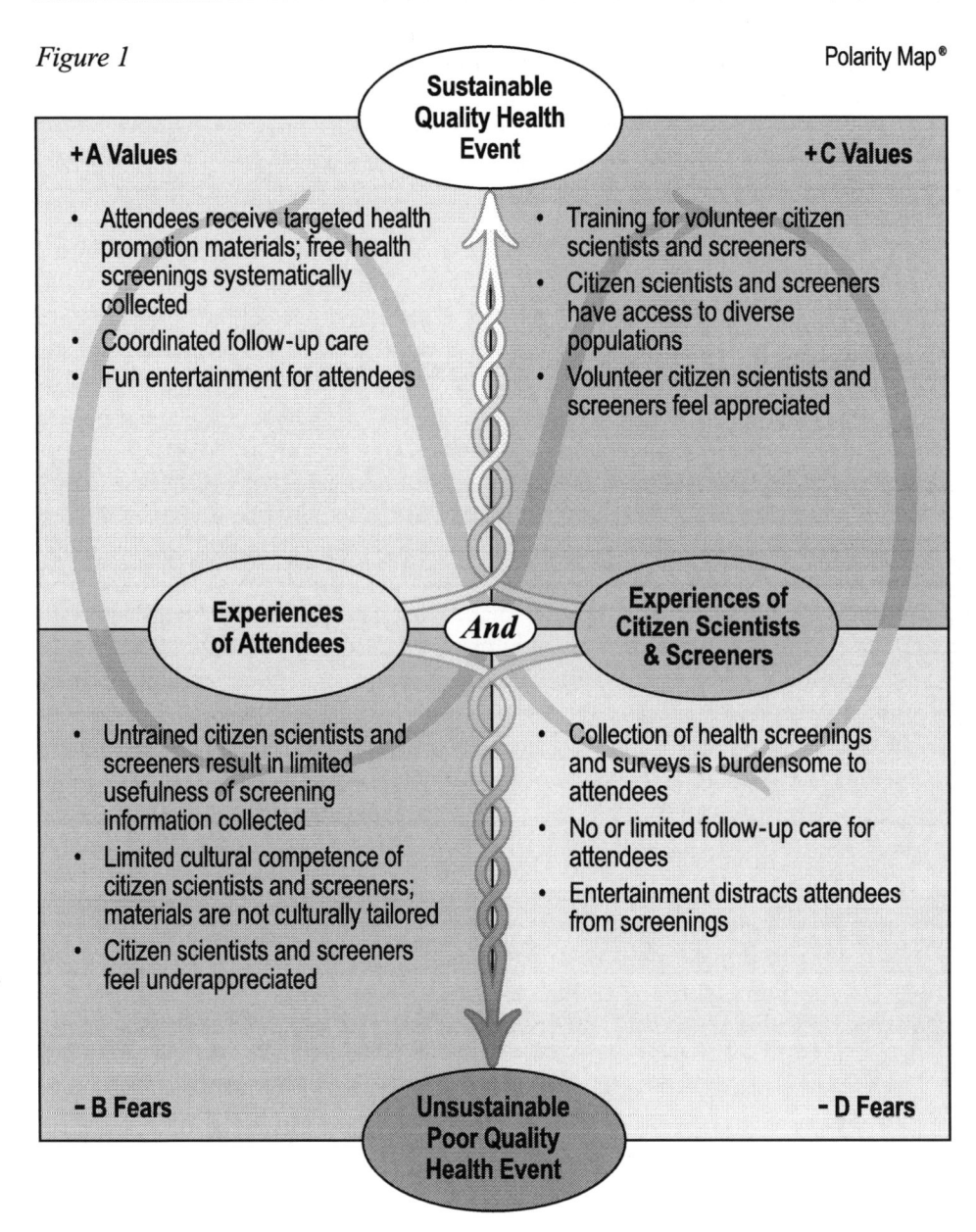

Sustainable Quality Health Event

+A Values
- Attendees receive targeted health promotion materials; free health screenings systematically collected
- Coordinated follow-up care
- Fun entertainment for attendees

+C Values
- Training for volunteer citizen scientists and screeners
- Citizen scientists and screeners have access to diverse populations
- Volunteer citizen scientists and screeners feel appreciated

Experiences of Attendees *And* **Experiences of Citizen Scientists & Screeners**

- Untrained citizen scientists and screeners result in limited usefulness of screening information collected
- Limited cultural competence of citizen scientists and screeners; materials are not culturally tailored
- Citizen scientists and screeners feel underappreciated

- Collection of health screenings and surveys is burdensome to attendees
- No or limited follow-up care for attendees
- Entertainment distracts attendees from screenings

− B Fears   **Unsustainable Poor Quality Health Event**   **− D Fears**

Since then, we have created a 15- to 20-member Community Research Advisory Board (ages 15-77) to meet with, advise, and contribute to academic researchers' studies while also utilizing institutional resources to support members' education as well as their outreach events. Four years in, its facilitator Julie and I are drafting a peer-review publication to highlight all of the groups' successes with the goal of encouraging other institutions to support similar endeavors.

Task-focused *And* People-focused

Unfortunately, as time went on, we became very focused on the task of optimizing the ePassport to the neglect of my relationship with Sherman. Our relationship ultimately was not sustainable. We hadn't clearly discussed our roles and expectations for working together and many unspoken expectations consequently went unmet. It is one of the hard lessons I learned early on in my journey to becoming community engaged. It is why I ask my new partners to develop both team charters and partnership agreements with me. Both have been useful in helping to avoid unanticipated partnership challenges by laying out our shared goals, establishing timelines, planning communication, and outlining expectations and commitments.

Structured *And* Flexible

Once Theresa joined me, we moved the community research forward much faster, and both of us spent energy cultivating the relationship with the center. She visited the center on a regular basis over the course of several weeks to observe and learn. We met frequently to discuss what she had observed. Throughout her time at the center, Theresa saw firsthand the staff's flexibility in caring for individual community members in unique ways and struggling to complete the documentation needed to justify the center's funding. After further examination, we realized that by making a few changes over time to some critical documents *And* training staff to utilize tools while catering to clients, the center would be able to leverage both the structure needed to stabilize the organization *And* the flexibility needed for each staff member to better serve.

Grounded *And* Visionary

As a result of my early successes with Alexis and Sherman, I was approached by a colleague, Victor, to support a team with a vision for utilizing systems thinking to combat poverty. Wanting to learn more about how social laboratories[154] could help positively improve the economic situations of lower income minority populations in our city, Theresa and I regularly met with Victor, his colleague Peter, and others to discuss our shared vision. However, we would often leave the meetings questioning how these often HUGE undertakings would be realized. In hindsight, we had been slow to ask several important practical questions like: "What is the budget?", "Who will fund it?", "Who and how many do we invite to participate?", and "What other political challenges will affect our timeline?". These grounding questions were required to make our vision a reality, but were absent. Still, our time with the system thinkers allowed us to cultivate a relationship with Peter, who later commissioned us to develop and test a Neighborhood Economic Vitality Index (NEVI). According to Peter, by labelling neighborhoods as impoverished, we declare that they must inherently be broken, incapable, and filled with needs. NEVI's purpose was to create a language of economic vitality or economic possibility by capturing the assets of underground GDP[155] that traditional measurements miss. By focusing on local assets, NEVI's discussions and surveys seek to grow social capital and productive capacities. Theresa and I were able to ground Peter's vision to create a uniquely useful tool. Further, as Victor introduced me to Polarity

---

[154] Kahane, Adam. *Collaborating with the Enemy: How to Work with People You Don't Agree with or Like or Trust*. Berrett-Koehler Publishers, 2017.

[155] Gross Domestic Product: An indicator used here to assess the health of a localized, underground economy.

Thinking™ Founder, Barry Johnson,[156] I was later offered a new tool that would help me consider the many polarities associated with all my ongoing work!

Standard *And* Tailored

It took many years of partnership before we first submitted a federal grant with our community partners. I wanted to make sure that our partnership was sustainable and had appropriate infrastructure to enable success. We proposed a program that would be mutually beneficial and not burden or distract our partners from the important community work. The "We Engage for Health (WE4H)"[157] program is now federally funded. With the help of our grant's program officer, we are collaborating with a complementary pair of academic researchers (Susan and Susan) from a nearby university. Together they had worked in curriculum development and graphic design for many years and provided the much-needed skills we desired to create standard stories tailored to underserved communities. Rather than a long list of dry facts, WE4H stories focus on three Big Ideas introduced by the stories' cast of characters. The stories include enough emotional detail so that participants much more vividly remember and share information with their families and friends. The stories not only increase our participants' health and science knowledge, but also their confidence in making positive health changes.

However, our goal was also to make these stories tailorable to better connect with specific target communities. For example, one of our community partners is most interested in childhood lead poisoning, while another is most concerned about heat islands[158] and their accompanying air pollution. The stories we offer can be easily switched out based on the needs of our partners as well as the hands and citizen science activities that support learning. Our overall program has standard offerings, while our offerings to communities can be tailored. Our approach differs from that often taken by traditional researchers who emphasize standardization, but we believe our tailored material will make a world of difference. Now, in year two, we are already seeing its growth possibilities. Further, our interdisciplinary research team is also benefiting. By seeing, mapping, and learning from the underlying tensions we experience together, we are now able to better leverage the infrastructure to support projects well beyond "We Engage for Health."

> Find bio and contact info for author Melinda Butsch Kovacic at
> www.polaritypartnerships.com/certified-polarity-practitioners

---

[156] Johnson, Barry. *And: Making a Difference by Leveraging Polarity, Paradox or Dilemma. Volume One – Foundations.* HRD Press, 2020.
[157] Please see web site for additional reading and expansion on these stories. www.WeEngage4Health.life; funded by a National Institute of General Medical Sciences Science Education Partnership Award.
[158] Heat Island: an urban area in which significantly more heat is absorbed and retained than in surrounding areas. www.merriam-webster.com/dictionary/heat%20island. Accessed February 2021.

Sacred Union of Masculine And Feminine Principles: Applying the Master Polarity to Leadership and Culture

Allison Conte, MS

As I was writing this chapter, the COVID-19 pandemic turned the world as we knew it upside down. Faced with an entirely new reality, it was clear I couldn't write this piece in the way I'd planned. So, I put down my laptop and went out to sit with a tree.

Planting my feet in the dirt and leaning back against a majestic white pine tree, I looked out at a beautiful bay that is home to seals, sea lions, and an occasional whale. From the depths of the earth, a message arose: "Shhh. Pause. Listen." (The polarity shift contained in this message will become clear later in this chapter.)

This pandemic had wreaked and continues to inflict more havoc around the world with loss of life and economic suffering than I ever imagined seeing in my lifetime. And right alongside that pain, there is also *promise*. I hope we will look back on this event as the catalyst that finally motivated humanity to change its life-disrespecting ways, inspired us to create The More Beautiful World Our Hearts Know is Possible,[159] and taught us to live in peace and harmony with all of creation.

To realize this opportunity, we are going to have to take a hard look at a code that has been broken for millennia – and rewrite that code. The broken code refers to a fundamental imbalance in a master polarity that is deeply embedded in humanity's collective consciousness: Masculine *And* Feminine.[160]

The Masculine *And* Feminine Principles

Masculine *And* Feminine Transcends *And* Includes a multitude of other polarities within it. For this reason, it is considered a "master polarity" whose poles are often referred to as the Masculine Principle *And* Feminine Principle. In this chapter, I share three lists of underlying polarities: General (*Figure 1*), Leadership (*Figure 3*), and Spiritual (*Figure 5*).

For the past 5,000 years, human culture has been dominated by the Masculine Principle: the get-it-done energy that builds (and conquers) cities, protects boundaries, puts satellites into space, and keeps trains running on time. As Barry Johnson would say, "There is good stuff in the Masculine."

However, an over-focus on the Masculine has led to "results" that nobody wants: the interlocking problems of war, climate change, environmental destruction, overpopulation, corporate greed, oppression, and inequality (particularly gender inequality, for obvious reasons).

---

[159] First coined by Charles Eisenstein as his book title, *The More Beautiful World Our Hearts Know is Possible*.
[160] Barry Johnson refers to this mastery polarity as Yang *And* Yin in *And: Volume One*, Chapter 32, p. 269.

Among the many downsides, the over-focus on Masculine values has created a culture of overgrowth and overwork. Our constant demand for more productivity, more consumption, and more wealth – combined with unchecked population growth – is unsustainable for humanity and for the planet. It is, frankly, anti-life.

The Feminine principle is required to sustain life (and counteract the downsides of overwork and overgrowth). The Feminine provides much-needed rest and nourishment, considers the interests of the whole, and expresses itself in cycles of birth, growth, decline and death. It was this energy that came forward with the message, "Pause. Listen," when I sat with the tree.

If we are to create a world that works for all, including humans, the earth, and all our relations,[161] we must uplift the Feminine and restore it to its rightful place of honor, alongside the Masculine (*Figure 1*). In other words, to correct the broken code, we must embrace a *sacred union* of the Masculine *And* Feminine.

Figure 1: General Polarities

Masculine Principle	*And*	Feminine Principle
Activity	And	Rest
Doing	And	Being
Part	And	Whole
Self	And	Other
Sovereignty	And	Inter-Being
Individual	And	Collective
Agency	And	Communion
Separate	And	Connected
Seeding	And	Gestating
Protecting	And	Nurturing
Giving	And	Receiving
Initiating	And	Responding
Thinking	And	Feeling
Evaluating	And	Appreciation
Logic/ Reason	And	Intuition/ Creativity
Focus	And	Flow
Structure	And	Flexibility
Determination	And	Passion
Concepts	And	Experiences

The Evolutionary Arc Moves Toward Integration

The Feminine principle first dominated on Earth from as far back as 25,000 BC to about 3,000 BC in the Archaic age, extending into the Tribal age. About 5,000 years ago, the Masculine principle came to dominance, first through the Warrior age, followed by the Traditional age, and finally Modern age. During that sweep of time, the Feminine principle was essentially suppressed.[162]

Most developmental theorists agree that the developed world is undergoing an historic paradigm shift in both consciousness and culture from Modern to Postmodern, with early signs of Integral.[163] The emerging Postmodern paradigm – with its values of caring for the planet, people over profits, empowerment of marginalized and oppressed groups, and the development of human "interiors" such as emotional and relational skills – is relatively more caring, inclusive, and connected (more

---

[161] *All my relations* is a Lakota term meaning *all of creation*.
[162] Eisler, R. *The Chalice and The Blade: Our History, Our Future*. Harper One, 1988.
[163] Beck, D., Cowan, C. *Spiral Dynamics*. Blackwell Business, 1996.

Feminine) than the previous Warrior, Traditional, and Modern paradigms. From this perspective of the long arc of human development, one can see that we are moving toward a healthy integration of the Masculine *And* Feminine master polarity, as depicted in *Figure 2*.[164]

Figure 2: Stages of Human Evolution

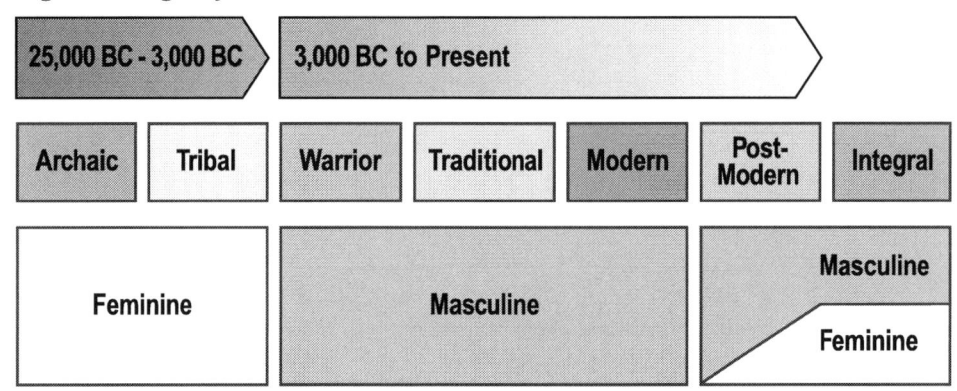

25,000 BC - 3,000 BC	3,000 BC to Present						
Archaic	Tribal	Warrior	Traditional	Modern	Post-Modern	Integral
Feminine		Masculine				Masculine / Feminine

In the short-term, however, we are not even close. As the entrenched patriarchal paradigm tries to hold onto power, we are seeing a major backlash happening now.

Case in point: During his four years in office, President Trump, who has bragged of sexual harassment and has been accused of rape many times over, systematically raped the earth as well. His administration eradicated life-giving reserves of land and water, while promoting unsustainable industries that damage the earth. These were an assault on the Feminine, both personal and planetary.

Biological Gender and the Masculine *And* Feminine Polarity

Although related to gender, the Masculine *And* Feminine principles do not refer specifically to gender; instead, they are universal values, energies, qualities, capacities, and essences. All men and women, regardless of gender or sexual orientation, have access to all of the values and energies contained in Masculine *And* Feminine and the polarities within.

Because the associations between Masculine-Male and Feminine-Female run deep, it can be challenging to discuss these energies without triggering reactions related to gender. By shifting the focus from gender to essence – principles, energies, values – we can level-up the conversation about gender dynamics.

With this in mind, it's useful to relax gender associations and look for a truth that transcends gender: *Both* men and women have an inner Feminine, *And* an inner Masculine. That said, it's also true that gender does indeed matter when talking about these principles.

---

[164] Susan Cannon, Ph.D., first published this chart in our co-authored 2015 white paper, "Integral Feminine Leadership."

With exceptions, most women tend to have a more Feminine essence and facility with Feminine capacities compared to most men (who, with exceptions, tend to have a more Masculine essence). There are a number of complex reasons for this, which meet at the intersection of biology, psychology, and sociology. As such, we have a different lived-experiences of the Masculine *And* Feminine polarity.

Because both men and women have an inner Feminine, we all suffer emotional, psychic, and spiritual pain as a result of the cultural devaluing of the Feminine and the long-term effects of Masculine dominance. But we suffer differently. Women with a feminine essence often feel this pain acutely, particularly at work.

How Does Masculine *And* Feminine Show Up in Leadership?

The increasingly outdated stereotype of a powerful leader is hyper-Masculine: driven, assertive, critical, cognitively intelligent, competitive. These energies can feel energizing and empowering at first, but over time, without the balance of the Feminine, they become draining and disempowering.

In a hyper-Masculine organizational culture, individual leaders are often driven to wield "power over" others, work excessive hours, and stifle emotions. They don't take in enough nourishment in the form of restorative sleep, rewarding relationships, and connection to Nature. They go through the motions even though success feels empty, their soul is slowly dying, and their health is deteriorating. Many suffer from stress-related health issues such as adrenal fatigue.[165]

Operating on overdrive blocks access to the intuition and inner guidance that could help leaders to make more effective decisions and find healthier, more fulfilling ways of working. It also robs them of what it takes to be inspirational leaders because they've lost touch with passion, creativity, and joy.

The hyper-Masculine paradigm affects teams and organizations by rendering them more likely to suffer from siloed thinking, unsustainable results, high turnover, low levels of employee engagement, lack of creativity/innovation, and projects that flounder or fail to get off the ground.

Integrated Leadership is Needed Now

What is needed at this pivotal time of ecological and social collapse is an uprising of ... full-spectrum leadership in every one of us. ~ Nina Simons[166]

In today's Volatile, Uncertain, Complex, and Ambiguous (VUCA) environment, many critically important leadership competencies are aligned with the Feminine principle: sensing and adapting to emerging realities, creativity, participative decision-making, emotional intelligence, social networks, intuitive awareness, and

---

[165] Adrenal fatigue is a condition caused by long-term stress and reportedly affects millions of people, but is not yet recognized by Western medicine as a distinct syndrome. Primary symptoms are fatigue that is not relieved by sleep and a general sense of un-wellness, tiredness or "gray" feelings. People with this condition often prop themselves up with caffeine and sugar to get through the day.
[166] Nina Simons is Co-Founder of Bioneers.

many others. In a VUCA world, the best leaders are able to work with – and embody – the integration of Masculine *And* Feminine (*Figure 3*). These "full spectrum" leaders are the ones who can help us rewrite the broken code and move humanity forward in a good way. I believe that, increasingly, those leaders will be women.

Women Will Lead the Way

The world would be a better place if women were in charge. ~ My father

My father's belief in the power of women's leadership was pretty far out on a limb in the 1960s. Today it's not so far out. In a study of 64,000 people surveyed in 13 countries, two-thirds believe the world would be a better place if men thought more like women.[167] The author of that study, John Gerzema, declared, "The Feminine is the operating system of the 21st century." The Dalai Lama has said that the world will be saved by women. And President Barack Obama has said, "If every nation on Earth was run by women, you would see a significant improvement across the board on just about everything ... living standards and outcomes."[168]

Figure 3: Leadership Polarities

Masculine Principle	And	Feminine Principle
Scale (Breadth)	And	Impact (Depth)
Shareholder Value	And	Stakeholder Value
Profitability	And	Sustainability
Competition	And	Collaboration
Quantity	And	Quality
Clear	And	Flexible
Drive	And	Devotion
Planning Ahead	And	Sensing What Is Emerging
Directive Decisions	And	Participative Decisions
Cognitive Intelligence	And	Emotional Intelligence
Standardization	And	Customization
Power of Hierarchy	And	Power of Network
Commanding	And	Inspiring

This perspective that women are more effective leaders is supported by a plethora of research from the leadership field that shows women leaders outperforming men in the boardroom, in the C-suite, and on 360-degree assessment surveys. And, so far, the most effective responses to the COVID-19 pandemic appear to have come from women leaders around the globe.[169]

From a polarity perspective, this is no surprise. As Johnson has pointed out, women tend to use *And*-thinking more than men – which makes sense, since the Feminine principle favors integration (Masculine favors differentiation). Women also have an adaptive advantage in leadership because we've already done the heavy lifting to develop Masculine leadership capacities in order to survive in a Masculine-dominant workplace.

---

[167] Gerzema, J., D'Antonio, M. *The Athena Doctrine: How Women (and the Men Who Think Like Them) Will Rule the Future.* Jossey-Bass, 2013.
[168] President Barack Obama, speaking at a private leadership event in Singapore, December 16, 2019. www.bbc.com/news/world-asia-50805822
[169] Wittenberg-Cox, Avivah. "What Do Countries With the Best Coronavirus Responses Have In Common? Women Leaders." Forbes Magazine, April 13, 2020.

For these reasons, women will be crucial way-showers of new-paradigm, integrated leadership.

A Model for Integration: Sophia Leadership

Building on Johnson's work, I began developing the Sophia Leadership model in 2012 with the overarching goal to help organizations create more balanced leadership cultures.

I sensed something was missing from Johnson's description of the Yang *And* Yin polarity: namely, the extraordinary power of Shakti, the Feminine energy that is creative, passionate, and pleasurable. Shakti is different from the kind of passive/receptive energy most Westerners think of when they hear the word, *yin*. This flavor of the Feminine is anything but still and passive: it is active and energetic, even fiery.

I felt as if I'd come home when I discovered the work of Jungian scholar Gareth Hill,[170] which brings an archetypal and developmental perspective to the Masculine *And* Feminine energies – and expands them to include this more active side of the Feminine.

According to Hill, healthy human development involves two aspects of Masculine *And* Feminine: Static *And* Dynamic (another polarity). Crossing Masculine *And* Feminine with Static *And* Dynamic yields four universal energies, which correspond to four archetypes in the human psyche. As we grow, we move through these energies in a developmental progression.[171]

The Sophia Leadership model is a blend of Johnson's work, Hill's work, and my own knowledge based on years of study in the fields of integral theory, developmental theory, leadership, organizational development, psychology, spirituality and energy work. The model itself is too robust to explain in full here, but below I share a brief summary of Hill's four universal energies/archetypes.

Four Universal Energies

Although the four energies/archetypes form a multarity (they are all interdependent), there are two primary polarity tensions that show up again and again in the human experience: Static Feminine *And* Dynamic Masculine, and Static Masculine *And* Dynamic Feminine (*Figure 4*).

1. **Static Feminine (Great Mother archetype):** Being. Interconnectedness and integration (of the whole). Everything included in a womb-like embrace. Unconditionally loving. Nurtures life. Cycles of birth-growth-decline-death.
    - Too much: Passive, victim, enmeshed, smothering, numb
    - Too little: Apathetic, neglectful, careless

---

[170] Hill, G. *Masculine and Feminine: the Natural Flow of Opposites in the Psyche.* Shambhala, 1992.
[171] Hill's developmental sequence, as well as an understanding of developmental theory in general, is beyond the scope of this chapter but remains an important component of the Sophia Leadership model.

2. **Dynamic Masculine (Warrior archetype):** Doing. Agency and self-determination (of the part). Initiates. Differentiates. Sets boundaries. Gets things done. Goal-oriented.

   - Too much: Inconsiderate of others, dominating, violent, abusive or destructive
   - Too little: Lacks confidence, abandons the goal, collapses

3. **Static Masculine (Great Father archetype):** Structure. Order. Containment. Rules of order, theories of knowledge, hierarchies of value. Analytical thinking.

   - Too much: Rigid, righteous, bureaucratic, oppressive, judgmental, dry/lifeless
   - Too little: Alienated, apathetic, disorganized

4. **Dynamic Feminine (Muse archetype):** Flow. Vision. Creativity. Play, sensuality, beauty, passion. Collaboration. Relationships. Process-oriented.

   - Too much: Irresponsible, hedonistic, addicted, manic
   - Too little: Repressed, bored, dry/lifeless

Figure 4: The Four Universal Energies of Integrated Leadership

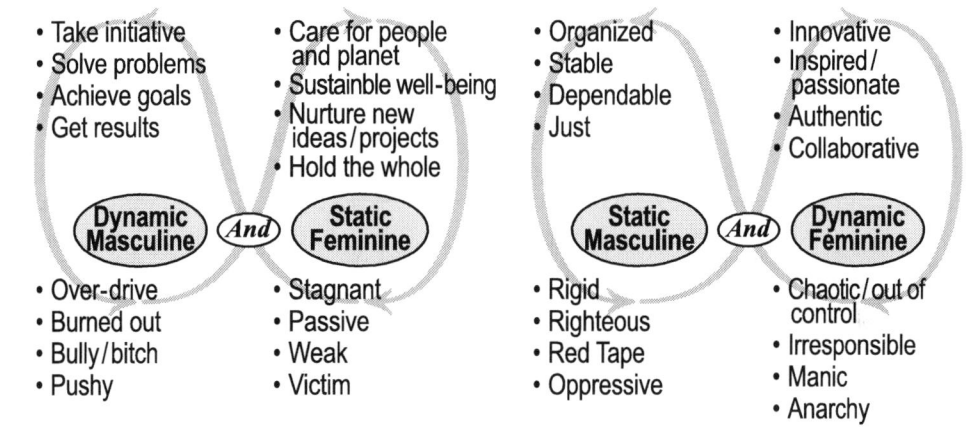

Dynamic Masculine *And* Static Feminine	Static Masculine *And* Dynamic Feminine
• Take initiative • Solve problems • Achieve goals • Get results	• Care for people and planet • Sustainable well-being • Nurture new ideas/projects • Hold the whole	• Organized • Stable • Dependable • Just	• Innovative • Inspired/passionate • Authentic • Collaborative
• Over-drive • Burned out • Bully/bitch • Pushy	• Stagnant • Passive • Weak • Victim	• Rigid • Righteous • Red Tape • Oppressive	• Chaotic/out of control • Irresponsible • Manic • Anarchy

Application: How Might We Move Toward Sacred Union?

Although sacred union is needed at all levels of system – families, teams, communities, organizations, and society as a whole – I believe we must start by doing the inner psycho-spiritual work to create coherence and integration within ourselves.

Doing the inner work to embody sacred union is a profoundly generous and generative act. Development of this kind requires dedication and patience; it is the work of a lifetime. From a place of integrity with our own personal development, we can begin to help others.

As mentioned, I initially began working with others around Masculine *And* Feminine energies when I was working as an executive coach and corporate consultant. Over the last few years, I've focused on Leadership Development *And* Spiritual

Development for changemakers (*Figure 5*). I've co-founded two organizations whose work aims to create a better world through sacred union.

Sophia Leadership's mission is to develop women changemakers to achieve their missions more effectively, with joy and ease. The Center for Sacred Union is a nonprofit spiritual community whose mission is to promote wholeness for people and planet by engaging the mystery of sacred union as a spiritual path.

In both organizations, we work deeply with the four universal energies in an embodied way. In addition to Polarity Thinking™, we use a variety of transformational tools including assessments, coaching, group work, shadow work, energy work, spiritual practices, ceremony, and ritual.

Figure 5: Spiritual Polarities

Masculine Principle	And	Feminine Principle
God	And	Goddess
Absolute Reality	And	Relative Reality
Emptiness	And	Form
Non-Duality	And	Duality
Un-Manifest	And	Manifest
Transcendent	And	Immanent
'Outer' World	And	'Inner' World
Heaven	And	Earth
Holy Word	And	Holy Spirit
Sun	And	Moon
Light	And	Dark
Unique	And	Universal
That Which Never Changes	And	That Which Is Constantly Changing

Whatever your focus in life and work, you can make a positive difference by consciously working with the master polarity of Masculine *And* Feminine and helping others to do the same. I invite you to join me walking the path toward sacred union for your own benefit, and for the benefit of all beings. One place to start can be, "Shhh. Pause. Listen."

Find bio and contact info for author Allison Conte at
www.polaritypartnerships.com/certified-polarity-practitioners

Polarity Thinking™:
The Foundation of Evolutionary Spirituality
Rev Kelly Isola, ThD

Evolution is a fundamental design of the human condition – biologically, socially, psychologically, and yes, even spiritually. Evolutionary spirituality is not a religion, faith, or particular belief system. In fact, one of the first thinkers around the idea of the evolution of spirituality, long before Darwin's "Origin of Species," was Friedrich Schelling who said, "History as a whole is a progressive, gradually self-disclosing revelation of the Absolute."

In other words, prior to theories of biological development, philosophers[172] such as Immanuel Kant and Georg Hegel had already intuited that reality as a whole was, in some essential way, going somewhere. Humanity had a purpose and direction towards ever-expanding expressions of "Universal Spirit." Concerns of ultimate reality were now driving our capacity to consciously evolve ourselves and our world.

In the 200 years plus between Hegel and now, there have been several champions of the theory of "spiritual evolution." Foremost among these were the French philosopher Henri Bergson, and the French paleontologist and Catholic priest Pierre Teilhard de Chardin. Other key figures include Ralph Waldo Emerson, Rudolph Steiner, and integral theorist Jean Gebser. It was the work of the Indian philosopher-sage Sri Aurobindo (1872-1950) though that brought new dimensions to the idea.

After experiencing a spiritual awakening, Aurobindo envisioned the possibilities we humans have for engaging with the same force that has been driving the evolution of the cosmos for 14 billion years. Since only human beings can look to their past and self-reflect, he realized that through this process we could consciously co-create our future. By looking inward, we could look outward in order to create a world that works for all – while simultaneously being directed to inner fulfillment. Aurobindo had translated the theory of spiritual evolution into a spiritual practice.

As you read this, you will likely identify several (of the hundreds) of polarities that are the foundations of Evolutionary Spirituality: Self *And* Other, Inner World *And* Outer World, Past *And* Future, Theory *And* Practice. If you consider that every spiritual truth is essentially a paradox – polarity – then the lens through which you see the evolution of humanity, as well as your own growth, becomes even more illuminated. Looking at the Polarity Maps® provided in this chapter, consider the content of every quadrant and recognize your own thoughts as we walk through them together.

---

[172] Charles Darwin (1809-1882); Friedrich Schelling (1775-1854); Immanuel Kant (1724-1804); Georg Hegel (1770-1831); Sri Aurobindo (1872-1950); Henri Bergson (1859-1941); Pierre Teilhard de Chardin (1881-1955); Ralph Waldo Emerson (1802-1882); Rudolf Steiner (1861-1925); Jean Gebser (1905-1973)

- Upper quadrants (+A, +C Values): What are the positive experiences I've had or my desired outcomes when I focus on each of these poles?
- Lower quadrants (-B, -D Fears): When I over-focus on one of these poles to the neglect of the other, what are the negative outcomes, or projected consequences I see, or what do I fear might happen?

Throughout the chapter you will notice polarities "jumping out" at you, make note of these and learn to draw your own maps, use the blank map available at the end of this book, or use the ones provided here as a template. What's not presented on the chapter maps are the extended quadrants to the left and right; places to discern Action Steps and Early Warnings for the left and right-hand poles. Using what you know of Polarity Thinking™ and mapping polarities, take some time to consider your next steps. The Action Steps are *you engaging* in Evolutionary Spirituality! The Early Warnings show us when we have stepped outside the natural evolutionary impulse wanting to be made manifest as your Higher Self.

Evolution is about the past *And* the future, a 14-billion-year-old story that we contemplate from our stance here in the *present*, about how our own lives can shape the future. Pondering the past and future, through the lens of Polarity Thinking in the present moment, gives us profoundly greater clarity and integrity for choosing our future. Our underlying drive in working with polarities is "seeing is relieving, seeing is changing, and seeing is loving."[173] By seeing these energy systems and engaging them – remember this is a practice – we become a more powerful, integrated, effective, and loving species.

Evolutionary spirituality, then, is about right relationship with reality. It is about understanding how evolution really happens, how it takes place, and the processes of growth to being *And* becoming (note the polarity) our most noble selves. Each one of us has a role to play in the future of our planet: of creating a socially just, environmentally sustainable and spiritually fulfilling world. This is also humanity's collective task right now.

Aligning ourselves with the reality we are in, not through the rose-colored glasses of how we would like it to be, is more than just cleaning up our internal messes, or as Carl Jung[174] calls it our "shadow," those unlived and unloved pieces of ourselves; it is also about tending to what is holy outside ourselves, our relationships with humans and all life. One thing that has become painfully obvious, looking at our history, is that as we awaken, as our spirituality evolves, we become more self-aware. We are learning and experiencing that the more out of alignment or disconnected we are with our present-day reality, the more we suffer, individually and collectively. Everything suffers. This is why the practices of evolutionary spirituality are vital to creating our preferred future, of coming into right relationship with our future.

---

[173] Johnson, Barry. Shared in conversation. See: *And: Making a Difference by Leveraging Polarity, Paradox or Dilemma. Volume One – Foundations.* HRD Press, 2020.
[174] Carl Jung (1875-1961)

Engaging in Polarity Thinking, of embodying paradox, is a quintessential practice of evolutionary spirituality for the 21st century. The power of this practice is that it is not necessarily dependent on your faith tradition, religion, or life philosophy. It is a practice that can uplift and inform, while relieving the tension we feel from thinking something has to be *either/Or*. In fact, it often provides a greater sense of connection across cultures, enhancing the beauty in the diversity of all life and providing clarity around our purpose and direction in this evolutionary journey.

As you look across cultures and current spiritual or religious practices, you see at the heart of it all is paradox – and the accompanying tension that comes with that mystery. Oftentimes, our dualistic mind can't reconcile the seeming contradictions of a paradox and abandons the mystery because the brain seeks certainty. These experiences of bumping up against tensions and contradictions are turning points for us; they are doorways into a deeper mystery of God, Ultimate Reality, Nature, the Cosmos, or whatever word you may use – doorways for being in alignment with reality, *with what is*. These are also opportunities to deny or resist that mystery. This is a hallmark of evolutionary spirituality.

As you look at the map (*Figure 1*), see if you can find yourself – have you become stagnant in some ways of thinking, or too rigid? When was the last time you took a risk and learned something new about spirituality outside your comfort zone? Ask yourself, "What practices can I engage in that would embody the upsides (+A, +C) of both Certainty *And* Mystery?" Perhaps begin a meditation or mindfulness practice, or if you already have one, try something new and different. Whatever you choose, practice every day for 90 days to see how your discomfort as well your self-awareness expands. This is the doorway for growth. Any mindfulness practice will invite you into pausing during your day, and when you do, start to notice the chatter in your mind; the dialogue taking place. This brings the unconscious into the conscious mind, and by doing this, you will tap into those internal "messes" that need your attention and intention.

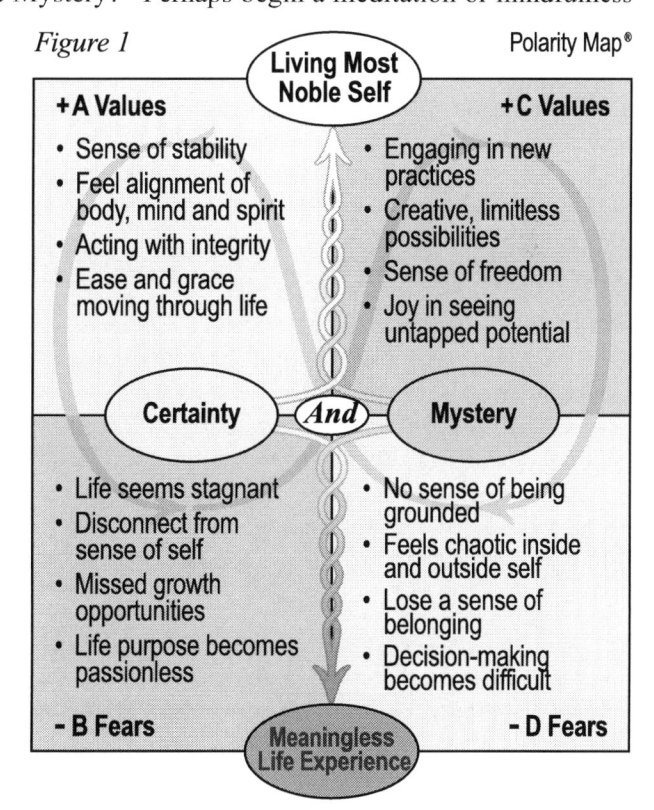

Figure 1 — Polarity Map®

Living Most Noble Self

+A Values
- Sense of stability
- Feel alignment of body, mind and spirit
- Acting with integrity
- Ease and grace moving through life

+C Values
- Engaging in new practices
- Creative, limitless possibilities
- Sense of freedom
- Joy in seeing untapped potential

Certainty —*And*— **Mystery**

- Life seems stagnant
- Disconnect from sense of self
- Missed growth opportunities
- Life purpose becomes passionless

- No sense of being grounded
- Feels chaotic inside and outside self
- Lose a sense of belonging
- Decision-making becomes difficult

– B Fears — Meaningless Life Experience — **– D Fears**

This healing brings you the expanded capacity to take actions for creating a future with more generosity, benevolence, and love. You are more "on purpose." If you hold both the Certainty *And* Mystery of our journey, you will grow in understanding of what *really* matters and dive deeper into the endless mystery of our 14-billion-year-old story more assuredly and compassionately. To live inside this tension is not to transcend one or the other values, but to include both because living as your Higher Self is bigger than either one alone. This is the evolution of consciousness at work in front of your eyes.

In evolutionary spirituality, we are intentionally pursuing the evolution of consciousness. Think of it as a spiritual calling. We are intuitively drawn to bring a higher order of love, compassion, equality, and belonging for all life, not just humanity. It is at the heart of the activist path, and whether we realize it or not, we are all activists in our own ways when we consciously engage in the evolutionary process at hand.

Gone are the days of defining an "activist" solely as someone out protesting, carrying signs, and toting megaphones shouting battle cries of injustices to rally the "troops." That is ONE form of being an activist, yet we must remain relevant. Evolutionary spirituality requires we stay connected to the evolving beliefs emerging in every generation around ideas of the Divine, God, spirituality, faith and being activists in the world. Another way of saying "co-creating our future."

Ironically, the root of the word "relevant" is to "lessen, or lighten." While the world is moving ever-faster, we need to remember that to be relevant we must lighten our load. Being relevant begins with the understanding that, outside of basic survival needs, everything changes - yes, EVERYTHING. While the rate of change increases around us, we don't need to speed up to hang on, we need to lighten our load, clean house as it were, not *in spite* of the world around us – but *because* of the world around us. With all this change, many express their fear that what is most sacred will be lost forever. What we have known and love as "spiritual" will be gone, and this can invoke great sadness and uncertainty.

Oftentimes with change comes great upheaval, discomfort, and a loss of direction and grounding. We long for more stability, calmer waters, the "good ole days." Yet, whenever I hear someone say, "We need to go back to____," I feel a little nervous. Go back to what? I'm not sure we need to "go back to" anything. I do believe though, in focusing some attention on bringing forward pieces of our roots, our heritage, the wisdom of the ages. We transcend or move beyond what no longer serves – this is relevance – and we include or bring forward that which continues to serve – this is reverence. Reverence is standing in the awe and wonder, without "going back" because we are afraid.

Today, how people choose to be "activists" is discerned through the process of an inner transformation, which guides the outer "revolution." Understanding the paradox of Reverence *And* Relevance (*Figure 2*), we work to awaken to the paradigms and structures created over time that make up our values, individually and collectively.

Being relevant means being in our preferred future now. To be relevant means to be "pertinent to the matter at hand."

Ask yourself, "Am I holding beliefs or ideas that are 'sacred cows' which perhaps no longer serve?" Maybe you have spiritual practices from ancient traditions that are just as relevant today? When we take time to consider these types of questions, we begin to work from that place of right relationship with the present and allow our discoveries to define what it means to be a spiritual activist. Essentially, we are changing the world from the inside-out.

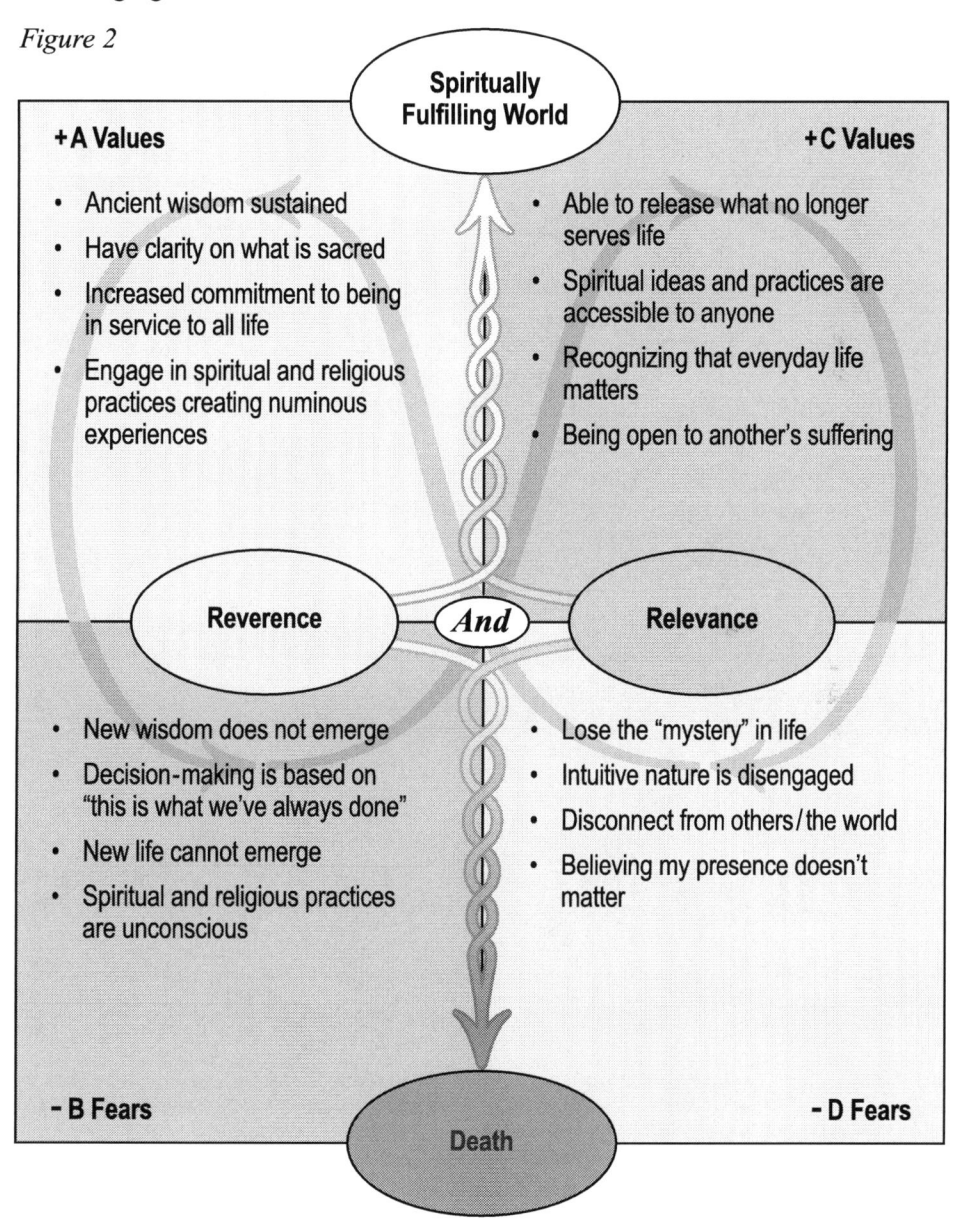

Figure 2

Spiritually Fulfilling World

+A Values
- Ancient wisdom sustained
- Have clarity on what is sacred
- Increased commitment to being in service to all life
- Engage in spiritual and religious practices creating numinous experiences

+C Values
- Able to release what no longer serves life
- Spiritual ideas and practices are accessible to anyone
- Recognizing that everyday life matters
- Being open to another's suffering

Reverence *And* **Relevance**

-B Fears
- New wisdom does not emerge
- Decision-making is based on "this is what we've always done"
- New life cannot emerge
- Spiritual and religious practices are unconscious

-D Fears
- Lose the "mystery" in life
- Intuitive nature is disengaged
- Disconnect from others/the world
- Believing my presence doesn't matter

Death

There are many different approaches to Evolutionary Spirituality. Some see it as simply a philosophy or theory, others view it through a particular religious lens, yet others engage with it as both philosophy *And* practice (note the polarity). If we understand Evolutionary Spirituality as both, then we are engaging the natural evolutionary impulse at work for billions of years. Essentially we are answering a "spiritual calling." Joseph Campbell[175] invited us to answer that call, to follow our bliss, which is not a cognitive pursuit, but rather a bliss that emerges by engaging the world. A bliss borne out of the intersection of your own gifts *And* what the world needs most (note the polarity).

The power of Polarity Thinking is harnessing that evolutionary energy system in order to lead us through a seemingly impossible paradox for the purposes of "clearing the decks" to live our "yes" to life. Remember Aurobindo's realization: by looking inward, we could look outward in order to create a world that works for all, while simultaneously being directed to inner fulfillment (note the polarity). By consciously engaging in practices that move us along this evolutionary path, we discover that our Higher Self emerges naturally within and through us. This clearing of the decks frees up energy which we can devote to our individual and collective good. This freedom is found in the synergy Contemplation *And* Action (*Figure 3*). The two are inseparable.

Contemplation means pausing, quieting our inner world, and giving ourselves over to that evolutionary impulse – whatever is ultimate reality beyond the cognitive mind – to inform us and grow us. Some may see contemplative practices as a way to escape the present reality; however, they are the exact opposite. Contemplation is consciously choosing to step away, to go apart for a while, so that we return to the attentiveness of daily life knowing what compassionate action is ours to take. We are better able to follow our bliss. We also have greater clarity on what is NOT ours to do.

What practices are you engaged in that are designed to still your interior world? How can you adopt a practice that embodies the best of contemplative practices *And* compassionate service? Have you ever walked a labyrinth, carrying *into* the center of the labyrinth the question "what is mine to do?" If not, try this, and as you walk out of the labyrinth notice what concrete next steps emerge from your own wisdom.

No matter how well-intentioned our actions may be, without our contemplative practices, we are more likely to cause harm than do good in the world. We are also more likely to experience burnout, essentially to come out of alignment with the present, thereby abandoning the evolutionary impulse, the spiritual calling. We stop practicing ways of healing the suffering in the world, and we stop co-creating a future where life thrives. And regrettably, we move from what is possible to thinking things are impossible. Contemplation helps us discern what is truly important, what really matters in the present and what to do – actions we can take – in the face of injustice.

---

[175] Joseph Campbell (1904-1987)

Figure 3

```
                    ┌─────────────────────┐
                    │  Healing All Life   │
                    └─────────────────────┘
```

+A Values

- Develop capacity for Higher Self to guide your actions
- Aligns our mind with what the world needs most
- Expands our nurturing capacities for others
- Discover places in myself that need self-compassion

+C Values

- Compassionate service brings meaning to my own life
- Experience the interconnectedness of all life
- Knowing my presence here matters
- Contributing to creating world that works for all

Contemplation *And* **Action**

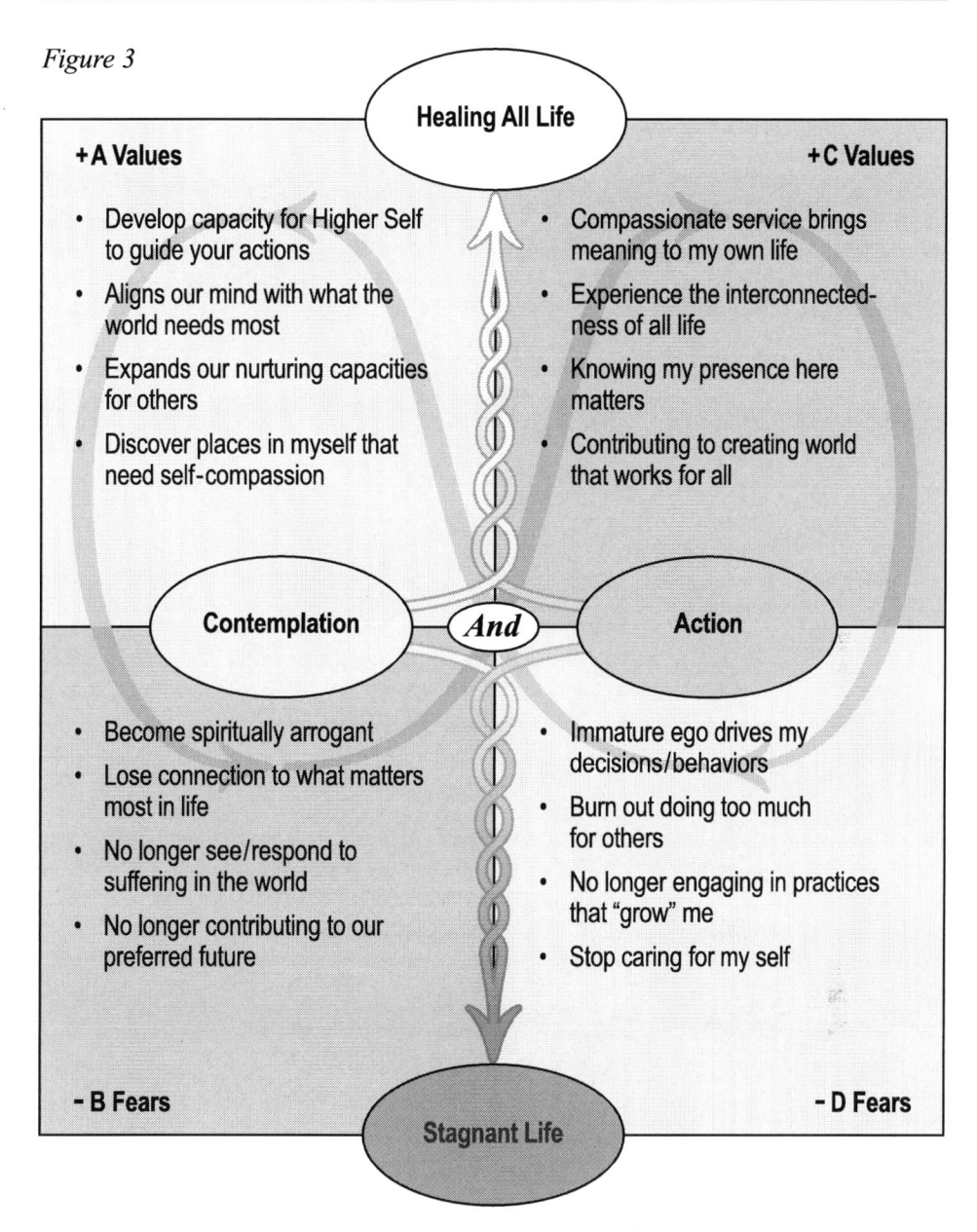

- Become spiritually arrogant
- Lose connection to what matters most in life
- No longer see/respond to suffering in the world
- No longer contributing to our preferred future

- Immature ego drives my decisions/behaviors
- Burn out doing too much for others
- No longer engaging in practices that "grow" me
- Stop caring for my self

– B Fears   **Stagnant Life**   **– D Fears**

Throughout our evolution from nomads to clans to tribes, communities, networks and beyond, an inner transformation has also been taking place. As our circles and connections have grown, so has our capacity for care and concern, in part out of necessity, and in part because we can self-reflect and consciously choose to act with generosity and benevolence. While the entire body of knowledge of Evolutionary Spirituality cannot be offered in these pages, hopefully there is enough to get you started on this journey: using the evolutionary creative spark inherent in you, as well as Polarity Thinking as a map for evolving your own consciousness, and stepping into your role as a co-creator of our future world. We can discover our next steps to organize ourselves globally, while enhancing the relationships we hold dearly. By doing this, we enhance our relationship with all Life. Evolutionary Spirituality comes down to making the infinite shine through the finite.

On your evolutionary journey toward spiritual discovery and expressing your Most Noble Self, these may be some notable polarities you will feel and can leverage during your process (*Figure 4*). This list is a few of the many you will likely discern over a lifetime of inner transformation and outer "revolution" as you awaken to co-creating a world that works for all.

Figure 4

Key Polarities for Spiritual Awakening *And* the Transformation of Culture		
Being	*And*	Becoming
Practice	*And*	Reflection
Intellect	*And*	Intuition
Ancient Wisdom	*And*	Current Events
Direct Experience	*And*	Numinous Experience
People	*And*	Planet
Letting In	*And*	Letting Go
Higher Self	*And*	Ego Self
Limited Reality (Human)	*And*	Infinite Potential (Divine)
Devotion	*And*	Questioning
Culture	*And*	Cosmos
Inner Transformation	*And*	Outer Revolution
Self-Awareness	*And*	Self-Expression
One's Gifts	*And*	World's Needs

Find bio and contact info for author Kelly Isola at
www.polaritypartnerships.com/certified-polarity-practitioners

Competing Visions: How Opposing, Underlying Feelings About Human Nature Lead to Political Polarization

Bert Parlee, PhD

Imagine there's no countries, It isn't hard to do. Nothing to kill or die for, And no religion too. Imagine all the people living life in peace ...

~ John Lennon

Lennon goes on to reaffirm this "Unlimited Vision" of human potential with his paean to peace anthem: "Give Peace a Chance." Those of us who share this vision believe that if our intentions are loving and fair-minded, we can apply our open hearts and minds to cultivating free and equal societies that will organically bring forth the natural and basic goodness in people; our better angels will soar. As these and related views shaped the emerging Social Justice culture in the 60s and 70s, today they fashion our culture of diversity, inclusivity, and in particular, of equity.

The intention here will be to show how God and evolution's purpose may conspire to populate societies with people who represent both the "Limited" and "Unlimited" visions of human nature. We are generally unaware of how much these visions animate the stands we take on specific topics. These opposite and complementary intimations about life remain largely unexamined by individuals and cultures alike. Relatedly, a fascinating feature about political opinions is how reliably the same individuals repeatedly line up together on the same side of a wide range of diverse issues. Whether it's climate change, abortion, gun control, health care, immigration, foreign affairs, etc., the same folks on one side end up uniting and generally feeling the same ways about all of these different topics. Meanwhile, those they oppose are themselves lining up, correspondingly, with similarly-minded others on the opposite side of these diverse matters. And they're both looking angrily at those with the opposing vision, about what constitutes the good, the true, and the beautiful in society. Are there any common dimensions we can look to that might help explain these all too reliable divides that both unite and divide good people? It turns out there are. More importantly, as with all polarities, there are good-hearted and well-intentioned individuals on either side. And we need all of them.

During the Enlightenment period of the 1700s, while reflecting on his vision of the "noble savage" of antiquity, Jean Jacques Rousseau famously stated, "Man is born free, and everywhere he is in chains." He was asserting that modern states repress the equality and freedom that is our birthright. Rousseau believed that egalitarian revolution led by the morally and intellectually evolved – in this case the French Revolution which he championed – is what would ultimately lead to a Utopian state. From this foundation, humankind was destined to become perfectible, living out its potential as realized beings. This Unlimited vision assumes that good and wise leaders are able to design and engineer equitable social systems, wherein care and fairness will be the order of the day, and where prosperity, property, and other assets will be distributed equitably for the benefit of all.

A vision has been described as a "pre-analytic cognitive act"; our gut feeling about what the world and its inhabitants are like, and how it works before we engage systematic reasoning. In A Conflict of Visions, Thomas Sowell, an African American economist, describes our visions as the silent shapers of our thoughts.[176] He claims that different people feel and reason from two fundamentally divergent premises and assumptions. Sowell uses the terms "Constrained" and "Unconstrained" to represent these opposing visions about how people come from countervailing presuppositions concerning why things unfold as they do. "Limited" and "Unlimited" are terms I'll use here interchangeably (*Figure 1*).

Visions comprise the underlying bedrock upon which theories are later constructed. Rousseau's Unlimited Vision paints a picture of what for him is our most natural human compassion and magnanimity. On the other hand, our Limited vision recognizes mankind as more fundamentally "fallen." Enlightenment philosopher Thomas Hobbes described man's naturally Limited condition in terms that omitted Rousseau's "noble" adjective. For Hobbes, "The armed power of political institutions was all that prevented the war of each against all, that would otherwise exist among men in their natural state, where life would be solitary, poor, nasty, brutish, and short."[177] These visions represent diametrically opposed intuitions about human nature that we, on either side, continue to subconsciously sense and "feel into" today.

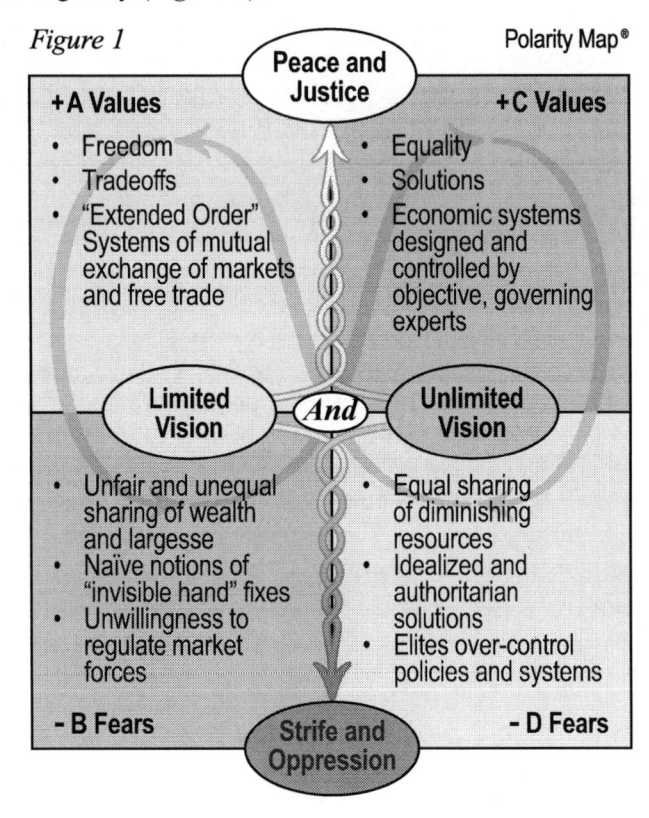

Figure 1 — Polarity Map®

Peace and Justice

+A Values
- Freedom
- Tradeoffs
- "Extended Order" Systems of mutual exchange of markets and free trade

+C Values
- Equality
- Solutions
- Economic systems designed and controlled by objective, governing experts

Limited Vision *And* Unlimited Vision

- Unfair and unequal sharing of wealth and largesse
- Naïve notions of "invisible hand" fixes
- Unwillingness to regulate market forces

- Equal sharing of diminishing resources
- Idealized and authoritarian solutions
- Elites over-control policies and systems

- B Fears — Strife and Oppression — **- D Fears**

Sowell references a hypothetical story about a tragedy in far-away China that Adam Smith used to illustrate our Constrained human nature. I'll adapt this story

---

[176] Sowell, Thomas. *A Conflict of Visions: Ideological Origins of Political Struggles.* Basic Books, 1987.
[177] Hobbes, Thomas. *Leviathan.* 1651.

to a relatively recent event from our own lifetime. The Indonesian tsunami in 2004 killed a quarter of a million people in Asia, evoking international shock and dismay. Many of us contributed to the Red Cross and other organizations assisting with the tragedy. Nonetheless, most of us quickly returned to our more immediate concerns, with a rapidly diminishing regard for the horror continuing to unfold on distant shores. This correlates with Smith's conclusion on a European's reaction to the Chinese catastrophe in 1760, "If he were to lose his little finger, he would not sleep that night; but, provided he never saw them, he would snore with the most profound security over the ruin of a hundred million of his human brothers and sisters."[178]

Smith felt that the moral limitations of man – his egocentricity in particular – were not to be lamented, nor regarded as things to remedy or change. The Constrained vision understands man's nature to be a fixed condition. If evolution caused us to continually wring our hands over the endless misfortunes that befall people, there would be no time left in which to learn, grow, advance, and transform. While this Limited vision allows for much development and increasingly civilized behavior as we have evolved, they would nevertheless point to the continuing strife of war, crime, and oppression, as well as the ongoing cruelties and pettiness that characterize town and even family life and other close relationships. "Everybody Wants to Rule the World" might serve as an anthem of this vision, with a paradoxical phrase that captures its continuing code from ancient times: "The more things change, the more they remain the same." Put in different "*both/And*" terms: Things are getting better. Things are getting worse. Things are the same as they've always been.

Aware of this inherent Constraint in man's nature, the essential social and moral challenge was to make the most of the possibilities existing within such limitations, rather than attempting to change the impossible. While educated to be a moral philosopher, Smith conceived of an economic framework that would allow men and women to bring their best selves forward in spite of these constraints. He brought structure and formality to free market ideas that evolution had been developing around the world for centuries. Outlining his capitalist system of the "extended order of voluntary exchange," this system would yield unintended benefits to others without people needing to become preoccupied with becoming intentionally charitable. He believed that as people practiced principles of honesty, mutual as well as reciprocal exchange, contract, civil liberties, private property, human rights, etc., under the rule of law, generative collaborations and innovative adaptations would create increasing prosperity for all involved; even as they were, paradoxically, pursuing their own interests. The Constrained vision thus began developing into what came to be called "Classical Liberalism."

Meanwhile, Rousseau, Thomas Paine, Edwin Godwin, and other Enlightenment philosophers with the Unlimited Vision, championed the French Revolution's Social Justice egalitarian ideal. As the process continued to unfold in France, eventually devolving into mob rule and the "reign of terror," Jefferson's earlier Unconstrained presumptions and unqualified support for unmarshalled equality became

---

[178] Smith, Adam. *The Theory of Moral Sentiments*. 1759.

tempered while witnessing the brutishness Hobbes had described. The experiment for absolute equality was increasingly difficult to secure without instituting the safeguards and constraints that were then considered unnecessary compromises of the full equality aspiration. Enlightenment French poet Antoine Baudot identified how the mix of liberty and equality became problematic during the Jacobin period, when equality was redefined as not only the judicial equality of rights based on impartiality and the objective weighing of evidence, but as also the equality of results. Baudot at the time considered that French temperament was inclined rather toward equality than liberty, a theme which would be reused by Alexis de Tocqueville, who believed that an equal society could only be founded on coercion.

The American revolution had itself been ignited by the passionate fervor of the Unconstrained Vision to overcome British tyranny and to create a more perfect union. Once free, it had then steered the governance structure toward a more Limited course, following constraint. Being astute students of history, the founders were well aware of earlier governmental experiments, and of the repetitive mischief that leaders and followers could fall prey to. Thus, they shepherded the initial dynamism of change toward constraining checks and balances, crafting a Republican system of limited, representative democracy. They were willing to compromise the aspirational "solution" of attaining complete equality. Instead, they chose to deliberately restrain their constitutional system with a series of "tradeoffs" in the form of checks and balances. Alexander Hamilton spoke of a "radical infirmity in all human contrivances, resulting from the imperfections of Man."

The other revolutionary change unfolding at this time was the industrial revolution. While it was true that man's quality of life was in many ways improving dramatically, it was doing so in a far too injurious fashion for those with the Unlimited Vision. The "disenchantment of the world" was a symptom of the new religion of scientism. People became cogs in large industrial machinery, marked by dehumanizing and barbaric effects in the service of productivity and profit. The Bohemian counterculture, rising up against the excesses of the new Bourgeoisie class, led the Unlimited Vision's fight against the injustices propagated by the rationalizing rapaciousness of "manifest destiny." Those with the Unconstrained vision lobbied for humane working conditions and better labor laws. Nonetheless, western governments chose to continue to work within the confines of these downsides as they experienced the benefits of capitalism to be outperforming the costs, as millions were lifted out of poverty. For the Limited vision: "The best is the enemy of the good," and "tradeoffs" are understood to be inevitable.

The Limited vision believes that "the good" in society is better achieved more from freedom than focusing on solutions that would create equality. Milton Friedman, a 20th century Nobel Prize winning economist, captures this sentiment: "A society that puts equality – in the sense of equality of outcome – ahead of freedom, will end up with neither equality nor freedom. A society that focuses on freedom will not secure equal outcomes, but it will render a better approximation of equality than any other system. The use of force to achieve equality will destroy freedom, and the force, introduced for good purposes, will end up in the hands of people who use it to promote their own interests."[179] Friedman and others of the Limited Vision reject direct political equalization of economic results, judging the process costs to be too high. At the same time, our Unlimited vision, when lionizing the virtues of equality, allows us to "break a few eggs to make an omelet (equitable solution)."

We can now draw correlations between the underlying ideologies of competing visions and how these respective "felt senses" of human nature get translated into political theories and movements.

Constrained *And* Unconstrained as Classical Liberalism *And* Social Justice Liberalism (*Figure 2*)

Traditional Justice, upon which the American Constitution is founded, is grounded in the image of "Lady Justice." She wears a blindfold that represents impartiality, not wishing to see any attributes that could bias her deliberations. She is only interested in the scales she holds, weighing the evidence objectively, unburdened by agendas that could unfairly tip the scales. She is interested in hearing extenuating evidence that would lean her toward mercy and aggravating evidence that would weigh her scales toward penalty. This form of justice is a hallmark of Classical Liberalism. Equality before the law is one mainstay of this political theory, as are human rights, civil liberties, economic freedom, limited government and democratic institutions, all operating under the rule of law. This political theory is built upon our felt sense of the Constrained Vision where freedom is more foundational than equality; an informed understanding of human self-interest is managed by exercising intervening factors such as devotion to moral principles and civility; and to concepts of honor and nobility rather than having to love all neighbors as oneself. Classical Liberalism believes that intentional care and compassion for all would be nice, but would be asking too much of people who perform better while incentivized with rewards; even to their self-esteem in the form of being highly regarded.

Social Justice Liberalism (our Unconstrained vision) posits man's understanding and disposition as capable of intentionally turning our will toward the creation of social benefits for their own sake. People should be able to be aware of inequalities where they exist and feel dutifully moved to redress them in compensatory manners that take all contributing factors into account. Social Justice Liberalism values equality first and foremost, along with diversity, inclusivity, sensitivity, pluralism, and multiculturalism; always with an eye to identifying currently or previously marginalized or de-privileged groups of people. This supports Lady Justice removing her blindfold and tipping the scales in their favor as a form of restorative redress in the service of "activist justice." This sentiment is complemented by public supports through extensive government services, leveraged toward providing deserved compensatory assistance. There is a deep focus on achieving greater fairness by not only supporting equal opportunities, but also in creating equal outcomes. Policies such as welfare, affirmative action, and redistribution of wealth are seen as solutions to inequality and a more directly caring approach to human challenges.

---

[179] Milton Friedman and Rose D. Friedman. *Free to Choose: A Personal Statement*. Harcourt, Inc., 1980.

Figure 2

Action Steps

- People enjoy free speech, ability to gather, protest, etc., while enjoying lifestyle choices of their own
- Opportunities for individual initiative and advancement
- Formation of civil empowerment groups (neighborhoods, churches, etc.) in service of self-governance

Early Warnings

- Unrealistic expectations for people to perform beyond their capabilities
- Unwillingness to establish fair rules/codes of conduct
- NIMBY-type mindsets that look out for their own while disregarding the needy in other areas of commons

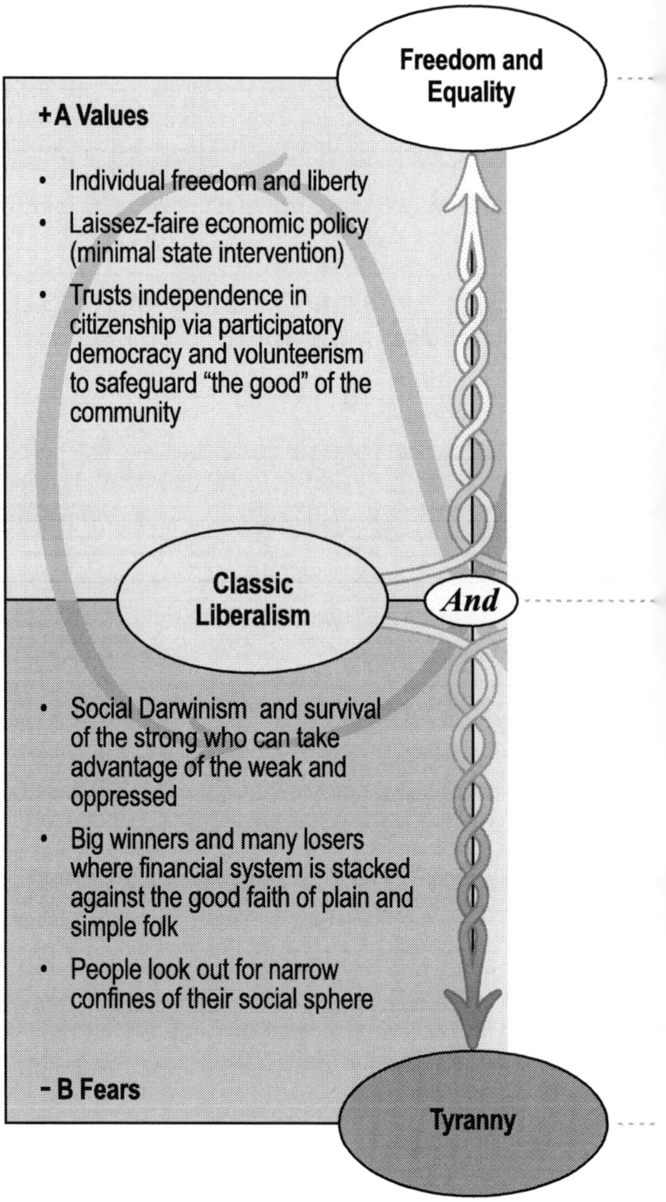

+A Values

- Individual freedom and liberty
- Laissez-faire economic policy (minimal state intervention)
- Trusts independence in citizenship via participatory democracy and volunteerism to safeguard "the good" of the community

Classic Liberalism *And*

- Social Darwinism and survival of the strong who can take advantage of the weak and oppressed
- Big winners and many losers where financial system is stacked against the good faith of plain and simple folk
- People look out for narrow confines of their social sphere

− B Fears

Freedom and Equality

Tyranny

Chapter 30: Parlee

Freedom and Equality

+C Values

- Group rights, based on privileging previously marginalized populations
- Significant state leadership and control in economic policy
- Trusts government to redistribute wealth and resources so as to engineer equality and outcomes based on fairness compensations

And

Social Justice Liberalism

- Exchange of one privileged (oppressive) group for another (*Animal Farm*)
- Social disintegration and loss of personal safety and property
- Perpetuation of "bad citizenship"; not checking behaviors of preferred groups as a means of assuaging guilt for acknowledged past wrongs

− D Fears

Tyranny

Action Steps

- Protect rights and actively advance prospects and opportunities for previously marginalized groups
- Activist government oversight with regulatory bodies to ensure fairness in business
- Progressive income tax and related policies to ensure equality

Early Warnings

- Lack of respect, and denial of "voice" for those outside preferred group or "correct" point of view
- Unfair burden on businesses, middle class, and wealthy in order to throw money at failing programs
- Lack of civil norms/codes of conduct, misunderstanding illiberal as "authentic" expression

Tradeoffs and Solutions: Differences of Emphasis

While valuing freedom over equality, Classical Liberalism grounded in the Constrained vision is aware that not only will inequalities exist, but that this will indeed result in undeserved disadvantages for those who will end up with less than others. For the Limited Vision, this is the cost of freedom. This Constrained vision also endeavors to support strivings toward equality, but not at the cost of creating unfairness or injury to innocent others in the process.

For Social Justice Liberalism, devotion to equality involves crafting solutions to inequities. If there are process costs associated with this in terms of compromised freedom or safety for others, this is a price that should be paid in the service of fairness, which is a higher order virtue than freedom.

Sowell offers an example to illustrate some costs associated with eliminating certain inequalities and injustices. "In San Francisco in 1996, a relative of one of the city's supervisors phoned a pizza company to request a pizza be delivered to his home. He was told that the company did not deliver pizza where he lived, which happened to be in a high-crime neighborhood. Immediately, there was an outburst of moral indignation. A law was passed decreeing that anyone who makes deliveries to the public in any part of the city must make deliveries to every part of the city."

This simple example highlights all the elements of our Unconstrained strivings for Social Justice. Most people in high crime neighborhoods are not criminals, and large numbers of innocent people have all sorts of added costs imposed on them through no fault of their own. In this instance, this is the cost of not being able to receive food or other orders that most of us take for granted. They are treated unequally and, to our Social Justice sensibility, unfairly.

On the other hand, a Classical Liberal would say that we must be prudent in our efforts to right all wrongs. Will we decide not to weigh the costs involved in such equalizing struggles? In the case above, the cost would involve impacted delivery drivers. Once we begin to consider how many deliveries are worth how many drivers being injured, or worse, we have modified our quest for Social Justice. We instead reduce our options to the more personal scale of weighing costs vs. benefits by allowing such a policy. Tradeoffs. The fundamental difference between the Limited and Unlimited vision, and that between Traditional and Social Justice, depends on how much process costs are weighed. Or not.

Most importantly, both those with the Limited and Unlimited Visions, Classical and Social Justice Liberals, all stand for their respective understandings of justice. The posture of their stance can vary as widely as the deep political divides that characterize our polarized times. With a generosity of spirit, may we hope to see those on our less-preferred pole as also well-intended champions of justice. Families, neighborhoods, and nations seem to want both sides to bring their collaborative selves and even better arguments to bear in the service of helping to bend the arc of the moral universe toward ever-greater degrees of justice in the time ahead.

About Bert Parlee ~ www.polaritypartnerships.com/certified-polarity-practitioners

Institute for Polarities of Democracy:
Leveraging Democratic Values
and Advancing Social Change

William Benet, PhD
Suzanne Rackl, MM, CFRE, CFRM
Cliff Kayser, MSHR, MSOD, PCC

In 2017, the Institute for Polarities of Democracy was established as a Washington, D.C.-based nonprofit organization to promote and advance the Polarity Thinking™ theory of Barry Johnson[180] and the Polarities of Democracy theory of Bill Benet.[181] The Institute's mission of positive social change is to train and educate scholars, researchers, and practitioners in educational and societal settings in using Polarity Thinking and Polarities of Democracy tools and processes to advance organizational well-being and to create healthy, sustainable, and just communities in the United States and internationally. Johnson's theories and the PACT™ tools, processes, and application are the main subject of this book. In this chapter, we focus primarily on the Polarities of Democracy theory and the role of the Institute for Polarities of Democracy.

Origins of the Polarities of Democracy Theory

The Polarities of Democracy theory was developed by Benet at the University of Toronto from 2001 to 2012.[182] The theory was published in the Journal of Social Change in 2013.[183] Since that time, a growing number of researchers and practitioners around the world have been using the theory to study and promote positive social change.

Incorporating Johnson's Polarity Thinking concepts as its conceptual framework, the Polarities of Democracy theory can be used to plan, guide, and evaluate social change efforts to address the social and environmental threats to our human survival and support building healthy, sustainable, and just communities. The theory includes

---

[180] Johnson, Barry. *Polarity Management.* HRD Press, 1992. And: *Making a Difference by Leveraging Polarity, Paradox or Dilemma. Volume One—Foundations.* HRD Press, 2020.
[181] Benet, W. J. *The Polarity Management Model of Workplace Democracy* (Doctoral dissertation, Ontario Institute for Studies in Education of the University of Toronto, Canada). Available from ProQuest Dissertations & Theses Global Full Text database, UMI Publishing (Order No. NR15724), 2006.
Benet, W. J. "The Polarities of Democracy: A Theoretical Framework for Building a Healthy, Sustainable, and Just World." Unpublished Manuscript. Social Economy Centre, Adult Education and Community Development Program of the Ontario Institute for Studies in Education of the University of Toronto, Canada. 2012.
[182] Ibid.
[183] Benet, W. J., 2013. "Managing the Polarities of Democracy: A Theoretical Framework for Positive Social Change." Journal of Social Change 5(1), 26-39. https://doi.org/10.5590/JOSC.2013.05.1.03

ten overarching values required to fully attain democracy and posits that each of these values are essential, yet none are sufficient alone. The ten values are arranged in five interrelated polarity pairs. (*Figure 1*)

Figure 1: Polarities of Democracy

Freedom	*And*	Authority
Justice	*And*	Due Process
Diversity	*And*	Equality
Human Rights	*And*	Communal Obligations
Participation	*And*	Representation

Two seminal works formed the foundation of Benet's approach. The first was the Managerial Grid theory of Robert Blake and Jane Mouton,[184] and the second was the Civic Education theory of R. Freeman Butts.[185] Benet used these works in concert with best practices from adult education, organizational development, public education, and social work research regarding how to attain freedom, justice, equality, and human rights in both the workplace and in society.

Blake and Mouton's Managerial Grid is a classic organizational development tool that Benet believes still provides the soundest description of the behaviors required for collaborative teamwork. The Managerial Grid theory is based on integrating a maximum concern for people or relationships with a maximum concern for tasks or results. R.Freeman Butts developed his Decalogue of Democratic Civic Values[186] as a framework for democratic societies. Butts is the former President of Teachers College at Columbia University, and he set forth what he believed to be the purpose of public education: to prepare students to be responsible citizens in a democratic society. He presented his ten values as five that enhance the worth of the individual and five that enhance the cohesiveness of society.

Benet was introduced to Johnson's seminal work on Polarity Thinking[187] while completing doctoral courses in research methodology at the University of Toronto and was immediately drawn to these concepts as a possible linkage between Blake and Mouton's Managerial Grid theory and Butt's Decalogue of Democratic Civic Values. In 2001, Benet began his dissertation work using Johnson's Polarity Management[188] as the conceptual framework to develop a unifying theory for democracy with exhaustive research of the literature that embraced not just Western thought, but also Eastern, African, and ancient Indigenous knowledge and wisdom.

Polarities of Democracy Theory

The Polarities of Democracy theory successfully integrates the seminal works of Johnson, Butts, and Blake and Mouton, as well as the concepts from Western, Eastern, African, and Indigenous wisdom, providing a theoretical framework for the democratization of workplaces and society in order to address the social and environmental challenges faced on a local, national, and global level. The theory

---

[184] Blake, R.R., and Mouton, J.S. *The Managerial Grid III*. Gulf publishing Company, 1985.
[185] Butts, R.F. *The Revival of Civic Learning*. Phi Delta Kappa Intl Inc., 1980.
[186] Ibid.
[187] Johnson, B. *Polarity Management*. HRD Press, 1992.
[188] Ibid.

promotes participatory practices that allow citizens, workers, families, organizations, and communities to unleash their creativity and strengthen their capacity for both research and social change initiatives that promote social and environmental justice and responsibility. The Polarities of Democracy is a unifying theory, anchored in ten non-partisan democratic values (*Figure 1*), with practical applications for advancing democratic workplaces and society.

The Polarities of Democracy theory uses Johnson's Polarity Thinking concepts to show how the energy system of interdependent pairs works over time in a pattern of shifting from one pole of a polarity to the other. Dysfunction in this natural dynamic occurs when *Or*-thinking – *either* this pole *Or* that pole, which assumes the two cannot coexist – is applied to interdependent pair polarities as a "solution" to the tension. This misdiagnosis of a polarity that requires *both/And*-thinking can interrupt the flow of energy creating vicious cycles and dysfunction.

As the downside of an overemphasized pole becomes stronger, oppositional forces – coming similarly, from an *either/Or* thinking perspective – begin to push for the benefits of the opposite pole because they tend to see only the positive aspects of that pole. Those who resist those changes see only the positive aspects of the current pole's values that they defend, and fear the negative results of the pole that could result from those advocating for change. Along with the ten values identified for the Polarities of Democracy theory, additional key findings suggested by Benet's research include:

- The concepts of democracy arose from our emerging consciousness as part of our evolutionary development, and the fundamental purpose of these is to overcome oppression.
- The principles of democracy have universal applicability to all cultures and time periods.
- The predominant Western philosophy of utility ignores the role that human altruism plays in our evolutionary and democratic development.
- Our societal origins provided a more democratic relationship between men and women than the patriarchal societies that have dominated modern history.
- Patriarchal societies have prevented us from attaining a full expression of democracy on a national or global level.
- If true democracy is to be attained, then these ten polarity values must be leveraged effectively in order to maximize the positive aspects of each value while minimizing the negative aspects of each value. (*Figure 2*)

Polarities of Democracy Introductory Maps

The Institute for Polarities of Democracy developed these maps (*Figure 2*) for use as a simple guide to leverage democratic values for positive social change. The Institute works with organizations and communities to create detailed and customized maps for specific democratic reforms, and it supplements them with action and execution. Viewing these five maps as a multarity, the *collective* deeper fear is oppression, systemic failures, and civic collapse. The *overarching* greater purpose of the multarity is the promise of democracy and human emancipation. (See Chapter 42, p. 321, for an introduction to multarities.)

Figure 2: The Five Polarities of Democracy

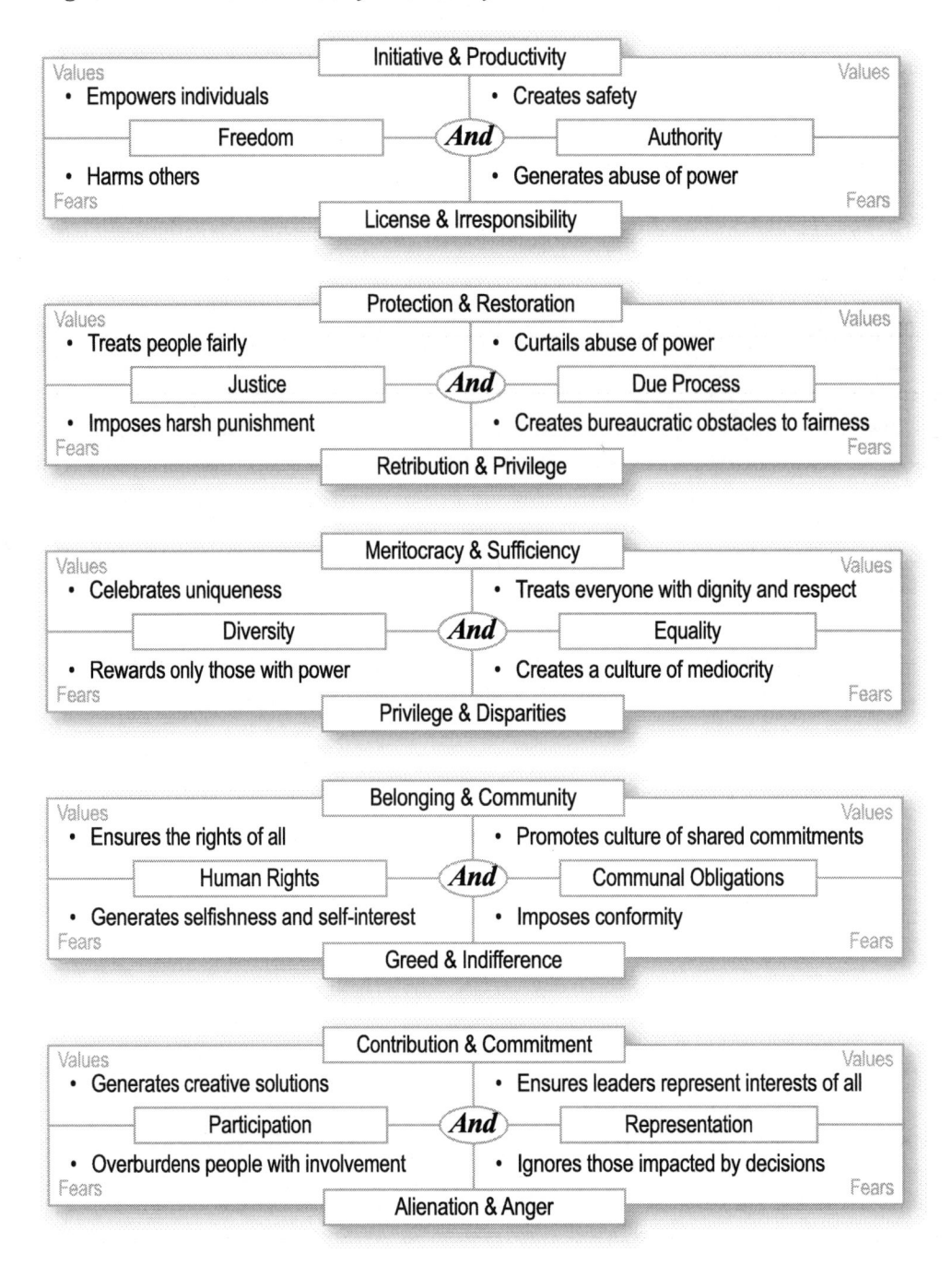

Initiative & Productivity

Values
- Empowers individuals

Freedom **And** Authority

Values
- Creates safety

- Harms others

- Generates abuse of power

Fears
License & Irresponsibility
Fears

Protection & Restoration

Values
- Treats people fairly

Justice **And** Due Process

Values
- Curtails abuse of power

- Imposes harsh punishment

- Creates bureaucratic obstacles to fairness

Fears
Retribution & Privilege
Fears

Meritocracy & Sufficiency

Values
- Celebrates uniqueness

Diversity **And** Equality

Values
- Treats everyone with dignity and respect

- Rewards only those with power

- Creates a culture of mediocrity

Fears
Privilege & Disparities
Fears

Belonging & Community

Values
- Ensures the rights of all

Human Rights **And** Communal Obligations

Values
- Promotes culture of shared commitments

- Generates selfishness and self-interest

- Imposes conformity

Fears
Greed & Indifference
Fears

Contribution & Commitment

Values
- Generates creative solutions

Participation **And** Representation

Values
- Ensures leaders represent interests of all

- Overburdens people with involvement

- Ignores those impacted by decisions

Fears
Alienation & Anger
Fears

Adding Practice to Theory

In 2013, Benet's article on the Polarities of Democracy theory was published in the *Journal of Social Change*. Almost immediately, doctoral students interested in democratic principles and social change began using his theory in their research studies. The largest cohort of doctoral students are from Walden University's School of Public Policy and Administration where Benet serves on the faculty and as a chair for doctoral dissertations. These doctoral students from across the globe have used the Polarities of Democracy as the theoretical framework for their dissertations, along with Polarity Thinking as their conceptual framework.

As of January 2020, fifteen doctoral studies have been completed using the Polarities of Democracy as a lens for interpreting findings, and an additional twenty-five studies are underway. This doctoral research is international in reach, covering studies from California to Nigeria and from London to Bangladesh. Thus, the Polarities of Democracy and Polarity Thinking are being used globally to achieve democratic solutions answering questions of oppression and marginalization, and leveraging democratic values to advance social change.

Establishing the Institute

Given the global success of the Polarities of Democracy theory in academic research, Benet, Johnson, and colleagues began exploring how to partner strategically to extend the reach of their combined work. They believed that the mapping and Polarity Assessment™,[189] tools Johnson and Polarity Partnerships, LLC, had developed could strengthen the application of Polarities of Democracy when used to guide social change projects in real world settings.

Cliff Kayser led an effort with Johnson and Benet to establish a charitable entity to further these goals. Polarity Partnerships was the founding donor with support from the Center for Democratic Values, Suzanne Rackl of Strategic Community Impact, and a cadre of volunteer colleagues and students. The Institute for Polarities of Democracy was created with these primary objectives:

- To promote the Polarities of Democracy as developed by Benet as a theoretical framework for progressive social change initiatives that advance healthy, sustainable, and just organizations and communities.
- To promote Polarity Thinking concepts as developed by Johnson as the foundational conceptual framework underlying the Polarities of Democracy theory.
- To articulate, communicate, and disseminate the fundamental values underlying our democratic republic, which are necessary to its survival.
- To be intentional about using Polarities of Democracy and Polarity Thinking to interrupt the abuse of power and privilege anywhere it might occur.
- To seek diversity in our board, staff, and partnering relationships and empower and leverage that diversity in support of the above objectives and purposes.

---

[189] The Polarity Assessment™. www.polaritypartnerships.com/our-impact. 2020.

Mission and Vision of the Institute

The power of the Institute's vision is marrying the tools and processes of over four decades of polarity approach development with the basic principles of democracy drawn from centuries of literature about freedom and governance into the one unifying Polarities of Democracy theory. The Institute's goal is to catalyze social progress through leveraging the positive aspects of democratic values at all levels of society. (See *Figure 2*.) The mission is to advance healthy, sustainable, and just organizations and communities by promoting the use of the Polarities of Democracy theory of positive social change. The Institute has been created to support researchers, social change activists, nonprofits, NGO's, policy makers, and government entities to use our tools and thinking as nonpartisan solutions to oppression, discrimination, injustice, and policy challenges.

Again, the theory is comprised of ten universal democratic values in five interdependent polarity pairs: Freedom *And* Authority; Justice *And* Due Process; Diversity *And* Equality; Human Rights *And* Communal Obligations; and Participation *And* Representation. The Institute combines this theory with research, tools, and action to promote positive social change in the U.S. and increasingly throughout the globe. It also works to articulate, communicate, and disseminate the critical values underlying our democratic republic – values fundamental to its survival.

Programs

The Institute's programs and activities range from resources, training, and research to consulting, evaluation, and applied social change projects. The Institute is investing in change and creating impact, as well as engaging in policy leadership and societal transformation initiatives. Its first two years were dedicated to creating tools and providing scholarships and training to post-doctoral Fellows, and future seasons will bring a broad spectrum of additional resources, initiatives, training, and partnerships – all dedicated to improving quality of life and strengthening democratic principles.

Investing in Change

- **Learning:** The Institute has welcomed two cohorts of scholars and practitioners to our Social Change Fellows Ranks in its first three years. These sixteen post-doctoral Fellows are deepening their understanding of polarity approaches and Polarities of Democracy theory and are already using their new learning in their writing, work, and dialogue for social change challenges and opportunities. As a result of this growing body of social change work, the Walden University Library has created the Polarities of Democracy collection. This is the first collection created under the banner of the Social Change Collection, which houses scholarly output of the Walden University community in order to generate, conserve, and transform knowledge to improve human and social conditions.

- **Empowerment:** In 2019, the Institute established the Desi Benet Social Change Fellow Scholarship to be awarded to a woman PhD social change agent in each Fellows cohort, memorializing the earliest supporter and champion of the Polarities of Democracy theory.

- **Teaching:** The Institute's Leadership and Fellows have developed a strong cadre of tools and resources including study guides, video courses, assessment training, maps, and writings that are available to students, researchers, trainers, and the wider learning community.

Creating Impact

- **Action:** The Institute has launched six positive social change projects located in community-based settings. These projects focus on leveraging the theory's non-partisan democratic values to strengthen organizations and communities working on issues ranging from economic revitalization to protecting voter's rights.

- **Leadership:** With the myriad of resources, researchers, and social change agents in place, the Institute launched consulting services in 2020 along with dialogue and direct-action seminars. It also supported the launch of Johnson's book *And:* Volume One – Foundations along with this second volume; each highlighting the role of polarities across a spectrum of issues.

- **Partnerships:** The Institute continues to develop strategic alliances within higher education institutions, social change organizations, charitable entities, NGOs, philanthropic organizations, colleagues, and activists. It also partners with leaders from national and international organizations to support and extend the reach and use of Polarities of Democracy theory as a tool for their work in social change and advancing democracy.

Policy Leadership and Societal Transformation

- **Policy Research Initiative:** The Institute formed a strategic alliance with the Center for Social Change at Walden University to apply the Polarities of Democracy theory to research and projects that lead to purposeful action for sustainable positive social change. The collaboration spans doctoral research, dissemination networks, and trans-disciplinary study across colleges and programs including public policy, criminal justice, and social work.

- **Transforming Policing Culture and Social Investment Reform Initiative:** Following the tragic murder of George Floyd by Minneapolis police in 2020 and the resultant national outcry calling for a transformation of how we treat Black people in America, the Institute created an Initiative with three broad components to address the challenges of structural and systemic racism underlying the vast racial disparities and inequities that exist in America. The Institute:

    1. Formed a strategic alliance with the National Organization of Black Law Enforcement Executives (NOBLE) to support transforming policing cultures in the U.S. from a warrior mentality to one of guardianship through reforms related to the 21st Century Policing report and the Justice in Policing Act.
    2. Identified an advocacy agenda to combat racial inequities that is focused on ensuring appropriate investment and commitment to societal systems including mental health, employment, the social economy, public education, healthcare, social work, housing, and the environment.

3. Developed a comprehensive approach that applies the Polarities of Democracy to organizational and systems transformation efforts at addressing police restructuring, and the structural and systemic racism in the U.S.

The Movement

The Institute has major practice hubs of fellows and colleagues in Washington D.C., U.S., Toronto, Canada, and London, England. In addition to our hub communities, there are multiple completed and in-progress research projects from the U.S., Europe, and Africa. Social change projects are currently underway in Zambia, Nigeria, and in the U.S. in California, Florida, Maryland, South Carolina, New York, and Virginia. The Institute also hosts a virtual learning community that currently includes colleagues and doctoral students across five continents. The Polarities of Democracy theory is being used to help people across disciplines, issues, and boundaries on campuses and in communities – in the classroom, the policy room, and in the boardroom.

Goals

Future Institute goals include long-term activism and resource training in the social justice arena. Through the Polarities of Democracy theory's alignment with the United Nation's Sustainable Development Goals, the Institute and its partners are working in the areas of ending poverty, increasing health and well-being, reduced inequalities, and creating sustainable cities and communities. Additionally, the Institute has a strong cadre of expertise around the UN's Sustainable Development Goal of peace, justice, and strong institutions, with particular expertise regarding peace and conflict mediation, anti-gun violence, counter-terrorism, and intelligence.

The impact of Institute programming is an ongoing, vibrant organization that activists, researchers, organizations, policy makers, and marginalized groups or communities can turn to for real-world tools and support to advance their rights through leveraging positive aspects of democratic values – Freedom *And* Authority; Justice *And* Due Process; Diversity *And* Equality; Human Rights *And* Communal Obligations; and Participation *And* Representation.

The Institute is an expanding organization with replicable, innovative initiatives, and partners in place to continue success. The long-term result will be a disruption of oppressive forces that stymie human creativity and societal possibilities.

To learn more and to support the Institute for Polarities of Democracy's continued growth and impact creating positive social change and strengthening democracy, please contact Suzanne Rackl, Managing Director at www.InstituteforPOD.org

---

Find bio and contact info for author Cliff Kayser at
www.polaritypartnerships.com/certified-polarity-practitioners

How Does Polarity Mapping Connect with Our Built-In Neurology?

Ann V. Deaton, PhD, PCC

"What do you mean people are just as important as products?" The COO raised his voice in disbelief as he challenged the HR recruiter. "If we don't have new products, we can't pay those people." The recruiter's face flushed with emotion as she responded, "I get it. But what you don't seem to get is that if you can't find and keep good people, you'll have no shot at delivering the innovative products you are so hot for. Focusing on your people is more critical every time."

Suddenly realizing I'd entered the room, the two of them looked to me before the COO asked pointedly, "I guess you heard all that. Which of us do you think is right?" Although thrown by his abruptness, I responded with assurance, "You are absolutely right – products are critical to your company's success." He smiled and gave me the thumbs up before realizing I was still speaking. I continued, "And what is also true is that if you focus only on products and never prioritize people, your results will spiral down before you know it."

Not the gentlest entrance for a new client, and I wondered whether my candor would cause me to lose the opportunity to work with them when we'd just barely begun. On the other hand, arriving at such a moment made me confident that I had a tool they needed – for their bottom line and their ability to use their time and energy for more effective discussions, instead of for angry arguments about who was right and who was wrong.

This vignette demonstrates what often happens with people who are deeply committed and passionate about what they are doing:

- Smart, experienced people develop strong opinions that differ from one another;
- Each feels certain they are right; and
- They focus on validating and justifying their own perspective rather than listening to those who see it differently.

This is a recipe for repeating the same cycle over and over again; it is not a formula for thriving.

My first career was as a Clinical Neuropsychologist. As a neuropsychologist, I studied neuroscience, learned how the brain and nervous system function, and had the opportunity to see what can go horribly wrong. In recent years, dynamic brain visualization and neuroscience research have dramatically expanded our knowledge of how our brains interact with our environments. We can now see how the neural and chemical activity in our brains influence (and are influenced by) our thoughts, emotions, and actions. The growth in our understanding of how our brains operate comes at a critical time as the world we are dealing with is increasingly challenging and complex.

In the scenario above, we can make several observations:

1. Both the COO and the HR recruiter got triggered and became defensive and protective. We are hardwired to be vigilant for danger and react instantly when our safety feels in jeopardy. The risk detected here is to each person's emotional well-being. Each time our danger antennae are raised, focus constricts as we zero in on the risk. We experience an amygdala hijack. Once hijacked, our thinking brains go offline for an estimated 17 minutes, unavailable for the complex cognitive tasks that our jobs and our relationships require (*Figure 1*). Our actions become limited to key survival behaviors. In the example above, the COO and the recruiter can continue the argument (Fight); leave the situation (Flee); shut down (Freeze); or pretend to agree with the other person for the sake of harmony (Appease). They are stuck, unable to move forward effectively.

Figure 1

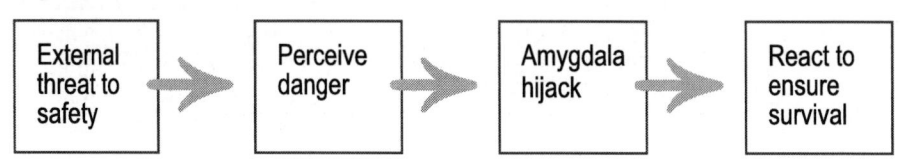

| External threat to safety | ⇒ | Perceive danger | ⇒ | Amygdala hijack | ⇒ | React to ensure survival |

When we are addicted to being right, we are mastered by our amygdala ... [specifically the] "fight" behaviors ... and we see the world through an I-Centric point of view. ~ Glaser[190]

2. When we assess that the other person is "not like me" (as the two do above), the brain activates our distrust response. Distrust causes us to be on guard, fearful of what may happen. When we experience threat and distrust, a torrent of Cortisol (stress hormone) is released, instructing the brain to cease executive functions. These higher-level functions become temporarily unavailable. In a fear state, our dialogue is limited by the neurochemistry of fear.

3. Our brain's confirmation bias means we scan for that which confirms what we already think, and disregard opinions that differ from ours. In the scenario above, the COO is only open to hearing that yes, he is right, products are critically important. When we are sure of our answer and convinced we are right, we stop being curious to learn more. The door closes to hearing what others have to offer; our brain fails to process disconfirming information. And we move forward on our own narrowly defined path with efficiency and certainty. It is not a path to thriving.

---

[190] Glaser, J. E. *Conversational Intelligence: How Great Leaders Build Trust and Get Extraordinary Results.* 2014, p. 42.

4. When we feel safe and trusting of others, we are able to listen instead of trying to win, partner rather than protecting or defending ourselves. The bonding hormone Oxytocin gets activated and we strive to connect and collaborate. We can experience the benefit of learning from those who think differently, valuing them as potential resources rather than risks. That is not yet happening above with the COO and HR leader we see here.

How Does Polarity Mapping Enhance Our Built-in Neurology?

Utilizing Polarity Thinking™ and mapping can create a sense of safety and clarity in many of the most difficult and complex situations faced by teams and organizations. Polarity Thinking and mapping provides an approach to leverage our knowledge of human behavior and the brain, and to enable individuals and teams to engage in interactions that contribute to trust, yielding greater effectiveness and enjoyment. This enables a virtuous cycle for sustainable results. Creating a Polarity Map® together is both an initiator of trust and a methodology for maintaining and restoring trust when conflict arises.

The approach of Polarity Thinking creates a predictable context where our sense of threat and the likelihood of being triggered is reduced. With this sense of safety present, we can focus on a common goal. In the situation above, the goal might be to recruit and keep key team members. Both the COO and HR leader agree on the importance of that goal. Because they now see the other as "like me," their connection (versus protection) mode gets activated and they are poised to partner. What is going on neurochemically behind the scenes is:

- Increased oxytocin (bonding hormone) enhances feelings of closeness to others, and desire to be open with them;
- Increased dopamine and serotonin give us a positive outlook and a sense of well-being; and
- The behavioral impact is to disclose more about what they perceive and what they are feeling, and to be interested and caring for others' perspectives.

When we hold strong opinions or beliefs, you might expect them to be modulated by disconfirming information or data, by differing perspectives. That's not what happens. Lacking the tools for *both/And*-thinking, "... we carefully edit our reality, searching for evidence that confirms what we already believe."[191] Barry Johnson refers to the Polarity Map as a "wisdom organizer." The structured methodology of the map gives us a place to value and validate our own perspective, making us feel safe. The map also provides a space to capture information that makes us aware of what we cannot yet see. Research suggests that the stronger our commitment to our own perspective (one pole of the Polarity Map), the LESS likely it is that data that disconfirms our view will be processed, as we selectively take in only what our brain expects to perceive. We need tools that ensure ongoing access to

---

[191] Lehrer, Jonah. "Accept Defeat: The Neuroscience of Screwing Up" www.wired.com/2009/12/fail-accept-defeat. December 21, 2009.

our reasoning brains so that when we experience contradictory information, we can bridge the gap between what we are thinking and what others are thinking. A Polarity Map offers a structure for that shared story.

What Difference Does This Make for Your Team and Organization?

High levels of trust impact productivity and an organization's ability to achieve its goals and objectives. In his work with organizations, Paul Zak quantified the dividends of trust.[192] Employees in high-trust environments, contrasted with those in low-trust settings, reported "74% less stress, 106% more energy at work, 50% higher productivity, 13% fewer sick days, 76% more engagement, 29% more satisfaction with their lives, and 40% less burnout." This makes it evident that accessing tools that enable an environment of trust will contribute to sustainable success – both on the people front, and on the side of results.

What does it look like when an organization uses polarity mapping to explore and take advantage of their differences? Revisiting the conversation of the HR leader and COO above, it might now look like this: Instead of believing that they have the sole right answer and digging in to defend their positions, these two experts are familiar with the polarities, and have learned that the best answer to a polarity is a *both/And* instead of an *either/Or*. A coach or a colleague volunteers to facilitate creating a Polarity Map for Products *And* People. They begin with highlighting the benefits of one of the poles, choosing the COO's preferred pole because he seems more certain that he is right, and more angry and defensive in this interaction. The facilitator walks our two experts through populating the map (see *Figure 2* on the following page) with their wisdom as follows:

The Upside of Product Focus (+A Values)

Facilitator invites the COO to articulate all the positive things that occur when the company focuses on Products. He notes the fact that team members feel informed and clear about expectations, and that financial bonuses for performance serve to motivate even greater productivity. Who wouldn't want this? Instead of countering his view or pointing out that it is limited, his colleague acknowledges and appreciates his wisdom. In fact, they document it on the following Polarity Map, encouraging the COO to add other positive impacts of this Products focus. Instead of feeling threatened and needing to justify his belief that Products are key, he now feels heard and understood. His brain is in a calm, trusting state and he can listen as the facilitator turns to the HR recruiter.

The Upside of People Focus (+C Values)

Facilitator then says to the recruiter, "Obviously, Products are critical to our success and creating good Products depends on People. What are all the positive things that happen when we focus on our People?" Glad to have a chance to weigh in, this leader notes that when People feel valued, they are happy and productive.

---

[192] Zak, Paul. J. "The Neuroscience of Trust." Harvard Business Review, January - February 2017.

Their sense of loyalty and care for other team members results in them helping one another overcome hurdles, working extra when needed, and remaining at the company even through challenging times. Clearly, a focus on People is essential for the company's success, and this leader is delighted to be able to articulate all the benefits of this. Her list is also captured in the Polarity Map.

All three map creators step back to appreciate all the upsides they have identified – the fact that with these two areas of focus, their team members see a clear connection between effort and outcomes and their interdependence. Asked about what they see, the COO and HR leader note that they want all of the positive outcomes identified so far. Who wouldn't? Basking in the glow of dopamine and oxytocin, they look at one another as allies and collaborators instead of adversaries. Each has provided a piece of the puzzle. Having a facilitated and structured dialogue has enabled them to trust the process and one another.

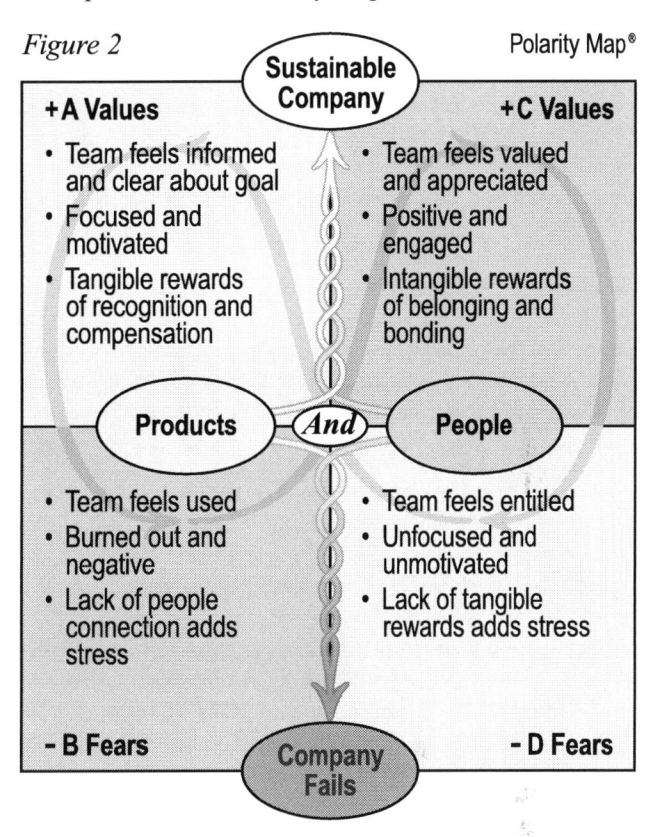

Figure 2 — Polarity Map®

Sustainable Company

+A Values
- Team feels informed and clear about goal
- Focused and motivated
- Tangible rewards of recognition and compensation

+C Values
- Team feels valued and appreciated
- Positive and engaged
- Intangible rewards of belonging and bonding

Products —(And)— People

- B Fears
- Team feels used
- Burned out and negative
- Lack of people connection adds stress

- D Fears
- Team feels entitled
- Unfocused and unmotivated
- Lack of tangible rewards adds stress

Company Fails

The Downside of People-Only Focus (–D Fears)

Now the facilitator asks a more challenging question. "Okay, so what would happen if we acted like only one *Or* the other were important instead of *both* Products *And* People? What negative things would result if we focused only on one and neglected the other?" Continuing from the upside of People, she invites the pair to envision what downsides they would experience if the company always focused on its People and never its Products. Both leaders contribute with possibilities, such as the COO's fear that, "We'd have these entitled people thinking they deserve a job and just want to hang out with their friends." The HR leader adds, "If we focus only on People, the best people leave, missing the sense of accomplishment they used to have when a new Product got launched." This wisdom is added to the downside of the People pole before going on.

The Downside of Product-Only Focus (–B Fears)

"Okay then, maybe People was the wrong focus after all. What if we stopped wasting energy on People and just focused on our Products?" Familiar with where this is going, both quickly offer their thoughts. "No, that can't work either. People would start to feel used, like cogs in a machine. They'd call out sick whenever they didn't feel like coming to work, and start competing to get individual rewards instead of collaborating. The impact would be poor quality and late products, even though we were focused exclusively on Products. People matter too."

Perhaps it seems too perfect, and yet the process itself is structured, predictable, and fair. As teams become more skilled in using Polarity Thinking, they quickly embrace the opportunity to generate better and more consistent results.

Long-term Sustainable Results

As an organization becomes familiar with Polarity Thinking, mapping can be a tool for understanding complex situations. Identifying key polarities activates hope in our brains. When hope is present, anxiety is reduced,[193] enabling us to recognize our own blind spots and build relationships with those who see things differently. We leverage our diversity. Instead of thinking, "This person is not like me; they are a threat," we consider, "This person does not think like me; they have a critical piece I need."

With Polarity Thinking available to our teams, we avoid getting triggered and defaulting to survival reactions. We trust that a divergent perspective is not just something to tolerate but something that brings value and will help us to generate better results. Rather than resisting difference, polarity mapping provides a mechanism to invite clarity about what the other offers, wisdom we may not easily access without their assistance. This structure and mindset of appreciation activates Oxytocin, the bonding neurochemical in our brains, and we tend to move towards the other person, to seek to understand their viewpoint, to benefit from what they see that we cannot.

Conclusions

Unfortunately, our brain's hardwiring to stay on familiar tracks of knowing and to be hypervigilant for threat is not a path to thriving. Our natural defaults are not so useful when the "danger" detected is the realization that our strongly held opinion might be wrong, or at least incomplete. In those challenging circumstances, it is more effective to keep our brain calm and access its capabilities for evaluating, strategizing, innovating, collaborating, and executing. Polarity Thinking and mapping helps the brain stay in that state where we can increase clarity and invite collaboration. In creating a map, we gain access to a more complete story, one of opportunity and connection.

About Ann Deaton ~ www.polaritypartnerships.com/certified-polarity-practitioners

---

[193] Wang, S., Xu, X., Chen, T., Yang, X., Chen, G., and Gong, Q. "Hope and the Brain: Trait hope mediates the protective role of medial orbitofrontal cortex spontaneous activity against anxiety". Neuroimage, August 15, 2017.

Polarity Thinking™ as a Catalyst for Experiential Learning
Kay Peterson, MN, MBA, PCC

Coaches and consultants are in the business of change and grow. The essential method of getting better at anything involves a process so automatic that it recedes into the background. This process is Experiential Learning. By making this simple, four-step, inside-out method of Experiential Learning explicit, coaches and consultants can empower people to improve performance, learn something new, make quality decisions, and achieve their goals. Using this process effectively is also the key to self-transformation and growth. The Polarity Thinking™ model provides a catalyst to unleash this learning potential.[194]

Experiential Learning as a Process

David Kolb synthesized the work of nine foundational scholars from education, psychology, and philosophy to develop an ideal process of learning and developing from experience (the learning cycle) and described nine approaches to using it (learning styles).[195] Experiential Learning is based on several unique perspectives on learning and development, beginning with the awareness that learning is present in every life experience and is an invitation to be engaged in each experience. Here, learning is viewed as a recursive cyclical process as opposed to a linear, traditional information transfer; a process rather than simply outcomes. The process is holistic since it involves all aspects of a whole person (affective, perceptual, cognitive, and behavioral), and can be applied to any life situation. Consider everyday decision-making, teamwork, or managing life transitions as learning.

The Learning Cycle

The Experiential Learning Cycle describes an ideal process of learning that includes four steps or modes: Experiencing, Reflecting, Thinking, and Acting. (See *Figure 1*.)[196]

The Experiential Learning Cycle (*Figure 1*)

In practice, the cycle is more dynamic and less prescribed, yet deep learning requires the use of all four modes regardless of the order. By doing this, people are able to experience an effective, well-balanced learning and living process that keeps their subjective experience at the center of learning. Although people can learn this mental model in just a few minutes, it is tricky to employ.

---

[194] Johnson, Barry. *Polarity Management: Identifying and Managing Unsolvable Problems.* HRD Press, 1996.
[195] Kolb, David A. *Experiential Learning: Experience as the Source of Learning and Development,* 2nd *Edition.* Pearson Education, 2015.
[196] Ibid as source, adapted. ©2017 Kay Peterson and David A. Kolb. All Rights Reserved.

Figure 1:
Experiential
Learning Cycle

Experiencing (Concrete Experiencing)
Attend to your experience in the moment.
Ask: Am I present in this moment?
What is happening?

Acting
(Active Experimentation)
Take action to implement your decision.
Ask: What can we do to progress? What action can we take now?

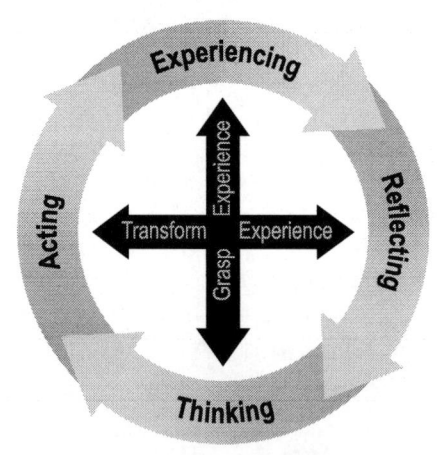

Reflecting
(Reflective Observation)
Pause to reflect on that experience to make meaning.
Ask: What are other points of view? Am I allowing time to make sense and examine assumptions?

Thinking (Abstract Thinking)
Next, engage abstract thinking to generalize and make a decision.
Ask: What does the evidence show? Am I accurate?

To be effective, the process of learning requires the resolution of conflicts between dialectically opposed modes that motivate learning. Notice that the learning cycle is comprised of two polarities. The north-south axis of Experiencing *And* Thinking are two interdependent and opposite ways of grasping information to understand the world. (See *Figure 2* for full Polarity Map®.) Experiencing is direct and subjective, while Thinking is an interpretation that is generalized and objective. Reflecting *And* Acting are two interdependent and opposite means of transforming or processing our experiences and thoughts. (See *Figure 3* for full Polarity Map.) We connect our direct Experience to our general knowledge by Reflecting about the meaning and implication of our experience. We transform our abstract Thinking and feelings into behavior by Acting.

How can we feel and think at the same time? How can we watch and do simultaneously? Due to this tension, most people find that they use preferred poles and avoid or underutilize others. These preferences lead to basic orientations to life. When people realize their preferences, they become aware of the results of using their preferred and avoiding their non-preferred poles, and supplement what is missing in their approach.

It helps to first value our current preference as one that may involve a more stable *"either/Or"* approach. This is a patterned way of responding to the constant stimuli in the environment that could otherwise prove overwhelming both psychologically and physically. Culture, personality, educational specialization, career choice, and the immediate demands of one's life situation influence the poles we preference, giving less attention and value to others. As we find a comfortable way of navigating the learning cycle – typically choosing Experiencing *Or* Thinking, Reflecting *Or* Acting – we accentuate the process that is comfortable, and it becomes self-reinforcing. We seek situations that call for those strengths. Ultimately, this specialized approach becomes a "possibility processing structure" that determines the range of choices and decisions we see, influencing the choices and decisions we access during the next situation we live through; each influencing future choices. This "steady-state" or habit is reinforced by the continuing choice of situations where the approach is successful.

By the time we reach adulthood, preferences for navigating the learning cycle are relatively stable, operating beneath the surface of our awareness. Entrenchment occurs when we habitually cling to these preferences for all situations, even those that demand more flexibility. Studies have shown that when people specialize in one field, especially highly technical or abstract fields like science, medicine, law, or engineering, they tend to be more rigidly attached to one approach. While this may make them more successful in their specialty, it also leaves them with less flexibility to meet other situations in life.[197] Over time, people typically face challenges that require more flexibility in addition to stability.

It is important to note that this is not a trait-based model that pigeonholes us into an entrenched, locked-in, stable pattern. Instead, when we apply the Polarity Thinking model, we find a fuller picture of the less-preferred pole and can supplement our approach to be more flexible over time. This can prove to be lifechanging, increasing our learning capability and moving us along the path to integration.

How does an *either/Or* approach show up over time? If we linger too long favoring one pole to the exclusion of the other, we experience the downside of our preferred pole and the downside of the non-preferred pole. For instance, if we value Experiencing, we may get inspired by what is happening now; yet, if we underutilize Thinking, we will lack a realistic view about the future. If we favor Thinking, we may focus on evidence as the basis for decision making; yet, without Experiencing, we may completely neglect emotional cues or intuition (*Figure 2*, Values/Fears). If we over-focus on Reflecting, we may create accurate plans; yet, without Acting, we may be overwhelmed by information. If we preference Acting, we may get things done on time; yet, without also using Reflecting, we may take unnecessary risks or make mistakes (*Figure 3*, Values/Fears).

The same concept holds true for different combinations of poles. If we linger too long in one part of the entire process or skip it entirely, we experience the downside. For instance, by attending to Experiencing *And* Reflecting, we raise our awareness, generate ideas, and attend to relationships; and, over-focusing impedes our ability to make a decision or accomplish an outcome.

---

[197] Sharma, G. and Kolb, David A. *The Learning Flexibility Index: Assessing Contextual Flexibility in Learning Style.* In S. Rayner and E. Cools (Eds.) *Style Differences in Cognition, Learning, and Management: Theory, Research and Practice.* Routledge, 2010, pp. 60-77.

Figure 2

Action Steps

- Practice mindfulness
- Track feelings before making decision
- Touch base with colleagues at beginning of each meeting

Early Warnings

- Regret over decision
- Experience overwhelm or upset
- Make snap decision without considering data

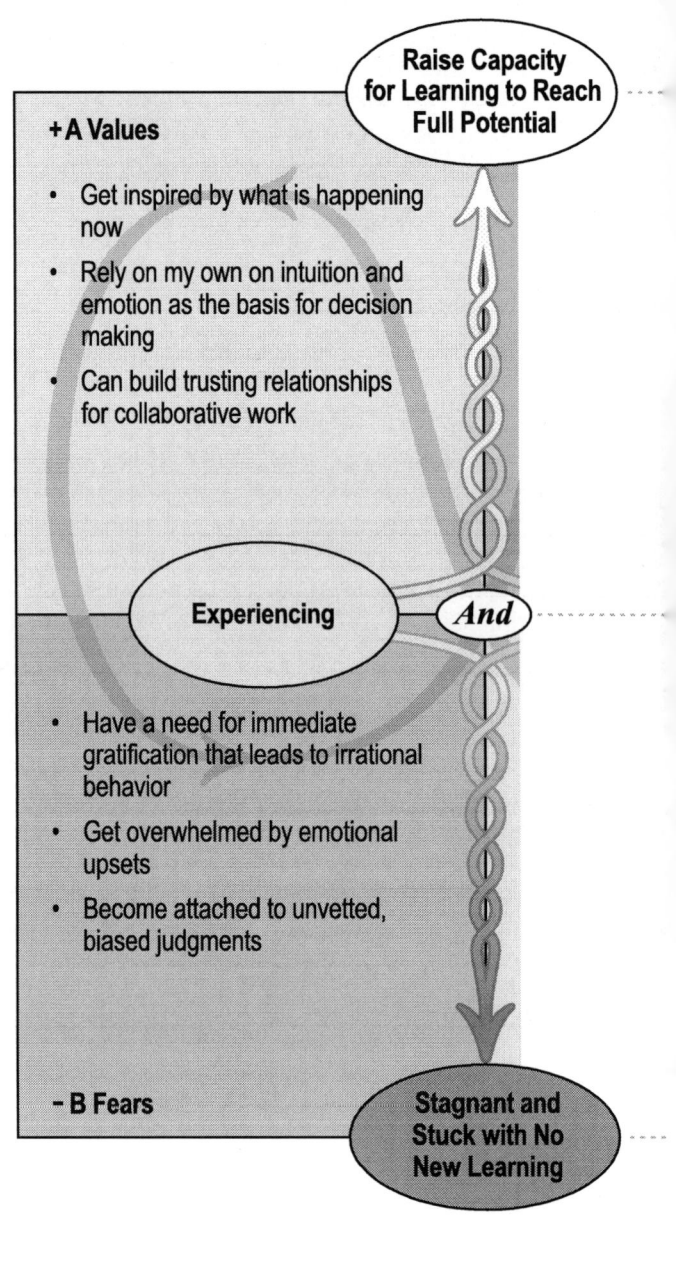

+A Values

- Get inspired by what is happening now
- Rely on my own on intuition and emotion as the basis for decision making
- Can build trusting relationships for collaborative work

Experiencing *And*

- Have a need for immediate gratification that leads to irrational behavior
- Get overwhelmed by emotional upsets
- Become attached to unvetted, biased judgments

− B Fears

Raise Capacity for Learning to Reach Full Potential

Stagnant and Stuck with No New Learning

Chapter 33: Peterson

Polarity Map®

Raise Capacity for Learning to Reach Full Potential

+C Values

- Have a realistic view about the future
- Focus on evidence as basis for decision making
- Make objective, deliberative judgments

And

Thinking

- Miss out on life (in the present) by "being in my head"
- Get overwhelmed by analysis paralysis
- Become detached from human factor causes poor judgment

− D Fears

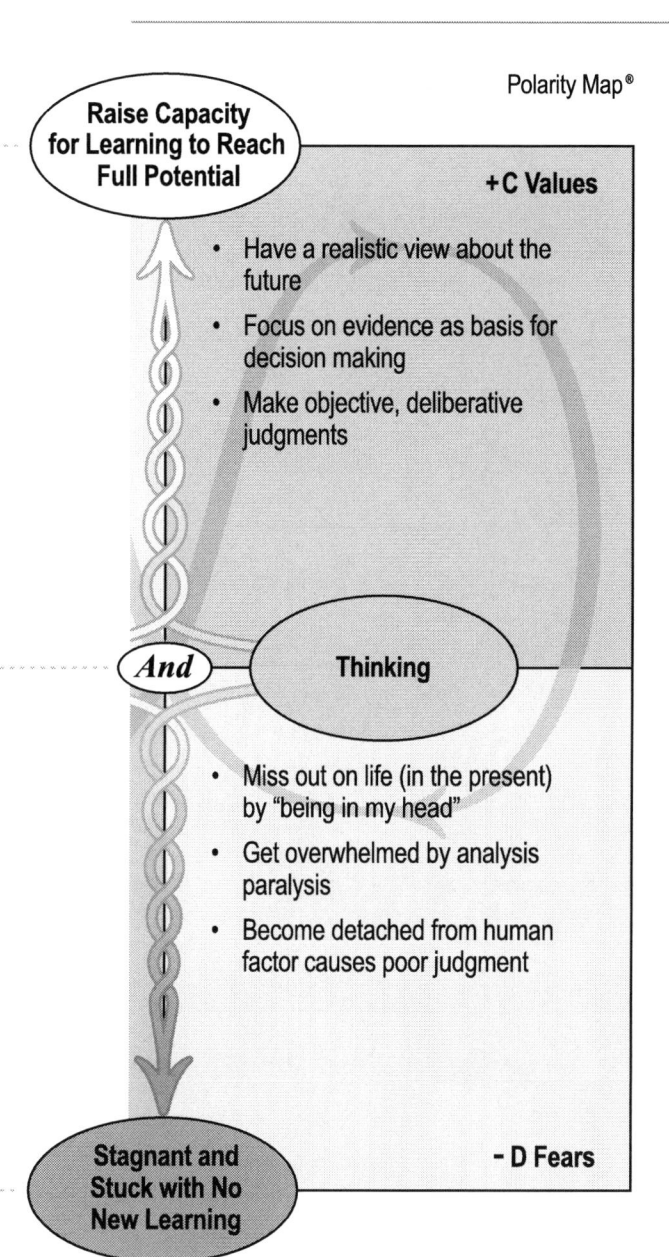

Stagnant and Stuck with No New Learning

Action Steps

- Have clear strategy
- Create model or diagram to explain the evidence
- Check on goal attainment daily/weekly

Early Warnings

- Cancel meetings or calls with people
- Sit at desk for over 1 hour without moving
- Lack enthusiasm or motivation

Figure 3

Action Steps

- Allow processing time for decisions
- Seek information and opinions of all stakeholders
- Ask clarifying questions

Early Warnings

- Postpone making decisions
- Exceed the time allotted to complete task
- Feel fearful of mistakes

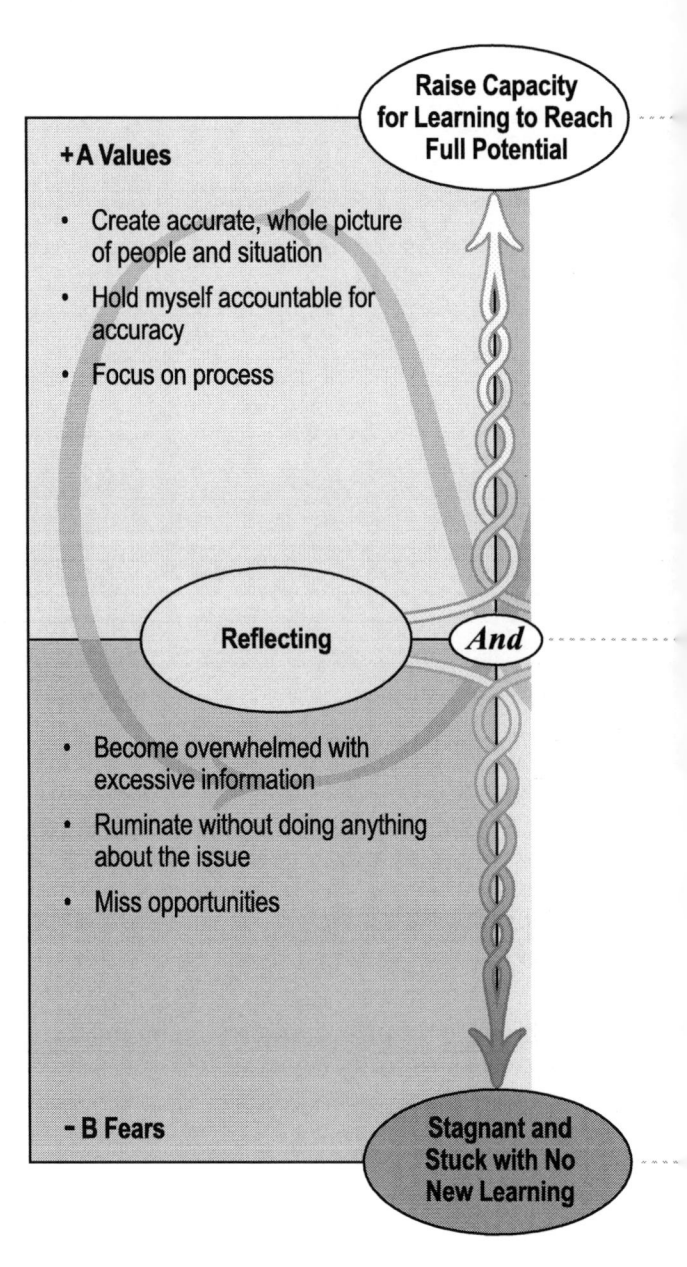

+A Values

- Create accurate, whole picture of people and situation
- Hold myself accountable for accuracy
- Focus on process

Reflecting *And*

- Become overwhelmed with excessive information
- Ruminate without doing anything about the issue
- Miss opportunities

−B Fears

Raise Capacity for Learning to Reach Full Potential

Stagnant and Stuck with No New Learning

Chapter 33: Peterson

Raise Capacity for Learning to Reach Full Potential

+C Values

- Create timely results and outcomes
- Hold myself accountable for time deadlines
- Focus on outcomes

And — **Acting**

- Become overwhelmed by busyness and activity
- Make mistakes and take unnecessary risks
- Get pushy or abusive

− D Fears

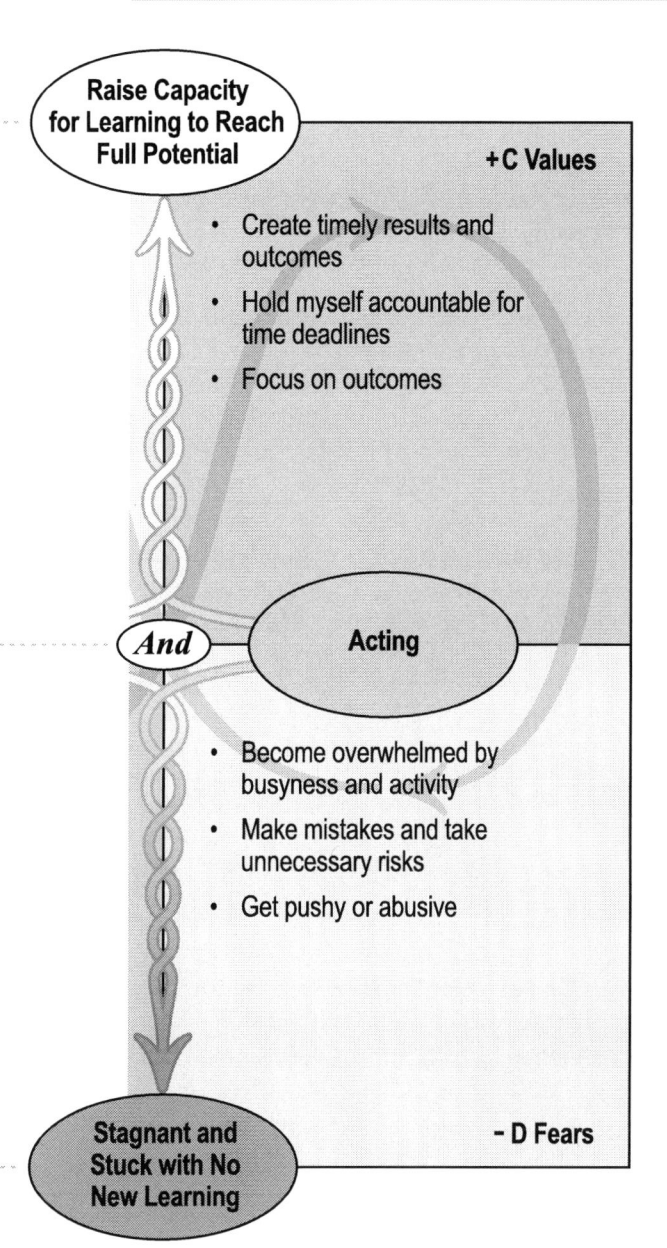

Stagnant and Stuck with No New Learning

Action Steps

- Set achievement goals (SMART)
- Set schedule to limit time on task
- Measure progress to goals every week

Early Warnings

- Rely on one source of information
- Skip process steps
- Find self apologizing to others

255

By using Reflecting *And* Thinking, we organize and attend to information and ideas, but without leverage from the other modes, we may be paralyzed in analysis. Thinking *And* Acting can ensure that we set our goals and know how to measure success; and, without the inclusion of the interdependent opposite modes, we may create the same results again and again. Acting *And* Experiencing allow us to experiment with new behaviors and seize new opportunities, but using on only those steps may create a "ready-fire-aim" approach that leaves us operating without a strategy.

To be most effective, to continue to mature, and to reach our full potential, we must learn to leverage the conflicts between dialectically opposed poles inherent in the learning process. We can change and expand the way we use the learning cycle to become flexible in order to adapt to situational needs and create more choice. Learning flexibility is the ability to use all modes of the learning cycle at will to modify our approach for the context. Flexibility has many benefits. People who have high learning flexibility are happier and have greater overall flexibility in life. They see more possibilities in any given moment, they experience less conflict and stress, and they are able to handle more complexity. Learning flexibility is related to more fulfilling personal relationships; flexible learners experience less conflict and stress, even in a more complex life situation. With flexibility, we perceive ourselves as self-directed and exhibit later stages of adult ego development.[198] Without flexibility, we may become stagnant and stuck.

Polarity Thinking is a catalyst for building flexibility. Recognizing our preferred pole in the interdependent pairs of the learning cycle raises awareness for self *And* others, and sheds light on strengths *And* blind spots/challenges. It draws attention to awareness *And* our unawareness, recognizing that what is less developed, out of awareness, unowned, or resisted can be as valuable to discover for our development as what is in awareness.

Examples of Polarity Maps for the Experiencing *And* Thinking, and Acting *And* Reflecting dimensions (*Figures 2* and *3*) of the learning cycle are pictured. These simple maps can form the foundation for a high level, impactful examination of our own ability to be flexible in our approach, as well as to help our clients do so. When working in more detail, we use the additional polarities included in the learning cycle defined by the learning styles. The concepts can be applied at all levels of a system: individual, team, organization, and community.

With awareness, we can harness the power of *both/And* Polarity Thinking to leverage our ability to use the entire learning cycle, overcoming the habit of being pulled to one extreme or the other. The impact of this dynamic approach to learning and life assures that we will continue to learn and develop every day of our lives.

About Kay Peterson ~ www.polaritypartnerships.com/certified-polarity-practitioners

---

[198] Sharma, G. and Kolb, David A. *The Learning Flexibility Index: Assessing Contextual Flexibility in Learning Style.* In S. Rayner and E. Cools (Eds.) *Style Differences in Cognition, Learning, and Management: Theory, Research and Practice.* Routledge, 2010, pp. 60-77.

Polarity Coaching®
Kathy Anderson, MBA, MAOD, CPCC

This chapter on Polarity Coaching®,[199] will overview how the traditional coaching principles and techniques of active listening, powerful questions, etc., easily and seamlessly fall into place and compliment use of the Polarity Map® and Polarity Thinking™ principles.[200] In fact, you will find that polarity mapping is a simple and natural extension of the coaching conversation and answers the question, "What do I do when I am coaching someone who is trying to solve a difficulty that is inherently unsolvable and unavoidable?"

Most often, a client hires a coach to help reach a goal or deal with an obstacle. The coach and client too often approach the coaching engagement with *either/Or*-thinking, often focusing on an issue that may look like a problem to solve. What is not readily understood is that much of the time, the issue is not a problem to solve, but rather a polarity to manage. Throughout this book, you have learned and now understand that when an *either/Or* approach is taken with a polarity, only half the issue is being addressed. And while there may be temporary success, unfortunately this approach will not ensure lasting success. When unseen and untapped, the inherent polarity actually works against long-term success and can cause frustration and an inability to sustain even initial gains.

Polarity Coaching combines the art and skill of coaching with the science and form of Polarity Thinking and works beyond *either/Or*-thinking using the power of *both/And*-thinking to help the client see the whole picture and the natural pattern of the polarity that is at work. Polarity Coaching is about coaching people, managing polarities, and the blending of the two disciplines that opens an opportunity to see and experience predictive patterns that would not otherwise be visible.

As coaches begin to recognize polarities and introduce polarities to their clients, they will come to understand the significant potential of blending traditional coaching methods and Polarity Thinking. Coaches and clients alike will see how this simple, yet powerful approach clarifies and identifies what really matters (the Greater Purpose Statement and Deeper Fear), breaks down barriers for sustaining success (naming of the interdependent pairs), identifies predictive patterns of behavior (infinity loop), finds solutions that work when incorporating the client's unique set of Values and Fears, and develops workable strategies in the form of Action Steps and Early Warnings that result in tactics designed to achieve client goals and visions.

---

[199] Anderson, Kathy. *Polarity Coaching®: Coaching People and Managing Polarities.* HRD Press, 2010.
[200] Johnson, Barry. *And: Making a Difference by Leveraging Polarity, Paradox or Dilemma. Volume One – Foundations.* HRD Press, 2020.

As Barry Johnson clarifies, The Polarity Map and principles can be used as a wisdom organizer, and the wisdom is in the life experience of the client. So true! As coaches, we want to bring as much wisdom – client life experience – into the coaching conversation for the benefit of the client as we can, and ultimately clarify and effectively communicate the client's wisdom back to the client. The Polarity Map makes this incredibly simple and transferable; clients uncover blind spots and get "unstuck." They learn how to manage the polarity.

Let's take a look at a coaching scenario that uncovers a fundamental polarity; Planned *And* Spontaneous. See how the client begins to understand that there is not a problem to solve, but rather, a polarity to be managed. Watch how polarity mapping techniques enrich the coaching conversation and effectively depict a visual structure of the whole picture and the natural pattern that is at play and that works for the client.

Planned *And* Spontaneous

Matt came to me for coaching. He and Annie had been married nearly ten years, and as they approached their ten-year wedding anniversary, they began talking about how they would celebrate. They agreed on a Florida vacation – a vacation they both wanted to remember for years to come. Problem solved, right? Wrong! Matt could not wait to begin planning each day of their vacation and decide where they would go, what they would do, and how it would fit into the budget. Annie saw things differently. She longed for two weeks of freedom and wanted to do whatever came their way – scheduling their flight and car rental was all the planning she needed. While Matt talked about wanting to plan, he also communicated concern about Annie's desire to be spontaneous. While it was clear that Matt came to me thinking he had a problem to solve, he did not see that he was really in the middle of a polarity to manage. Indeed, this was not the first time Matt's natural tendency to carefully plan various aspects of their lives created tension with Annie's more spontaneous nature and her tendency to be more spur-of-the moment in decision making. Matt's reaction was to resist the spontaneity, which he feared would lead to unavoidable and unforeseen negative consequences, and to try to impress upon Annie the need for planning – something Matt really valued. Unfortunately, when that didn't work, both Matt and Annie would experience significant frustration and disappointment.

The following excerpt is from our coaching conversation.

"It sounds like there may be wisdom in the resistance. As we coach, Matt, see if you are able to move toward the resistance, rather than away from it. What I mean by that is it would seem Annie values planning in some instances, and you have been able to relax a little when Annie is more laid back or spontaneous," I said. Then to clarify, I asked, *"Is spontaneous the right word to describe Annie?"*

"Definitely, she's spontaneous, and sometimes I love that about her," Matt agreed. *"It has helped me to relax more about some things. I can see that sometimes I'm too inflexible, which Annie tends to point out from time-to-time,"* Matt added with a blush.

Chapter 34: Anderson

"What I think I'm hearing is that both of you recognize each other's preferred pattern of behavior; you are more on the planning side and Annie more on the spontaneous side," I shared, trying to distill down what Matt had said.

"Yes, I would agree with that," Matt responded.

"It also sounds like you've been able to accept your differences," I said to confirm, *"and as you've experienced each other's natural tendencies, you've even grown to appreciate and engage these natural tendencies as your own from time-to-time."*

"Yes, I believe that's true," Matt agreed in reflection.

"So Matt, tell me what is getting in the way now?" I asked.

Matt started slowly, *"I feel we need to plan our vacation carefully. I try to explain this to Annie, but every time I talk about it, Annie resists even more, and we don't get anywhere. This is taking all the fun out of planning, and the clearer I communicate my point of view, the more Annie resists. Like I said, I'm stuck!"*

"Matt, what might the spontaneous part of you say?"

"I don't understand," Matt answered.

"I heard you say that Annie is naturally drawn toward the spontaneous part of her – it's what I would call her natural tendency, or motivational value. And she also sees the value of planning, what I would call your natural tendency or motivational value. I also heard you say that even as a natural planner, you can see the value of being spontaneous from time-to-time."

"Yes, that's true," Matt mused.

"Tell me then, what might the spontaneous part of you say about your vacation?" I repeated.

Matt hesitated, *"I guess I'm not looking at this from a spontaneous point of view. I've been focused on trying to plan the vacation,"* Matt answered thoughtfully.

"What perspective do you think Annie is looking at this vacation from, Matt, planned or spontaneous?"

"I know it's not from a planning perspective!" Matt said confidently.

"Do you think this is to be expected?" I continued.

"Yes, you're right; I should expect this," Matt sighed.

"Matt, do you see how Annie might resist a process of planning your vacation that does not include spontaneity?"

"Yes, I can see that now," Matt answered keenly, *"but I really want to solve this problem."*

I continued, *"I believe, Matt, this is a polarity to manage, not a problem to solve."*

Matt puzzled, *"A polarity to manage?"*

"Yes," I answered. *"Let me explain. Deciding where to go on your vacation is a problem to solve, and you have both agreed on Florida. You basically made a decision and you moved on. A polarity to manage is different, and when a polarity to manage is treated as a decision to be made (problem to solve), resistance occurs. With a polarity to manage, both points of view are accurate, and neither is complete in and of itself. In fact, both points of view are dependent on one another for a successful outcome."* I paused as Matt thought this through.

"I think I understand what you are saying." Matt stated a bit apprehensively.

"What polarities do you think are at work here, Matt?"

"Well, I'm not sure," Matt hesitated. *"But we've been talking a lot about planning and being spontaneous – would the polarity be Planned And Spontaneous?"*

"Yes," I continued, excited that Matt could see this. *"I agree – the polarity to manage is Planned And Spontaneous and focusing on either one and neglecting the other brings resistance, and adds to the frustration and disappointment you have been experiencing."*

"This sounds interesting," Matt enthused. *"I've been experiencing resistance, and yes, frustration and disappointment. Let's tackle this!"*

Before our initial coaching session was over, Matt and I put together a Polarity Map (*Figure 1*). I still remember when Matt realized the power of the Planned *And* Spontaneous polarity; tears came to his eyes as it really sunk in what had been happening and that he and Annie had so often been seeing and reacting to the down side of each other's natural tendencies. As a coach, this was amazingly wonderful!

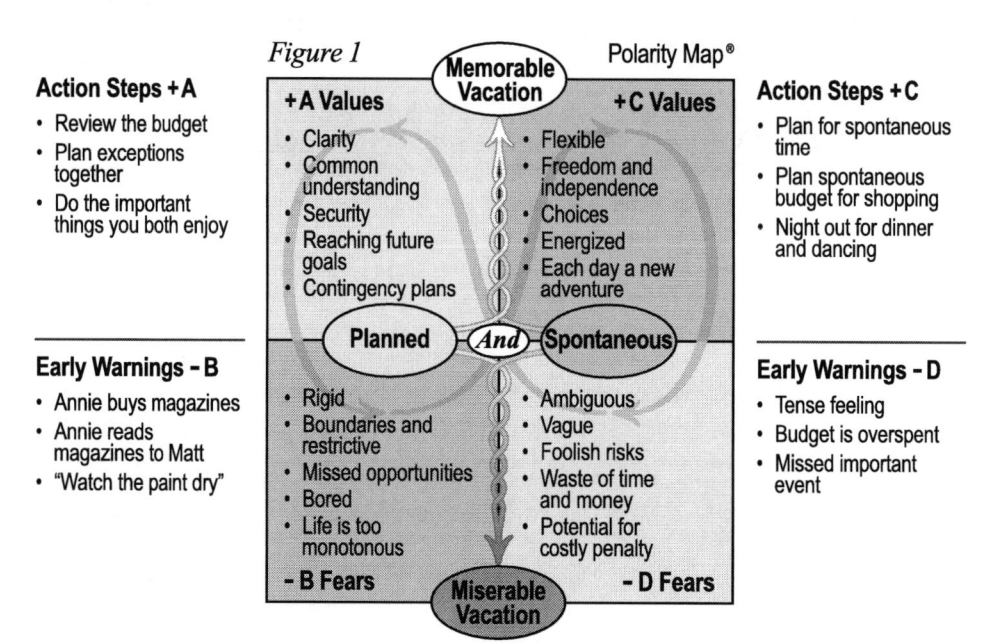

Figure 1 — Polarity Map®

Action Steps +A
- Review the budget
- Plan exceptions together
- Do the important things you both enjoy

Early Warnings −B
- Annie buys magazines
- Annie reads magazines to Matt
- "Watch the paint dry"

+A Values (Planned)
- Clarity
- Common understanding
- Security
- Reaching future goals
- Contingency plans

−B Fears
- Rigid
- Boundaries and restrictive
- Missed opportunities
- Bored
- Life is too monotonous

+C Values (Spontaneous)
- Flexible
- Freedom and independence
- Choices
- Energized
- Each day a new adventure

−D Fears
- Ambiguous
- Vague
- Foolish risks
- Waste of time and money
- Potential for costly penalty

Action Steps +C
- Plan for spontaneous time
- Plan spontaneous budget for shopping
- Night out for dinner and dancing

Early Warnings −D
- Tense feeling
- Budget is overspent
- Missed important event

Greater Purpose: Memorable Vacation
Deeper Fear: Miserable Vacation

We could now coach around the infinity loop, and through the values and fears of both Matt and Annie as he saw them. And, rather than working against the resistance he was experiencing and pushing against a natural energy flow, it was now okay to embrace the natural flow of the polarity and work with it.

Summary

Understanding the client's goal, motivational values, and fears, and designing a strategy in the form of action steps and early warnings is key to the coaching experience. With Polarity Coaching, coach and client are able to understand the interdependent polarities at play, providing powerful insights to important predictive patterns that enhance the coaching conversation, and helping achieve progress and sustain success. The Polarity Map is a wisdom organizer and an effective supplement to traditional coaching methods. Polarity Coaching uses the Polarity Map within the coaching conversation to create a visual structure that informs the client, while uncovering the whole picture and the interplay of the Greater Purpose and Deeper Fear, as well as the interdependent polarities, Fears, Values, Action Steps, and Early Warnings. This simple, yet powerful approach will enable clients to not only make change, but to sustain success, which will enhance your effectiveness as a coach.

Whether dealing with chronic problems, developing teams or leaders, making key decisions, or developing best practices within your organization, Polarity Thinking and Polarity Coaching are tools that will clarify and map the way to make and help sustain the change you are looking for.

For more Polarity Coaching scenarios, my book, <u>Polarity Coaching®: Coaching People and Managing Polarities</u>, offers coaching case studies starting from the simple to more complex. The book demonstrates that there is no single starting point with the Polarity Map; the coach simply starts where the client is, whether it's naming the poles, stating the Greater Purpose, identifying a Fear or concern, or focusing on an important Value. Each scenario is approached in a slightly different way, including walking through the map with a client, either face-to-face or by phone appointment, as well as being used by the coach, alone, as a personal wisdom organizer. There is no one recommended way – whatever works best with your client is the best method for Polarity Coaching.

Find bio and contact info for author Kathy Anderson at
www.polaritypartnerships.com/certified-polarity-practitioners

Polarities Are Generative Tensions at the Heart of Organization Evolution: A Living Systems Approach to Creating Conditions for Flourishing

Sally Breyley Parker

In 1997, I assumed the presidency of a commercial architectural firm. In the early days of my tenure, I suggested to my partners that we consider using the human body as a living systems model for the design and operations of the company. Enthusiastically, I talked about how our bodies naturally fostered both structure and flow; facilitated both stability and flexibility; cared both for the parts and for the whole; and ensured both nutrient intake and waste removal. I wondered, if we could somehow "mimic" the body's design, could we better optimize our energy and resource utilization? While not yet familiar with the language of polarities, I was aware of their power and the need to facilitate their flow. I still remember the look on my partners faces as they listened. Suffice it to say, I did not get much, if any, traction. A living systems model would have to wait.

Later that year I was invited to hear Dee Hock tell his story of the founding of VISA using a chaordic structure. According to Hock, given their growing complexities, organizations needed a new model, one which acknowledged both their chaotic and orderly dimensions. He even used the human body as an example of a chaordic structure that seamlessly marries the tensions of chaos and order. Although he did not refer to chaos and order as a polarity, by naming this tension as core to a new business model, he was giving voice and value to a critical energy system in organizations that traditional business models tended to ignore and consequently devalue. For me, he underscored the need for *both/And*-thinking to supplement *either/Or* – and he validated the power of a living systems lens for organization design and operations. I was on fire!

Soon after hearing Hock speak, I left architecture to pursue organization design and development, ultimately founding TimeZero Enterprises. Our systems approach is inspired by nature's wisdom. Because polarities are inherent in all living systems – human and non-human – polarities are central to our living systems framework. In fact, we find that Polarity Thinking™ is an essential capacity for living systems work. Our premise is that polarities are the generative tensions at the heart of an organization's ability to evolve and thrive. As energy systems, polarities have fueled life's evolution for more than 3.8 billion years. I think it is safe to say that when it comes to Polarity Thinking, nature has a lot to teach us.

Take a tree for instance. Its structure not only provides stability, it also enables nutrient flow to all of its parts. What can trees teach us about optimizing the health and performance of organizations by leveraging *both* structure *And* flow? Birds amaze us with their acrobatics as they flock. Flying at high speeds and in close proximity, they continuously self-organize in ever-changing formations. This not only improves their chance of survival against predators, it enables them to fly further using less energy, with less fatigue. These movements would be dangerous, if not impossible, without clear direction afforded through simple rules. What can we learn from birds about how to leverage *both* direction (simple rules) *And* self-organization to create cultures of innovation and creativity?

This chapter describes how Polarity Thinking inherently informs and shapes our work with organizations as living systems.

Polarity Thinking is Integral to a Living Systems Approach

We typically introduce the concept of polarities by talking about them as energy systems that "live within" an organization, its members, and its broader ecosystem. Breathing is the first polarity we have participants experience. A universal polarity, breathing involves *both* Inhaling *And* Exhaling. One is not better than the other. If we don't do both, we die. When we ask participants to hold an inhale and then exhale for an unnatural period of time, they personally feel the anxiety created when an energy system, in this case breathing, is interrupted or stuck. They also begin to see how polarities each have their own natural pace, flow, and rhythm. In the case of breathing, the way we manage and leverage the pace, flow, and rhythm of our breath has a profound impact on the quality of our life. This is why breathing is so central to practices like mindfulness.

Next, we examine Activity *And* Rest – a very familiar polarity that shapes the rhythm and quality of our lives. Many of us are familiar with the downside of over-focusing on activity at the expense of rest. This pattern highlights how willing we are to suffer the downside of activity (illness, burnout, injury) because of our culturally conditioned distaste for the downside of rest (unproductive, feeling worthless ...). This over-focus on one side of a polarity demonstrates the power of organizational and cultural preferences that keep individuals and organizations stuck in the downside of a pole – even when that downside is harming us.

Just think about how wellness programs often fail to get purchase within an organization because the organization overvalues activity and undervalues rest. Until the full polarity is seen as an essential energy system and rest is valued and authorized as part of that system, the organization's members will continue to suffer burnout.

I experienced a similar phenomenon when I was working in architecture back in the late 1990s. We were designing the corporate headquarters of a polymer elastomer company in the Midwest. The client design team included visionary and non-traditional leaders who wanted the office layout to be punctuated by open, communal areas where people could go to relax, read, reflect. We designed a beautiful space, but after the client moved in, people rarely used it. Why? Because relaxation and reflection were not yet authorized within the organization's culture. In two years, new leaders came in, saw the area as a waste of space, and had it reworked to be "far more productive."

The better we see and understand these energy systems, the healthier and higher performing we can be.

The Polarities of Flourishing

All healthy and productive ecosystems have three properties in common: Resilience, Self-Organization, and Hierarchy.[201] Existing at the level of the whole ecosystem, these properties emerge when conditions are conducive and are inherently interdependent. *Figure 1* briefly describes each property and the polarities within it.

Figure 1

Resilience	Polarities
The measure of a system's ability to survive and persist within a variable environment, to function in face of stress and disruption. A resilient individual or organization can recover in a timely fashion and even grow stronger. Feedback loops are essential to resilience... many working in different ways, through different mechanisms, at different scales, with redundancy. Too many layers within a system create delay and distortion to feedback and ultimately undermine its resiliency. Because it is hard to "see" resilience, it is easy to sacrifice for other short-term aims. But we know when we have exceeded its limits and the system structure breaks down.	Activity *And* Rest Continuity *And* Transformation Part *And* Whole Short-term *And* Long-term Autonomy *And* Coordination Growth *And* Development Structure *And* Flow

Self-Organization	Polarities
A system's ability to learn, diversify, complexify, and evolve. It naturally produced heterogeneity and unpredictability, often resulting in new structures, new designs, and new ways of doing things. It requires freedom for experimentation and a certain amount of disorder. At the heart of all self-organizing systems are simple rules and organizing principles that enable a wide diversity of organizational structures. Self-organization can threaten power structures.	Leadership *And* Followership Part *And* Whole Planned *And* Emergent Self *And* Other Action *And* Reflection Structure *And* Flow

Hierarchy	Polarities
Recurring "branching" patterns that arise naturally to enhance flow (e.g., materials, information, nutrients, resources, etc.). Their purpose is to help sub-systems do their jobs better. Hierarchies give a system stability and resilience, reduce the amount of information that any part has to track, and balance the welfare, freedoms, and responsibilities of the sub-systems and total.	Autonomy *And* Coordination Freedom *And* Responsibility Part *And* Whole Structure *And* Flow Stability *And* Change Include *And* Transcend Centralize *And* Distribute

[201] Meadows, Donella H. *Thinking in Systems: A Primer.* Chelsea Green Publishing, 2008.

Resilience requires self-organization and natural hierarchy; self-organization fosters resilience and naturally creates hierarchies; and hierarchy supports resilience and is created through and enables self-organization. Polarities are at play in all of these properties.

As living systems strategists and designers, our charge is to cultivate the conditions for these properties to emerge and sustain. When we can see and understand these properties and their dynamics, we are better equipped to foster the conditions for a thriving organization.

Some polarities – Part *And* Whole, Structure *And* Flow – appear in multiple properties. These are macro polarities in a living systems perspective, and they represent high leverage points within an organizational system.

Mechanistic *And* Organic: A Macro Polarity for Flourishing

Business as machine has long been a primary metaphor for organizations. As a result, we have naturally valued stability, certainty, and control, placing a premium on problem solving (*either/Or*-thinking), planning, and managing change. While these capacities are essential for organizations, in a world that is increasingly Volatile, Uncertain, Complex, and Ambiguous (VUCA), we find them far from sufficient.

Organizations today also need to be adaptive and agile. In other words, they need *both* the Stability and order of the traditional "Mechanistic" mindset (+A) *And* the Adaptability and agility afforded through "Organic" capabilities (+C). An organization that values and can leverage both will flourish (*Figure 2*).

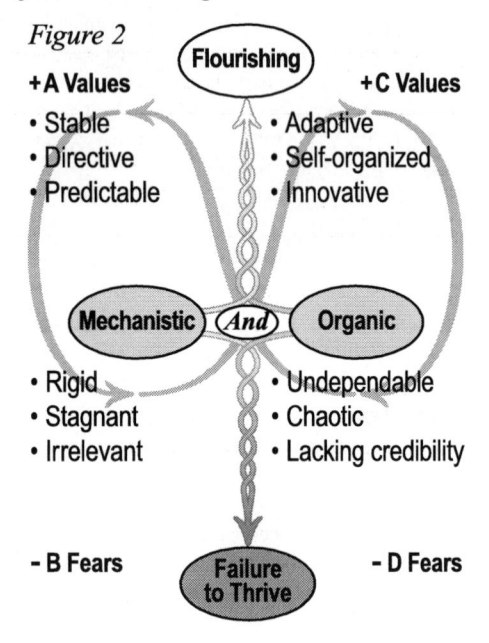

Figure 2

Flourishing

+A Values
• Stable
• Directive
• Predictable

+C Values
• Adaptive
• Self-organized
• Innovative

Mechanistic *And* Organic

• Rigid
• Stagnant
• Irrelevant

• Undependable
• Chaotic
• Lacking credibility

− B Fears

Failure to Thrive

− D Fears

However, fear of the downside of Organic (-D), becoming Undependable, Chaotic, Lacking credibility or even anarchical, is often enough to keep an organization stuck in the downside of the mechanistic pole (-B) where they become Rigid, Stagnant, Irrelevant, and lose energy.

As we explore the Mechanistic *And* Organic polarity with organizations, we introduce numerous polarities that are nested within (*Figure 3*). Doing so allows the organization to unpack this critical polarity for themselves.

It is important to name poles using language that resonates – language that its members find recognizable and transformative. There are no "right" names for polarity poles. The key is supporting an organization to find the words that capture their experiences of each energy system. This helps legitimize the *both/And* of the Mechanistic *And* Organic polarity so that the organization can begin the process of seeing and leveraging the inherent potential in this generative tension.

Leveraging Mechanistic *And* Organic

Today, most organizations have experienced, at least to some degree, the downside of an overemphasis on mechanistic values and capabilities. However, their change efforts often fail to gain desired results. We see two reasons for this: 1) an overemphasis on *either/Or*-thinking and 2) a "From→To" mindset.

Figure 3

Mechanistic	*And*	Organic
Continuity	*And*	Transformation
Planned	*And*	Emergent
Individual	*And*	Team
Structure	*And*	Flow
Stability	*And*	Change
Part	*And*	Whole
Directive	*And*	Self-organized
Data	*And*	Intuition
Predictability	*And*	Novelty
Responsibility	*And*	Risk
Action	*And*	Reflection
Task	*And*	Relationship
Independent Work	*And*	Collaborative Work

***Either/Or*-Thinking:** *Either/Or*-thinking is central to a mechanistic mindset. While *either/Or*-thinking is essential for problem solving, without *both/And*-thinking, organizations fail to see and value *both* Mechanistic *And* Organic capabilities as equally essential for thriving. If an organization's value system continues to prefer the mechanistic pole, the attributes of the organic pole will remain unauthorized within the system. Until the organization places equal value on developing its organic capabilities, there will be insufficient "authority" within the organizational system to sustain the growth and development of those capacities.

We use polarity mapping, particularly the Past *And* Present, Present *And* Future approach combined with the getting unstuck process, to help organizations break through the limits of *either/Or*-thinking to embrace the power of *both* Mechanistic *And* Organic attributes and values. This positions them to begin the work of "authorizing" the organic within the organizational.

From → To Mindset: Like *either/Or*-thinking, a From→To mindset forms the basis of nearly all prevailing leadership, team, and organization effectiveness models. It sets in motion an inevitable "pendulum swing" because it sees change as an event; as something to drive, manage, and control in order to reach a new state of stability and equilibrium. It fails to see change as integral to the ongoing cycle of an organization's evolution, as essential to its ability to achieve and sustain success over time. It also obfuscates the power of the Continuity *And* Transformation energy system.

With a From→To mindset, a battle between change champions and change resistors is inevitable. In the case of living systems, change champions believe that the current mechanistic mindset (Continuity) is the problem and their goal is to drive change toward the solution of an organic mindset (Transformation), as seen in *Figure 4*.

On the other hand, change resistors see an organic mindset (Transformation) as the problem and the current mechanistic mindset (Continuity) as the solution, as seen in *Figure 5*. With a From → To mindset, both change champions and resistors find themselves stuck in their perceived problems and hooked on their perceived solutions.

Once again, Polarity Thinking is essential to expanding beyond this dominant approach to change. We often begin by sharing a simple statement inspired by nature: "Nature doesn't change, it creates new in the midst of what is." This statement is a beautiful example of the Include *And* Transcend polarity, which is at the heart of evolution. Life evolves by building on what works, reshuffling information to create new forms and solutions, and incorporating surprise (often in the form of mistakes). In other words, it is constantly in the flow of Continuity *And* Transformation, where change happens naturally, and adaptability is critical.

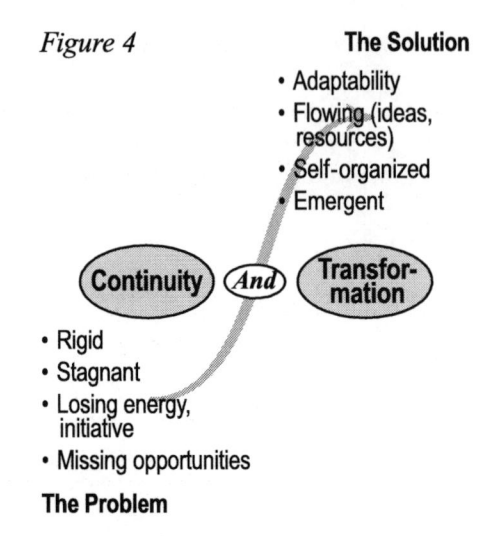

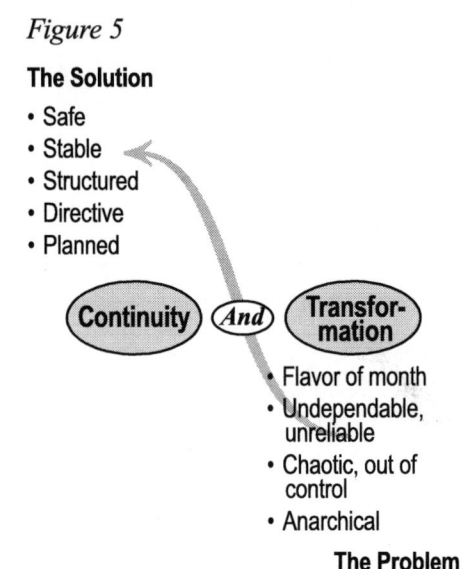

Figure 4

The Solution
- Adaptability
- Flowing (ideas, resources)
- Self-organized
- Emergent

Continuity *And* Transformation

- Rigid
- Stagnant
- Losing energy, initiative
- Missing opportunities

The Problem

Figure 5

The Solution
- Safe
- Stable
- Structured
- Directive
- Planned

Continuity *And* Transformation

- Flavor of month
- Undependable, unreliable
- Chaotic, out of control
- Anarchical

The Problem

Let's look at an example that illustrates the power of these two phenomena. In 2008, we were approached by a county planning commission to "design" a new organization to champion the regeneration of a river valley that had long been subject to industry pollution and environmental degradation. We agreed to engage with one caveat. Rather than assume that a new organization was the solution, our approach was to explore ways of organizing, which may or may not result in a new organization. The area of focus was multi-county and touched many different types of organizations, businesses, government entities, and non-profits, whose missions and/or livelihoods somehow touched or depended on the valley. To represent the diversity of the valley, we convened a design collaborative whose membership reflected the diversity of place.

Our process was designed to surface *both* Mechanistic *And* Organic values and needs and early in our conversations, two "camps" emerged. One camp, composed primarily of government representatives, felt that an entity responsible for the valley's regeneration must have "teeth" – it needed to be big with authority to direct the actions of others and be able to control and enforce those actions. The other group argued that it needed to accomplish its mission in a more grassroots fashion – that it needed to start small and earn trust and leverage shared vision to foster self-organization. The design that ultimately emerged reflected this *both/And*. Implementation would start through the formation of small and stealth-like organization. We were thrilled!

However, when the design collaborative's work was complete and the director of county planning pulled implementation of the initiative back into the county, the process stalled almost immediately. In hindsight, I now realize (after developing deeper capability in Polarity Thinking) that our process never explicitly addressed the impact of *either/Or*-thinking and a From→To mindset.

Although the design reflected an integration of *both/And*-thinking, the head of county planning retained the belief that you *either* led through authority and size *Or* you were controlled by others. Additionally, his predominant mindset was that people and organizations could not be trusted because they would act in their own self-interest which would undermine the aim of regenerating the valley (the problem), so a big organization with "teeth" was essential (the solution).

Consequently, he defaulted to a more traditional top-down design solution in which the County would retain control but was destined to fail.

Had we been more aware of the power of these forces, our outcomes may very well have been different. If we had introduced Polarity Thinking from the start, we would have recognized these key tensions – Directive Leadership *And* Shared Leadership as well as Directive *And* Self-Organized – as polarities to manage, not problems to solve. Moreover, had we mapped these polarities, we would have established a shared understanding of the upsides and downsides of each pole, and that our work as designers was to enable an organization that could leverage these tensions in service to the regeneration of the Cuyahoga River Valley as a sustainable and prosperous place to live and work.

Life Creates Conditions Conducive to Life

As we work with organizations as living systems, we continue to experience the transformative and life-giving power of Polarity Thinking. Polarities are at the heart of our ability to evolve. The more able we are able to see, understand, and leverage these critical energy systems, the more equipped we are to create and sustain life-giving organizations where:

- Structure enables, rather than constricts, flow
- Planning processes foster learning because they embrace *both* the known *And* the emergent

- Purpose *And* value provide simple rules for behavior, negating the need for overly prescriptive, directive environments
- Trust in *both* data *And* intuition grounds decisions that foster *both* performance *And* health

Conclusion

Polarities are energy systems inherent in all living systems, including organizations. Using a Living Systems Approach, we view the polarities in systems as generative tensions, necessary for the ability of organizations to evolve and thrive. We can leverage the polarities that are most critical to organizations' evolution, creating conditions for these generative tensions to produce resilience, self-organization, and natural hierarchy that serve the whole.

Many organization development and design professionals are used to designing and re-engineering structures, such as policies, strategies, competency models, and processes. Less often do we tend to the intangible flows of energy enabled by those structures. But Nature shows us it is important to do both. Polarity Thinking is an essential capability for organizations and communities to flourish.

Find bio and contact info for author Sally Breyley Parker at www.polaritypartnerships.com/certified-polarity-practitioners

Polarity Thinking™ and Oshry's Organic Systems Framework
Cliff Kayser, MSHR, MSOD, PCC

The fundamental business of all human systems is based in a dual need to survive and develop. A system expresses its power through individuation and differentiation, its love through homogenization and integration.

~ Barry Oshry

Power without love is reckless and abusive, and love without power is sentimental and anemic.[202]

~ Dr. Martin Luther King, Jr.

This chapter explores powerful intersections between the work of Barry Oshry[203] and Barry Johnson[204] to support robust system outcomes for leaders, teams, and organization systems. Specific focus is given to key stakeholder conditions contributing to empowerment and avoiding disempowerment in the context of two polarities inherent to Oshry's Organic System Framework. Note that key stakeholders are those who are or will be impacted by a planned change process.

Engaging Key Stakeholders

Oshry's work examines the power of key stakeholders in organization systems from "Top, Middle, Bottom, and Customer" (TMBC) perspectives. His new perspective expands on our general view of TMBC as only hierarchal. This supplemental perspective revealed that, depending on the context of work processes, all of us can function in any of the TMBC role relationships regardless of our hierarchal position. The choices we make as key stakeholders in our TMBC roles and relationships as they relate to *both* the hierarchy *And* the conditions have a profound impact on power.

The following *Figures 1-4* provide a high-level summary of the process framed as "stories" – conditions, responses, and outcomes – that each key stakeholder might follow when leading from any TMBC condition. In summary, when key stakeholders make Conscious Choice Responses in the context of each condition, it leads to Empowerment and Robust System Outcomes while Blind/Reflexive Responses in the context of each condition leads to Disempowerment and Weak System Outcomes. Seeing these TMBC conditions improves capability and capacity of key stakeholders to attain and sustain Oshry's "Total System Empowerment."[205]

---

[202] www.goodreads.com/quotes/134364-power-without-love-is-reckless-and-abusive-and-love-without
[203] Oshry, Barry. *Seeing Systems: Unlocking the Mysteries of Organizational Life.* Berrett-Koehler, 1995.
[204] Johnson, Barry. *And: Making a Difference by Leveraging Polarity, Paradox or Dilemma. Volume One – Foundations.* HRD Press, 2020.
[205] www.govleaders.org/total-system-power.htm

Figure 1: Leading From the Top

	Robust System Outcome	I/Others Share Power
EMPOWERING	Empowerment ↑	*"I'm shaping the system, diagnosing the dangers and opportunities structuring and resourcing the system so that it is better able to cope and prospect."*
EMPOWERING	Conscious Choice Response ↑	*"I'm a Developer. My work is strengthening the capacity of the system to cope and prospect."*
EMPOWERING	Condition ↑	*"Things are complex, complicated, changing, and uncertain. Danger and opportunity are everywhere."*
	Relationship Role	**When You're Leading From the Top**
DISEMPOWERING	Condition ↓	*"Things are complex, complicated, changing, and uncertain. Danger and opportunity are everywhere."*
DISEMPOWERING	Blind/Reflexive Response ↓	*"I'm responsible, so I will shoulder all responsibility."*
DISEMPOWERING	Disempowerment ↓	*"I'm not doing enough or doing it well-enough. I'm letting everyone (people) and everything (system) down."*
	Weak System Outcome	**I/Others Lose Power**

Figure 2: Leading From the Middle

	Robust System Outcome	I/Others Share Power
EMPOWERING	Empowerment ↑	*"I'm sharing system 'intelligence' to resolve issues that otherwise land on Tops or Bottoms."*
EMPOWERING	Conscious Choice Response ↑	*"I'm an Integrator. My work is to help others deal with their issues, which are not mine."*
EMPOWERING	Condition ↑	*"Things are so conflicted. Demands, priorities, and pressures constantly change."*
	Relationship Role	**When You're Leading From the Middle**
DISEMPOWERING	Condition ↓	*"Things are so conflicted. Demands, priorities, and pressures constantly change."*
DISEMPOWERING	Blind/Reflexive Response ↓	*"I'm responsible, so I try to resolve everyone's issues or try to resolve others' conflicts."*
DISEMPOWERING	Disempowerment ↓	*"I'm not pleasing others. I'm feeling weak, incompetent."*
	Weak System Outcome	**I/Others Lose Power**

Figure 3: Leading From the Bottom

	Robust System Outcome	**I/Others Share Power**
EMPOWERING	Empowerment ↑	"I'm closest to Customer work and I'm using that closeness together with my brain power, experience, and expertise to fix problems or see they they get fixed."
	Conscious Choice Response ↑	"I'm a Fixer. My work is a shift from 'they are responsible' to 'I am responsible'."
	Condition ↑	"Things don't work (tools, structure, rules, procedures), and there's a lack of information."
	Relationship Role	**When You're Leading From the Bottom**
DISEMPOWERING	Condition ↓	"Things don't work (tools, structure, rules, procedures), and there's a lack of information."
	Blind/Reflexive Response ↓	"I'm suffering from the actions/inactions of insensitive, incompetent, or malicious Tops and Middles."
	Disempowerment ↓	"I'm looking up the chain to those responsible for fixing these problems."
	Weak System Outcome	**I/Others Lose Power**

Figure 4: Leading as a Customer

	Robust System Outcome	**I/Others Share Power**
EMPOWERING	Empowerment ↑	"I let the system know how well it is doing or what it thinks it is doing, and the degree to which parts are working together to deliver outcomes."
	Conscious Choice Response ↑	"I'm a Validator. My work is to share responsibility for process and outcomes."
	Condition ↑	"Things are not coming as fast as I want/need, at the quality I want/need, and at a fair cost."
	Relationship Role	**When You're Leading as a Customer**
DISEMPOWERING	Condition ↓	"Things are not coming as fast as I want/need, at the quality I want/need, and at a fair cost."
	Blind/Reflexive Response ↓	"I'm angry about irrelevance of my input and being told 'Be patient' or 'We know better'."
	Disempowerment ↓	"I'm the customer, I'm not responsible for the craziness of this system – others are."
	Weak System Outcome	**I/Others Lose Power**

In the next section, we explore two polarities that all key stakeholders in organization systems face. First, the interdependent processes involving Power *And* Love. The second, the interdependency between Survive *And* Develop. For both of these, harnessing key stakeholder power is a critical factor in sustainable success.

Two Polarities in Oshry's Organic Systems

We use the 5-Step SMALL Process™ and Polarity Maps® to make the two implicit polarities in Oshry's work explicit; Power Processes *And* Love Processes, and Survive *And* Develop. The generic wisdom of Oshry's Organic Systems Framework has been organized in universal Polarity Map templates (*Figures 5* and *6*). Similarly, organization systems can capture their specific/unique Top, Middle, Bottom, Customer (TMBC) wisdom using their own Polarity Map templates and the 5-Step SMALL Process.

Power Process *And* Love Process (*Figure 5*)

Step 1) TMBC Seeing: According to Oshry, "A system expresses its power through individuation and differentiation, its love through homogenization and integration." Power *And* Love each comprise unique *systems processes*. Power Processes involves "Differentiation" – processing difference – and "Individuation" – processing separateness (+A Values). The Love Processes involves "Homogenization" – processing commonality – and "Integration" – processing togetherness (+C Values).

Step 2) TMBC Mapping: The upside benefits of Power Processes appear in the upper left quadrant (+A). An over-focus on Power Processes without focus on Love Processes appear in the lower left quadrant (-B). The upside benefits of Love Processes appear in the upper right quadrant (+C). An over-focus on Love Processes without focus on Power Processes appear in the lower right quadrant (-D).

Steps 3 and 4) TMBC Assessing and Learning: It is important to measure the degree to which individuals and the system are experiencing a maximization of benefits of both poles (+A, +C Values) and minimizing the limitations (-B, -D Fears). This can occur through dialogue or, with more precision, by using the Polarity Assessment™.[206] In Learning, we make meaning of assessment results including factors that may be contributing to or mitigating high performance.

Step 5) TMBC Leveraging: Achieving and sustaining a "Robust System/Empowering" (Greater Purpose) and avoiding a "Weak System/Disempowering" (Deeper Fear) is illustrated in *Figure 5* with a well-leveraged infinity loop; both upsides of Power *And* Love are being maximized and both downsides of Power *And* Love are being minimized. This outcome is the result of Steps 1-4 above, plus identifying and implementing Action Steps and Early Warnings:

- **Action Steps:** What are the Conscious Choice Responses by TMBC's that will empower both Power/Differentiating *And* Love/Integrating, including strategies for *Developing, Integrating, Fixing,* and *Validating*?

---

[206] The Polarity Assessment™. www.polaritypartnerships.com/our-impact. 2020.

- **Early Warnings:** What will key stakeholders track to help ensure blind/reflexive responses don't lead to disempowering outcomes for Power *And* Love?

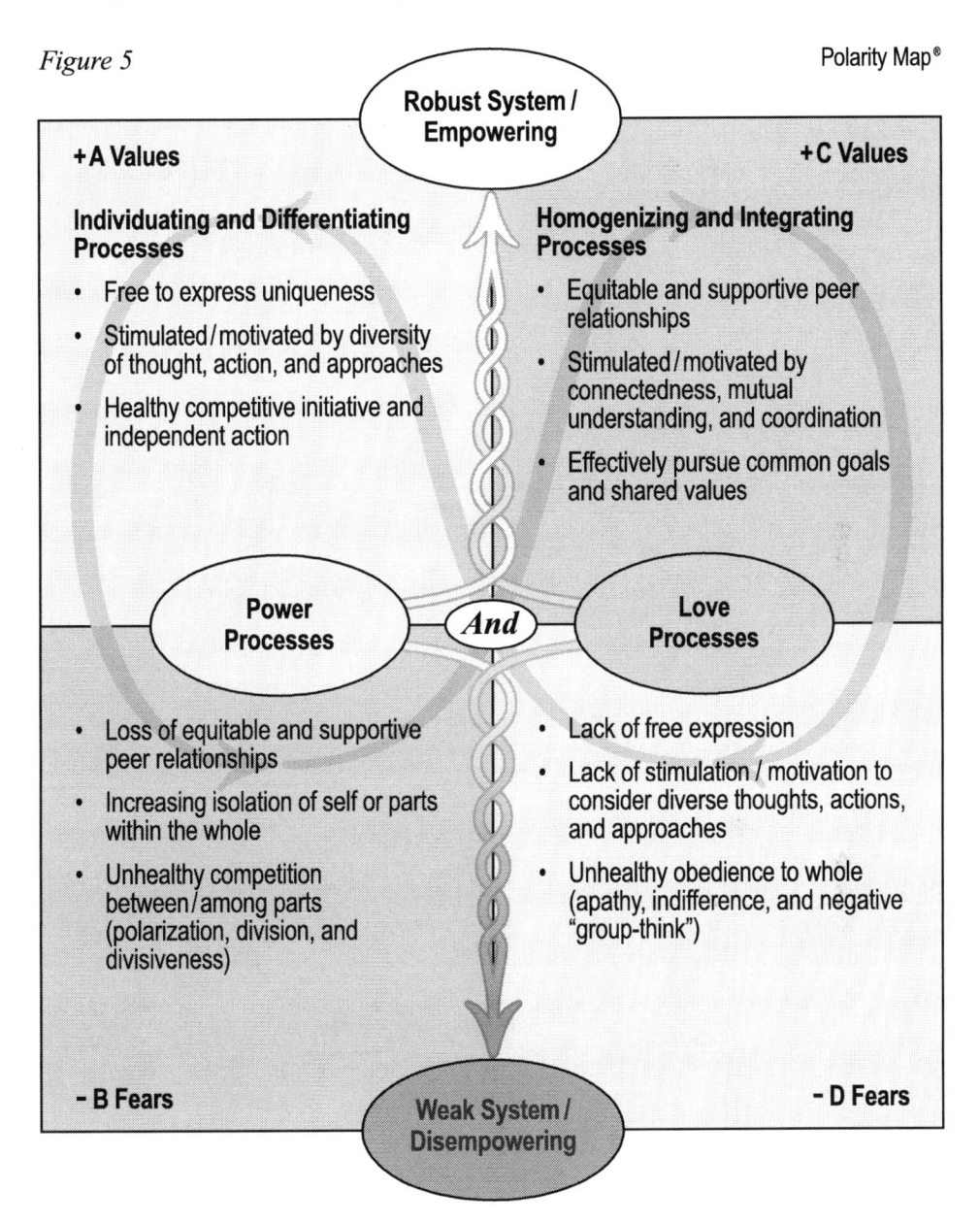

Figure 5   Polarity Map®

Robust System / Empowering

+A Values

Individuating and Differentiating Processes

- Free to express uniqueness
- Stimulated/motivated by diversity of thought, action, and approaches
- Healthy competitive initiative and independent action

+C Values

Homogenizing and Integrating Processes

- Equitable and supportive peer relationships
- Stimulated/motivated by connectedness, mutual understanding, and coordination
- Effectively pursue common goals and shared values

Power Processes *And* **Love Processes**

- Loss of equitable and supportive peer relationships
- Increasing isolation of self or parts within the whole
- Unhealthy competition between/among parts (polarization, division, and divisiveness)

- Lack of free expression
- Lack of stimulation / motivation to consider diverse thoughts, actions, and approaches
- Unhealthy obedience to whole (apathy, indifference, and negative "group-think")

- B Fears   **- D Fears**

Weak System / Disempowering

Power without love is reckless and abusive (-B), and love without power is sentimental and anemic (-D). Power at its best (+A) is love implementing the demands of justice, and justice at its best is power correcting everything that stands against love (+C). ~ Dr. Martin Luther King, Jr.

Survive *And* Develop (*Figure 6*)

Step 1) TMBC Seeing: According to Oshry, the fundamental business of all human systems is based in a dual need to Survive *And* Develop.

Step 2) TMBC Mapping: To Survive, organization systems Cope with Dangers (+A). To Develop, systems Prospect for Opportunities (+C). An over-focus on the Survive pole, without consideration for the Develop pole, leads to an Inability to Prospect for Opportunities (-B). This, in turn, will have the organization seek out the benefits of the Develop pole; Prospect for Opportunities (+C). An over-focus on the Develop pole to the neglect of the Survive pole leads to the Inability to Cope with Dangers (-D). When an organization system becomes aware of this inability, it returns to seeking the benefits of the Survive pole (+A). This oscillating interdependency between Survive *And* Develop is then inherently part of the fundamental business of all human systems.

Figure 6: Survive And Develop, Integrating TMBC Perspectives

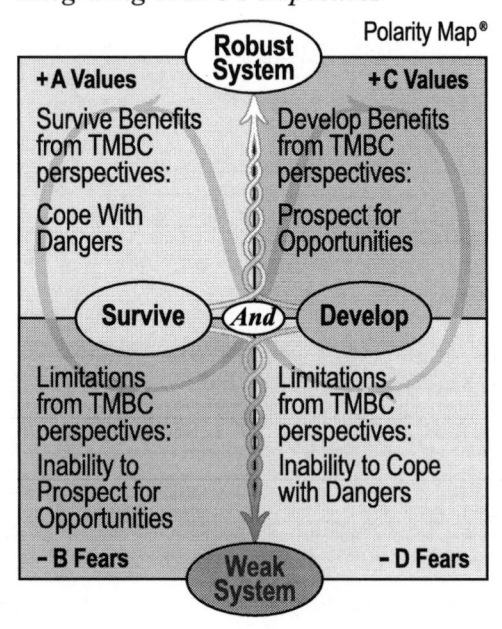

+A Values	Robust System	+C Values
Survive Benefits from TMBC perspectives: Cope With Dangers		Develop Benefits from TMBC perspectives: Prospect for Opportunities
Survive	*And*	Develop
Limitations from TMBC perspectives: Inability to Prospect for Opportunities		Limitations from TMBC perspectives: Inability to Cope with Dangers
- B Fears	Weak System	- D Fears

Polarity Map®

Steps 3 and 4) Assessing and Learning: Though identical to the previous Steps 3 and 4, this is worth repeating. It is important to measure the degree to which individuals and the system are experiencing a maximization of benefits of both poles (+A, +C Values) and minimizing the limitations (-B, -D Fears). This can occur through dialogue or, with more precision, by using the Polarity Assessment. In Learning, we make meaning of assessment results including factors that may be contributing to or mitigating high performance.

Step 5) TMBC Leveraging: Achieving and sustaining a "Robust System/Empowering" (Greater Purpose) and avoiding a "Weak System/Disempowering" (Deeper Fear) involves developing Action Steps and Early Warnings strategies:

- **Action Steps:** What are the Conscious Choice Responses by TMBC Relationship Roles for empowering Survive (to cope) *And* Develop (to prospect), including leveraging strategies for *Developing, Integrating, Fixing,* and *Validating*?

- **Early Warnings:** What will key stakeholders track to help ensure blind/reflexive responses don't lead to disempowering outcomes for Survive *And* Develop?

***Or*-thinking Without *And*-thinking: Getting Hooked and Stuck by Power *Or* Love**

Exploring weak systems and disempowering outcomes through a polarity lens begins by looking at the root source – misapplying the *Or*-thinking competency to polarities that require *And*-thinking. *Figures 7* and *8* show how leaders, teams, and organization systems get hooked and stuck as they over-focus – or "choose between" – *either* Power Process *Or* Love Process. Both figures illustrate Reality 51 from Volume One, "A powerful value/fear diagonal when combined with *Or*-thinking gets us 'hooked' by a false choice between the poles. We become blind to the other value/fear diagonal and over-tolerate the downside of our valued pole. We then get 'stuck' there – unable to access the upside of the pole that is feared."[207]

How Key Stakeholders Get Hooked and Stuck by Power

Figure 7: Hooked and Stuck in Power Processes

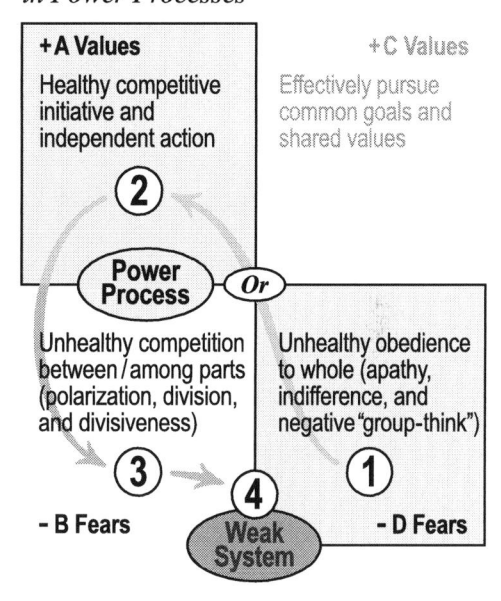

In *Figure 7*, you have an organization that recognizes that there is an "Unhealthy obedience to the whole" (1), and sees employees becoming apathetic, indifferent, and giving into group-think (-D Fears). Overall, there is a sense of disempowerment and a Weak System (4). *Or*-thinking is a seductive setup, as it provides a "solution" that seems obvious; *either* have unhealthy obedience to the whole, *Or* have healthy competition.

Key Stakeholders rally around the Power Process and use incentives and recognition to promote healthy competitive initiatives and independent action (2). This "solution" can become so appealing, it might even be embedded in the "Value Pillars" of the organization or competency models; we Value Independent Action!

Getting Hooked lies here; the actions *did* move the organization from a problem toward their perceived solution. But the *narrative was incomplete*, and the solution became another setup. As the organization focused only on competitive initiatives and independence, unhealthy competition between and among the parts started to show up (-B Fears). The resulting polarization, division, and divisiveness (3) brings them full circle; disempowerment and a Weak System (4).

Now they're stuck. They've embedded Independent Action (2) into the corporate "Value Pillars," and caused an implicit or explicit disdain/fear of Unhealthy obedience to the whole (1), effectively sidelining common goals and shared values (+C Values). Herein lies the paradoxical twist; the organization will not only feel the down sides of Power Process (3) but will *also* start to embody what they

---

[207] Johnson, Barry. *And: Making a Difference by Leveraging Polarity, Paradox or Dilemma. Volume One – Foundations*. HRD Press, 2020.

originally feared from the very beginning – apathy, indifference, and negative "group think" (1) – as employees feel disempowered inside a polarized, divided, and weak system (4). Has this ever been your experience?

How Key Stakeholders Get Hooked and Stuck by Love

A run through *Figure 8* shows the results of another organizational setup; you *either* have unhealthy competition, *Or* you have common goals.

Figure 8: Hooked and Stuck in Love Processes

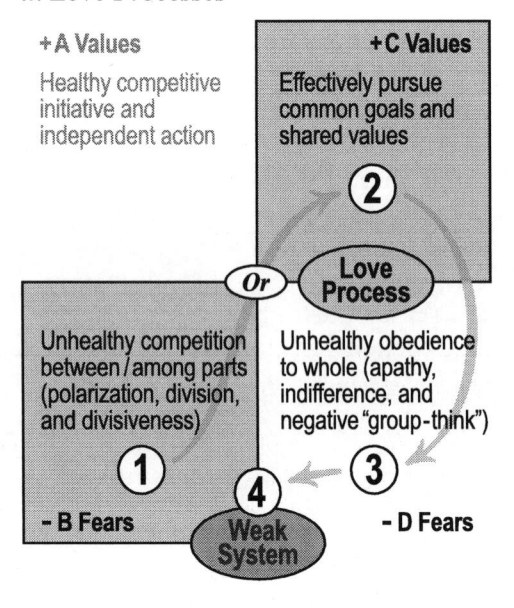

(1) The organization feels there is unhealthy competition between and among the parts. (2) A "charge!" is led toward the pursuit of common goals, and "Shared Values" becomes a corporate slogan reinforced with competency models, incentives, and reward programs. (3) The over-emphasis on having common goals and values lead to an unhealthy obedience to the whole. The lack of seeing the benefits (+A Values) associated with independent action and fear of returning to unhealthy competition (1) keeps Key Stakeholders from moving toward healthy competition and the system becomes disempowered and weak (4). Have you ever seen this happen?

As seen in *Figure 7* and *Figure 8*, when dealing with a polarity, misapplying *Or*-thinking is the root source of becoming stuck in the disempowering fears of the preferred pole. In an ironic twist, you *also* end up with the negative consequences of the unseen or ignored pole so you inhabit the down sides of both. *And*-thinking is antidotal and a necessary process for empowerment.

Summary

This chapter explored the Key Stakeholder engagement intersections in Oshry and Johnson's work that supports systems in leveraging interdependent challenges *And* opportunities. Oshry's examination of disempowering and empowering conditions was viewed through the 5-Step SMALL Process for two inherent polarities. Lastly, Key Stakeholder disempowerment through the misapplication of *Or*-thinking was identified.

A deep bow of gratitude to "Barrys" Oshry and Johnson for supporting this chapter, for the grandness of their hearts / minds, and for each living-out their theories.

About Cliff Kayser ~ www.polaritypartnerships.com/certified-polarity-practitioners

Alleviating the Suffering of Paradox by Mapping Polarities
Brian Emerson, PhD

In 1988, Van DeVen and Poole predicted future significant advances in organizational theory would "require ways to address the paradoxes inherent in human beings and their social organizations."[208] It seems they were right. In the past several decades, there has been an increasing focus on paradox in both leadership and organizations. The discussion about paradox – the need to effectively attend to opposing, yet interrelated, tensions over time – and the research suggesting the benefits of dealing with it effectively have become robust.[209] However, while many talk about the importance of navigating paradox, few are offering pragmatic methods how to do so.

One exception is Barry Johnson's work with Polarity Maps®. The process of mapping provides a practical way for groups to deal with polarities and avoid the negative repercussions so often associated with paradox.[210] Or does it?

While it is relatively easy to find anecdotal evidence from consultants who have used various forms of Polarity Maps over the past two decades, there is little empirical evidence as to how, or if, mapping polarities is effective in helping address competing needs. That lack of evidence sparked the desire for this research. What happens when a group uses a Polarity Map to make sense of paradox? Does using a map make a difference, and if so how? What follows is a short description of the research and the theories it produced.

The Study

Because the desire was to find out "what's really going on" for groups that use Polarity Maps, this study used a Grounded Theory research methodology. Grounded Theory is a good choice for research not trying to prove or predict anything. Instead, the methodology allows one to examine something in depth so that a theory can be created to describe what is happening with the topic being studied.

To conduct this type of study, a researcher interviews people to explore their experience of the phenomenon. Interviews are conducted in a non-leading fashion, so instead of a prescribed list of questions, the interviewer simply digs more deeply into the participant's experience. Interviews are conducted until the researcher begins to hear the same things time and time again and thinks there is enough data to move to analysis. Typically, Grounded Theory researchers interview 12-20 people before final data analysis.

During analysis, information from all of the interviews is sorted, putting common ideas together into groups. These themes are then fit together to explain the experience. This creates a theory that can then be used to understand the phenomenon more deeply.

For this particular study, 25 participants from the United States and Canada were recruited from past clients of Polarity Mastery alumni. The initial interview prompt was, "Tell me about your experience using a Polarity Map." From there, participants described their experience and follow-up questions were asked to dig deeper into their responses. There was not a prescribed set of questions that led participants in any particular direction or that searched for specific data. After talking to 14 people, the data began to repeat itself, so final analysis began using the method describe above. The transcripts of each interview were coded, and these codes were grouped into themes. As the themes began to connect, two different yet related theories emerged, outlined in *Figures 1* and *2* and discussed below.

As part of a Grounded Theory study, after theories are created to describe what is going on, the researcher investigates literature from various fields as a way to explore and explain why it might be going on. The sections below discuss the possible "why" for each stage of the theories of Suffering Paradox and Navigating Paradox.[211]

Suffering Paradox

The first theory that emerged from the research is an explanation of what happens when groups are Suffering Paradox. Not surprisingly, when describing their experience with Polarity Maps, participants often juxtaposed their stories against what happened in groups that did not use Polarity Maps. From the descriptions of the latter, a theory emerged about what happens when groups encounter a paradoxical situation but do not have a productive way to make sense of it.

The process of Suffering Paradox (*Figure 1*) begins when a group experiences a paradoxical situation and moves forward without some sort of sensemaking tool to map the polarity. That is, they approach the polarity as any other problematic situation. In these instances, it seems people in the group can begin Preferencing one pole over the other and then Attaching themselves to it. In order to make themselves right, they begin looking for ways to make the Other pole, and the people who prefer it, wrong. This leads to an *either/Or*-ing mindset that creates a Destructive Tension impacting results, communication, morale, and relationships. Although they are not necessarily linear in nature, the phases are presented sequentially here for ease of discussion.

Preferencing: When encountering paradox, it seems that individuals quickly begin Preferencing one pole over the other. There are several explanations why this might be. First, at least for groups from Western cultures, are the traditions of *either/Or* logic,[212] the belief that the world requires tradeoffs – you "can't have your cake and eat it too,"[213] and the need to maintain an orderly society that has right or wrong alternatives.[214]

Another possible explanation can be found in personal construct theory, which suggests we often make sense of the world by using bipolar constructs such as safe-unsafe, smart-stupid, etc.[215] These quick, and often unconscious, decisions create the platform from which we solve problems and take action.[216] While breaking the world into discrete opposites can be beneficial, it can also lead to bias and entrenchment,[217] which is what happens as individuals begin Attaching.

Figure 1: The Process of Suffering Paradox to Experience Destructive Tension

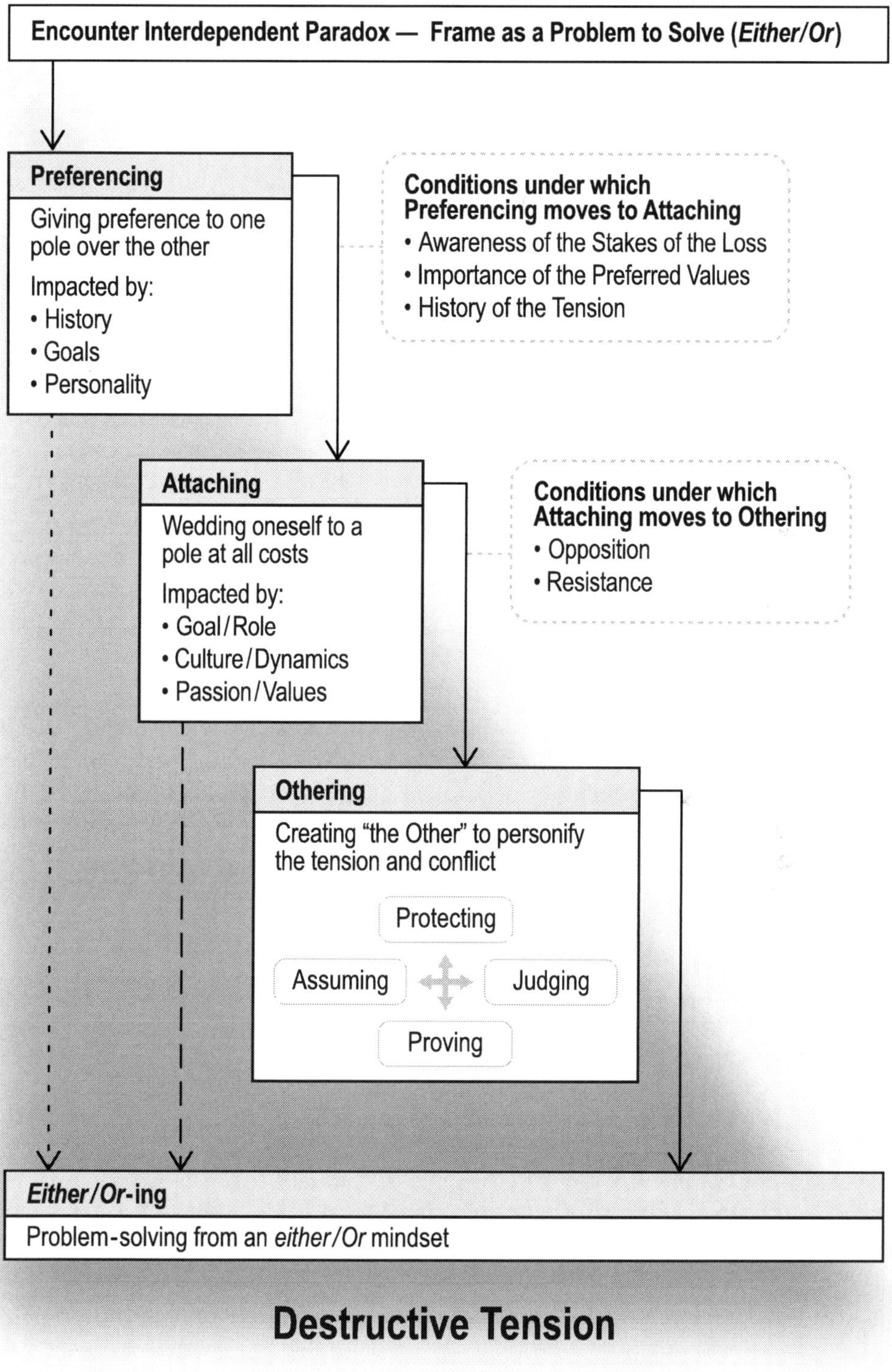

```
┌─────────────────────────────────────────────────────────────────────┐
│ Encounter Interdependent Paradox — Frame as a Problem to Solve (Either/Or) │
└─────────────────────────────────────────────────────────────────────┘
                    │
                    ▼
┌──────────────────────────────┐
│ **Preferencing**             │      Conditions under which
│ Giving preference to one     │      Preferencing moves to Attaching
│ pole over the other          │      • Awareness of the Stakes of the Loss
│ Impacted by:                 │      • Importance of the Preferred Values
│ • History                    │      • History of the Tension
│ • Goals                      │
│ • Personality                │
└──────────────────────────────┘
          │         │
          │         ▼
          │   ┌──────────────────────────────┐
          │   │ **Attaching**                │    Conditions under which
          │   │ Wedding oneself to a         │    Attaching moves to Othering
          │   │ pole at all costs            │    • Opposition
          │   │ Impacted by:                 │    • Resistance
          │   │ • Goal/Role                  │
          │   │ • Culture/Dynamics           │
          │   │ • Passion/Values             │
          │   └──────────────────────────────┘
          │         │         │
          │         │         ▼
          │         │   ┌──────────────────────────────────┐
          │         │   │ **Othering**                     │
          │         │   │ Creating "the Other" to personify│
          │         │   │ the tension and conflict         │
          │         │   │          [Protecting]            │
          │         │   │  [Assuming] ↔ [Judging]          │
          │         │   │           [Proving]              │
          │         │   └──────────────────────────────────┘
          ▼         ▼                    ▼
┌─────────────────────────────────────────────────────────────────────┐
│ *Either/Or-ing*                                                     │
│ Problem-solving from an *either/Or* mindset                         │
└─────────────────────────────────────────────────────────────────────┘
```

Destructive Tension

Attaching: Attaching occurs when individuals begin to associate part of "who they are" with the pole they prefer. This is not surprising given that individuals often define part of themselves based on bipolar values.[210] For example, an individual who values speed over deliberateness might pride themselves on being someone who "gets the job done quickly," thereby Attaching part of their identity to that pole. This finding about how polarities play a part in our identity and ego formation is explored more deeply in the book, Navigating Polarities.[218]

Attaching creates what Ford and Ford[219] refer to as the logic individuals use to determine who they are and who they are not. These logics are typically unconscious until they are brought to light by an event, which, in the case of paradox, happens when people come into contact with individuals attached to the other pole. This leads to Othering.

Othering: A likely explanation for Othering is disidentification – defining who one is by what one is not.[220] For example, part of how one understands being Brazilian is that they are not Japanese. With paradox, when individuals Attach to a pole, part of how they make sense of themselves is because they are not the Other pole. This can create an "us vs. them" mentality that leads to Protecting, Proving, Assuming, and Judging.

When an individual or group's identity or point of view is threatened, they quickly move to defend the values that make up their logic and delegitimize the Other as a way to maintain one's own legitimacy.[220] This seems to hold true when Suffering Paradox, as people begin Protecting the pole they have Attached to and work at Judging and Proving the Other wrong. In these situations, groups seem to focus more on the negation of the Other than on working to find a solution to the problem at hand.

Another key aspect of Othering involves individuals Assuming they fully understand the point of view of those Attached to the opposite pole, which Quinn and Cameron[210] have suggested is a main source of the problems that stem from paradox. These assumptions are used as further ammunition in Proving and Judging, which virtually guarantees the Other will be vilified.[214] This us-against-them mentality serves to entrench groups in their positions[221] and leads the group to approach problem solving through *Either/Or*-ing.

***Either/Or*-ing:** The *Either/Or*-ing mindset is based in hierarchical logic, which assumes one pole is good and the other pole is bad,[208] one is right and the other is wrong. It can begin at any point when Suffering Paradox, and does not require Preferencing, Attaching, or Othering. Instead of an integrative solution, individuals who are *Either/Or*-ing see the paradox as a win-lose situation in which the most powerful group will prevail. The adverse emotions inherent in such a competition, especially if they are compounded by Preferencing, Attaching, and Othering, lead to a negativity experienced as the Destructive Tension associated with Suffering Paradox.

Destructive Tension: It appears that when a group is Suffering Paradox, the inherent tension in the polarity turns Destructive. It is easy to find examples in the literature that support this notion.[222,210] It seems Destructive Tension can be experienced at any point during the process of Suffering Paradox, and impacts at least four different areas: Results, Moral, Communication, and Relationships. This is supported by other studies that suggest ineffectively dealing with paradox can lead to a decline in performance,[210] impaired decision-making quality,[223] and the overall state of being stuck.[224] In short, when Suffering Paradox, not only does the issue at hand not get resolved, negative repercussions ripple through the group that go well beyond the "problem" being solved and impact other areas of effectiveness.

Based on the description of Suffering Paradox, it would be easy to assume that the dimensions of Destructive Tension are synonymous with paradox. However, little could be further from the truth. In fact (and paradoxically), when groups use a sensemaking tool such as Polarity Maps to address paradox, what arises is not a Destructive Tension, but a condition that appears to be its exact opposite – Creative Tension, a byproduct of Navigating Paradox.

Navigating Paradox

The theory of Navigating Paradox explains what happens when a group maps the polarity to make sense of organizational paradox. Johnson's[214] simple and complex sensemaking tool helps people navigate paradox through the process of Seeing It, Discussing It, and Embodying It (*Figure 2* on the following page: move bottom to top). This gives way to Divining and Synthesizing which creates a *Both/And*-ing approach and allows a Creative Tension to manifest in the system.

Polarity Maps and Sensemaking: This study supports the notion that the Polarity Map is a tool that helps groups make sense of, and reframe, paradox – which, according to multiple scholars, is key to effectively dealing with the phenomenon.[209,224] Though it sounds simple, reframing paradox is a tall task given that it relies on an individual's or group's cognitive capacity to hold multiple, complex, and oppositional pieces of information in the brain at one time.[225] According to Kegan,[226] this is a difficult, if not nearly impossible, endeavor for most adults to do on their own without a sensemaking tool.

According to Stigliani and Ravasi,[227] when dealing with particularly complex circumstances, effective individuals and groups often rely on sensemaking tools; things such as visual maps, to make sense and take action. Having a way to capture and discuss a process that is difficult to observe is crucial to acting in the midst of complexity.[228] This is consistent with the experience of people who used Polarity Maps to Navigate Paradox. What follows is a description of how the literature supports what is going on for people during each stage of the process.

Mapping: The process of Mapping allows groups to See, Discuss, and Embody paradox. It appears that Seeing It is vital to dealing with the complexity as it allows the group to make what was subject into object so they can "have it" rather than "be had" by it.[226] This helps reduce some of the potential emotionally charged dynamic as groups enter into Discussing It and allows for a more robust reframing process, which depends on the extent to which the different perspectives feel heard and accepted by others.[225]

Figure 2: The Process of Navigating Paradox to Experience Creative Tension

Creative Tension

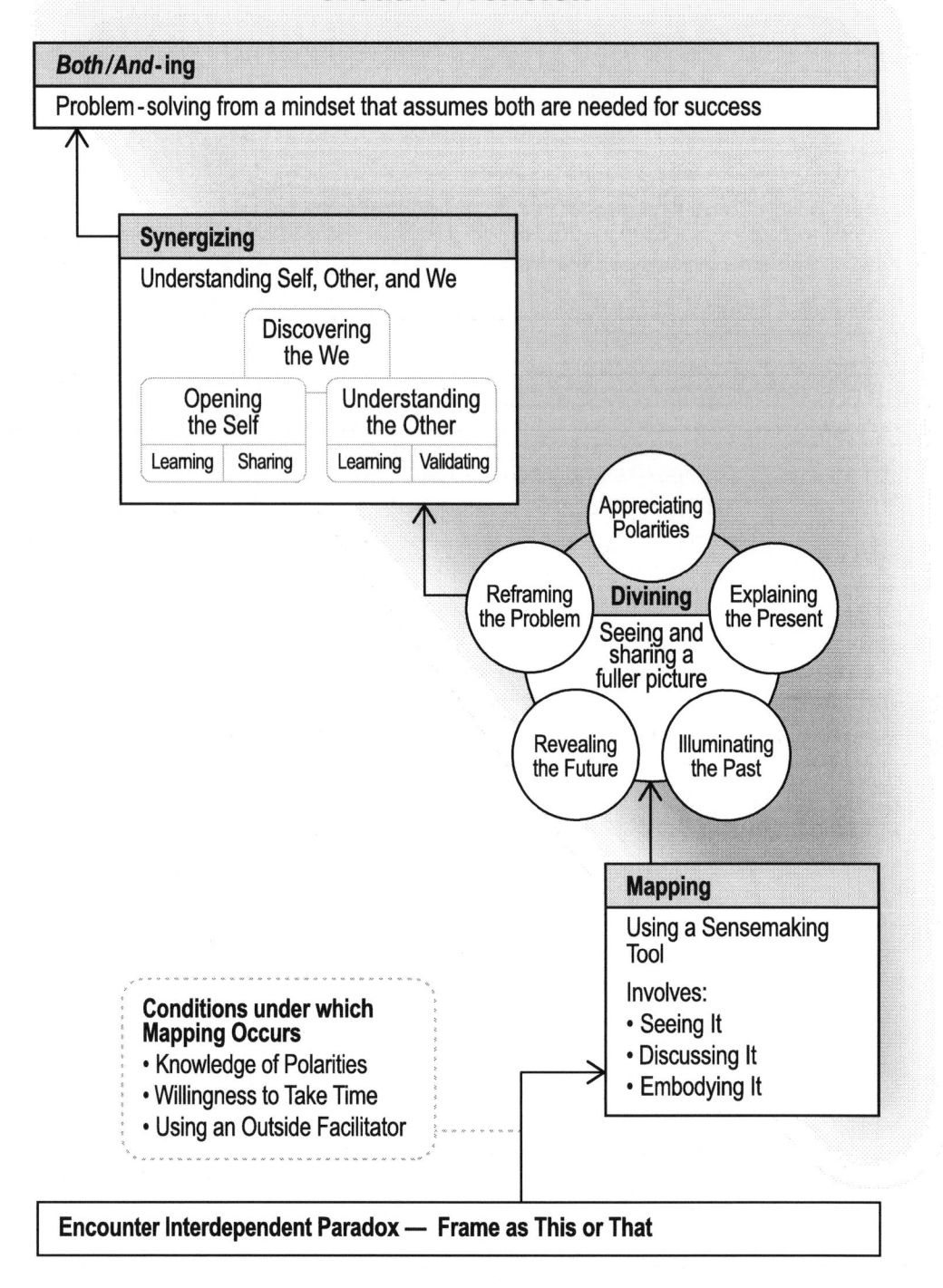

Both/And-ing
Problem-solving from a mindset that assumes both are needed for success

Synergizing
Understanding Self, Other, and We
- Discovering the We
- Opening the Self — Learning | Sharing
- Understanding the Other — Learning | Validating

Divining
Seeing and sharing a fuller picture
- Appreciating Polarities
- Explaining the Present
- Illuminating the Past
- Revealing the Future
- Reframing the Problem

Mapping
Using a Sensemaking Tool

Involves:
- Seeing It
- Discussing It
- Embodying It

Conditions under which Mapping Occurs
- Knowledge of Polarities
- Willingness to Take Time
- Using an Outside Facilitator

Encounter Interdependent Paradox — Frame as This or That

The majority of participants in the study mentioned the importance of "moving around the room" as they were mapping. This supports Stigliani and Ravasi's[227] notion that the ability to physically move and interact with parts of a sensemaking tool creates deeper understanding among group members. Likewise, it is easier to understand and consider multiple unique perspectives when one can move to different points on the map.[228] Combined with Seeing It and Discussing It, Embodying It creates the platform for individuals to enter two of the most powerful stages of Navigating Paradox — Divining and Synthesizing.

Divining: During Divining, a group experiences one or more stages that help them see and share a fuller picture of the issue at hand. This is consistent with the work of Lewis and Dehler,[229] who suggest Polarity Maps afford people a more robust view of their situation. In this case, that involves Appreciating Polarities, Explaining the Present, Illuminating the Past, Revealing the Future, and Reframing the Problem.

Appreciating Polarities: The findings of this study are different than Bartunek's[225] report that the process of reframing paradox can leave people paralyzed, defensive, and damaged. This study's data suggest that those affective aspects are more consistent with groups Suffering Paradox and almost completely opposite of those Navigating Paradox. This is likely due to the dimension of Appreciating Polarities.

Polarity Maps allow groups to see paradox in a positive light, which is likely due to W. K. Smith et al.'s[230] suggestion that accepting paradox is aided by having a way to differentiate the "unique contribution of each alternative" and then integrating "both alternatives and seeking synergies between them."[230] Mapping creates a situation in which the perspective of those who hold each of the poles is valued, it is made obvious both poles are needed for success, and it is clear that each pole has downsides – all of which help individuals accept and Appreciate Polarities.

Explaining the Present, Illuminating the Past, Revealing the Future: Because of the cyclical and ongoing nature of paradox,[214] groups can use the map to understand what is happening for them in the present moment, trace backwards the events of the past, and look into the future of the moving energy loop in order to create a more robust and unequivocal view of their reality. The ability for members of a group to take action based on the discovery of a shared understanding of their situation is a key component of any sensemaking process,[231] and in this case is likely a key contributor to the Creative Tension that is part of Navigating Paradox.

Reframing the Problem: The concept of Reframing the Problem is an important element of Divining, for it appears to ease a significant degree of harmful tension and stress in the group. The realization that the situation is not actually a problem to solve, but an ongoing and unsolvable paradox to manage, likely helps avoid the condition alluded to by Weick who says, "Those who get demobilized, defensive, and angry in organizations are those who see the world as a place filled with problems that could be solved once and for all."[232] While not specifically talking about paradox, Weick's point applies here. Reframing the polarities for what they are – never-ending energy systems to manage, and not solvable problems – leads to less stress and frustration and makes Synergizing and Creative Tension possible.

Synergizing: Finding the synergy between two poles of a paradox is key to developing a paradox frame.[230] The power of paradox lies not in compromise between the two poles, but in the ability to synthesize both of the opposites in their full strength.[233] The concept of Synergizing supports these thoughts and takes them one step further.

When Navigating Paradox, Synergizing means not just bringing together the poles but also, and perhaps more importantly, bringing together the individuals who have been Attaching to them. Several dimensions play into this process. The first seems to be an Opening of Self, which is the increased self-awareness that happens when people are introduced to new frames from which to view themselves and their preferences.[219] The second, Understanding the Other, occurs as people listen and understand why others hold different viewpoints. According to Proctor,[215] this is a way to create higher levels of intergroup connection, which is consistent with the experience of participants in this study.

The final component of Synergizing, Discovering the We, is perhaps the most critical. Smith and Berg suggest that groups will stay stuck in paradox until they stop the process of disidentification: "By defining 'others' as the opposite of 'self,' individuals and groups ... constrain their ability to move in the service of reducing anxiety."[221] It seems that Polarity Maps help individuals Discover the We by illuminating that both points of view are not opposites but actually interrelated, which can spur the group to *Both/And*-ing.

***Both/And*-ing:** *Both/And*-ing refers to taking action that combines or synergizes the two poles, which is one way to effectively deal with paradox.[209] This synergized action is similar to Emerson and Lewis' Transformational Third Way, which is a space that integrates both poles and denies neither,[218] and Rothenberg's[234] concept of Janusian thinking, which involves holding and acting with two oppositional concepts in mind at once. It appears that Polarity Maps might achieve this by helping groups take "a leap that transcends ordinary logic"[234] through *Both/And*-ing, which contributes to a Creative Tension.

Creative Tension: The dimensions of Creative Tension can be experienced at any point during the Navigating Paradox process. The group's experience of collaborative mindset, positive energy, connection to others, and dynamic synergy can be likened to Csikszentmihalyi's flow state[235] and appears to be virtually opposite of the Destructive Tension experienced when Suffering Paradox. Not surprisingly, the four areas negatively impacted by the Destructive Tension—Results, Morale, Communication, and Relationships, are positively impacted by the Creative Tension of Navigating Paradox.

The notion that Results are positively impacted when Navigating Paradox is consistent with the wide range of documentation in the literature.[209, 210, 213] The explanation for positive impacts on Morale could lie in the linkage between Smith and Berg's[221] proposal that the perceived oscillation between two poles of a paradox produces hope, which Lindsley et al.[223] suggest impacts morale and increased performance. It is not ironic that this state is exactly opposite the inflexibility and lack of creativity experienced in organizations[220] mired in the Destructive Tension of Suffering Paradox.

The rationale for positive impacts on Communication and Relationships is multifold. Highlighted here is the possibility that by using Polarity Maps to make the situation object,[226] groups are able to shift from what Amason[236] calls affective conflict to cognitive conflict. Because individuals are then making sense of the paradoxical tension from a different frame, they are able to listen better to the Other's meanings and rationales, which can increase the level of interpersonal and intergroup understanding and connection.[215]

Conclusion

This study set out to discover "what's going on" when groups map polarities and what difference does using a sensemaking tool make? The theories of Suffering Paradox and Navigating Paradox shed light on both questions and provide empirical evidence that mapping polarities is an effective and practical way to help groups deal with paradox.

This study did not examine the effectiveness of the actions created by using a Polarity Map, which is a possibility for future study. However, this does not diminish the power of the Polarity Map, for in the end, the most important byproduct of Navigating Paradox might not be the actual actions taken to manage the polarity. Instead, the power might be in how the map helps groups think about polarities and "dancing with the opposites."[237] As Luscher et al.[238] contend, we cannot get rid of paradox, we can only live it and appreciate how paradoxical tension "creates circles of reflection ... and sparks circles of even greater complexity" that can propel us into a shared and creative future. Knowing how to Navigate Paradox to harness that complexity is a great step in that direction.

> Find bio and contact info for author Brian Emerson at
> www.polaritypartnerships.com/certified-polarity-practitioners

References

[208] Van de Ven, A. H., & Poole, M. S. "Paradoxical Requirements for a Theory of Change." In R. E. Quinn & K. S. Cameron (Eds.), *Paradox and Transformation: Toward a Theory of Change in Organization and Management* (pp. 19-64). Ballinger, 1988.

[209] Smith, W. K., & Lewis, M. W. "Toward a Theory of Paradox: A Dynamic Equilibrium Model of Organizing." Academy of Management Review, 36(2), 381-403, 2011.

[210] Quinn, R. E., & Cameron, K. S. "Pardox and Transformation: A Dynamic Theory of Organization and Management." In R. E. Quinn & K. S. Cameron (Eds.), *Paradox and transformation: Toward a theory of change in organization and management* (pp. 289-308). Ballinger, 1988.

[211] Emerson, B. "Navigating Organizational Paradox With Polarity Mapping: A Classic Grounded Theory Study." 2013. Retrieved from https://search.proquest.com/docview/1357148735. For a more detailed description of Grounded Theory, this study's methodology, or the two theories it produced, please reach out to the author directly at brian@andiron.com or www.polaritypartnerships.com/certified-polarity-practitioners.

[212] Hampden-Turner, C. *Maps of the Mind: Charts and Concepts of the Mind and Its Labyrinths*. Macmillian, 1981.
[213] Eisenhardt, K. M., & Westcott, B. J. "Paradoxical Demands and the Creation of Excellence: The Case of Just-in-Time Manufacturing." In R. E. Quinn & K. S. Cameron (Eds.), *Paradox and Transformation: Toward a Theory of Change in Organization and Management*. Ballinger, 1988, pp. 169-194.
[214] Johnson, B. *Polarity Management: Identifying and Managing Unsolvable Problems*. HRD Press. 1992.
[215] Procter, H. "The Construct." In R. Butler (Ed.), *Reflections in Personal Construct Theory*. Wiley, 2009, pp. 49-68.
[216] Horley, J. "Personal Construct Theory and Human Values." Journal of Human Values, 18(2), 161-171. 2012.
[217] Lewis, M. W. "Exploring Paradox: Toward a More Comprehensive Guide." The Academy of Management Review, 25(4), 760-776. 2000.
[218] Emerson, B., & Lewis, K. *Navigating Polarities: Using Both/and Thinking To Lead Transformation*. Paradoxical Press, 2019.
[219] Ford, J. D., & Ford, L. W. "Logics of Identity, Contradiction, and Attraction in Change." The Academy of Management Review, 19(4), 756-756. 1994.
[220] Fiol, C. M., Pratt, Michael G., & O'Connor, E. J. "Managing Intractable Identity Conflicts." The Academy of Management Review, 34(1), 32-55. 2009.
[221] Smith, K. K., & Berg, D. N. *Paradoxes of Group Life: Understanding Conflict, Paralysis, and Movement in Group Dynamics* (1st ed.). Jossey Bass, 1987.
[222] Tracy, S. J. "Dialectic, Contradiction, or Double Bind? Analyzing and Theorizing Employee Reactions To Organizational Tension." Journal of Applied Communication Research, 32(2), 119-146. 2004.
[223] Lindsley, D. H., Brass, D. J., & Thomas, J. B. "Efficacy-Performance Spirals: A Multilevel Perspective." The Academy of Management Review, 20(3), 645. 1995.
[224] Smith, W. K., & Tushman, M. "Managing Strategic Contradictions: A Top Management Model for Managing Innovation Streams." Organization Science, 16(5), 522-536. 2005.
[225] Bartunek, J. M. "The Dynamics of Personal and Organizational Reframing." In R. E. Quinn & K. S. Cameron (Eds.), *Paradox and Transformation: Toward a Theory of Change in Organization and Management* (pp. 1137-1162). Ballinger, 1988.
[226] Kegan, Robert. *In Over Our Heads: The Mental Demands of Modern Life*. Harvard University Press, 1994.
[227] Stigliani, I., & Ravasi, D. "Organizing Thoughts and Connecting Brains: Material Practices and the Transition From Individual to Group-Level Prospective Sensemaking." Academy of Management Journal, 55(5), 1232-1259. 2012.
[228] Huff, A. S., & Jenkins, M. "Introduction." In A. S. Huff & M. Jenkins (Eds.), *Mapping Strategic Knowledge* (pp. 17-32). SAGE Publications, 2002.
[229] Lewis, M. W., & Dehler, G. E. "Learning Through Paradox: A Pedagogical Strategy for Exploring Contradictions and Complexity." Journal of Management Education, 24(6), 708-725. 2000.
[230] Smith, W. K., Besharov, M. L., Wessels, A. K., & Chertok, M. "A Paradoxical Leadership Model for Social Entrepreneurs:..." Academy of Management Learning & Education, 11(3), 463-478. 2012.
[231] Weick, K. E., Sutcliffe, K., M., & Obstfeld, D. "Organizing and the Process of Sensemaking." Organization Science, 16(4), 409-421. 2005.
[232] Weick, K. E., *Sensemaking In Organizations*. Sage, 1995.
[233] Clegg, S. R., Cunha, J. Vieira da, & Cunha, M. Pina e. "Management Paradoxes: A Relational View." Human Relations, 55(5), 483-503. 2002.
[234] Rothenberg, A. *The Emerging Goddess*. Univ of Chicago Press, 1979.
[235] Csikszentmihalyi, M. *Beyond Boredom and Anxiety*. Jossey-Bass, 1976.
[236] Amason, A. C. "Distinguishing the Effects of Functional and Dysfunctional Conflict on Strategic Decision Making: Resolving a Paradox for Top Management Teams." Academy of Management Journal, 39(1), 123. 1996.
[237] Holt, K., & Seki, K. "Global Leadership: A Developmental Shift for Everyone." Industrial and Organizational Psychology, 5(2), 196-215. 2012.
[238] Luscher, L. S., Lewis, M., & Ingram, A. "The Social Construction of Organizational Change Paradoxes." Journal of Organizational Change Management, 19(4), 491-502. 2006.

Polarity-Based Inquiry

Cliff Kayser, MSHR, MSOD, PCC

The art of progress is to preserve order amid change and to preserve change amid order. ~ Alfred North Whitehead[239]

The first responsibility of a leader is to define reality. The last is to say thank you. In between the two, the leader must become a servant and a debtor. That sums up the progress of an artful leader. ~ Max DePree[240]

You know the adage "People resist change." It is not really true. People are not stupid. People love change when they know it is a good thing. No one gives back a winning lottery ticket. What people resist is not change per se, but loss. When change involves real or potential loss, people hold on to what they have and resist the change. ~ Ronald A. Heifetz[241]

The quotes above capture the essence of Arnold Beisser's Paradoxical Theory of Change[242] which Barry Johnson discussed in <u>And:</u> Volume One – Foundations, Chapter 13.[243] This chapter is a Paradoxical Theory of Change "how-to" for the art of progress and artful leadership that relies on using people's "resistance" as wisdom for defining reality in order *And* change. We explore how the impact of thinking competencies in order *And* change makes the difference between dueling gap polarization and leveraging dual gaps. Variations of this approach appear in <u>Volume One</u>, Chapters 16 and 17, while unique support for this chapter is provided by Chapters 29, 30, 37, and 38.[244] Following are details and discussion of the case application.

Case Description

The Office of Personnel Management (OPM) measures employees' perceptions of whether – and to what extent – conditions characteristic of successful organizations are present in their agencies by administering the Federal Employee Viewpoint Survey (FEVS). A department ("Department") focused on biotechnology in global health and safety for one of the nation's oldest and largest agencies requested Polarity Thinking™ principles, tools, and consulting/coaching support in an effort to improve the Department's low FEVS scores. In the 2014 project-launch meeting

---

[239] Whitehead, A. N. From the series "Great Ideas of Western Man." Smithsonian American Art Museum, 1964.
[240] DePree, Max. *Leadership is an Art.* Michigan State University Press, 1987.
[241] Heifetz, R. A., Linsky, M., and Grashow, A. *The Practice of Adaptive Leadership: Tools and Tactics for Changing Your Organization and the World.* Harvard Business Press, 2009.
[242] Beisser, A. "The Paradoxical Theory of Change." In Fagan, J. and Shepherd, I.L., (Eds.) *Gestalt Therapy Now.* Harper & Row, 1970.
[243] Johnson, Barry. *And: Making a Difference by Leveraging Polarity, Paradox or Dilemma. Volume One – Foundations.* HRD Press, 2020.
[244] Ibid.

with his senior team, the leader ("Leader") shared a number of complex issues he believed were responsible for the Department's low FEVS scores. We had no idea how those challenges would be compounded, or how the success of Polarity Thinking in this Department would initiate its use throughout the organization.

Outcomes: Short and Long Term Success

Between 2015-2018, the Leader and his Department faced a change of agency leadership, a new administration post-presidential election, and an escalation of global disruptions in the industry the agency serves. Despite multiplying and escalating challenges, FEVS scores in the Leader's Department improved as scores in other agency Departments declined. In 2018, to expand the use of Polarity Thinking principles, the Department's Center for Training and Organization Development (CTOD) received training and access to a suite of online resource tools available through Polarity Partnerships. Today, CTOD's Training curriculum offers a basics course in Polarity Thinking, and mapping polarities is part of skill and competency development in training for courses in communication, change, and conflict. CTOD's internal OD consulting work is enhanced by its ability to use the Polarity Assessment™ (another tool in the suite of online resources) to create custom polarity-based performance assessments for individuals, teams, and the organization.

Overview of a Polarity-Based Inquiry

The mantra is: *Start slow with SMALL to go big and go fast.*

- Seeing: Start slow by answering "where" are we going, "why" are we going there, and "who" needs to be part of the process for getting there.
- Mapping: Answers "how" the process will happen and "what" questions will be addressed.
- Assessing: Answers "where" are we now in the dual gaps of order *And* change.
- Learning: Answers "what" questions are emerging.
- Leveraging: Go big and go fast by answering "what now" for dual-gap strategies.

Step 1: Seeing

Where and Why

The top of the Polarity Map® provides a place for the Greater Purpose Statement "GPS" to function as a "Global Positioning System." The GPS "pins" the end point for the effort to determine "where we're going" and "why we're going there." Going slow to get these questions answered early and clearly has great payoff both in the short and long-term.

When the Leader answered the GPS questions, a concern quickly arose. Internally focused FEVS scores were low, while external performance indicators relating to the Department's mission of protecting the health and safety of the American people were quite high. The Leader wanted to ensure that focus on internal performance didn't compromise the external performance successes. Therefore, both internal and external performance dimensions were included in the GPS to:

> *Gain and sustain improvement in FEVS scores, while continuing to deliver on the Department's vision and mission.*

Who

Who needs to be on-board for this challenge and/or opportunity if we are to be fully successful now, and over time?

Involving key stakeholders reduces risk of a future breakdown the same way preventative maintenance on a vehicle does before taking a long or important trip. The engine for progress in order *And* change is people. Failing to engage the people who will be impacted likely contributes to the reason there is a 70% breakdown rate of organizational change efforts.[245] When a malfunctioning GPS is part of the story, drama and frustration becomes another dimension in the failure.

Because of its size, a small cross-section of the Department was recruited and selected to act as a "design team" to represent key stakeholders across the system. They named it the "Polarity Design Team" (PDT). Diversity on design teams is crucial, and the Department sought to recruit between 8-12 people who had: 1) strong opinions, 2) broad knowledge of external client needs, and 3) internal organization perspectives from the top, mid-level, and front-line staff.

Fast-forward to the end of 2019. The Leader was a guest presenter sharing the case study of his Department's success at a 3-day network leadership course at American University with over fifty of his fellow agency leaders from around the world in attendance. In his response to a question about the recruitment and selection of PDT members, the Leader shared a few unexpected "byproducts" of that process. First, the recruiting proved to be quite effective as a way to "market" and communicate the initiative. Second, the Leader had either not been aware or was reminded of several existing initiatives with similar goals. For example, an Employee Engagement Committee had been established a year prior, but was poorly resourced yet rich in member dedication and passion. By selecting individuals from those initiatives to serve on the PDT aligned the Department's limited internal resources.

Step 2: Mapping
How

How will key stakeholders (or a design team) answer key questions?

Figure 1 on the following page shows the Polarity Map for the Continuity (order) *And* Transformation (change) Polarity-based Inquiry that also integrates Past/Present *And* Present/Future.

What

Realities, defined by key stakeholders or design team, are based on four "what" questions that are focused on particular quadrants of the polarity. Each question is also considered from different stakeholder perspectives: Leader, Team, Organization, Customer, Broader Community, etc. This list can be modified based on the context and input from key stakeholders or design team.

---

[245] Nohria, N. and Beer, M. "Cracking the Code of Change." Harvard Business Review, May-June 2000, p. 133. hbr.org/2000/05/cracking-the-code-of-change. Accessed February 26, 2020.

The Four "What" Questions of Polarity-Based Inquiry

Starting in the lower-left quadrant of *Figure 1*:

- "What problems are there?" Move *from* **Pain**: (-B)
- "What are the solutions to the problems?" Move *to* **Attain**: (+C)
- "What are the risks in the solutions?" Move *from* **Refrain**: (-D)
- "What must we not lose in the process?" Move *to* **Retain**: (+A)

These four questions align closely with two inquiry-based approaches: "S.W.O.T. Analysis" and Kegan and Lahey's Immunity to Change.[246] Following is a summary of the four questions each asks in their inquiry process and the connection to the Polarity-based Inquiry questions. All of these are incorporated into the Polarity-based Inquiry template (*Figure 1*).

Figure 1

	Sustainable	
+A Stakeholders* **Retain** the benefits of a valued **Strength** or **Current Commitment**		**+C** Stakeholders* **Attain** the benefits of an **Opportunity** or **Improvement Goal**
Continuity Past/Present	*And*	Transformation Present/Future
Stakeholders* stop the **Pain** from limiting **Weaknesses** or what's **Being Done/Not Being Done**		Stakeholders* **Refrain** from **Threats** or limiting **Big Assumptions/Beliefs**
-B	Unsustainable	**-D**

* Stakeholders are Leaders, Teams, Organizations, Customers, or Broader Communities

SWOT/Polarity-Based Inquiry Comparison

SWOT is a popular inquiry method used by leaders, teams, and organizations to conduct strategic planning and adapt to change. Starting in the upper left quadrant of *Figure 1*:

- What are the **Strengths** to **Retain**: (+A)
- What are the **Weaknesses** or the **Pain** to move from: (-B)
- What are the **Opportunities** to **Attain**: (+C)
- What are the **Threats** to **Refrain** from: (-D)

Immunity to Change/Polarity-Based Inquiry Comparison

Immunity to Change transforms people's way of talking to help them avoid the causes of failed change. Starting in the upper right quadrant of *Figure 1*:

- What is the Commitment to an **Improvement Goal** to **Attain**: (+C)
- What is **Being Done/Not Being Done** Instead causing **Pain**: (-B)
- What is/are the Hidden/Competing **Commitments** to **Retain**: (+A)
- What are the **Big Assumptions/Beliefs** to **Refrain** from: (-D)

---

[246] Kegan, R., and Lahey, L. L. *Immunity to Change: How to Overcome It and Unlock Potential in Yourself and Your Organization.* Harvard Business Press, 2009.

Tips for the Step 2 Mapping Process

There are no "hard-and-fast" rules for the order of quadrants key stakeholders or a design team addresses first, second, third, or fourth.

If, in a particular organization system's context the negative emotion level is high, trust level is low, or there is a combination of the two, it is helpful to start with the two upside quadrants, (+C) Attain and (+A) Retain, and then move to the two lower quadrants, (-B) Pain and (-D) Refrain. In addition, it may be advisable to engage support from an experienced external or internal facilitator who has a background and/or training certification in PACT™ (Polarity Approach for Continuity and Transformation).

Be creative about how to populate each of the quadrants. Use your entire room to physically move to locations as each quadrant is populated. Leverage the polarity of Fun *And* Serious.

Dual Gaps in Step 2

Gap-analysis is a common term in change management and typically refers to the gap between where you are and where you want to go, or the perception of a gap between negative and positive performance. *Figures 2* and *3* identify the dual gaps in Continuity *And* Transformation revealed in the Polarity-based Inquiry.

Figure 2: Present/Future – Transformation Gap

The Gap presents when you move *from* (-B: **Pain** from limiting Weakness or what's Being Done/Not Being Done) *to* (+C: **Attain** the benefits of an Opportunity or Improvement Goal).

Figure 3: Past/Present – Continuity Gap

The Gap presents when you move *from* (-D: **Refrain** from Threats or limiting Big Assumptions/Beliefs) *to* (+A: **Retain** Strength or Current Commitment).

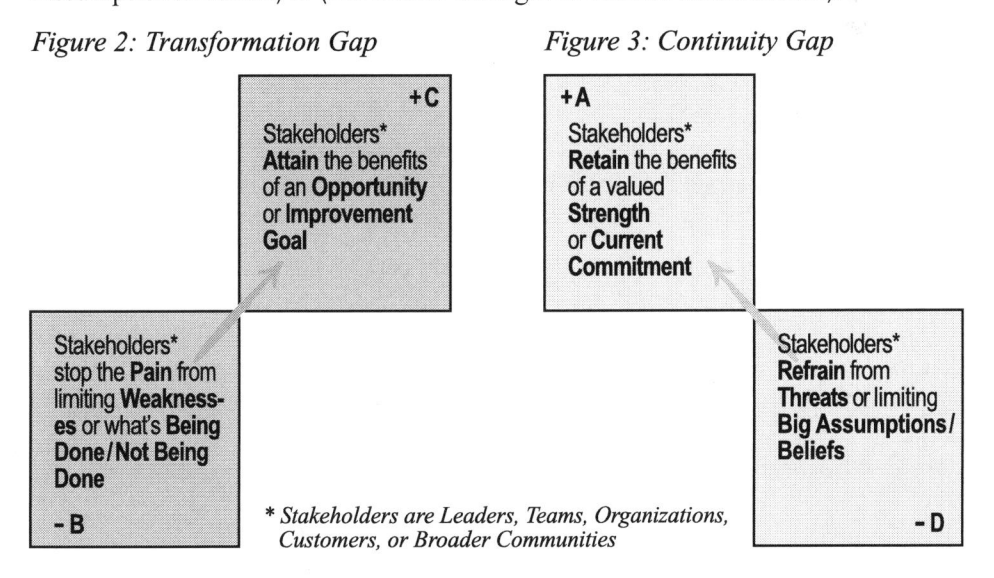

Figure 2: Transformation Gap

+C
Stakeholders*
Attain the benefits of an **Opportunity** or **Improvement Goal**

Stakeholders* stop the **Pain** from limiting **Weaknesses** or what's **Being Done/Not Being Done**
-B

Figure 3: Continuity Gap

+A
Stakeholders*
Retain the benefits of a valued **Strength** or **Current Commitment**

Stakeholders*
Refrain from **Threats** or limiting **Big Assumptions/Beliefs**
-D

* Stakeholders are Leaders, Teams, Organizations, Customers, or Broader Communities

Dueling Gap Polarization – Misapplying *Or*-thinking

There is wisdom in both diagonals. Each gap focuses on an important dimension of the Continuity (order) *And* Transformation (change) polarity and each is technically correct, but incomplete. It is not unusual for people to hold a preference, a strong preference, or even view one or the other of the gaps as clearly superior. When *Or*-thinking is misapplied to preferences in an effort to alleviate or "solve" the tension between the gaps, dueling gap polarization results. This polarization undermines the ability to utilize the wisdom in both gaps. Often, the dysfunction escalates over time or flips back and forth between the gap "solutions." In either case, the dysfunction escalation or negative pendulum swings is unsustainable.

Leveraging Dual Gaps – Applying *And*-thinking

The Step 2 mapping process increases awareness of the interdependent dynamic inherent to the four quadrants and dual gaps. This awareness creates an increased willingness and desire to apply *And*-thinking as the best and most creative approach to fully leverage people's wisdom in the dynamic. This awareness of the interdependence is a significant supplement and enhancement to S.W.O.T. analysis and Immunity to Change. The Polarity-based Inquiry defines reality for people's wisdom by:

- Differentiating the dual gaps in the four-question inquiry in the context of the interdependency;
- Integrating the dimensions of the four-question inquiry in the context of the interdependency;
- Highlighting the role *And*-thinking plays in leveraging dual gaps; and,
- Highlighting the role *Or*-thinking plays in dueling gap polarization.

Steps 3 and 4: Assessing and Learning
Where Are We

Building capability to use people's "resistance" as a resource to define reality supports a solid foundation of trust for open and honest dialogue that has the capability to hold missing or avoided conversations. The quality and safety these types of spaces provided make possible the vulnerability and courage it takes to ask bolder questions and explore answers more confidently. Conversation that was previously transactional or positional becomes more engaging and creative.

During the guest presentation in 2019 discussed earlier, the Leader described this phase of the process as, "building the bridge as they walked on it." Under the umbrella polarity of order *And* change, the PDT identified additional polarities they believed required focus and attention to sustainably achieve the GPS. They were: Tactical *And* Strategic; Timeliness/Efficiency *And* Quality Service Delivery; Employee Empowerment *And* Employee Compliance; and, Employee Interests *And* Organizational Interests.

Step 5: Leveraging
What Now

Leveraging a polarity involves developing dual strategy execution plans to maximize benefits for both poles and minimize limitations that result from over-focus on one pole to the neglect of the other. Together, the Action Steps and Early Warning Signs create conditions for the system to "go big and go fast" to achieve the GPS sustainably.

Action Steps: *Who will do what, by when, to maximize upside benefits for each pole of the polarity?*

Early Warnings: *What are the unique and measurable indicators for both poles of the polarity that indicate – early – you're getting into the downsides?*

There are two additional categories of Action Steps:

High-Leverage Action Steps: *Are there Action Steps that could serve to benefit the upside of both poles of a polarity?*

An example of a High-Leverage Action Step the PDT identified was the decision to conduct a custom Polarity Assessment for the additional polarities identified in Steps 3 and 4. This single action benefitted each of the poles of the polarity (Continuity – Past/Present *And* Transformation – Present/Future). The additional data gathered established an aggregate performance benchmark and supported informed choices for the Department's actions. Additionally, individual Programs received their own reports as benchmarks. A total of 70 Action Steps emerged from this High-Leverage Action Step.

Super High-Leverage Action Steps: *Is there an Action Step that supports the upside benefits of both poles of multiple polarities?*

The PDT examined the 70 Action Steps identified to determine if there were any Super-high leverage Action Steps among them. Three fit the criterion. A fourth Super-high leverage Action Step was identified to take full advantage of the other three, and was used in performance plans for all front-line managers and senior leaders in the Department to ensure implementation.

In the guest presentation at American University described earlier, the Leader said of these Super high-leverage Action Steps:

> *I'm pretty convinced they played a critical role improving the low FEVS scores related to employee engagement. However, I'm also convinced that if in 2014 we would have said to our front-line managers and senior leaders, 'Do these three things that are now in your new performance plan' – I honestly don't think it would have worked... The process was ultimately as important or perhaps even more so, than the actions themselves.*

Conclusion

This chapter shared an artful leadership "how-to" process to define reality, capture "resistance" wisdom, and artfully progress order *And* change. *And*-thinking for leveraging dual gaps was recognized as a key to avoid dueling gap polarization caused by misapplying *Or*-thinking.

> Find bio and contact info for author Cliff Kayser at
> www.polaritypartnerships.com/certified-polarity-practitioners

*Shifting from Drama to Empowerment:
Using The Empowerment Dynamic* and
Polarity Thinking™ to Engage Key Stakeholders*

Cliff Kayser, MSHR, MSOD, PCC
Bert Parlee, PhD
Ann V. Deaton, PhD, PCC, CTPC

Here be dragons

This chapter is for current-day cartographers who guide leaders, teams, and organizational systems through fearful territories using Polarity Maps® and the Polarity Approach for Continuity and Transformation (PACT™).[247] Our expedition begins with two methodologies for navigating fear-based territories: the Dreaded Drama Triangle (DDT) – disempowerment through "drama" story dynamics – and The Empowerment Dynamic* (TED*) – enabling shifts from drama to empowerment.[248]

Three key reference points guide the integration of our DDT/TED* and PACT. The first two provide orientation for DDT/TED* shifts on Polarity Maps. The final reference point explores how the PACT process accelerates shifts from disempowering drama (DDT) to sustained empowerment (TED*) for the broad range of fear conditions key stakeholders encounter. We trust you will find the integration of these powerful approaches to be a valuable legend as you map out journeys with key stakeholders.

Overview of Drama and Empowerment Methodologies (*Figure 1*)

Our natural default (preferred pole) as humans is to protect ourselves against threat so we are problem focused. In the Dreaded Drama Triangle that results from this focus, we tend to relate in predictable roles – Victims, Persecutors, and Rescuers (*Figure 1*, lower triangle).

Figure 1

DDT: Victim, Persecutor, Rescuer (*Or*-thinking)

Victim: "Poor Me"

- Feels powerless, oppressed, helpless, hopeless, and ashamed.
- Looks for a Rescuer to alleviate their negative feelings.

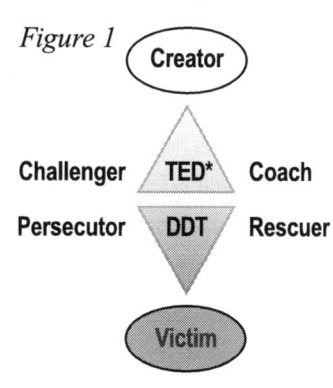

---

[247] Johnson, Barry. *And: Making a Difference by Leveraging Polarity, Paradox or Dilemma. Volume One – Foundations.* HRD Press, 2020; *Polarity Management.* HRD Press, 1992.

[248] Emerald, D. *The Power of TED* (The Empowerment Dynamic).* Polaris Publishing, 2006, 2016.

Rescuer: "I'll Help You"
- Feels best when needed and fears not being needed.
- Rescues on own terms and keeps the Victim dependent.

Persecutor: "It's All Your Fault"
- Mobilized by anger and/or instilling fear – blaming, criticizing, oppressing Victim(s).
- Fears and defends against becoming a Victim.

TED*: Creator, Challenger, Coach (*And*-thinking)

The Empowerment Dynamic (TED*) offers the antidote to drama, shifting from a problem focus to a focus on our vision, or desired outcome. When we focus on what we want rather than what we fear, there is a related shift in the roles we play (*Figure 1*, upper triangle):

From Victim To Creator: with passionate intention, Creators focus on propelling the person, team, or system previously identifying as Victim(s) to take steps as Creator(s). Empowered Creators own their ability to choose responses to life circumstances.

From Persecutor To Challenger: is focused on learning and growth, holding Creator(s) accountable while encouraging learning, action, and next steps. A Challenger intentionally builds others up, instead of putting them down using criticism, blame, or control. They challenge by encouraging others to stretch, believing in their potential, inviting them to step into growth opportunities. Challengers evoke and provoke learning as an accountability partner.

From Rescuer To Coach: uses compassion and questions to help Creator(s) develop a vision and action plan. Rather than doing for the other and taking on responsibility for "rescuing" other(s), Coaches provide safety through a witnessing presence and encouraging support partner.

Reference Points One and Two

The first reference point orients the shifts from DDT to TED*, illustrating two shifts from downside limitations (-Fears) to upside benefits (+Values). One is from the Persecutor limitations (-B) to Challenger benefits (+A). The second is the limitations of Rescuer (-D) to the benefits of Coach (+C). *Figure 2* provides the Polarity Map for Challenge *And* Support from which we can consider these Leveraging possibilities – Action Steps and Early Warning Signs – in our shift toward TED*.

Action Steps and Early Warning Signs

Early warnings or signs that inform us that we have slipped from Challenger (+A) to Persecutor (-B) include sarcasm, blame, judgment, and loneliness. These warnings are often the manifestation of having a Dominating approach, being Defensive, and can Create adversaries. Early signs that we've moved from Coach (+C) to Rescuer (-D) are others' responsibilities ending up on our own "to do" lists, and when we find ourselves delighting in opportunities to swoop in and save the day; corollary actions to Creating dependence, being Needy, and a Savior approach.

When experiencing these warnings, we can take Action Steps to minimize the downsides and again gain the benefits of Challenger (+A) and Coach (+C). We do so by acknowledging mistakes as an opportunity to learn and grow rather than cause for judgment or rescue. Action steps also include asking curious questions that provoke learning and enable the other to solve their own challenges, and then celebrating their success. These signs and actions all support focusing on what we want, not what we fear.

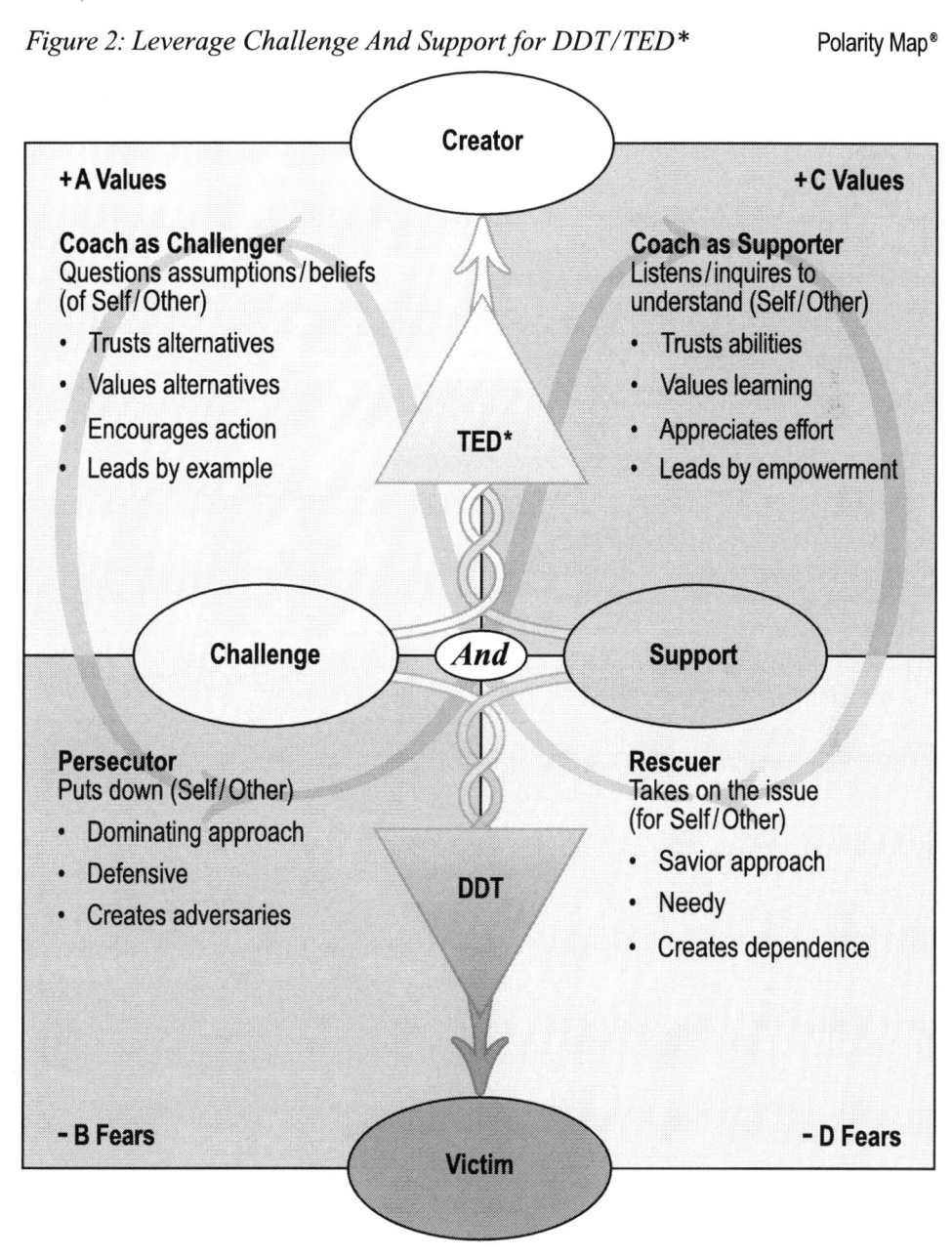

Figure 2: Leverage Challenge And Support for DDT/TED*   Polarity Map®

Creator

+A Values

Coach as Challenger
Questions assumptions/beliefs
(of Self/Other)

- Trusts alternatives
- Values alternatives
- Encourages action
- Leads by example

TED*

+C Values

Coach as Supporter
Listens/inquires to
understand (Self/Other)

- Trusts abilities
- Values learning
- Appreciates effort
- Leads by empowerment

Challenge *And* **Support**

Persecutor
Puts down (Self/Other)

- Dominating approach
- Defensive
- Creates adversaries

DDT

Rescuer
Takes on the issue
(for Self/Other)

- Savior approach
- Needy
- Creates dependence

− B Fears   **Victim**   **− D Fears**

The second reference point orients the shift from DDT to TED* using the polarity Focus on Current Reality *And* Focus on Desired Outcome (*Figure 4*, pp. 302-303). It is important to recognize DDT's could result from getting "hooked" by over-focusing on one point of view to the neglect of the other. Drama results when, let's say, an over-focus on Current Reality has kept stakeholders from focusing on Desired Outcome (-B), so there is a charge to shift focus to Desired Outcome (+C). But the passionate charge toward and over-emphasis on Desired Outcome inevitably leads to being out of touch with the Current Reality (-D). This is one DDT triangle. Then it happens again, but in the opposite direction. The fear of being "out of touch" (-D) yields another passionate charge toward Current Reality (+A), fatefully leading to unaddressed Desired Outcome (back to -B). This triangle of movement, "solving a problem" by focusing on *either* the Current Reality *Or* the Desired Outcome, will almost always bring the stakeholders into the Dreaded Drama Triangle. The Empowerment Dynamic* is designed to navigate effectively between the Current Reality *And* Desired Outcome, acknowledging the importance of *both,* and leveraging the tension generated by the gap between what is and what could be. To dispel the DDT, what is needed is the power of *And*-thinking.

Perception vs. Thinking Competency

Researchers from the U.S. Army used mathematical models to demonstrate how *Or*-thinking to the neglect of *And*-thinking leads to the inevitability of another world war.[249] Similarly, misapplying *Or*-thinking to *Figure 3* could invite a "war" of sorts — in the form of a Victim/Persecutor. Misapplying *Or*-thinking results in each stakeholder seeing the other as the Persecutor who is wrong, stupid, evil (or all the above), and themselves as Victim. Add a Rescuer to the scene and you have a triangle, where the roles can begin to shift in a full-blown DDT. If retaliatory cycles become increasingly vicious, staggering levels of cruelty is justified by fear — or the reverse. And cruel outcomes are then defended with self-righteous indignation *Or*-thinking.

Fig 3: Differences in Perception

Reference Point Three – the PACT 5-Step SMALL Process™

Key stakeholder challenges and opportunities bring a broad range of fear conditions that require specialized focus to navigate. Complex situations require using both *Or*-thinking *And And*-thinking competencies. Engaging key stakeholders in this process helps ensure both thinking competencies are engaged for a range of fear conditions key stakeholders experience and navigate.

Seeing helps orient key stakeholders in the thinking competency required to address the Current Reality *And* Desired Outcomes with less fear/drama and more empowerment.

---

[249] West, B., Mahmoodi, K., and Grigolini, P. *Empirical Paradox, Complexity Thinking and Generating New Kinds of Knowledge.* Cambridge Scholars Publishing, 2019.

Following are five scenarios to help illustrate how the PACT™ process can accelerate shifts from DDT (*Or*-thinking), and sustain outcomes for TED* (*And*-thinking). DDT's *either/Or* false choice can create incredible drama for the stakeholder, as they feel forced to choose between them. With *both/And*, the stakeholder can *both* see *And* powerfully leverage both poles to gain and sustain their goals!

1. **Leader Career Decision:** A current job lacks in fulfillment of purpose, but pays well. An alternative job opportunity is in line with personal mission, but pays less. The impact of the decision has profound impact on key stakeholders.

    The poles at play: Leader/Family, Money/Mission, Continuity/Transformation. The drama, DDT (*Or*-thinking), is in having to choose between these poles. The power, TED* (*And*-thinking), is when you know you can leverage these polarities toward a powerful career track and work-life balance, while still coming to closure by making a decision between the current job or the alternate job.

2. **Healthcare Leaders Reduction in Force:** Efficiently and effectively responding to the impact on key stakeholders.

    The poles at play: Patients/Staff, Empathy/Performance, Margin/Mission, Continuity/Transformation. DDT (*Or*-thinking) can overwhelm when the belief is that there is a singular choice between these poles. TED* (*And*-thinking) lets you empower both to the benefit of the Healthcare company *And* employees, while still reducing the workforce.

3. **Key Stakeholder Performance Focus in an IT Start-up:** Customer support for the existing product helps the organization hit the numbers for the board, but siphons resources for innovation that's central to their brand.

    The poles at play: Service on Current/Innovation on Current, Tactical/Strategic, Customer/Organization. DDT may have you feeling caught between these poles while TED* leverages the polarities in support of satisfying both company *And* customer with current products *And* innovation.

4. **National Leadership of COVID-19 Pandemic Response:** Decisions that support efficient and effective responses for protecting lives and economic well-being of key stakeholders in the nation.

    The poles at play: Human Health/Economic Health, Short-term/Long-term, Anticipate/Respond, Deliberate/Emergent, Individual Rights/Communal Obligations, State Responsibility/Federal Responsibility, National Needs/Global Needs. Choose between these and your nation can quickly descend into chaos, while actively leveraging each pair will create a healthy and well-run nation.

Figure 4: Leverage Current Reality and Desired Outcome for DDT/TED*

Action Steps

- Commit to the power of **TED*** (Emerald, 2016) to address the Current Reality
- Practice 3VQ for the Current Reality (Emerald, 2016)
- Practice Conversational Intelligence™ (Glasser, 2014) for the Current Reality
- Practice Appreciative Inquiry (Mohr and Watkins, 2002) for the Current Reality
- Practice the Stockdale Paradox (Collins, 2001) in the Current Reality (confront the brutal facts)

Early Warnings

- Complaints about neglecting attention for Desired Outcome
- Increased pattern of Desired Outcome dialogue neglected
- Increasing difficulty avoiding DDTs related to the neglect of Desired Outcome dialogue

+A Values

- Current Reality dialogue using TED*
- Current Reality learning from thoughts, emotions, and actions

Focus on Current Reality

- Unaddressed Desired Outcome fears from too much focus on Current Reality
- DDTs

− B Fears

Sustainable Progress

TED*

And

DDT

Swirl of Confusion

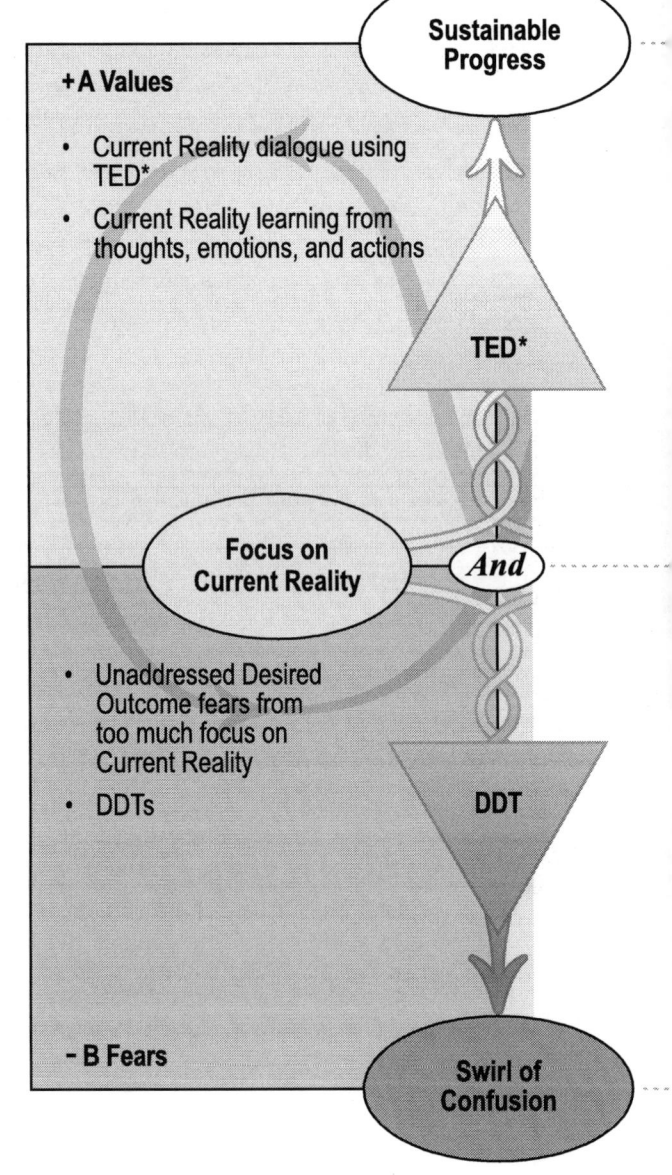

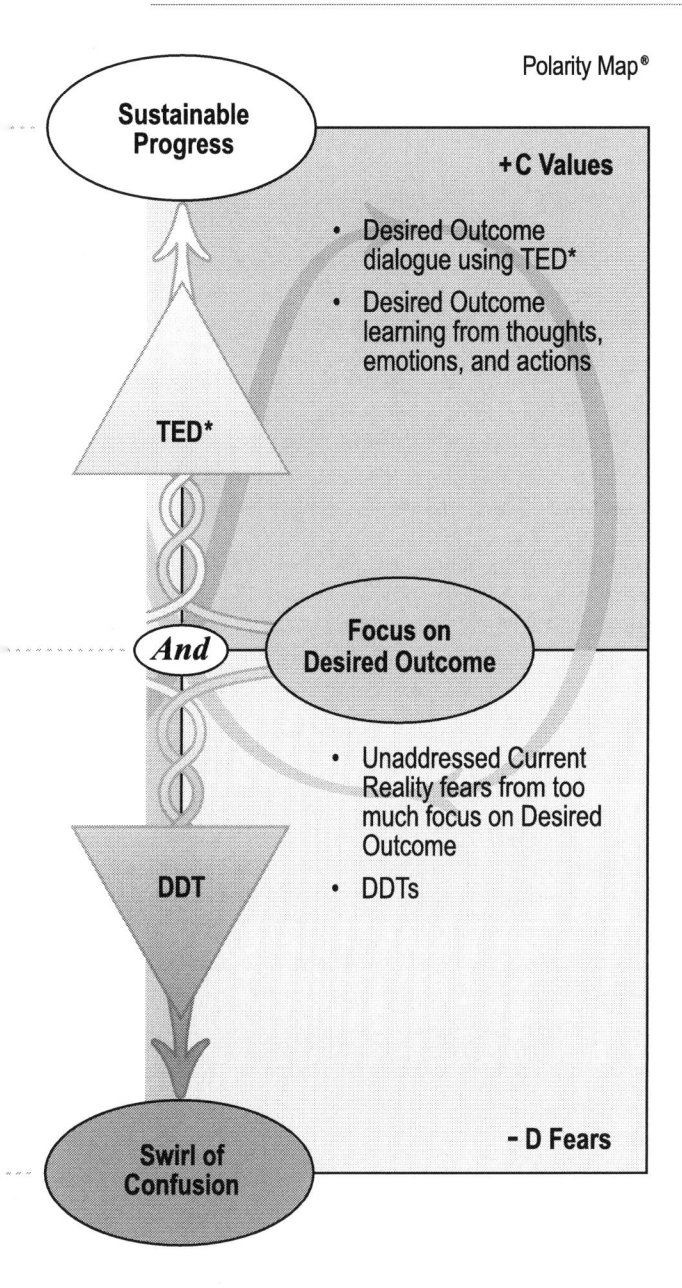

Polarity Map®

Sustainable Progress

+C Values

- Desired Outcome dialogue using TED*
- Desired Outcome learning from thoughts, emotions, and actions

TED*

And

Focus on Desired Outcome

- Unaddressed Current Reality fears from too much focus on Desired Outcome
- DDTs

DDT

− D Fears

Swirl of Confusion

Action Steps

- Commit to the power of **TED*** (Emerald, 2016) to address the Desired Outcome
- Practice 3VQ for the Desired Outcome (Emerald, 2016)
- Practice Conversational Intelligence™ (Glasser, 2014) for the Desired Outcome
- Practice Appreciative Inquiry (Mohr and Watkins, 2002) for the Desired Outcome
- Practice the Stockdale Paradox (Collins, 2001) for the Desired Outcome (unwavering faith for prevailing)

Early Warnings

- Complaints about neglecting attention to Current Reality
- Increased pattern of Current Reality dialogue neglected
- Increasing difficulty avoiding DDTs related to neglect of Current Reality dialogue

5. **Global Leadership Climate Crisis Response:** Decisions that support efficient and effective responses for protecting lives and the economic well-being of key stakeholders on the planet.

The poles at play: Economic Health/Climate Health, Study/Respond, Deliberate/ Act, Human Health/Economic Health, Individual Rights/Communal Obligations, National Needs/Global Needs. As with the others, to choose *either/Or* will, over time, lead to negative outcomes regardless of which pole is chosen. Choosing *both/And* will lead to powerful and world changing responses to this crisis.

Mapping key underlying polarities in the drama enhance the seeing. Mapping the polarity tensions identified by key stakeholders explores unique contexts of the challenge/opportunity territories. As key stakeholders improve their capability for mapping uncharted territories, their capacity for TED* improves in parallel.

Assessing how well upside benefits are being maximized and downside limitations are being minimized can take place through one or a combination of navigation tools: dialogue; manually assessing polarities; or using the online Polarity Assessment™. **Learning** supports key stakeholders making meaning of their challenges and opportunities based on the Assessing. **Leveraging** supports the developing Creator Action Step strategies and Early Warning Signs to avoid Victim.

Conclusion

Medieval cartographers often depicted unknown territory with "Here be dragons." In this chapter, we explored the integration of powerful methodologies to help dispel or reduce fears when navigating in difficult or unknown territory. With the shift from focusing on the problem as a Victim, toward focusing on what we want as Creators, what formerly appeared as dragons may now be seen more clearly as often harmless souls, or even beings amenable to strategically creative solutions, having the transformative power to fundamentally change what appears to be their core nature. We first oriented DDT/TED* fear-to-empowerment shifts on two Polarity Maps: Support *And* Challenge; and Current Reality *And* Desired Outcome. We then explored how the PACT process supports navigating unique key stakeholder fear conditions to do as Wayne Dyer's quote suggested, "Change the way you look at things and the things you look at change."

The authors would like to say a special thanks to Donna Zajonc of The Power of TED* for her thoughts and insights to this chapter. www.powerofted.com

---

Find info for authors Cliff Kayser, Bert Parlee, and Ann V. Deaton at www.polaritypartnerships.com/certified-polarity-practitioners

Creating and Sustaining Virtual Teamwork Effectiveness: Final Research Report

Center for Creative Leadership®

Executive Summary[250]

Background

Challenged by constant reliance on technology, lack of face-to-face interactions, and working across time zones, virtual teams often encounter tensions and challenges to effectiveness. This research was conducted to help virtual teams achieve greater success; not by eliminating these challenges, but by teaching members ways to leverage polarities underlying virtual teamwork. Polarities, also known as contradictions or paradoxes, are ongoing themes that appear to be in opposition to each other but in reality can be complementary and synergistic. It is increasingly recognized that understanding polarities in business management is paramount because organizations and the people working in them find themselves in environments that are increasingly Volatile, Uncertain, Complex, and Ambiguous (VUCA).

Through this research we explored the role of polarities in virtual teams' effectiveness. Our central research premise is that teams who understand and are able to leverage polarities will achieve and maintain greater effectiveness over time. We engaged with 140 teams globally from a wide range of industries. The research was conducted over time, with most teams completing a polarities assessment two times, six months apart. This allowed us to explore how the polarities change over time and what impact this has on the effectiveness of the virtual team. More details regarding the research design and teams can be found at the end of this report.

Research Findings

Positive Outcomes

- As anticipated, leveraged polarities (maximizing benefits and minimizing the downsides of both poles) are positively associated with virtual team effectiveness. What this means is that teams who were able to have sufficient focus on both poles (either naturally or through concerted focus and effort) had higher ratings of team effectiveness. Polarity management is an important leadership capability.

- The polarity Task Focused *And* Relationship Focused is positively associated with team effectiveness. In other words, team effectiveness requires individuals

[250] ©2017 Center for Creative Leadership. All Rights Reserved. CVD011217.

who focus on the tasks of the team *And* focus on building relationships to facilitate working together as a team.

- The polarity Unified Team *And* Diverse Individuals is positively associated with a number of individual-level effects including individual team members' satisfaction working on the team, trust in the team, commitment to the team, opportunities for professional growth and development, professional and work-related learning, and sustainability/viability (intent to remain). In other words, team effectiveness requires individuals who can work apart effectively *And* bring their diverse individual perspectives together to work as a unified team.

How Other Aspects of Virtual Teams Influence and Interact With the Polarities

- Team commitment had significant interactions with team members' geographic dispersion. The highest levels of overall teamwork polarity occurred at high levels of team commitment and low levels of max time differences (maximum number of time zoned between members ranged from 0 to 12 hours). Clearly, time differences are a teamwork hindrance.

- Team structural "togetherness" (i.e., hours per week spent on this team) and team attitudinal "togetherness" (i.e., team commitment) were both significantly positively related to the polarities.

- When team members are over-committed (members of multiple teams), the polarities suffer and this negatively impacts team effectiveness.

- When team members are more geographically dispersed (higher maximum time zone difference between team members), there tends to be lower levels of commitment to the team and, in turn, more challenges leveraging polarities.

- None of the team composition diversity measures (e.g., diversity of gender, age, education, team tenure, position, geographic region of origin) were significantly related to the polarities. This finding is consistent with logic underlying the team cohesion polarity, which suggests teams need *both* diverse individuals *And* a unified team to have a high functioning team – simply having a team composed of diverse individuals is insufficient.

Change Over Time

- Polarities affect teamwork and individual team members. Changes in polarities are related to changes in team effectiveness and individual team members' learning, satisfaction, and desire to remain with the team. In other words, virtual teams who actively work on polarities benefit both the team as a whole *And* its team members.

Training

- Overall, the polarity training, which included information on the polarities concept and feedback on the team's current status on eight polarities, had less impact on changes in polarities than we had expected. It seems that awareness of the polarities was not enough to help teams improve; high levels of information sharing among team members was also required for polarities improvement.

Information sharing includes team members sharing their opinions when making decisions, effectively sharing large amounts of important information, getting relevant information in a timely manner, not allowing a few vocal team members dominate discussions and asking all team members to share their thoughts while discussing issues.

- The teams most effective at leveraging technology for communication and coordination so that members feel more connected and less virtual (virtual teams who are less virtual) benefited the most from polarity training.

Actions Team and Organizations Can Take

1. Team members need support to integrate polarity management into their practice. Organizations can help teams tie action plans and efforts to leverage polarities to broader organizational outcomes (e.g., strategy, culture).
2. Provide increased education about polarity management, coupled with increased emphasis on information sharing between team members.
3. Identify polarity management champions on teams and in the organization.
4. Integrate polarity management as a teamwork leadership competency.
5. Foster a culture that supports the use of polarity management.
6. Managers should be aware of the possible positive and negative impacts of scheduling a person simultaneously in too many or few project teams on their performance.
7. Teams need to be supported in their team (work) processes and to this end, organizations can assign team coaches to each team and provide teams with technology that facilitates processes such as communication and coordination.
8. Assist individual employees in their time management because multiple team memberships put employees under considerable time pressure in each team context.

Conclusion

Teams of the future need to be able to thrive in a world of polarities. This research shows that the team's ability to leverage polarities positively relates to team effectiveness indicators including team performance as well as individual team members' satisfaction, trust, commitment, professional development, learning, sustainability/viability (intent to remain). Organizations should provide increased education about polarity management, coupled with increased emphasis on information sharing between team members. This is particularly important to the extent to which team members are spread out across time zones (more geographic dispersion) and use more asynchronous virtual tools (such as email and online collaborative websites) to coordinate and execute team processes. Finally, organizations should carefully consider how many virtual teams each member works on. Team structural "togetherness" (i.e., hours per week spent on this team) and team attitudinal "togetherness" (i.e., team commitment) were key drivers of polarities.

We hope that these findings will stimulate discussions and highlight possibilities for further action.

Feedback From Study Participants

- *The polarity approach is quite an intriguing new way of looking at things. It helps you to achieve more than balance; it provides a way to achieve growth and progress.* (Leader of Team 1000)

- *Thank you for all your time; you know, a few months ago ... we had no idea that opposing entities, polarities, could be used to benefit teams. It has been an educational experience for me personally, watching how these small things make a big difference.* (Leader of Team 1059)

- *This is good timing for this, as [team member] knows our team has changed quite a bit over the past twelve months. We've had different people taking on different challenges, the org structure has changed, we've had a lot of movement, and we're almost on a monthly basis still trying to figure out the best way to get the most out of our team ... I think this [Polarity Thinking] gives us a lot more concrete theory.* (Leader of Team 1008)

- *On behalf of the team, I would like to express my appreciation for the time you spent with our team. I had never considered the concept of how polarities can coexist in our business environment. We now are empowered with this knowledge.* (Leader of Team 1053)

- *On behalf of the Team, I would like to thank you and the wider CCL team for including [organization name removed] in the Virtual Team Polarity Research. As a team, we have gained substantially from working with CCL and hope to continue to develop our polarities thinking now and into the future. We look forward to reviewing the findings from your research.* (Leader of Team 1037)

The research team wants to thank every team member for their participation in this research project. We also want to thank the SHRM Foundation for their financial support of this project.

About the Research

Introduction to Polarities and the Polarity Map®

Polarities are ongoing pairs that appear to be in opposition to each other, but in truth, are complimentary and interdependent. You may be more familiar with the concept of polarities under a different name, such as paradox, conundrum, dilemma, dual tensions, and wicked problems. Whatever your preferred terminology, there is an underlying phenomenon that works in predictable ways. The more we understand the elements of this phenomenon and the dynamics by which it functions, the more effective we can be at reaping the benefits of two apparently opposite poles.

Given the explosive growth in virtual teams worldwide, developing effective techniques for such teams is rapidly becoming a core business competency and a competitive advantage. One way to develop effective virtual teams is by enhancing their functioning through Polarity Thinking. The ability to see, frame, and reframe unsolvable situations is a critical skill for making a better future in the VUCA world of Volatility, Uncertainty, Complexity, and Ambiguity.

Barry Johnson introduced the Polarity Map in 1975 to facilitate exploring tensions, reinforcing cycles, and the potential for leveraging paradox. The user-friendly framework is distinguishable by its symbolic representation of the "why," "what," and "how" to take advantage of paradox. The Polarity Map as a whole raises awareness of the connection between competing interests with predictable cycles that align energy in a dynamic and diagonal flow. Simply, the graphic tool shows the upsides and downsides of interdependent pairs, warning signs of over-focusing on one of the two poles, and finally, potential action steps to leverage the paradox and reach desired goals.

In Short:

- Some leadership problems can be addressed with *either/Or*-thinking, but polarities must be addressed with *both/And*-thinking.

- Polarities are interdependent pairs that need each other over time to achieve a higher purpose.

- While polarities are unavoidable and unsolvable, they are leverageable. Understanding how to leverage, how to maximize the upsides of both poles while minimizing the downsides, enables you to do more with less, with greater speed and sustainability.

Use Polarity Thinking and the Maps To:

- Explore opportunities and advantages in tensions or contradictions rather than suppress or deny them.

- Illustrate perceptual differences and hidden views when debating topics of the contrasting value.

- Shift views that only a "few" people are responsible for managing polarities to it being a process of the group.

- Sensitize the organization to a paradoxical lens.

- Reframe your organization's wicked problems so they become complementary and codependent (a healthier stance).

- Interpret and expose reoccurring chronic issues, especially those that might be globally based.

- Look for clues in mixed messages for a source of hidden paradox.

- Escape vicious cycles. Work towards continuous improvement (virtuous cycles), moving from good to great.

- Be observant of the contexts and times when contradictions are present (e.g., the times when the organization is in profitability mode and when it is in growth mode).
- Help leaders understand how to effectively handle paradoxes (e.g., direct and coach).
- Work through resistance to change.

Eight Polarities Researched

Based on an exhaustive review of the virtual teams' literature as well as a variety of team member experiences, we have identified eight "classic" challenges that virtual teams face. Below is a brief description of each of the polarities assessed in this study.

Figure 1: Eight Polarities Researched

Map Title / Poles	Polarity Description
COLLABORATIVE LEARNING (Advocacy *And* Inquiry)	Team members will advocate for ideas and decisions that they believe are best. At the same time, team members will genuinely inquire about and be open to alternative viewpoints.
COMMUNICATION (Formal *And* Informal Communication Communication)	Team members must utilize formal communication to align member efforts and share information. At the same time, informal communication provides quick responses and fosters teamwork.
DEPENDABILITY (Verify *And* Trust)	Team members must verify work quality. At the same time, they will trust one another to be effective team members.
GEOGRAPHIC DISPERSION (Physically *And* Physically Apart Together)	Team members work towards common goals while geographically dispersed. At the same time, they need face-to-face time to bond as a team and accomplish complex tasks.
MANAGED WORK SCHEDULES (Flexible *And* Traditional Schedule Schedule)	Team members will need to be available to work outside hours of the traditional business day. At the same time, team members need to respect each other's need to maintain their usual schedule.
TEAM COHESIVENESS (Unified *And* Diverse Team Individuals)	Team members need to act as a unified team. At the same time, they should maintain and make use of their distinct perspectives and identities.
TEAM EFFECTIVENESS (Task *And* Relationship Focused Oriented)	Team members focus on task work. At the same time, they must also focus on building relationships to facilitate working together as a team.
WORK PROCESSES (Create New *And* Use Existing Processes Processes)	Team members invent new processes for working together more productively. At the same time, they must make use of proven processes and be mindful of their ability to interface effectively with the broader organization.

Research Design

This study employed a multi-treatment pretest-posttest quasi-experimental research design to explore the role of managed polarities in the effectiveness of virtual teams. The original design included 120 teams in total, 30 in each of 4 groups (1 control, 3 treatment). All three treatment groups completed the pre-survey assessment; they differ in terms of the treatment received. After completing the pre-survey assessment, the first treatment group received a feedback session. The feedback session consisted of a team debrief of aggregated item and scale level scores for each polarity, an overview (based on composite score) of how well the team has been managing the polarities to date, and a discussion of how the team achieved the current results. The second treatment group received the feedback session and in addition received a standardized action planning session. The researchers worked with these teams to develop action plans for managing the polarities including identification of action steps the teams can take to leverage the upsides of the polarities, identification of "early warnings" or measurable indicators that a team is getting into the downsides of the polarities, and instructions for using a log for the six months of the implementation period based on the action steps and early warnings. The third treatment group received the feedback session, standardized action planning session, and a follow-up session. The follow-up session included a progress check-in conducted at the mid-point. Approximately six months after the initial assessment, each virtual team (treatment and control) is assessed again on the eight polarities and asked to complete a measure of team effectiveness.

Surveys were administered to all team members and the team leaders. Measures of team performance and task interdependence were collected from the team leaders; all other variables were collected from the team members and aggregated to the team-level.

Who Participated

One hundred and forty-one teams were recruited from 56 for-profit, non-profit, and government organizations from a wide variety of industries (e.g., manufacturing, education, technology, food/beverage, healthcare, philanthropy/humanitarian aid), and geographic regions (e.g., Africa, Eastern Europe, Western Europe, South America, North America). Forty-five teams withdrew after Time 1 (T1) surveys were completed or were non-responsive.

Two-wave data were collected approximately 6 months apart. Time 1 (T1) yielded responses from 141 teams and 831 team members. The T1 data collection also generated survey responses from 68 team leaders and 99 team supervisors. Time 2 (T2) yielded responses from 96 teams and 432 team members. The T2 data collection also generated survey responses from 46 team leaders and 25 team supervisors.

Modeling the dynamics between the team polarities and team effectiveness, at both the team and individual levels, required survey responses from two+ members per team at both T1 and T2 and an external rating of team performance (e.g., from a team supervisor). The final sample consisted of 55 teams and 221 members. These teams were from 32 different organizations, which included for-profit, non-profit, and government organizations from a wide variety of industries (e.g., manufacturing, education, technology, healthcare, philanthropy/humanitarian aid) and geographic regions. The majority of team members included were originally from the North American region (45.2%), Western Europe (20.4%), Latin America (10.4%), Asia Pacific (12.7%), South Asia (7.7%), with the remaining few members being from the Middle East, Eastern Europe, Africa, and Oceania. The sample average was 41.19 (SD = 10.12) with an average team tenure of 2.99 years (SD = 2.92). Males comprised 43% of the sample and females 57%. The sample was generally well-educated with 14.5% having doctoral level degrees, 37.1% master's level degrees, 34.4% bachelor's degrees, 6.3% with some college, and only 7.7% with a high-school diploma or equivalent.

Key Terms and Measures

Members of Multiple Teams – average number of teams that team members are currently on.

Team Effectiveness – a measure of overall team performance, team viability (intent to stay) and team satisfaction.

Virtual Teams – groups of geographically, organizationally, and/or time dispersed, mutually dependent workers brought together through technologies to work on the same objectives.

Virtuality – the extent to which team members use virtual tools to coordinate and execute team processes. Includes percent of time working face-to-face, utilizing video conferencing, phone, email, text, shareware/knowledge tools. For example, if a team primarily uses asynchronous technology of low informational value (e.g., email), the team has a relatively high level of virtuality. Conversely, if team members meet face-to-face more frequently and often use information-rich, synchronous technology (e.g., video conferencing), the team has a relatively lower level of virtuality.

Research Partners
- Jean Brittain Leslie, Emily Hoole, Rebecca Anderson: Center for Creative Leadership
- Margaret Luciano, Ph.D., Arizona State University
- John Mathieu, Ph.D., University of Connecticut
- Leslie DePol, Polarity Partnerships, LLC
- SHRM Foundation

Resources
- Johnson, B. Polarity Management: Identifying and Managing Unsolvable Problems. HRD Press, 1992.
- Polarity Partnerships. www.polaritypartnerships.com
- "Managing Paradox Blending East and West Philosophies to Unlock Its Advantages and Opportunities." www.ccl.org
- Virtuality. "The Dimensions and Antecedents of Team Virtuality." psycnet.apa.org/psycinfo/2005-11387-004

For partnership information contact Leslie DePol at www.polaritypartnerships.com.
For questions about CCL research please contact Jean Leslie at lesliej@ccl.org.

Polarity Thinking™ and Vertical Development

Beena Sharma

Do you think that some people are more mature than others?

Most likely, your answer is a 'yes' to this question. I now ask you to describe some characteristics that indicate maturity. What comes to your mind? Take a moment.

You may list some of the following: not blaming others or circumstances; controlling one's emotions; considering others' viewpoints; pausing to reflect; recognizing one's assumptions; thinking long-term or even in historical and multi-generational time; systems thinking; having "beginner's mind"; seeing humanity as one.

Notice that you have a pretty good idea about what are more mature ways of responding to life's issues. (You may notice that items in the above list also reflect progressively more mature ways of being.) You will perhaps agree with me that maturity is not about getting more degrees, learning more skills, gathering more information, or producing more knowledge. In doing so, you have just made an important distinction between two kinds of development. In the first kind, called horizontal development, we "gain" more information and knowledge. In the second, called vertical development, we "become" more mature. Both are important and necessary for human development. In horizontal development, new information is used to solve problems at the current order of complexity. In contrast, vertical development transforms the way we look at problems and our relationship to our struggles. Vertical development helps us move beyond earlier, less functional ways of dealing with personal and professional issues. It helps individuals become wiser through a series of perspective shifts. It looks at development as an ongoing, dynamic process: we become increasingly aware of our attachments and preferences and learn to transcend them. Vertical development increases one's capacity for seeing the bigger picture and is *rarer* than horizontal growth.

This chapter explores the relationship between Polarity Thinking™ and vertical development. The evolution of human maturity is a dynamic, vital, messy, and fundamentally mysterious process. I posit that individuals who are more mature acquire a greater capacity to integrate polarities. By learning, practicing, and applying Polarity Thinking, individuals can acquire and integrate new perspectives, including those excluded before. By teaching how to observe, name, and leverage polarities that show up every day and over time, we can facilitate vertical growth in individuals, teams, and organizations. I submit that continuously practicing seeing a more "complete" picture of reality by *integrating* interdependent pairs is fundamental to being integral.[251] Integration fuels evolution.

---

[251] Wilber, K. *Integral Psychology: Consciousness, Spirit, Psychology, Therapy.* Shambhala Publications, 2000.

Measuring Vertical Development

Within the discipline of western modern psychology, researchers, psychometricians, and theorists exploring adult development have inquired for over six decades into how we make meaning and how we continue to step into new understandings in our journey through life. Some of the central questions of this quest related to investigating vertical development are: How do adults continue to develop throughout their life span? Are there universal "stages" of development that adults go through in the same way that Piaget described children develop in stages?[252] Does everyone go through these stages? Is there a universal trajectory of development, and what does it look like? What prompts people to move through the stages?

The Leadership Maturity Framework (*Figure 1*: LMF) is an empirically-derived theory that maps vertical development and describes the journey of the adult through various stages of development and maturity. The LMF defines a sequence of eight stages of increasing self-awareness and capacity, based on ego-development theory.[253]

Figure 1: Leadership Maturity Framework (LMF)   VeDA

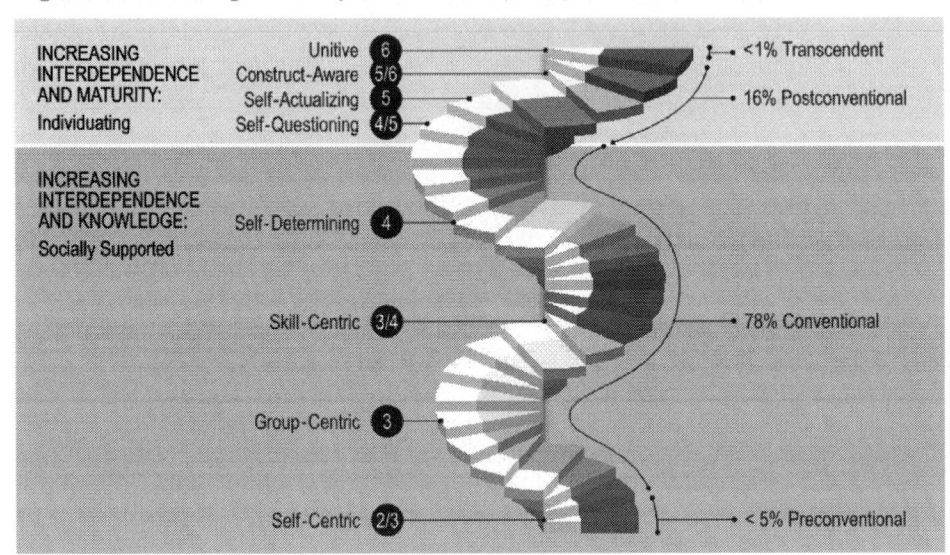

© 2020 Vertical Development Academy. LMF © Dr. Susanne Cook-Greuter. LMF labels © Cook-Greuter & Sharma.

The eight stages in the LMF span four broad tiers of development: preconventional, conventional, postconventional, and transcendent. Percentages indicate number of individuals rated at each of the four tiers, derived from a general adult population with subsamples drawn from diverse occupations and backgrounds.[254]

---

[252] Piaget, J. *The Theory of Stages in Cognitive Development.* In D.R. Green, M.P. Ford, & G.B. Flamer, *Measurement and Piaget.* McGraw-Hill, 1971.

[253] Ego development theory was developed by Dr. Jane Loevinger in the early '60s and further refined and validated by Dr. Susanne Cook-Greuter in the '90s.

[254] Cook-Greuter, S. R. "Postautonomous Ego Development: A Study of Its Nature and Measurement." Doctoral dissertation. Harvard Graduate School of Education, 1999.

Each stage describes a different way of seeing the world with a different set of assumptions. At each stage we make meaning in unique and new ways that are qualitatively different from the way we made sense before our ideas were challenged by our experiences. Each later stage constitutes a transformation of the previous perspective, including and transcending it. As we progress through each stage, we acquire greater capacity for dealing with life's challenges. Research shows that people at later stages are able to deal with greater complexity, are more tolerant of uncertainty, and can more flexibly adapt to what is needed in real time.

The overall human development trajectory can be seen as the progression of stories we tell about who we are, what is important to us, where we're going, what we conceive the world to be, and what we hold as real and/or true. One could say it is about making sense of our sense-making. *The LMF is a story about human story-making.*

The Maturity Assessment Profile (MAP[255, 256]) is an instrument used to assess a person's stage of vertical development. It reveals in great detail the major stage-related themes, preoccupations, and unique concerns of individuals. Dr. Susanne Cook-Greuter developed the MAP instrument, and expanded Jane Loevinger's theory (1970) into the present-day LMF. Cook-Greuter's work since the 1980s, and VeDA's more recent research using the MAP instrument, has shown that the LMF is a valid, robust, and comprehensive model of vertical growth and is predictive. By analyzing the responses from people who have taken the Maturity Profile, we find that *either/Or*-thinking is prevalent in conventional stage respondents, and *both/And*-thinking explicitly demonstrated in those assessed at later, postconventional stages.

Polarities Related to Adult Stage Development

Research using the MAP instrument indicates that *both/And*-thinking is an observable[257] marker of an individual's later-stage evolution. At each level in the sequence, we see stage-specific pole identifications or preferences that relate to the assumptions and beliefs held at that stage. Additionally, the development of the concept and understanding of polarities itself can be traced along the vertical developmental trajectory. *Polarity Thinking is a capacity that comes online with more maturity.*

As meaning-makers, we are all subject to "the polarity dynamic" as a function of what is important to us, and what we identify with, regardless of our stage of development. We interpret our experiences in value-laden terms and are subject to the tensions generated due to our preferences. Our pole preferences are influenced by all aspects that contribute to the variability of human beings: historical, geographical, cultural and linguistic context, family history, biological differences, individual

---

[255] Dr. Cook-Greuter and Vertical Development Academy (VeDA) have profiled ~14,000+ people from all walks of life with the MAP. This represents the largest number of developmental profiles archived in one database.

[256] Note: The Maturity Profile (MAP) is a measure of adult development and distinct from The Polarity Map® which is a methodology and toolkit for working with polarities. Both are tools that facilitate human maturity.

[257] Tracking a person's stated or implicit preferences in their responses to the MAP is one criteria we use to assess their level of ego maturity.

orientations, preferred sensory modalities, as well as special gifts and talents. How much we are defined by our predispositions, how tightly we hold on to them, how we judge others' preferences, how attached we are to one pole over its interdependent pair, and how capable we are of embracing the neglected pole – these are used as indicators of relative maturity. In the conventional realm (see *Figure 1*) we *are* our preferences. They define us. It is therefore more accurate to say that they are identifications and come more from our conditioning than from our conscious choices. At stage 4 (Self-determining) we begin to choose our values, and can struggle with pairs of values that appear to be competing for our attention and energy. As we grow into postconventional stage perspectives, we are able to notice our preferences, challenge our assumptions, and learn to see the "other point of view" as valuable and complimentary – not opposing or contradictory. As we go further along, we are more capable of reintegrating what we excluded before and are no longer in the grip of *Or*-thinking as the only way of parsing our world. Later-stage meaning-makers can often embrace, integrate and let go, on their own, whatever subtle preferences they discover. Indeed, unearthing blind spots (and neglected poles) can become a valued, intentional, and internalized "practice" over time.

Polarities at Play Within Each Stage of Adult Development

Our current-stage perspective offers us a particular sense of self and certainty, and a set of clear values. We might consciously or unconsciously hold on to one pole, either unaware of what we exclude, or choose to reject a competing value, sometimes seeing it only in terms of its downside. As our worldview expands to include more complexity, we can sense the need for the missing interdependent pair in our search for a resolution. We learn to embrace what was neglected, and experience the relief in not having to struggle with making that *either/Or* choice. Once we have entered a new stage, we may, at first, reject the pole(s) we embraced at the previous stage because we are now aware of its limits and downsides. The later the stage, the less likely one rejects previously held values.

Figures 2-8 on the following pages are illustrative lists of some polarities that show up in the foreground of experience for each stage in *Figure 1*. The pole one is attached to, or identified with, is listed in the left column. The interdependent pole is listed in the right column and indicates the neglected or unavailable (as the not seen, accessible, or valued perspective). Sometimes, the other pole is simply not yet on one's radar because the stage capacity itself limits what one can pay attention to. Along with the illustrative list at each stage, I call out one polarity (poles are in bold), to provide a brief, descriptive example.

To get a sense of the mindset at each stage, read the list of poles in the left column sequentially and you will get a feel of the world-view at that stage. To get an idea of what is next for the person in terms of their development, read the list of poles in the right column. This list on the right offers the "missing" interdependent values for a given stage. Healing and growth can come when the perspective expands to include those on the right. (I use the symbol of the infinity loop instead of the "*And*" between the poles to reflect the dynamic and all the principles underpinning the ongoing movement between the poles.)

Illustrative List of Polarities by Stage of Development (*Figures 2-8*)

Self-Centric Stage (2/3) – Preconventional: the core drivers are self-protection and survival. Others can become instruments for one's benefit. Learning to consider what is in **"Our" Benefit**, not just in **"My" Benefit** is a move towards the missing pole and leads into making meaning at the next stage.

Figure 2: Polarities Related to the Self-Centric Stage (2/3)

Pole Identified With	Interdependent Pole
Self-Interests and Needs ∞	Others' Interests and Needs
Acting, Doing ∞	Pausing, Thinking
Intent, Action ∞	Effect, Consequence
Urgent, Immediate ∞	Patience, Short-Term
Protecting Self ∞	Taking Responsibility

Group-Centric Stage (3) – Early Conventional: identity comes from membership in a group, and safety comes from **Keeping Peace and Harmony**. Learning to **Speak Up**, to even find one's voice and express one's own thoughts, is a move towards embracing the other pole, and the next stage.

Figure 3: Polarities Related to the Group-Centric Stage (3)

Pole Identified With	Interdependent Pole
Caring for Others ∞	Self-Care
Following Norms ∞	Questioning Tradition
Keeping Harmony ∞	Speaking Up
Belonging ∞	Independence
Doing What Others Expect ∞	Identifying What I Want
Unconditional ∞	Conditional

Skill-Centric Stage (3/4) – Mid-Conventional: perfecting procedure and being **Efficient** is of great importance at this stage. Adding the focus on **Effectiveness** (interdependent pole) of what one is doing, paying attention to timing and whether the outcomes serve a larger goal, leads one to the next stage of development.

Figure 4: Polarities Related to the Skill-Centric Stage (3/4)

Pole Identified With	Interdependent Pole
Being Efficient ∞	Being Effective
Contributing Individually ∞	Collaborating
Being Right ∞	Willing To Align
Respect for Credentials ∞	Respect for Performance
Advocating ∞	Inquiring
Directive Leadership ∞	Participative Leadership

Self-Determining Stage (4) – Late Conventional: successfully **Accomplishing** what was planned based on desired outcomes is an overriding focus here. Being comfortable with "failure," and **Learning From Failing**, to achieve what was desired is one step towards the next stage and represents the interdependent pole.

Figure 5: Polarities Related to the Self-Determining Stage (4)

Preferred Pole		Interdependent Pole
Goal Oriented	∞	Process Oriented
Objective	∞	Subjective
Driving Agenda	∞	Open to What Emerges
Success Focused	∞	Freedom To Fail
Performing	∞	Learning
I Change the World	∞	I Am Changed

As mentioned earlier, with the transition from conventional to postconventional – considered a major milestone in adult development – the capacity to see *both/And* and to integrate polarities increases significantly.

Self-Questioning Stage (4/5) – Early Postconventional: individuals are really **Invested in Diverse Perspectives**, holding all of them to be equally valid. Growth involves also being **Able To Take a Stand**, integrating multiple perspectives and identifying the view that stands above others, based on higher principles.

Figure 6: Polarities Related to the Self-Questioning Stage (4/5)

Preferred Pole		Interdependent Pole
Inquiring	∞	Integrating
Exploring Multiple Perspectives	∞	Taking a Stand
Participative	∞	Systemic
Consensual	∞	Taking the Lead
Negotiable, Flexible	∞	Non-Negotiable, Higher Principles
Being in the Flow	∞	Enacting

At the next stage there is a great capacity to integrate multiple polarities, and navigate nested and stacked polarities as well.[258] However, subtle preferences tend to persist because of the value given to an integrated perspective, which is seen as preferable to the limitations of the earlier, partial views. This may translate into a reluctance or inability to tap the wisdom of earlier views for oneself, even while appreciating those that hold the earlier views.

---

[258] Johnson, Barry. *And: Making a Difference by Leveraging Polarity, Paradox or Dilemma. Volume One – Foundations.* HRD Press, 2020, Chapter 10, "The Part *And* Whole Energy Chain," pp. 83-87.

Self-Actualizing Stage (5) – Mid-Postconventional: one zealously explores one's blind spots in order to master **Self-Knowledge**. This effort can eclipse the wisdom of allowing for the unknowable, for **Mystery**. Embracing mystery leads to questioning one's ideas about oneself, a capacity that comes online at the next stage of development.

Figure 7: Polarities Related to the Self-Actualizing Stage (5)

Preferred Pole		Interdependent Pole
Overarching System Goals	∞	+ Individual Needs/Goals
Visioning	∞	+ Actualizing
Mastery, Much Is Known	∞	Mystery, Much Is Unknown
Seeking	∞	Non-Seeking
Deep Self-Exploration	∞	Holding Oneself Lightly
Self-Transforming	∞	Self-Accepting

Construct-Aware Stage (5/6) – Late Postconventional: brings a momentous realization: all frames are constructed. One realizes whatever one holds as real in life is one's **Story About Living**, created to explain it. **Experiencing Living**, in the eternal now, without the habit of explaining it with the mind, is the new move.

Figure 8: Polarities Related to the Construct-Aware Stage (5/6)

Preferred Pole		Interdependent Pole
Complexity	∞	Simplicity
Naming	∞	Un-Naming
Storying What Is	∞	Living in What Is
Extraordinary Self	∞	Ordinary Self
Radical Doubt	∞	Radical Acceptance
Questing	∞	Non-Seeking

Unitive Stage (6) – Transcendent: all kinds of polarities, contrasts, and dualisms – among them the dualism of "dualism and non-dualism" – are integrated. All concepts, feelings, ambivalences are embraced. Language and mind are seen for what they are – an incessant activity of meaning-making that can only approximate reality, and never fully grasp it. Flux and no-boundary now can only be lived, never adequately defined or explained.

> *When the opposites are realized to be one, discord melts into concord, battles become dances, and old enemies become lovers. We are then in a position to make friends with all of our universe, not just one half of it.*[259]
>
> ~ Ken Wilber on the
> transcendent consciousness

---

[259] Wilber, Ken. *No Boundary: Eastern and Western Approaches to Personal Growth.* Shambhala, 1979, p. 29.

The Development of One's Understanding of Polarities Across Stages

Generally speaking, at conventional stages we tend to have an attachment, identification, or preference for one value over another value that feels conflicting. That is, we tend to operate from an *either/Or* mindset. As we mature, we are more aware of *how* we think about our experiences; we learn that our framing of experience in *either/Or* terms itself limits our understanding of life. We see our habituated black and white thinking now as "false choices." We are able to appreciate a more complex world in which there are seemingly competing twin values, that both carry wisdom, and we understand these as *both/And* choices. Next, we can reclaim the wisdom of *either/Or*-thinking, no longer holding that *both/And*-thinking to be "better" than *either/Or*-thinking. Further along the growth path, we begin to notice that even the interdependent pairs include two concepts, where one concept can only be known through the other. Eventually, we can learn to embrace an unfiltered experience of reality beyond our ideas, representations, and stories. Thus, the capacity to deal with opposites evolves all the way to dissolving the very definitions and boundaries used to make meaning earlier.

Leveraging Development Using the Polarity Lens

Working with polarities helps reveal the connections between two elements earlier seen as separate. Once one begins to see the interdependence of two, it becomes easier to recognize them in three, four, or more elements and at multiple levels of a system, allowing for a more systemic and mature grasp of complexity.

When caught in the up-and-down dynamic of a polarity, there is a profound opportunity to notice our attachments and preferences in action. Using the polarity perspective, a coach can help clients gain a perspective on the attachments that solidify their identity. In becoming aware of their preferences, clients learn to recognize their fears. The process of owning the disowned releases developmental energy. This work can support both horizontal and vertical growth.

When the client is willing, ready, and able, a coach can identify the critical stage-related polarities that need attention for transition to the next stage. I refer to these polarities as "*high developmental leverage*" (HDL) polarities, which means working with these polarities are more likely to yield developmental dividends. In my experience, harmonizing HDL polarities provides greater potential for vertical development. In an individual, the HDL polarities may be those that I have identified as typical for various stage transitions; or they may be other polarities reflecting specific tensions in the client's world that come in the way of their growth.

Research shows that polarity wisdom emerges as human beings develop vertically. I posit that Polarity Thinking is a marker of postconventional adult development. I assert that vertical growth can be facilitated when people learn to intentionally use the Polarity Thinking toolkit, i.e., learn the dynamics and realities of how polarities work, and polarity mapping. It is part of the art of coaching to name and work with polarities that offer the most potential for facilitating maturity. I advocate tailored coaching using HDL polarities to foster and develop human maturity.

About Beena Sharma ~ www.polaritypartnerships.com/certified-polarity-practitioners

Multarities™: Interdependencies of More Than Two

Cliff Kayser, MSHR, MSOD, PCC
Shalom Bruhn, MAOB
Luke Massman-Johnson

A complex system that works is invariably found to have evolved from a simple system that worked. ~ Gall's Law [260]

This chapter recognizes the evolution of practice from seeing and leveraging the simplest *both/And* interdependency – a polarity – to more complex applications that include multarities™: *interdependencies of more than two poles, which synergistically contribute to a greater purpose that is more than the sum of the parts.*[R121, 261] The more we see these multiple interdependencies, the greater our ability to map, assess, learn and leverage key chosen polarities within the multarity in support of making our difference in the world.

The introduction of polarities in *And:* Volume One uses breathing as an analogy; the life-long interdependence of inhale *And* exhale. Activity *And* rest and the two hemispheres of the human brain are also used to illustrate interdependencies. The human body is useful for looking at multarities because of its inherent multitude of systems, including respiratory, muscular, skeletal, etc. These interdependent systems operate mostly in the background of our lives – on autopilot. However, there are times when we notice our body is not working as well as we'd like it to. Symptoms arise, perhaps as early warning signs, that help us diagnose which system or combinations of systems need attention. To return our health to an optimized state, we take certain steps – action steps – to help our system improve. Over time, the systems in need and the directions of our focused energy and efforts will change. What will stay the same, for as long as we occupy our body, is the monitoring and managing of the interdependence among our many systems. Just like polarities, multarities are not new. And you, with your marvelous multitude of interdependent working parts, are a multarity. This chapter explores seeing and thinking about interdependencies to enhance our quality of life on this wonderful planet.

Illustrating Multarities

Figure 1: Polarity

To address the complexity of multarities, new illustrations were crafted with stylized parts. *Figure 1* is a polarity: each pole is a simple circle, while *And* is represented by a dot connecting the poles. The infinity loop continues to identify the energy that is *both* differentiating: energy crossing between,

---

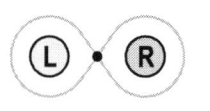

[260] Gall, J. *Systemantics: How Systems Work and Especially How They Fail.* General Systemantics Press. 1975.
[261] "Realities", e.g.[R121], are principles that apply to all polarities and multarities. See Appendix C.

keeping poles separate, *And* <u>integrating</u>: wrapping energy holding both poles in infinite connection. This interdependence is true for every pole in relation to every other pole in any multarity; a multitude of polarities.

Figure 2a shares the rich interdependent synergy of all poles, contributing to an exponential Greater Purpose (GP^5) *that is more than the sum of the 5 parts.* The superscript "x" in (GP^X) identifies the number of available poles supporting the exponential Greater Purpose of the multarity. In *Figure 2a* and *Figure 2b* it is (GP^5).

Figure 2a: 5-Pole Multarity

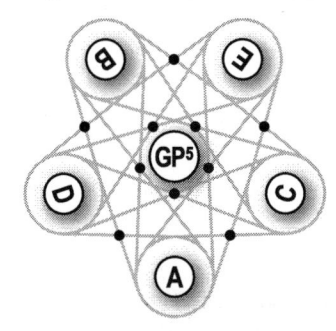

The black dots – the connecting *And* – help you spot the polarities among the lines generated by a multarity. With multarities, the energy system between one pole and any of the other poles is unique to each polarity, but the labeling of left or right pole can vary for each set. With that in mind, as we shift into multarities we no longer identify poles as "L" or "R" as we do with a singular polarity.

You can see how a single pole (A) shares an interdependence with each and every other pole; (A•B), (A•C), (A•D), and (A•E). This is true for (B), (C), (D) and (E) as well. As you increase the number of poles in a multarity, the number of polarities available increases geometrically. Ten polarities show up in our 5-pole multarity and this can feel overwhelming. In *Figure 2b* we have highlighted two polarities in a 5-pole multarity to show that working with multarities is not about just building but selecting and focusing on specific polarities inside a multarity, like we have done with (A•B) and (A•C). Though our graphics may show the full web of interconnected poles, as you work with multarities you can select those that are brought to the foreground; those that provide the greatest opportunity for improvement at a given point in time. Other polarities, as we noted with our body analogy, can run in the background on autopilot. It is also true that to the extent you can optimize the polarities in a multarity, you optimize the synergy of the system toward your (GP^X).[R122]

Figure 2b: Two Polarities in a 5-Pole Multarity

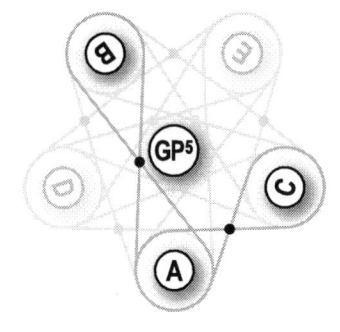

Basic Multarity Examples: From Analogy to Application

As our body analogy noted, you are already immersed in multarities. This entire book shows how prolific multarities are, as authors suggest multiple polarities that synergistically support their larger goals (GP^X) for individuals, companies, industries and the world. We are simply making explicit – Seeing – that interdependencies of more than two are a reality in our lives. Following are examples of well-known models/theories that are used every day to optimize systems. Each can be enhanced when seen through a multarity lens.

3-Pole Multarities (*Figure 3*)

- The three branches/poles of the U.S. Federal Government are intended to create a dynamic balance of power for Effective Governance (GP³): (F) Legislative, (G) Executive, *And* (H) Judicial.
- An oft-cited trio supporting Well-being (GP³): (F) Mind (G) Body, *And* (H) Spirit

4-Pole Multarities (*Figure 4*)

- The Myers-Briggs Type Indicator™ (MBTI) looks at 4-pole dimensions of personality[262] to enhance Personal Effectiveness (GP⁴): (I) Information, (J) Structure, (K) Decisions, *And* (L) Favorite World.
- Peter Koestenbaum's Leadership Diamond optimizes Leadership Effectiveness (GP⁴): (I) Ethics, (J) Vision, (K) Reality, *And* (L) Courage.[263]

Figure 3: 3-Pole Multarity

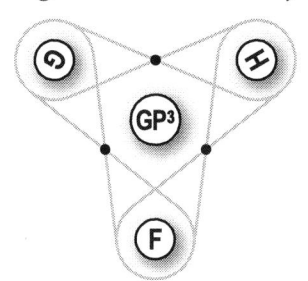

Figure 4: 4-Pole Multarity

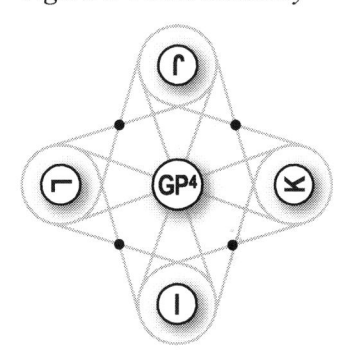

7-Pole Multarity (*Figure 5*)

Figure 5 is a rich example of a multarity supporting and enhancing multiple models. The 7-poles of the multarity represent The Barrett Model's seven levels of human consciousness: (M) Viability, (N) Relationships, (O) Performance, (P) Evolution, (Q) Alignment, (R) Collaboration, *And* (S) Contribution.[264] Barrett's breakthrough work also incorporates PEMS: Physical, Emotional, Mental, *And* Spiritual; a move inspired by Maslow's Hierarchy of Needs.[265] As you assess your needs, you can choose those polarities that provide the greatest opportunity for Personal Development (GP⁷) at any given time.

Figure 5: Maslow's Human Needs and The Barrett Model align with a 7-Pole Multarity

		7	Contribution (S)
Spiritual		6	Collaboration (R)
		5	Alignment (Q)
Mental		4	Evolution (P)
Emotional		3	Performance (O)
		2	Relationships (N)
Physical		1	Viability (M)

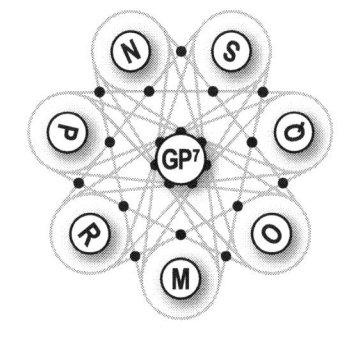

---

[262] www.myersbriggs.org/my-mbti-personality-type/mbti-basics.
[263] Koestenbaum, P. *Leadership: The Inner Side of Greatness: A Philosophy for Leaders*. Jossey-Bass, 1991.
[264] www.valuescentre.com/barrett-model. Accessed March, 2021.
[265] Maslow, A. H. "A Theory of Human Motivation." Psychological Review, 50(4), pp. 370-396.

Multarity Poles With Underlying Polarities

In Volume One, we learned, "The Greater Purpose of one polarity can be a pole of a larger polarity in which it is 'nested.'"[R68] The same holds for a multarity: The Greater Purpose of a polarity can be a pole of a multarity in which it is nested.[R123] So, it is possible for a pole in a multarity to *also* be the Greater Purpose of the underlying supporting polarity. For example, in *Figure 6a*, the polarity Fun *And* Seriousness (T•T) has Home (T) as its GPS. Home (T) is *also* one of five poles in this multarity which, in turn, supports a Thriving Southridge Shelter (GP⁵).

Figure 6a: One Polarity Supporting One Pole of a 5-Pole Multarity

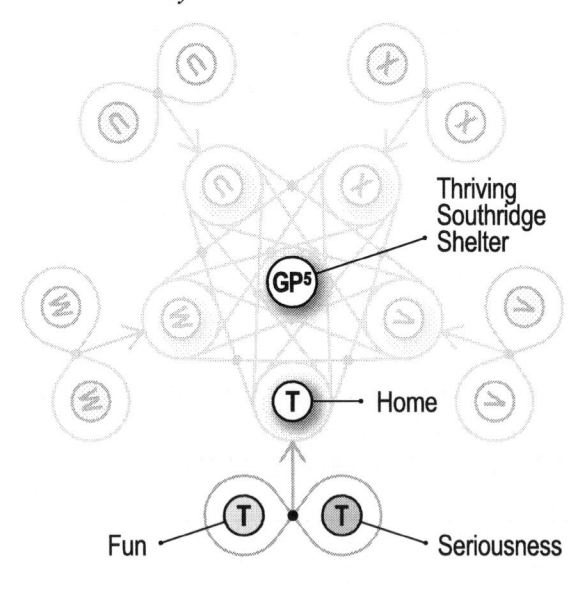

5-Pole Multarity with Five Supporting Polarities

Expanding on our example above, listed below are Southridge Center's supporting polarities as identified by Tim Arnold in Chapter 19, *Figure 3*, p. 147. *Figure 6b* shows the GPS of each polarity becoming one of the 5-poles in the shelter's chosen multarity. All five GPS experiences support a Thriving Southridge Shelter (GP⁵).

- Leveraging Fun *And* Seriousness (T•T) in order to experience Home (T)
- Unconditional Acceptance *And* Accountability (U•U) to experience Love (U)
- Reliance on a Higher Power *And* Personal Responsibility (V•V) in order to experience Hope (V)
- Consistency *And* Individuality (W•W) in order to experience Fairness (W)
- Embracing Our Brokenness *And* Embracing Our Excellence (X•X) in order to experience Beauty (X)

Figure 6b: 5-Pole Multarity w/ Supporting Polarities

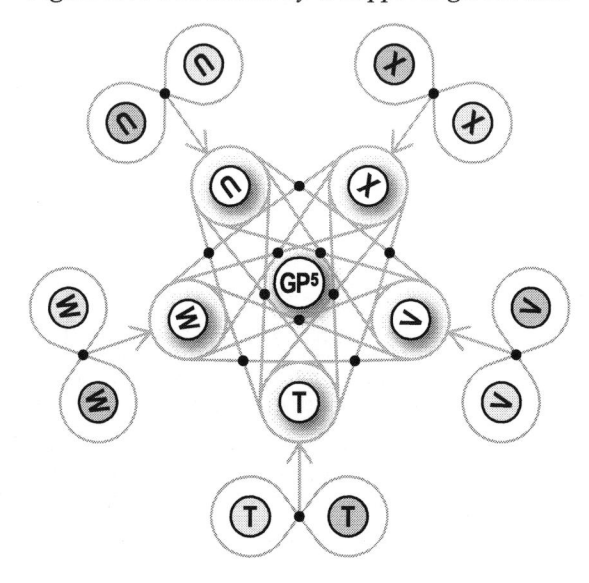

The Polarities of Democracy in Chapter 31, *Figure 2*, p.238, is another 5-pole multarity example. Listed below are their five polarities which support the five poles that make up their chosen multarity. A multarity they then leverage to attain their objective – an overarching greater purpose (GP[5]) – of Advancing Healthy, Sustainable, and Just Communities.

- Freedom *And* Authority supports the Initiative/Productivity pole
- Justice *And* Due Process supports the Protection/Restoration pole
- Diversity *And* Equality supports the Meritocracy/Sufficiency pole
- Human Rights *And* Communal Obligations supports the Belonging/Community pole
- Participation *And* Representation supports the Contribution/Commitment pole

3-Pole Multarity with Three Supporting Polarities

For each of the 3-poles of Judith Glaser's Conversational Intelligence (CI) multarity, we can identify polarities that support each pole.

- Ask *And* Tell supports the Transactional pole
- Advocacy *And* Inquiry support the Positional pole
- Share *And* Discover supports the Transformational pole

4-Pole Multarity with Four Supporting Polarities

In the Myers Briggs 4-pole multarity, each pole of the MBTI is the GPS of a well-leveraged supporting polarity:

- Extroversion *And* Introversion supports the Favorite World pole
- Sensing *And* Intuition supports the Information pole
- Thinking *And* Feeling supports the Decisions pole
- Judging *And* Perceiving supports the Structure pole

6-Pole Multarity with Six Supporting Polarities

In Chapter 8, *Figure 1*, p.67, Robert "Jake" Jacobs' Real Time Strategic Change (RTSC) principles are beautifully laid out as a multarity of six polarities.

From Analogy to Application to *Ands*

The analogies and examples shared so far were chosen for a few reasons. First, to introduce our new visual language for multarities. Second, to show the polarity and multarity dynamics imbedded in the common competencies we all navigate: our bodies, well-being, change, communication, personality types, and principles of governance and human organization. And third, to recognize that many of the theories and models used all over the world contain multarities as an intrinsic tappable resource. We are "in" polarities and multarities regardless of whether we see them, how we describe them, or our ability leverage them. The key factor determining the degree of leverage is thinking competency, starting with supplementing *Or*-thinking with *And*-thinking, then moving into *Ands*-thinking. The following *Figure 7* map summarizes how *Ands*-thinking supports the (GP[X]) Solve Problems, Leverage Polarities, and Leverage Multarities.

Figure 7

Action Steps

- Engage key stakeholders by meeting clients and their challenges "where they are" (HL)
- Measure performance solving specific problems and leveraging specific polarities
- Provide facilitation, training, and tools to develop capacity and capability to solve problems and leverage polarities

Early Warnings

- Increased complaints like, "We're not addressing big and critical issues."
- Delays due to the inability to address complex issues and opportunities
- Issues that affect peoples' well-being are poorly addressed or unaddressed at scale

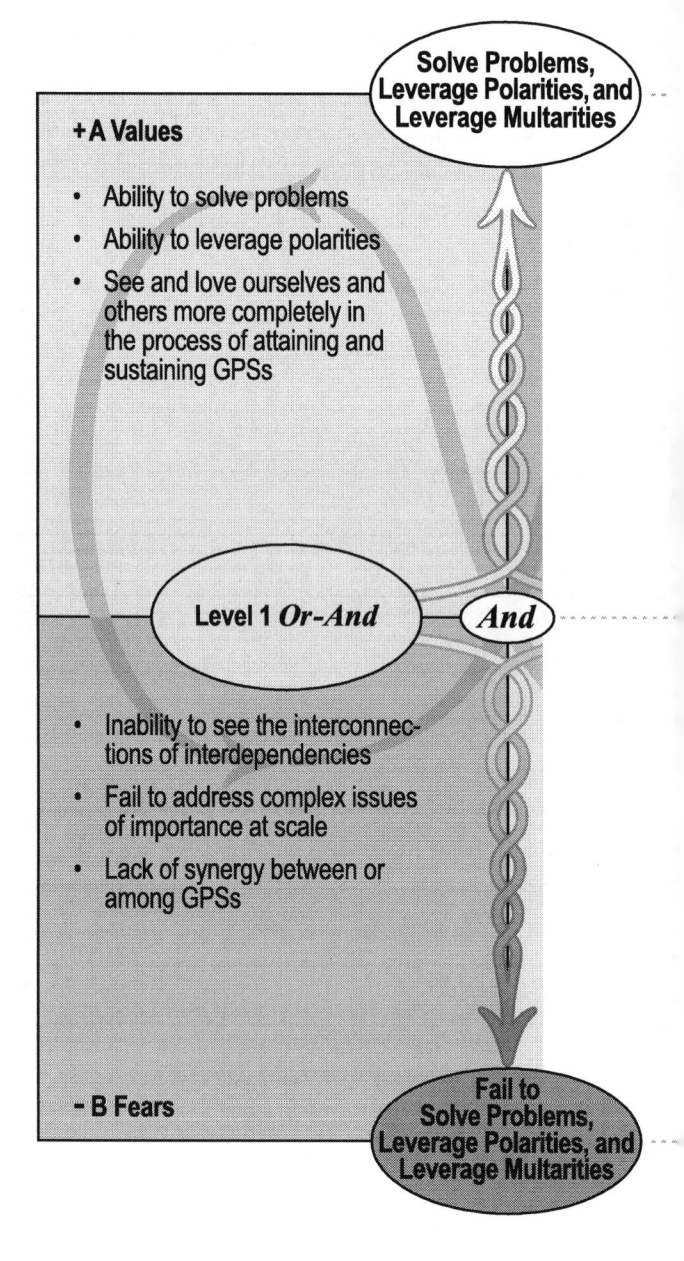

+A Values

- Ability to solve problems
- Ability to leverage polarities
- See and love ourselves and others more completely in the process of attaining and sustaining GPSs

Level 1 *Or-And*   *And*

- Inability to see the interconnections of interdependencies
- Fail to address complex issues of importance at scale
- Lack of synergy between or among GPSs

− B Fears

Solve Problems, Leverage Polarities, and Leverage Multarities

Fail to Solve Problems, Leverage Polarities, and Leverage Multarities

Polarity Map®

Solve Problems, Leverage Polarities, and Leverage Multarities

+ C Values

- Ability to leverage multarities
- Ability to address critical complex issues at scale
- Synergy from attaining and sustaining multiple interrelated GPSs

And — Level 2 *Ands*

- Inability to simplify complexity by breaking problems and polarities down to actionable size
- Lack of urgency addressing specific or local issues

− D Fears

Fail to Solve Problems, Leverage Polarities, and Leverage Multarities

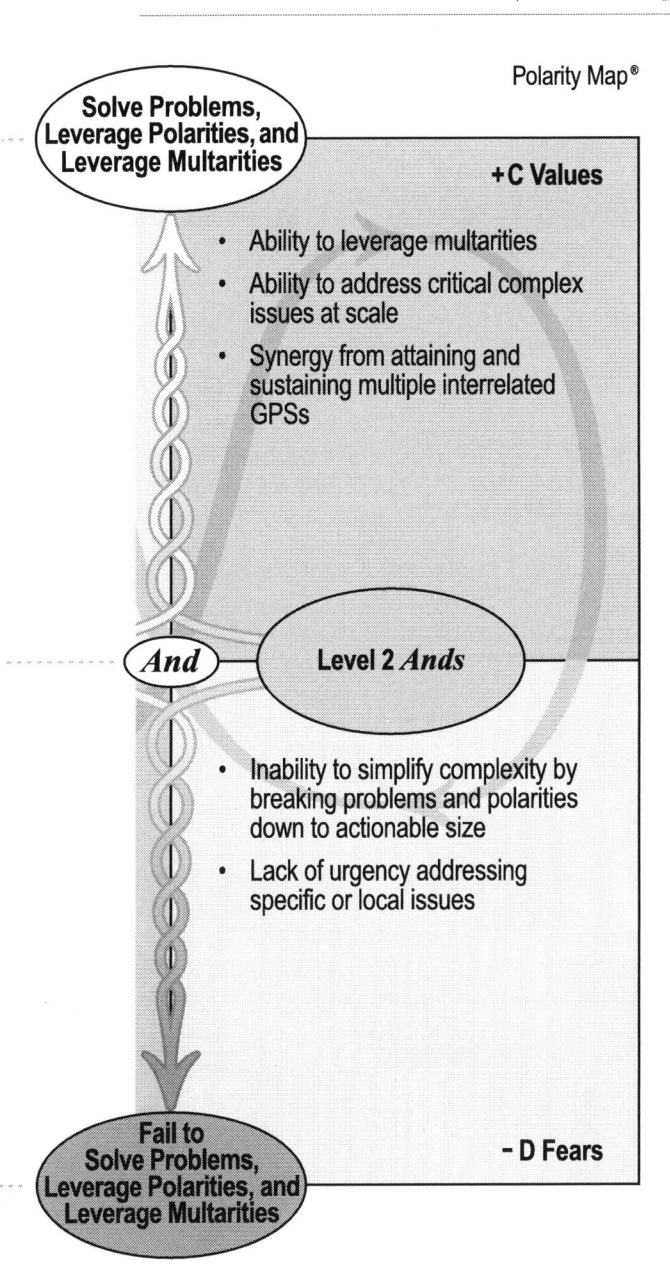

Action Steps

- Engage key stakeholders by meeting clients and their challenges "where they are" (HL)
- Measure performance leveraging multarities
- Provide facilitation, training, and tools to develop capacity and capability to leverage multarities
- Address complex issues that involve multarities: poverty, racism, sexism, and climate change

Early Warnings

- Increased complaints about particular problems not solved
- Increased complaints about particular polarities being poorly leveraged
- Inaction due to overwhelm

Evolution of Thinking and Practice

When we supplement *Or*-thinking with *And*-thinking we have stepped mentally from the world of independent variables into the world of interdependency. At the entrance we meet the smallest possible interdependency, the interdependent pair or polarity. We bring *Or*-thinking with us. Part of the beauty of *And*-thinking is the ready access we have to both – *Or*-thinking and *And*-thinking in combination. Once this mental threshold is crossed into what might be called a "Level 1" awareness of interdependent pairs, the next steps get easier. Volume One, Chapter 26, shares, "The Genius of *Or And* the Genius of *And*," and provides a rich Polarity Map®, *Figure 5*, pp. 212-213, that illuminates Level 1 awareness.[266] This *Or And And* mapped polarity is "nested" under and supports the left pole in *Figure 7*, p. 326. What might be called "Level 2" awareness within the world of interdependency includes: *Or*-thinking, *And*-thinking, and *Ands*-thinking, which focuses on interdependencies beyond two – multarities.

At its largest scope, the world of interdependent multarities includes everything that exists and has existed, seen and unseen. The more expansive our thinking, the smaller we know we are and the less it matters. We can just be in awe of the interconnected beauty of our interdependency in and with all – every thing/everything.

At a more pragmatic scope, we can appreciate that Level 1 *And*-thinking in polarity terms is not enough. We can recognize the wisdom of those whose models and theories were shared earlier in this chapter and earlier in this book. Though they may not have used the word "multarities," they have helped us begin to understand how to see and leverage them using more than one "*And*." Level 2 thinking in multarity terms requires multiple "*Ands*." For now, we suggest using *And*-thinking for polarities while using *Ands*-thinking for multarities.

Multarity Practice Considerations

Ands-thinking can be explored as a supplement to *And*-thinking the same way *And*-thinking was explored as a supplement to *Or*-thinking. *Figure 7*, pp. 326-327, provides a Polarity Map of the Level 1 *And* Level 2 thinking polarity. *Or*-thinking and *And*-thinking is a competency polarity to leverage at Level 1. *Or*-thinking and *And*-thinking *And Ands*-thinking is a competency multarity to leverage at Level 2. As noted, our *Figure 7* map summarizes how *Ands*-thinking at Level 2 supports the (GP^X) Solve Problems, Leverage Polarities, and Leverage Multarities.

Conclusion

This chapter explored application practices involving multarities and supplementing *And*-thinking with *Ands*-thinking. We look forward to our continued exploration and to the evolution of thinking and practice to be shared in future volumes.

About Cliff Kayser ~ www.polaritypartnerships.com/certified-polarity-practitioners

---

[266] Johnson, Barry. *And: Making a Difference by Leveraging Polarity, Paradox or Dilemma. Volume One– Foundations.* HRD Press, 2020.

RESOURCES

We Want to Partner With You

Our company name, **Polarity Partnerships**, was chosen because of our desire to partner with individuals and organizations whose work is congruent with our mission: "Enhance our quality of life on the planet by supplementing *Or*-thinking with *And*-thinking." The set of appendices and resources that follow are intended to support your work while helping to scale the positive impact and sustainability of our mission. For more information on these resources and how we might partner together, please visit us at www.polaritypartnerships.com.

Appendix A

Themes Found in <u>And:</u> Volume Two

<u>Volume Two</u> is more of a resource book than a linear narrative; every chapter can be referenced by theme. The authors have identified up to three themes their chapters most directly address. One way you may find this book useful is to identify the theme(s) of greatest interest to you and focus on the chapters that include them.

Theme	Chapter
• Consulting & Leadership	1, 2, 4-23, 25, 26, 28, 33-42
• IT & Tech	6, 18, 22
• Healthcare	19-24, 32
• Learning & Education	2, 9-12, 14, 17, 19, 24, 27, 30, 32, 34, 40, 41
• Social & Cultural	1-5, 26-29, 31, 35-39, 42
• Faith & Spiritual	3, 11, 28, 29
• Democracy & Politics	1, 4, 5, 25, 30, 31
• Methodology & Model	3, 6-10, 12-14, 17, 20-24, 26, 27, 29-42

Appendix B
Foundational Polarities and the Polarity Resource Portal

The Polarity Resource Portal™ is a secure, cloud-based application with access to instructional videos, case studies, best practices, Polarity Map® Libraries, and Polarity Assessments™. It supports practitioners and clients in their conceptual learning *And* real-world application to achieve measurable and sustainable results. Below are some of the most commonly experienced polarities. An expanded library is available at the Polarity Resource Portal: www.polarityresources.com.

Figure 1: Foundational Polarities

Or-Thinking	*And*	*And*-Thinking
Part	*And*	Whole
Part	*And*	Part
Care for Organization	*And*	Care for Community
Organization	*And*	Customer
Employee Interests	*And*	Organization Interests
Margin	*And*	Mission
Decentralize	*And*	Centralize
Short Term	*And*	Long Term
Continuity	*And*	Transformation
Proven	*And*	Cutting Edge
Individual	*And*	Team
Care for Self	*And*	Care for Others
Tasks	*And*	Relationships
Develop Existing Talent	*And*	Acquire New Talent
Challenge / Conditional Respect	*And*	Support / Unconditional Respect
Intent	*And*	Impact
Masculine	*And*	Feminine
Assertive in Conflict	*And*	Cooperative in Conflict
Physical Health	*And*	Emotional Health
Civil / Citizen Health	*And*	Soul / Spiritual Health
Make A Difference	*And*	Enjoy Life
Claiming Power	*And*	Sharing Power
Dominant Culture	*And*	Marginalized Cultures
Justice	*And*	Mercy
I-It / Differentiation	*And*	I-Thou / Oneness

Appendix C
New Realities in *And: Volume Two*

Volume One contains 120 polarity realities – principles that apply to all polarities and multarities. Volume Two adds two new polarity realities and introduces three multarity realities.

New Polarity Realities in Chapter 14

Reality 121 Even if something is not a preferred pole, it still lives within you or near you, and you are able to access it as a resource. (p. 108)

Reality 122 It takes risk, courage, and vulnerability to name and hold a pole in a system where that pole is not valued. (p. 110)

New Multarity Realities in Chapter 42

Reality 123 Multarities™: interdependencies of more than two poles, which synergistically contribute to a greater purpose that is more than the sum of the parts. (p. 321)

Reality 124 To the extent you can optimize the polarities in a multarity, you optimize the synergy of the system toward the Greater Purpose of the multarity. (p. 322)

Reality 125 The Greater Purpose of a polarity can be a pole of a multarity in which it is nested. (p. 324)

More Praise for *And*

"... issues that consume energy and time in our medical schools, all seemed to bow in front of the polarity mindset and map."

"In healthcare there are many takes and opposing views that are rarely discussed in the open because they pose unsolvable problems. It was enlightening to learn Polarity Thinking and the inclusiveness and acceptance it posed in dilemmas we considered, for a long time, better left unstirred.

Concepts like interprofessional education in healthcare and whether or not it was a good choice, managing school and hospital accreditation standards as fixed or dynamic boundaries, and so many more issues that consume energy and time in our medical schools, all seemed to bow in front of the polarity mindset and map.

The take-home message is loud and clear and a reminder for self that usually 'It is not a problem to solve, but a polarity to leverage.'"

> *Professor Samar A. Ahmed MD MHPE*
> *Trainer, UNESCO*
> *Fellow/Director, Ain Shams University-Middle East North Africa-FAIMER Regional Institute, Egypt*
> *Director, Centre of Excellence in Forensic Psychiatric Research*
> *Faculty of Medicine, Forensic Medicine Department, Ain Shams University*

> *"... a humanistic and loving platform to assess challenges and leverage resources ..."*

"Timeless and authentic ... Polarity Thinking has exposed a new strategic way of viewing social and global initiatives. Every day we encounter ... situations that require a decision which we believe is an *either/Or* conundrum, without realizing *both/And*-thinking can be applied. In today's society, we are faced with creating successful organizational equity and unified harmony, which is why <u>And:</u> Volume One and Volume Two are must-reads. Provided is a systematic thinking process which offers a humanistic and loving platform to assess challenges and leverage resources to delicately handle complex conversations. Polarity Thinking adequately stretches and expands the collaborative processes, which is needed to address racial, ethnical, and culturally diverse situations. This book embodies, in the most harmonious way, innovative and forward progressive thinking solutions that 'Make A Difference.'"

> *Nicole Hayes PhD*
> *Lieutenant Colonel, USA Ret.*
> *Founder/President, Organizational Solutions and Strategic Assessment Group, LLC*
> *Inaugural Desi Benet Social Change Fellow, Institute for Polarities of Democracy*

> *"... bound to radically change the way we lead, and in fact, the way we conduct our lives as a whole."*

"Here's a rich resource that goes well beyond impressive theories into actual, concrete, and highly diverse applications of Polarity Thinking that are bound to radically change the way we lead, and in fact, the way we conduct our lives as a whole. Practitioners Barry Johnson and his colleagues are offering us an exceptional gift through their valuable contribution to this expanding field. Better take it all in as it's worth every whit of it!"

> *Wil Hernandez, PhD*
> *Founder/Executive Director, CenterQuest*
> *Author, Henri Nouwen and Spiritual Polarities: A Life of Tension*

> "... I consider Polarity Thinking as a legitimate 6th Discipline."

"How to convert those resisting change into a resource to support effective change is the promise Johnson makes in his book. A promise all leaders at all levels of the system should take. Having embraced Peter Senge's The Fifth Discipline, I consider Polarity Thinking as a legitimate 6th Discipline. As a surgeon at a leading children's hospital, community activist and cofounder of a non-profit whose mission is to bring health equity, peace and prosperity to all children of all species for all generations, I can attest that *And* offers a way towards and to unprecedented and transformative collaboration – necessary if we are to address the social and environmental challenges that jeopardize the well-being of the present and future generations and of our planet."

Victor F Garcia MD
Founding Director, Trauma Services
Cincinnati Children's Hospital Medical Center
Co-founder of CoreChange

Action Steps +A

Early Warnings −B

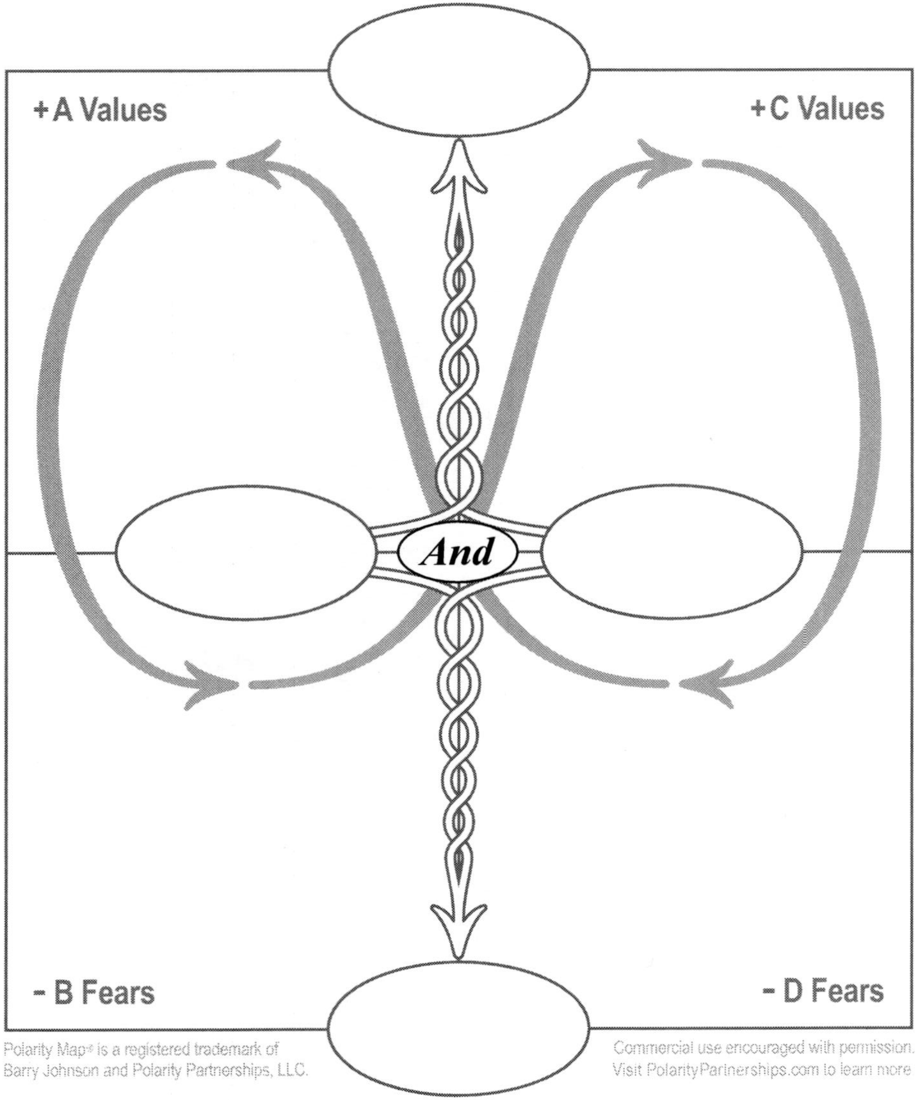

+A Values

−B Fears

And

+C Values

−D Fears

Early Warnings −D

Action Steps +C

Polarity Map® is a registered trademark of Barry Johnson and Polarity Partnerships, LLC.

Commercial use encouraged with permission. Visit PolarityPartnerships.com to learn more.

Made in the USA
Middletown, DE
22 September 2022